This Grand Experiment

CIVIL WAR AMERICA

Peter S. Carmichael, Caroline E. Janney, and Aaron Sheehan-Dean, *editors*

This landmark series interprets broadly the history and culture of the Civil War era through the long nineteenth century and beyond. Drawing on diverse approaches and methods, the series publishes historical works that explore all aspects of the war, biographies of leading commanders, and tactical and campaign studies, along with select editions of primary sources. Together, these books shed new light on an era that remains central to our understanding of American and world history.

JESSICA ZIPARO

This Grand Experiment

When Women Entered the Federal Workforce
in Civil War–Era Washington, D.C.

The University of North Carolina Press *Chapel Hill*

This book was published with the assistance of the Thornton H. Brooks Fund of the University of North Carolina Press.

© 2017 The University of North Carolina Press
Set in Arno Pro by Westchester Publishing Services
Manufactured in the United States of America

The University of North Carolina Press has been a member of the
Green Press Initiative since 2003.

Library of Congress Cataloging-in-Publication Data
Names: Ziparo, Jessica, author.
Title: This grand experiment : when women entered the federal workforce
    in Civil War–era Washington, D.C. / Jessica Ziparo.
Other titles: Civil War America (Series)
Description: Chapel Hill : University of North Carolina Press, [2017] | Series:
    Civil War America | Includes bibliographical references and index.
Identifiers: LCCN 2017013226 | ISBN 9781469635972 (cloth : alk. paper) |
    ISBN 9781469635989 (ebook)
Subjects: LCSH: United States—History—Civil War, 1861–1865—Women. |
    Women—Employment—Washington (D.C.)—History—19th century. | Sex role—
    Washington (D.C.)—History—19th century. | United States—Officials and
    employees—History—19th century. | Women—United States—Social conditions—
    History—19th century. | Women's rights—United States—History—19th century.
Classification: LCC E628 .Z58 2017 | DDC 973.7082—dc23
    LC record available at https://lccn.loc.gov/2017013226

Cover illustrations: *Top portraits from left to right*: Unidentified woman, photographed by
J. C. Potter (courtesy of the Library of Congress, LC-DIG-ppmsca-51386); Mary E. Walker,
photographed by J. Holyland (courtesy of the Library of Congress, LC-DIG-ppmsca-19911);
Jane Swisshelm, photographed by Joel Emmons Whitney (albumen silver print, National
Portrait Gallery, Smithsonian Institution); Unidentified woman, photographed by
D. C. Dinsmore (courtesy of the Library of Congress, LC-DIG-ppmsca-51390);
Clara Barton, "from portrait taken in Civil War and authorized by her as the one she
wished to be remembered by" (courtesy of the Library of Congress, LC-USZ62-108564).
Center: *View of Washington City*, print by E. Sachse & Co. (courtesy of the Library of
Congress, LC-DIG-pga-02599). *Bottom*: From the front and back of U.S. ten dollar bill, 1863
(National Numismatic Collection, National Museum of American History, courtesy of
Wikipedia.com).

As I wrote this book, my father, David Allen Ziparo, died
and my son, Zane David McHugh, was born.
This book is dedicated to them.

Contents

Illustrations

Acknowledgments

Most of this book was written at home, with only my faithful dog, Lincoln, for company. My isolated drafting experience obscures the tremendous professional and personal support I was fortunate enough to receive as I wrote *This Grand Experiment*. I have been looking forward to writing these acknowledgments for years, for the chance it affords me to offer my heartfelt thanks to those who have helped me along the way.

This work would not have been possible without the guidance and tutelage of my advisors, Michael Johnson and Mary Ryan, and all of my professors at Johns Hopkins University. I am so grateful that they were willing to take a chance on a "retired" lawyer, and I appreciate their careful reading of my work. Lou Galambos also deserves a special acknowledgment for his confidence in my abilities, his support, and his understanding. Thank you to all of the history teachers who have nurtured my love of history, including Skip Hyser and Michael Galgano at James Madison University and Paul Bass at Westhampton Beach High School. I am especially indebted to Harvard Law School's Low Income Protection Program which gave me the financial freedom to attend graduate school and produce this book.

The strength of this book lies in the voices of the women that I uncovered in my research. This would not have been possible without the archives and archivists, librarians, and staff at the National Archives at Washington, D.C., and College Park, Maryland, the Library of Congress, the Congressional Cemetery, the D.C. Historical Society, and the resources of the Chicago Public Library, Baltimore Public Library, Boston Public Library, and Milton S. Eisenhower Library at Johns Hopkins University. A special thank you is owed to Rod Ross, the legislative archivist at the National Archives in Washington, D.C., who went above and beyond in his assistance.

Most of my research was performed at the National Archives in Washington, D.C., and College Park, Maryland, and I could not have afforded it financially or survived it mentally without the incredibly generous support and assistance of Karyn and Kuba Szczypiorski. Karyn and Kuba not only gave me a bed to sleep in during my research trips, they fed me, chauffeured me, listened to my research triumphs and woes, and made me take breaks to watch truly terrible television. Thank you as well to all of my friends—especially the

B Squad and the JMU Crew—who supported me as sounding boards, frustration vents, distractions, and moral supporters. Thank you especially to Bethany Jay, Drew Darien, Donna Seger, Jennifer Woodrome, Amy Holliday, and Lindsay Jones, who read drafts of my chapters. I am so lucky to have you all in my life. Thank you to Lisa Tuttle who shares my interest in the Treasury Scandal of 1864 and was so generous with her research. Regina Starace not only read drafts of my chapters, she designed the cover of the book you are holding. Thank you, Regina, for being more like a sister than a cousin. Thanks also to my students and advisees at Pritzker College Prep in Chicago for teaching me about grit and to the folks at the Harvard College Writing Program, especially Karen Heath, and at Salem State University for your unflagging support.

Getting a book through the publishing process is harder than one might expect. Thank you to Chuck Grench, Jad Adkins, and Ian Oakes at UNC Press for all of your help and support. Thank you especially to Chuck for your patience as I weathered job changes, moves, illnesses and injuries, and having a baby. I appreciate your not giving up on this book or me.

It is impossible for me to ever adequately thank my family, Patricia Dalton, Judson Ziparo, Luke Dalton, Billy Dalton, Mary Lou McHugh, Dan McHugh, and John McHugh, as well as the Stoehrs, Powers, and Sherwood clans, but as my deepest gratitude is reserved for them, I will try. They were unwavering in their faith in me and my ability to get the job done, believing in me, and urging me on with humor and patience. Like every other accomplishment in my life, I could not have done it without my mother. She is, quite simply, "the best," and everything good I have ever done is a direct result of her parenting. John, your name should be next to mine on the title page. Thank you for our life together.

Finally, to the thieves who broke into my house and stole my laptop with all of my research halfway through graduate school, thank you for not using the giant knife you left on my couch and for teaching me, the very hard way, the importance of backing things up.

Introduction

We Are Not Playthings

We do not want to be petted. We want simply justice. We ask no advantage.
We ask for Equal Rights. Can we ever have them? We are not playthings.
We are not dolls. We are human beings.

—Gertrude, clerk in the Department of the Treasury, quoted in
The Revolution, Dec. 16, 1869

During the Civil War era, thousands of bright, spirited women like Gertrude came to Washington, D.C., to pursue a new opportunity: working for the United States of America. The supply of women seeking the well-paid, intellectually challenging civil service work far exceeded the number of jobs available. Federal supervisors did not anticipate this groundswell of ambitious and independent women. Nor were they entirely receptive to it. Female applicants in the 1860s were caught in a struggle between traditional, cultural notions of female dependence and an evolving movement of female autonomy in a new economic reality that was beginning to require that middle-class women enter the labor force. This burgeoning female autonomy was complicated, and made more complex by the manner in which the government incorporated women into the federal workforce. Supervisors hired independent women who feigned dependence. The government assigned women the same work as men, but did not pay them the same salaries. The nation alternatively believed them to be noble war widows or the "playthings" of politicians. Female federal employees, discouraged from advocating for political equality, sought greater labor equality without the help of the women's rights movement. The Civil War era female federal workforce was an important, though often overlooked, cadre of labor feminists in the struggle for women's rights in America.

The federal government did not generally employ women prior to the Civil War.[1] In 1859, there were eighteen female names listed in the biennial *Register of All Officers and Agents, Civil, Military, and Naval, in the Service of the United States*, all in the Government Hospital for the Insane.[2] By 1871 that publication included the names of over 900 women in seven different departments, an increase of over 5,000 percent. Not listed in the *Federal Register* were at least an additional three hundred women in the Government Printing

Office (GPO) and hundreds more in the Treasury Department's Bureau of Engraving and Printing, whose employment began in the Civil War era. Looking at these numbers does not, however, capture the full extent of the workforce transformation during the 1860s. Women's job tenures in federal work were often brief; many worked for the government for less than one year. Thus, the federal government employed several thousands of women during the 1860s. Additional thousands more applied for federal positions, but were unsuccessful. This book explains and explores the experiences of these women who were added to the federal payroll during the upheaval and turmoil of the Civil War era, the opportunities that federal employment created for women, and the dashed possibilities for labor equality in nineteenth-century America.

Newly available federal clerkships were the best paying positions open to Civil War–era American women. Women from across the country attempted to acquire these coveted spots because the pay was so much greater than they could earn almost anywhere else. Not only did they pay well; federal clerkships could also be intellectually stimulating. The work federal clerks performed was exactly the type War Department clerk Jane G. Swisshelm described as causing great discomfort to a "Mr. Propriety"—labor that required women "to use [their] mental powers," thus forsaking the "woman's sphere" and mixing in the "wicked" (presumably public) world.[3]

Civil War–era female federal employees were not simply tokens or assistants, either. The work they performed was interesting and had national importance. Mere hours after Abraham Lincoln informed his Cabinet of his intention to issue a proclamation to free the slaves in the South, the GPO, the staff of which was at least one-third female in 1862, set to printing the preliminary Emancipation Proclamation for distribution to the press, military commanders, foreign nations, and government agencies.[4] The women working in the Treasury Department helped to nurture our national currency through its infancy. In the Patent Office, female federal employees were among the first to learn of the newest inventions in the country. Moreover, the work was in Washington, D.C., and the capital during the Civil War era was exciting. The women who came to work in Washington in the 1860s prayed at the same churches, shopped in the same markets, and walked the same streets and hallways as the men prosecuting and coordinating the war and determining how to put the country back together once it was over.

While federal employment offered the dynamic and ambitious women of nineteenth-century America a long-desired chance to secure, even if only temporarily, intellectual fulfillment and independence, America was not prepared for women's attempts to seize it so enthusiastically. In 1864, early in the "experiment" of women's federal employment, an investigation into the Treasury Department aimed at disproving charges of fraud among the male employees became fodder for rumors about the sexual availability and deviancy of the female ones. Then, at the end of the decade, women's campaign to earn equal pay to men—one forged without the assistance of the women's equal rights movement—maintained momentum through four debates in Congress, but was ultimately defeated by a failure to see women as employees rather than as objects of paternal pity or sexual desire, and what could have been a pivotal moment in the achievement of gender labor equality—meaning equal access for men and women to positions, promotions, and pay—became something less.

This Grand Experiment reveals the complicated relationship between female federal employees and the suffrage movement. Because of how difficult it was to obtain and retain federal jobs, female federal employees and applicants were not motivated or incentivized to engage in controversial group action, and were actively discouraged from participating in the suffrage movement. Concessions to female weakness by female federal applicants and employees may have been detrimental to suffragists' efforts as women submitted to marginalization in order to obtain and retain jobs. Across multiple fields, including civil service, women performed critical work during the war, but a veil of subordination shielded the true extent of those contributions from the public and politicians, making their contribution less valuable in women's rights advocates' demands for economic and political equality.

Although there were important exceptions, few of the women who worked for the federal government during the Civil War era were suffragists or consciously part of what historians usually describe as the women's rights movement. We can, however, see an inchoate form of "labor feminism" emerging from the efforts of these Civil War–era female federal employees. "Labor feminism" could be considered a problematic designation to describe the activities of early female federal employees. As historian Nancy Cott has noted, "feminism" was not a word people in the nineteenth century used. Instead, she explains, they used phrases like "the advancement of woman" or "the cause of woman" and "most inclusively, they spoke of the woman movement." The use of the singular "woman," Cott argues, "symbolized . . . the unity of the female sex [and] proposed that all women have one cause, one movement." Of course, as Cott recognized, such unity is a fiction and was certainly absent in the ranks of the first female federal employees.[5] Other historians, including Ellen Carol DuBois, are more comfortable applying the term "feminism" to nineteenth-century activities aimed at expanding the rights and opportunities of women.[6] In their study of the century after women secured the right to vote, historians Dorothy Sue Cobble, Linda Gordon, and Astrid Henry use the plural "feminisms" to "emphasize that there have always been a variety of approaches to advancing women's well-being."[7]

In her book examining the labor of post–Depression-era women, *The Other Women's Movement: Workplace Justice and Social Rights in Modern America*, Cobble refers to the women under her study as "labor feminists," explaining: "I consider them feminists because they recognized that women suffer disadvantages due to their sex and because they sought to eliminate sex-based disadvantages. I call them '*labor* feminists' because they articulated a particular variant of feminism that put the needs of working-class women at its core and because they championed the labor movement as the principle [*sic*] vehicle through which the lives of the majority of women could be bettered." Lacking the ballot and among the first middle-class white women to work outside of the home for wages in very precariously held positions, early female federal employees do not neatly fit Cobble's definition. However, her ideas are instructive. Here, I consider Civil War–era female federal employees "feminists" because, much like Cobble's subjects, they recognized that they experienced disadvantages in their work due to their sex and those who felt secure enough to do so sought to eliminate those sex-based disadvantages. Cobble also found that her subjects "wanted equality *and* special treatment, and they did not think of the two as incompatible. They argued that gender differences must be accommodated and that equality cannot always be achieved through identity in treatment. Theirs was a vision of equality that claimed justice on the basis of their humanity, not on the basis of their sameness with men." Cobble's elaboration closely aligns with early female federal employees who were still navigating how to retain their reputations and rights as "ladies" while securing the advantages of federal employees. The "labor" half of Cobble's definition is less appropriate as applied to Civil War–era federal female employees because it implies collective action and shared vision. Because of how easily and frequently women were removed from federal payrolls, and because those women had no other labor options as financially rewarding as federal work, few women were vocal about the rights of female federal employees as a class, instead saving their energy and influence to safeguard their own jobs. Moreover, I found essentially no evidence of support from white female federal employees for the rights of their African American female coworkers. In working to retain their positions, however, female federal employees did see federal employment as "the principle [*sic*] vehicle" through which *their* lives "could be bettered."[8]

In addition to the female federal employees who did actively and publicly agitate for fairer wages and greater opportunities in federal service, one important way in which most Civil War–era female federal employees acted as labor feminists in the struggle for women's rights in America was by serving as an example. In defying conventional norms (even as they professed to be conventionally dependent women), by seeking and accepting jobs that had been "male" in newly mixed-sex workplaces and pushing into public spaces, these women concretized in the streets of Washington and the offices of the federal government the arguments the suffragists had been making prior to the conflict, and would make when the country was reunited. Female federal employees, even if not working consciously or collectively to improve the rights and status of women, were nevertheless challenging prevailing expectations about women's abilities through their individual examples. In so doing, these women helped to begin to break down some of the cultural and economic restrictions that constrained nineteenth-century middle-class white women.[9]

Framing these women as early, often unconscious, labor feminists underscores that the struggle for women's rights was broader than just the organized women's rights movement. Although the Civil War was not as transformative an event as suffragists believed it should have been, women including female federal employees did help to expand the social and political boundaries that continued to confine them. Those boundaries would never return to their antebellum perimeters and would continue to grow as female federal employees maintained their positions after the war and beyond, incrementally expanding possibilities open to women. Ultimately, female federal employees and other women of the Civil War era came to learn that they would never be able to transcend the limitations placed upon them without greater political power, eventually helping to push forward the women's rights agenda.

AS WAR DEPARTMENT CLERK Jane G. Swisshelm described it in 1865, this federal employment of women was a "grand experiment."[10] While it may have been grand, it was but one of many experiments in gender undertaken throughout the North in the Civil War era. The crisis of war opened opportunities to women throughout northern society. During the 1860s, women organized complex benevolence efforts on behalf of soldiers, widows, and freedmen; worked as nurses; served as soldiers and spies; became more in-volved in politics; petitioned Congress in unprecedented numbers; provided for families through manufacturing, textile, and munitions jobs; and moved more comfortably outside of the private sphere in which they had long been confined.

Some of these Civil War–era experiments have received the careful atten-tion of historians. Judith Ann Giesberg, Jeanie Attie, and Lori Ginzberg have extensively studied benevolence work, and their analyses reveal that women's work in soldiers' relief, while hindered by notions of their innate abilities and weaknesses, was nonetheless instructive to, and confidence building for, a generation of women who would go on to reform work in the late nineteenth and early twentieth centuries.[11] Carol Faulkner argues that the labor of white and black women was critical to the freedmen's aid movement. Although women sought opportunities to shape Reconstruction policy, however, they were largely excluded from leadership positions and their suggestions were often dismissed as too emotional (female). Still, women's involvement with the movement, finds Faulkner, "proved an important stage in the develop-ment of postwar women's political culture."[12] Historians, including Jane Schultz, who has studied female hospital workers during the Civil War, un-covered a diverse group of women who leveraged gendered notions of women's natural-born care-taking abilities into entry and acceptance into the masculine world of military hospitals, but who struggled for greater auton-omy and professionalization once there.[13]

Historians who have examined rural women during the Civil War, includ-ing Judith Giesberg, Nancy Grey Osterud, Ginette Aley, and J. L. Anderson, argue that while women were critical to the maintenance and survival of the farms of the North during the conflict, the federal government did not recog-nize their contributions, and that after the war, farm women on the whole gained no greater freedoms or rights.[14] Elizabeth R. Varon, Elizabeth D. Leon-ard, Deanne Blanton, and Lauren M. Cook have found, in their investigations of female soldiers and spies, women having to disguise or misrepresent them-selves in order to be allowed to demonstrate the heroism and sacrifice that were often only associated with men.[15] Scholars who have investigated women's efforts toward abolition and civil rights for African Americans and women demonstrate that women performed important political work, despite being disenfranchised and, until the Civil War era, often even prevented from tak-ing the podium in mixed-sex speaking halls.[16] Furthermore, even though women could not vote, historians have also found that at least some women were seriously involved in partisan politics.[17] Less work has been done squarely on the hundreds of thousands of women who worked in arsenals and for private manufacturers filling government contracts, though historians including Judith Giesberg, Nina Silber, and Mark Wilson have made important contributions, finding women energetically, though not always successfully, agitating for higher pay and better working conditions.[18]

With few exceptions, for women of the Civil War era to be successful and effective in the public—be it nursing, soldier relief, factory labor, or government work—they had to appear deferential to men. Whether or not this deference was genuine, across all fields these small concessions cumulatively reinforced for the public and the male power structure that women accepted and agreed with their subservient place in organizations and agencies and, as Giesberg notes, hid the contributions of necessarily modest women behind the egos of men in power.[19] Historians who have studied women of the Civil War era have largely found that the organizations, associations, and activities of the women they examined presented short-term opportunities, but that women's involvement in them had a lasting impact on female participants and began to expand perceptions of what was possible and desirable for nineteenth-century women.

Federal employment was not a short-term opportunity. While it might be expected that the end of the war would be a major and disruptive event in the narrative of female employment during the Civil War era, that was not the case. War-related bureaucratic work did not immediately abate at the end of hostilities; unlike the usurpation of Rosie the Riveters' positions by returning soldiers, Civil War–era female federal employees did not lose their positions en masse to boys in blue. Government work opened the door in the late nineteenth and early twentieth centuries to clerical occupations for women in the private sector as well. As this book will show, at least during the unsettled decade of the 1860s, female federal employment also provided a national stage on which women presented a clear argument to a receptive audience that women's labor was equal to men's labor—an early but brief, and ultimately failed, attempt to break free of the narrative of female deference to men.

Thus, while women moved into many new areas during the Civil War, the female federal employees who are the focus of this book are especially significant and worthy of historians' consideration. Study of these women reveals much about what Civil War–era women wanted, and how they went about obtaining what were the most coveted jobs for women in the country in the face of institutional and societal limitations. Equally important is a consideration of how politicians understood and responded to these women. Once supervisors began placing female names on federal payrolls, women never left. This first wave of female federal employees—those who joined the federal workforce during the Civil War era (which in this book will be considered to be the years 1859–71)—proved to government supervisors and to private industry that women were capable of performing clerical work, opening what would become a significant labor sector to women across the country. During the Civil War era, individual women formed entirely new relationships with the federal government, and thousands of ordinary, anonymous women were an active part in one of the central events of the nation's history. Female federal employees changed more than the federal bureaucracy. The presence of thousands of women in the streets, on the omnibuses, and in the hallways of federal buildings normalized the presence of women in the capital and in the government. The struggles and achievements of female federal employees occurred in full view of the nation's politicians and policymakers. Although politicians may have had contact with female nurses and aid workers, many of these women, though not all, left Washington, D.C., after the war. Female federal employees, as a group, never did. When politicians considered female suffragists' petitions and the Fourteenth and Fifteenth Amendments, one class of women that was prominent in their daily lives in Washington was the female federal workforce.

Although there were positive developments for women's labor during the Civil War era, this is not a triumphant narrative. Women's entrance into the federal workforce certainly destabilized some conventional notions about women and work, but legal, cultural, and personal considerations ultimately limited their prospects in federal employment and those limitations carried into the private sector. By proving women's abilities equal to that of men and by creating mixed-sex, nonfamilial workspaces, for which there was little precedent, female federal employees threatened gender norms and experienced the backlash of a society that was not entirely ready for such changes. Women often performed the same work as men, or work that was comparable, but they were paid only a fraction of men's salaries. Female federal employees challenged the inequity, but their efforts to obtain equal pay failed, and as women moved into the private clerical workforce, their smaller salaries followed.

Over the 1860s, women applying for government jobs came to realize that they were judged, not by their fitness for the position or the strength of their skills, but by the influence of their recommenders and the depths of their need. Successful applicants were those who marshaled a good deal of male support and presented themselves as in need of male protection. Women also had to maintain this constructed narrative of dependence to retain their positions. This hiring and retention practice filled the federal payrolls with women who were not necessarily the most qualified for the positions and obscured the intelligence and industriousness of those who were, adding fuel to allegations that female federal employees were at best government charity recipients and at worst sexually promiscuous opportunists. Women working for the government had to endure slander about their reputations in the streets of the capital and in the pages of newspapers around the United States. Female federal employees were often maligned as dangerous prostitutes or pitied as noble Civil War widows, but rarely publicly respected as employees.

Female federal employees were part of a generation of women who Nina Silber has argued "emerged from the Civil War not with a sense of empowerment and opportunity but with a profound sense of civic estrangement, political weakness, and even economic victimization."[20] Upon entering positions available to them—including nursing, benevolence work, and manufacturing— women encountered the same dynamic: in order to be able to participate, they had to accept limitations on, and judgment of, their participation. To secure and retain these coveted federal jobs, women had to appeal to the gentlemanly sympathy of recommenders and supervisors, acquiesce to a subordinate place in civil service, and expose themselves to public scrutiny of their private lives. In working for the federal government and living in Washington, D.C., women became aware of the value of their contributions and the inequity of their remuneration as well as the excitement and possibilities of the city streets. When female federal employees fought for promotions and equal pay to better recognize their labor, they found support among some supervisors and politicians who could not deny the injustice of unequally paying for work they knew to be equal.

Ultimately, however, the narratives of subordination and desperate need that women had, out of necessity, rehearsed in applications to supervisors and Congressmen, and that had been spread on newsprint throughout the nation, helped to defeat those efforts. As they become more comfortable in their roles and confident in their abilities, female federal employees found themselves trapped in cages they had been forced to help create. In order to obtain and retain their positions, women had to act as individuals, focused on personal needs. In order to achieve equality in the government workforce, however, women had to act collectively, focused on universal justice. Their failed plight in the latter goal buttressed the arguments of women's rights advocates that there could be no equality without the ballot.

This Grand Experiment is not the first book to examine women in the civil service. Most notable among past examinations is historian Cindy Sondik Aron's seminal monograph *Ladies and Gentlemen of the Civil Service: Middle-Class Workers in Victorian America*, which analyzed male and female clerical workers in the period between 1860 and 1900.[21] Aron's central findings concern how this new class of white-collar workers, comprised of men and women, balanced their identities as middle class with their identities as clerks. *This Grand Experiment*, which examines only female federal employees from 1859 through 1871, differs from *Ladies and Gentlemen of the Civil Service* in both breadth and depth.[22] In the pages that follow, I analyze female federal employment more broadly (including manual laborers where possible)—and deeply—considering the experiences of female federal employees at work, at home, and on the streets of the city.

My work deepens and expands in important ways our understanding of these women who were not the sole focus of Aron's work, looking at their lives holistically, providing detailed biographical details that reveal a less homogeneous experience, and finding thousands more women involved than historians had recognized. The composite portraits of female federal employees that emerge from the many assembled biographies portray women who were more heterogeneous, ambitious, and numerous than existing histories of early civil service employment have described. *This Grand Experiment* adds to existing literature on northern women during the Civil War era by providing further evidence of the deep desire so many women felt for intellectually stimulating work and by adding to the narrative of women learning to temper expressions of ambition and ability in order to obtain those positions. This book provides greater texture to the experiences of female federal employees by teasing out the distinctions among the federal departments. While employing women may have been an "experiment," it was not a closely controlled or uniformly administered undertaking. Across and within departments, individual supervisors regulated male and female employees according to their own idiosyncratic mixture of labor needs and personal beliefs. Supervisors incorporated women into different departments, offices, and bureaus in a myriad of ways and governed women by a variety of labor practices. The manner in which women would be integrated into the federal workforce, including issues such as hiring criteria, job assignments, opportunities for advancement, and compensation, was contested throughout the Civil War era. The compromises reached had lasting significance.

There was no existing archive or database that would provide answers to all of the questions asked in this book. In order to obtain a more intimate understanding of the experience of early female federal employees, I created individual files for more than three thousand women who were employed by, or who applied to, the federal government during the period under examination.[23] Some files contain only the information available in a *Federal Register* entry: the department and office a woman worked, the year she worked there, where she was from, where she was appointed, and how much she was paid. Other files contain information culled from a combination of the *Federal Register*, application materials, census data, diaries, newspapers, employee files, divorce cases, petitions, photographs, and congressional reports.[24] Additionally, to gain a better understanding of the daily lives of female federal employees and how they were perceived in the capital and across the country, I read at least one, and as many as four, Washington, D.C., newspapers for each day from January 1862 to October 20, 1870.[25] I also used targeted searches in online newspaper databases to capture reports on female federal employees in states from Maine to Hawaii. These newspaper articles not only provided insight into the public perceptions of female federal employees, but also gave color and vitality to the city of Washington during the Civil War era. The diary of Patent Office clerk Julia Wilbur provides a consistent narrative thread to give color to the life of female federal clerks, at least in the later part of the period under examination. This methodology has uncovered a diverse array of remarkable women who became female federal employees.

My research has uncovered extraordinary stories and evidence, but it does have limitations. Record keeping was not as systematic during the 1860s as it would become in later years, making quantification difficult. While my evidence is largely anecdotal, it is nevertheless extensive and thorough. Where possible, I have attempted to quantify data based on the materials available.

Additionally, while I have uncovered evidence of African American and poor clerks and laborers, the vast majority of materials describe white, middle-class female clerical workers. This is a problem of extant sources. Many women in the GPO, for example, obtained positions through the recommendations of prominent men, but their applications no longer survive, if application files were ever created. The GPO's annual reports provide female employees' names, but no additional demographic information. Additionally, while the female sweepers and scrubbers of federal buildings appear sporadically in local newspaper articles, employee files for these laborers are rare in the evidentiary record. I have included evidence of laborers where I have been able to find it, but the voices and stories of the white, middle-class clerical workers predominate. The unsettledness of female federal employment during the 1860s also makes it difficult to differentiate between types of labor, manual and clerical. Because the government was hiring women in multiple departments in informal ways, they did not always create or use the clear and explicit classifications of women's labor that they would eventually construct, nor did they have uniformity among the departments.

Moreover, demonstrating clear patterns of change over time is challenging. Because of their varying missions and responsibilities, departments experienced the war differently—the War Department, for example, felt the end of the war more acutely than did the Patent Office. Additionally, the mountain of bureaucratic labor the war produced kept the machine churning long beyond the cessation of hostilities, and the size and scope of the federal government continued to grow in the peace that followed war. Finally, the war was omnipresent in Washington, D.C., in some ways even after it ended. Female clerks attended memorial events and parades commemorating soldiers. In the summer of 1870, five years after the end of the conflict, Patent Office clerk Julia Wilbur was happy to receive the gift of a fan from a friend, which she had purchased in Gettysburg noting, "I appreciate it, as it shows the sympathies for the soldier."[26] Soldiers, war, and conflict did not disappear from Washington, D.C., after Appomattox. As a result, there is not an overarching sequence of events of female federal employment that can be neatly traced and tied to the commission, end, and aftermath of the war. I have endeavored to make these issues clear when possible, but such clarity was not always possible.

This Grand Experiment is structured to follow the life cycle of a woman's federal employment. Chapter 1, "I Wonder if I Cannot Make Application for an Appointment Too: Women Join the Federal Workforce," explores how women came to work for the federal government. During the early years of the war, different supervisors, scattered across various executive departments, created individualized and ad hoc policies regarding female workers based on their immediate labor needs and budget constraints. As evidenced in application letters, employee files, and department ledgers, women across the country and the socioeconomic spectrum responded to the opportunity in overwhelming numbers. Women's letters reveal that they yearned for intellectually demanding and high-paying jobs in a land of limited options for female employment.

The next chapter, "Telling Her Story to a Man: Applying for Government Work," examines how women applied for federal positions and details the criteria department heads used for selection. In general, supervisors chose female applicants who presented themselves as dependent and helpless over applicants who displayed independence and ambition. While many women and their recommenders adhered to this narrative of dependence, women's actions during the application process—including self-advocacy, working other jobs to stay afloat, and keeping abreast of developments in the departments—revealed significant independence and ambition.

The third chapter, "Teapots in the Treasury of the Nation: Gendering Work and Space," addresses the types of work that women performed for the federal government and how they were received and regulated as employees by male coworkers and supervisors. Because supervisors enjoyed great autonomy and because clerical work in the 1860s was largely undifferentiated, supervisors, male coworkers, and female clerks had choices to make as to how to incorporate women into federal employment. While some women were able to secure positions that were worthy of their abilities, traditional conceptions of gender ultimately hamstrung female clerks' efforts to achieve the respect and advancement potential available to men.

The daily lives of female federal employees, outside of work, are the focus of chapter 4, "A Strange Time to Seek a Residence in Washington: Perils and Possibilities of Life for Female Federal Clerks." This chapter describes the challenges and opportunities of life for women in the nation's capital during the 1860s. During the Civil War, Washington, D.C., was on the front lines of the conflict. After the war, annual reports of the Board of Metropolitan Police to Congress make clear that Washingtonians continued to endure overcrowding, public utility inadequacies, and disease. Women not only survived in this chaotic context; many—including Patent Office clerk Julia Wilbur, whose diary offers an intriguing window into the everyday life of a female federal employee—thrived in this tough city and under difficult circumstances, enjoying independence and changing the demographics of the city.

Chapter 5, "The Picked Prostitutes of the Land: Reputations of Female Federal Employees," explores how conceptions of women's sexuality complicated female employment and were exploited within and outside of the federal departments. The national rumor mongering about female federal employees burst forth after a scandal in the Treasury Department in 1864. That year, an investigation into fraud and counterfeiting in the department's Bureau of Engraving and Printing morphed into a salacious sex scandal that absorbed the country, even in the midst of a particularly bloody portion of the Civil War. The ramifications of that scandal would plague female federal employees for decades to come. By laboring as public servants in a mixed-sex workspace, female clerks were uniquely accessible to male attention, and while individually deprived of basic political rights, as a class they became an exploitable political tool in the press and in Congress.

The sixth chapter, "I Am Now Exerting All My Thinking Powers: Women's Struggle to Retain and to Regain Federal Positions," addresses female employees' struggles to keep their positions with the federal government. The number and percentage of women in the federal labor force grew fairly steadily throughout the 1860s, but volatility characterized federal employment due to the unrelenting pressure of applicants and some postwar decrease in and modification of workloads. This atmosphere of uncertainty forced female federal employees to utilize aggressive strategies to retain and regain the positions they had become reliant upon and viewed with a sense of ownership.

Women's government salaries are the focus of the final chapter, "What Makes Us to Differ from Them? The Argument for Equal Pay in the Nation's Capital." The government did not pay women the same salaries it paid men, although many performed the same work as men, or work that was considered to be equivalent with men's work. Early female federal employees' efforts to obtain equal pay for equal work engendered a precocious debate in Congress about equality that almost succeeded in earning equal pay for women and forced Congressmen to engage in dialogues about gender equality and the role the federal government should play in society. Despite this exciting rhetoric of equality and justice, Congress declined to set the standard of equal pay for women underscoring that although women had made much progress in federal work during the Civil War era, much work remained to be done.

IN 1870, Representative Anthony Rogers of Arkansas, a staunch opponent of female federal employment, "insist[ed]" that the "system of female clerks" be abolished. The Civil War was over and Rogers argued that "all these irregularities which grew up during the war shall be cut off, and that we shall return to the principles of government which were introduced by our fathers, and practiced by them."[27] Despite his statements and subsequent efforts in Congress, Rogers failed. Women working for the federal government, what Rogers decried as an irregularity, had become a regular part of the nation's bureaucratic operation. The government employment of women was a system forged in the exigencies of the Civil War and hardened by the ambitions and persistence of the women of America.

I Wonder if I Cannot Make Application for an Appointment Too

Women Join the Federal Workforce

On February 25, 1861, one week after Jefferson Davis delivered his inaugural address as the president of the Confederate States of America in Montgomery, Alabama, Sarah A. Robison sat at a desk at No. 79 East 15th Street in New York City, and composed a letter to president-elect Abraham Lincoln. The twenty-year-old orphan lived with her brother, a Republican who had cast his vote for Lincoln. Her brother's business suffered in the upheaval following Lincoln's election and Robison felt she could no longer look to him for support. In that morning's newspaper she read that "numerous persons" were applying to Lincoln for minor positions in Washington, D.C., including one man who had attempted to bribe his way into office with the gift of apples. Aware that she was on uncharted ground, Robison inquired of Lincoln: "I wonder if I cannot make application for an appointment too." Self-consciously joking that she did "not aspire to a foreign mission," she asked to be appointed governess to the Lincoln children.[1]

Less than two weeks later, Lydia Sayer Hasbrouck, M.D., wrote to newly inaugurated President Lincoln from Middletown, New York, on stationery that introduced her to be, "Devoted to Dress Reform [and] Women's Rights." Hasbrouck, a self-described "wife, mother tax payer and hard working woman of America," asked Lincoln to expand the role of women in the federal workforce. She presumed Lincoln, as "an intelagent citizen of our progressive west," was aware "of the growing spirit of discontent among the hard working, *unrepresented tax paying women* of America in relation to the manner in which men arrogate to themselves all power offices &c &c." Women did not want "merely" those "unprofitable offices which men refuse to accept," Hasbrouck explained to Lincoln. They wanted "the places of trust and good pay." She urged the president to appoint women to significant federal positions based on their personal abilities and strengths, asking for "a juster recognition of woman's individuality than has hitherto been shown her in the distribution of such offices as she is well fitted to fill."[2]

Eleven days after Hasbrouck penned her letter, Elsie Marsteller wrote to Lincoln from Prince William County in Virginia. Marsteller explained that though her husband was a doctor, a bad land deal had left them financially unable to educate their children. She asked President Lincoln to give her "one of the many offices you have to dispose of, that of Librarian at the Capital or indeed any that you would give to one entirely unknown to you as an act of Charity for which you will be rewarded hereafter."[3]

As historian Seth Rockman noted in his study of working people in antebellum Baltimore, women in all urban centers faced "narrow occupational choices and low wages" in early America.[4] These three women's letters indicate that American women in the mid-nineteenth century were hungry for the opportunity of government employment for different reasons. Like Robison, many women needed work to support themselves through the economic and social chaos wrought by the strained political times. Other women, including Marsteller, needed jobs to provide for their families because forces unrelated to the national conflict had left them in difficult financial situations. Like Hasbrouck, some women yearned for intellectually demanding and high-paying jobs in a land of limited options for female employment. Prior to the federal government hiring women, few options existed for women seeking well paid intellectual labor.

Not until the upheaval of the Civil War did the federal government begin to see a demand for this supply of female workers. Hiring women was not a conscious decision made by a monolithic federal government, however. Congress passed no law in the 1860s mandating that the federal departments hire females, but neither did it pass a law forbidding the practice.[5] During the early years of the war, different supervisors, scattered across various executive departments, created individualized and ad hoc policies regarding female workers based on their immediate labor needs and budget constraints. Such policies were also shaped by supervisors' personal views on the wisdom and propriety of female employment.[6]

Initially, these limited openings might have appeared novel and innocuous. Then they met with "the growing spirit of discontent" Hasbrouck had warned Lincoln that American women harbored, combined with an increasing number of families facing war-related financial crises. Women from across the country and the socioeconomic spectrum responded to the opportunity of federal employment in overwhelming numbers during the Civil War era, surprising supervisors who were unprepared for the flood of female applicants.

"An Outgrowth of Expediency":
Government Expansion of Female Employment

In 1873, journalist Mary Clemmer Ames described women's entry into the federal departments as "an outgrowth of expediency" that "soon proved its own right to existence, and refused to be extinguished."[7] Although the sea change of female federal employment occurred in the turbulent waters of the Civil War, the government had been quietly employing women prior to the national conflict. Before the war, federal supervisors took one of three positions on the subject of female employment. The first regarded women's only potential contributions to be labor that resembled domestic work. The second considered female employment by the government as charity, employing a handful of politically or personally connected middle and upper class "respectable" ladies enduring financial problems to perform copy work at their own homes. Finally, at least one, and perhaps only one, supervisor recognized that women could be valuable federal employees working alongside and performing the same work as men.

Supervisors subscribing to the first position employed females only in manual and low paying jobs. Most women working for the government in the antebellum period performed labor that could be categorized as "domestic" in government buildings. For example, in the Capitol, women scrubbed floors, polished railings, and washed drapery.[8] Prior to the Civil War, the largest federal employers of women were the Government Hospital for the Insane and the Government Printing Office, both of which hired women mainly for manual labor.

Established by Congress in 1852, the Government Hospital for the Insane admitted its first patient in January 1855.[9] Also known as St. Elizabeths, the institution admitted female patients and hired female attendants to care for them.[10] The facility also employed women to feed, clothe, and clean up after the patients and resident staff. These attendants, cooks, seamstresses, dairymaids, and housekeepers were the first women to appear in the *Federal Register*. Despite the arduous and unrelenting toil of their jobs, the hospital's superintendent professed in 1865 that he had "generally been able to secure the services of excellent female attendants."[11] His observation foreshadowed what later federal supervisors would discover: finding qualified female applicants would not pose a problem for the government in the 1860s.

The employment of women by the Government Printing Office (GPO) was less conventional, though far from radical.[12] In June 1860, Congress passed

a joint resolution authorizing the superintendent of Public Printing to establish the Government Printing Office to print, bind, and engrave federal reports as ordered by Congress, work that previously had been contracted out
to private firms.[13] Women's employment at the GPO was assumed from the
outset. In his annual report to Congress in 1860, the GPO's superintendent
attached several illustrations of the building. Depictions of the power-
press, folding, and stitching rooms all included female employees, and among
the "Schedule of materials, machinery, and fixtures" for the Folding Room
were "chairs, tables, counters, shelving, &.c, for 200 girls." Employing hundreds of women, the GPO was the largest federal employer of women in the
antebellum period. The work that women performed there was manual,
tedious, and reminiscent of women's domestic chores—folding, stitching,
and pressing.[14]

Not all female federal employees prior to the Civil War were manual laborers, however.[15] Some antebellum supervisors hired a small number of
middle- and upper-class women to perform copy work inside their own
homes—the second position taken on antebellum female federal employment. Women obtained these jobs through personal connections, and they
were seen as respectable because the work occurred in their domestic space.
For example, on Ash Wednesday in 1854, Elizabeth Lindsay Lomax, a military widow with six children, walked home from church with a colonel. The
two "had a pleasant time talking over old Newport days" and "he kindly said
he would try to secure [Lomax] some writing to do for the War Department."
The colonel was good to his word, and work flowed between the War Department and Lomax's house by messenger. In September 1854, after Lomax had
been copying for several months, she decided "after much consideration" to
also give piano and harp lessons to supplement her income. She agonized
over whether her deceased husband would "be displeased with me for desert-
ing my woman's sphere—the home fireside," to give these lessons. Neither
Lomax nor her War Department employers suffered any similar anxieties
over Lomax working for the government in her own home. In fact, Lomax
was proud of her government employment. On August 1, 1855, the diarist recorded that the month "was ushered in by a very pleasurable event. [A mes-
senger] brought a ponderous volume of papers from the War Department for
me to copy, which means that I am regularly installed as a worker for the Government, which pleases me mightily."[16]

Commissioner Charles Mason of the Patent Office took the third, and
most radical, position on women's antebellum federal employment. His practice of hiring women met with failure and foreshadowed the complications

that would arise in the coming decade.[17] On his own initiative, Mason hired a handful of women, including Clara Barton, in the 1850s as regular "temporary clerks." He purportedly paid the women the same amount he paid the men for the same work and brought the women into a government building to perform their labor.[18]

Mason's decision to employ women in a government building and pay them the same wages as men was not well received, and consequently was short-lived. In July 1855, Mason resigned his position, and the secretary of the interior began firing clerks, starting with the women.[19] Clara Barton was among those he dismissed. Attempting to save her job, Barton wrote to her congressman, Alexander Dewitt of Massachusetts, who appealed to the secretary of the interior on her behalf. The secretary replied to DeWitt on September 27, 1855, explaining:

> There is every disposition on my part, to do anything for the lady in question, except to retain her, or any of the other females. . . . I have no objection to the employment of the females by the Patent Office, or any other of the Bureaus of the Department, in a performance of such duties as they are competent to discharge, but there is such obvious impropriety in mixing of the sexes within the walls of a public office, that I determined to arrest the practice. . . . If the Patent Office . . . can find any work for Miss Barton, out of the office, I have not only no objection [to it], but it would give me a pleasure to know that whilst the public business is being performed, it is made instrumental to the comfort of an aged patriot, through the ministrations of a kind and dutiful daughter.[20]

The secretary's letter presaged themes that would recur during the 1860s and which will be explored in the chapters to follow. Female federal employment would be dictated by the prejudices of individual supervisors. Entrenched notions of gender propriety would limit what jobs would be made available to women, and the places women could work. Rather than basing employment decisions on a woman's abilities or intelligence, supervisors would be swayed by paternalistic appeals to charity and would consider the services of her male relatives in making decisions about her employment. Word of the secretary's firings reached Mason, then in New York, who noted the news in his diary on October 15, 1855. He was displeased: "They were some of my best clerks and besides, charity dictated their appointment and retention."[21] While women continued to work for the Patent Office during the 1860s, performing the work in their homes, no woman appeared in the *Federal Register* for that office until 1869.[22]

Thus, when urgent workloads and limited budgets motivated Civil War–era supervisors to consider bringing women into their departments, they had three examples they could follow. Instead, as we will see, many charted a fourth strategy: hiring women to work in government buildings, but paying them less and sometimes segregating them by space or task. Women's ingress began somewhat covertly in the Treasury Department in 1861. As the Civil War intensified work pressures on all federal departments, the other overtaxed and underbudgeted supervisors also turned to women. By 1863, over two hundred women were listed in the *Federal Register* in four departments.[23] Initially, supervisors employed women quietly, and without official congressional approval. As the practice spread, Congress began to address and codify the federal employment of women based on the existing practices of the various supervisors.

Although the Patent Office may have been first to experiment with employing women to perform clerical work in a government building, the Treasury Department is often cited as the entry point of females into the federal workforce because women entered that department in 1861 in large numbers and never left its payroll.[24] In his 1873 guidebook, *Behind the Scenes in Washington*, Edward Winslow Martin describes women as being smuggled into the Treasury Department, as their initial employment was informal and they "had no official existence."[25] Treasurer Francis E. Spinner was the man responsible for smuggling women in. When Spinner was a banker in New York, he claimed that he discovered his "wife and daughters could trim bank-notes faster and more neatly than my clerks or I could." He became treasurer of the United States in 1861 and soon went about, as he later put it, "hunt[ing] for a chance to carry out what were called my 'peculiar ideas' in regard to women."[26] Upon his inspection of the Treasury, he found men performing tasks he thought were better suited to, and could be more cheaply performed by, the fairer sex. Spinner informed Secretary of the Treasury Salmon P. Chase that he believed men, "'ought to be handling muskets instead of shears.'"[27]

Possibly because of Spinner's comment, some historians have claimed that the government began hiring women to meet an acute labor shortage engendered by men enlisting in the war.[28] This was not the case. The federal government never suffered from a dearth of male applicants in the 1860s. The problem faced by some supervisors, including Spinner, who was quite vocal on the issue, was a combination of ever-increasing workloads with a lack of *qualified* male applicants who were—critically—willing to work for the salaries offered by the government, which could not match the pay offered by private banks and merchant houses booming with war-generated business.[29]

In women, supervisors found capable employees happy to work for half of the pay that many men found too low.

When Spinner proposed the idea to Secretary of the Treasury Chase, the secretary "hesitated for some time, fearing that the introduction of women would demoralize the department." Chase allowed Spinner to send him one woman to test his "peculiar idea." Spinner sent Jennie Douglass.[30] Douglass had been a teacher at the school Spinner's daughter attended, but the school had failed due to the war, as did the school Douglass started to replace it. Unemployed, Douglass jumped at the chance Spinner offered. She agreed to perform the work for fifty dollars a month—less than one-half of the salary men received for the same work. Spinner provided her with a set of shears to cut and trim the currency notes and "set her to work beside the [male] clerks." He reported: "The result was, she did more work than any one of the clerks on the very first day. This decided the whole matter. The men were soon all replaced by women." So, in late 1861, women entered the Treasury Department to perform the manual labor of clipping notes at half the compensation men had been paid for the same job.[31] Here was the fourth position most federal supervisors took with regard to female employees—employ them in government buildings to do work men had been doing, and pay them significantly less for it.

Women soon found other jobs in the Department of the Treasury. As the paper currency circulated, it became worn and dirty, and citizens returned it for replacement. The department needed clerks to count the new notes going out of the Treasury Department and to count the old ones coming back in. Spinner, who fancied himself a champion of women, later told a newspaper reporter, "Now came my opportunity to have women appointed as clerks to do this work." Spinner presented Chase with the names of seven women he believed would be appropriate for the job. All seven received their appointments on October 9, 1862, as clerks in the United States Treasury Department—the first women, Spinner claimed, "who ever received appointments as clerks in any executive department of the National Government at Washington."[32]

The Treasury Department was not alone in discreetly bringing women into its workforce. As the war dragged on, supervisors in various departments, offices, and bureaus turned to women to help with increasing workloads at lower salaries. For example, seemingly of his own volition, Lieutenant Colonel George D. Ramsay, commander of the Washington Arsenal, began to use women to work in the laboratory as early as December 1861.[33] Other departments also began to incorporate women.

The Post Office was the next department to "smuggle in" women. The Post Office faced a crippling workload during the Civil War.[34] Soldiers' letters did not require postage, and they sent and received an enormous amount of mail during the war years.[35] In the North, all such letters went through the Washington City Post Office, which was described by a local newspaper in 1863 as "the great heart through which all the letters and newspapers between the troops and their families must pass."[36] The burden was not merely the volume of mail, but the manner in which it was, or was not, addressed. Deciphering handwriting and improper addresses on millions of pieces of mail was laborious. In 1862, Congress passed "An Act to Promote the Efficiency of the Dead Letter Office," authorizing the postmaster-general to return dead letters, and to employ twenty-five clerks to do so. Congress did not specify the gender of the clerks.[37] On February 5, 1862, two weeks after Congress passed the act, a Philadelphia newspaper reported "new appointments of ladies in the Dead Letter Office."[38] The postmaster had granted eight of the twenty-five positions to women.[39]

The War Department's Quartermaster General's Office followed suit. By the end of 1862, the unceasing torrent of bills, invoices, reports, statements, and itemized accounts sent to that office in the capital from quartermasters throughout the Union Army had completely overwhelmed the office. A local newspaper reported in November that the office had a "large force" engaged to address the work, but that the backlog of work already amounted to $130 million worth of accounts. To address the problem, the paper explained, Quartermaster General Meigs rented additional office space to accommodate the expanded staff he intended to request from Congress, "the greater portion of which it is said will be composed of ladies."[40] On December 12, prior to Meigs receiving approval from Congress, the local press announced that the quartermaster general had appointed three women to clerkships.[41]

These first supervisors to hire women did so without official congressional approval. Yet the addition of female names to the government payrolls did not go unnoticed by Congress. While Congress had not formally sanctioned supervisors' employment of women, the practice was far from a secret and enjoyed tacit congressional approval. Many of these women owed their appointments to the recommendations of congressmen and senators. Especially apparent must have been the large numbers of women who had begun working in the Treasury Department. By 1863, almost 14 percent of the Treasury Department employees in Washington listed in the *Federal Register* were female.[42]

Congress offered blanket legitimacy to the practices of Spinner and others in hiring women in the March 1864 Deficiency Act. The purpose of the act was to apportion funds to the strapped department budgets for deficiencies in their appropriations caused by the ever-increasing workload of the Civil War. It explicitly authorized the employment of women: "the heads of the said several departments are hereby authorized to employ females instead of any of the clerks hereinbefore designated . . . whenever, in their opinion, the same can be done consistently with the interests of the public service." The act also formalized the custom of paying women half of what the lowest paid male clerks earned, capping their salaries at $600 per year.[43] For the remainder of the decade, Congress wrestled with questions regarding the sagacity and logistics of female federal employment.

Congress's action was, of course, simply codifying what supervisors had already been doing, and so the question becomes: why did supervisors decide to embark on this experiment of expanded female federal employment? Of course, there was no single reason. Men hired women for different positions based on idiosyncratic motivations. Generally speaking however, supervisors, and later Congress, brought women as a group into the federal government because the growing mountain of war-related work had created workload crises and women could do the work well and for a mere fraction of what would have had to be paid to men. Paternalistic notions of charity to helpless women made this radical move palatable to supervisors, politicians, and the public.[44] Of little or no concern was any real intention to work toward gender equality.[45] These factors—original and ad hoc—shaped the system of the federal employment for women across all of the executive departments. To remain desirable as employees to the government, women had to be underpaid and somehow "deserving," which typically meant desperate, respectable, and bereaved.

Although economic and benevolent incentives motivated the government to employ females, the issue of which specific women to employ hinged on other concerns. Deciding on the hiring criteria for female federal employees became an acutely pressing consideration. Once the federal government had created the demand for female employment, it was quickly overrun by the supply of eager applicants.

"Hard Working Women of America" Respond to the Opportunity

There was no nationwide solicitation of female applicants when the Treasury Department opened its doors and payroll to women.[46] Women, however, did not need one. As the letters which opened this chapter demonstrated, women had been applying to jobs that were not yet officially open to them, and the government already employed hundreds of women at the GPO and the Government Hospital for the Insane. In newspapers, handwritten letters, and conversations between friends and strangers, word spread that the government was hiring women. The occasional applicant of the fairer sex quickly grew to a horde of office-seekers in skirts.

Residents of Washington, D.C., were the first to hear of the development. Journalist Mary Clemmer Ames described Washington, D.C., of the 1860s as "full of needy women."[47] In 1863, 49 percent of the women listed in the *Federal Register* as working in the Treasury Department, for example, were either from the district or had been appointed in the district.[48] The female Washingtonians who sought federal positions generally had connections to or experience in federal employment. Some of these women obtained their jobs by virtue of male federal employees. In March 1862, for instance, nineteen Treasury Department employees petitioned Secretary Chase to give Rosa Perry a position in the department. The young woman's father had been a Treasury Department clerk. When he died, his coworkers asked that Rosa, Perry's eldest child, be given a position "to clip Treasury notes in order that the family may be enabled to live."[49] Other early applicants to the new positions were themselves antebellum federal employees who had been performing work at home. Sisters and Washingtonians Elizabeth and Columbia Adams had been employed for a year by the Patent Office. After Lincoln's election, their brother, chief messenger of the Patent Office, was removed, presumably for political reasons. The sisters also lost their positions. A third sister wrote to Secretary Chase in April 1862 asking that Elizabeth and Columbia be given jobs, or even a single job, the salary of which they could split, though the family's pleas were unsuccessful.[50]

Early applications also came from outside of Washington demonstrating that news of the government's employment of women travelled quickly and that there was a receptive audience of women anxious for such opportunities. In the first seven months of 1862, for example, Letitia Arnold applied for a position in the Treasury Department from Philadelphia, a recommender sent a letter to the Treasury on behalf of Jarvis Adams of New Hampshire, Julia Richards applied from New York, and Adelaide Adams applied from Michigan.[51] Exactly how women from Michigan to New Hampshire learned that the government was hiring women is unknown. Most application materials do not contain such information, and those that do make only vague reference to "having heard" of it.[52] Julia Richards's application evidences how little some women understood the kinds of government employment that might be available to them. "I have heard that there [are] situations that can be and are filled by women, something in connection with the manufacture or getting ready for serculation of the currency something called *your currency* or Green backs," she wrote to Abraham Lincoln from her home in Schenectady, New York, in April 1862.[53] What is clear is that the news spread quickly, and enjoyed an enthusiastic and hungry audience.

The writer of a late nineteenth-century Washington, D.C., guidebook informed his readers that "when it was noised abroad that employment was given in Washington to women, crowds of them from almost all parts of the country began to flock here."[54] The volume of applications, the distance from which the applicants hailed, and the aggressiveness with which women pursued employment increased as the decade progressed. The war demanded an enormous amount of bureaucratic labor not only during, but after, its commission. Newspapers across the United States ran articles on the crush of female applicants. A Philadelphia paper reported in 1865 that it was "well known" that the Treasury Department "is continually badgered by applications for positions by females."[55] "The pressure for appointments [for women] is overwhelming," declared the *Troy Weekly Times* in 1866. The paper described the Presidential Mansion, General Grant's headquarters, and the Department of the Treasury as "besieged continually" by female applicants.[56] Later that month, San Francisco's *Evening Bulletin* reported that "hopeful [female] applicants without number are continually pouring into the Capital."[57] An 1867 Baltimore *Sun* article described the quantity of female applicants as "innumerable."[58]

Unlike Civil War nurses and benevolence workers, the primary motivation of female applicants to the federal government was not patriotism. "Necessity, exaggeration, romance and sorrow, combined as propelling motives, and the Capital was soon overrun with women seeking Government employment," explained Mary Clemmer Ames in her 1873 book on Washington.[59] Contrary to Ames's assertion, the motives of female applicants were more economic than emotional. Two reasons explain women's astounding response to the prospect of federal employment: familial financial crises due to the Civil War and its aftermath and the paucity of employment opportunities available to women. In 1863, Virginia Penny, realizing the precarious financial situation many women faced during the Civil War, published a work she intended to serve "as a business manual for women." Penny wrote: "At no time in our country's history have so many women been thrown upon their own exertions. A million of men are on the battlefield, and thousands of women, formerly dependent on them, have lost or may lose their only support.

Some of the mothers, wives, sisters, and daughters of soldiers, may take the vacancies created in business by their absence–others must seek new channels of labor."[60] Historians have found that, unsurprisingly, women suffered financial strains when men left for the battlefield.[61] "I would not have been compelled to seek a situation for myself were it not for this War and its sad consequences," Carrie Montgomery of Brooklyn, New York, explained to the War Department in her March 1865 application for employment.[62]

These wives, daughters, and sisters of soldiers did not simply want jobs, however, they wanted jobs with the federal government. Penny's *The Employments of Women: A Cyclopedia of Women's Work* presented women with hundreds of possible jobs they might try to pursue, ranging from Actresses to Window Shade Upholsters and over five hundred other vocations in between. Penny was exhaustive in her cataloguing, including entries for such niche occupations as "Makers of Artificial Eyes" (No. 439) and "Backgammon-Board Finishers" (No. 456).[63] But federal positions paid far more and were less physically demanding than these and almost every other job available to women at the time, most notably the more common occupations of teaching, farming, and domestic work.[64] Because of this, many women, including those who had been supporting themselves before the war or who lacked male breadwinners due to reasons unrelated to the conflict, also coveted the premium government positions. Former commissioner of patents Samuel S. Fisher explained to a lecture audience at an Ohio YMCA in 1871: "It must be remembered in justification of the number of applications [from women for federal work] that the number of occupations which an educated woman can enter is very limited; that the salaries paid in the departments are above the average wages which a woman can obtain in any other office, while every department of life is open to young men, with the reasonable hope of soon obtaining better compensation than any government office can afford to pay."[65]

Historian Ellen Carol DuBois found that in 1870, 1.3 million women worked for wages in nonagricultural jobs. Of these, 70 percent were domestic workers and 24 percent worked in factories making textiles, clothing, or shoes.[66] Such jobs did not command decent wages. As Rachel M. Yoe wrote in her 1864 application for a position as copyist in the Quartermaster General's Office: "I find it quite impossible to find suitable employment in any other vocation outside of the Departments of the Government."[67] Women working in factories, for example, earned more than most working women, and they typically brought home around fifty cents per day.[68] At $600 per year, a woman cutting or counting notes in the Treasury Department in 1865 earned more than three times that.[69] Teachers in Washington, D.C., in the late 1860s earned only $150 to $500 per year.[70] One Philadelphia newspaper reported in 1865 that the Treasury Department was "continually badgered by applications for positions by females who would receive a larger salary in the Treasury than they could otherwise make outside of the Department."[71] Ironically, federal supervisors hired women because they could pay them so little, and women sought out those jobs because they paid so much.

When the government opened office doors to women then, it was not only war widows and orphans who tried to walk through. Across occupations, women's low salaries prompted them to attempt a move into government service. Mary A. Locke explained in her multiple letters seeking work in the Treasury Department in 1861 and 1862 that she was having a difficult time supporting her family on the money she was able to make at her trade as a seamstress.[72] Locke found that with "no support but the neidle" it was "more then one can do times like the present" to provide for a family.[73] The "mere pittance" Mary F. Shockley earned teaching "at colored schools" was not enough to support her and her widowed sister's family.[74] "My employment hereto-fore has been that of a copyist, and also a teacher in music," explained Annie M. Peters in her application to the Treasury Department, continuing, "having failed to find either of these sufficiently remunerative, now appeal to you for that employment."[75] Another woman who applied to the Post Office in 1869 "had been trying to make a living by selling books . . . but was then literally starving for the want of bread."[76]

Women who had been laboring in other professions were eager to secure a government clerical position not only because it paid more, but because it was, in most cases, also less physically taxing than jobs they had been performing. Teachers expressed this sentiment most often.[77] Emma W. Abbot of Vermont sought a job with the Treasury Department in 1867 after "several years" of teaching in that state had "proved very detrimental" to her health.[78] Annie M. T. Adams wrote to the Treasury Department, being "extremely desirous of obtaining some employment, which will be less of a tax on my strengths, than that of teaching."[79] Mary F. Shockley explained to Secretary of the Treasury Hugh McCulloch in 1868 that the "arduous duties" of teaching had "very much exhausted my energies and weakened my nervous system; so that I require more quiet employment."[80]

Women's other professions, including washing, domestic work, nursing, and boardinghouse keeping, were also physically demanding, making government work an attractive alternative.[81] Jane Grey Swisshelm explained the relative comfort of clerical work to the readers of the Minnesota *St. Cloud Democrat*. Swisshelm obtained a job at the War Department through Secretary of War Edwin Stanton, whom she had met prior to the conflict's outbreak. The job did not begin immediately, so Swisshelm volunteered as a nurse at Washington's Campbell Hospital and continued to volunteer there during her employment at the War Department.[82] In July 1863, she wrote in her newspaper column that due to her work in the hospital she "had partial paralysis of the feet . . . so I have gone to work in the Department where I must sit seven hours a day."[83] Sitting and writing in an office was a far preferable occupation to many women who had been engaged in more physically taxing labor.

Some women, Swisshelm included, sought to join the civil service not only because of the higher salaries and relative physical ease of the work, but because government positions presented women with a rare opportunity to perform intellectual work and be involved in the operations of the nation. A federal clerkship appealed to sharp and ambitious women who yearned for the challenge and prestige of a job in the heart of the nation's capital, and had the freedom to move to Washington, D.C., if hired.[84] Antislavery champion and woman's rights activist Josephine S. Griffing came to Washington in 1864 to work for the National Freedmen's Relief Association and became one of the most visible employees of the federal Freedmen's Bureau.[85] Jane Grey Swisshelm was a well-known newspaper editor and journalist before clerking in the War Department.[86] Prior to joining the Department of Agriculture, Lois Bryan Adams was a newspaper editor, journalist, and poet. During her time in the government service, she wrote for the *Detroit Advertiser*, *Michigan Farmer*, and *New York Tribune*.[87] Julia A. Wilbur was heavily involved in freedmen's relief efforts before joining the Patent Office in 1869.[88] Smart, motivated women like Swisshelm, Griffing, Adams, and Wilbur were eager for the chance to be involved in crafting America's future. Even if their contributions seemed meager, the proximity to decision makers and decision making offered by federal employment was unparalleled in any other profession open to women.

Other women simply desired or required an opportunity to procure some measure of autonomy.[89] Sallie Bridges applied to the Treasury Department in 1865 because, she explained, she wanted to "render myself independent." Her recommender echoed her motivation in his letter, describing "her spirit to be independent of others."[90] Maria E. Baker was an orphan when she applied to the War Department in 1865. She was "compelled to self-support, or receive a home with either of my sisters" and asserted, "I prefer an honorable independence."[91] As we will see in the following chapter, however, such explicit expressions of a desire to be independent, absent evidence of the loss of a male breadwinner, rarely resulted in a job.[92]

"A Juster Recognition of Woman's Individuality":
Female Applicants of the 1860s

In 1861 Lydia Sayer Hasbrouck asked Lincoln for "a juster recognition of woman's individuality" in the distribution of federal jobs.[93] Such recognition is also called for in describing the early wave of female federal employees. Although journalist Mary Clemmer Ames acknowledged in 1873 that the nearly one thousand women then employed in the Treasury Department, "from the toilers of the tubs under its roof, to the Brush-and-Broom Brigade in its basement," represented "the entire gamut of society" and performed tasks ranging "from the lowliest manual toil, to the highest intellectual employment," historians have typically focused their examinations on the white, middle-class clerical force, often to the exclusion of African American women, female manual laborers, and working-class female clerks.[94]

This focus on middle-class, white clerical workers is the result of an imbalance in the evidentiary record. The richest sources available to historians researching early female federal employees are women's applications and employee files. Such documents survive for only a handful of female manual laborers; the overwhelming majority of the files of female federal applicants and employees from the 1860s belongs to clerical workers in the Treasury and War Departments. Moreover, women seeking clerical work in Washington, D.C., in the 1860s likely *were* predominantly white, middle-class women who had the connections to obtain the job, the financial wherewithal to move to the capital to accept the position, and the education required to perform it.

Yet there are problems with this description of early female federal employees—they were not all white, middle-class clerical workers. Female manual laborers become hidden by the comparatively massive record left by their clerical sisters. Although some of the experiences and identities of female federal manual laborers may be recreated from ephemera of evidence gathered from third-party sources, mainly newspapers, by virtue of their volume and richness, the voices of clerical workers predominate. The second problem is that the generalization of early female federal clerical workers as white and middle class, while perhaps generally true, suggests a uniform reality and obscures the true variety of experience.[95] Because the federal government established stricter criteria for employment and began to keep more extensive employee records after the Civil War era, historians researching female civil service workers after the 1860s enjoy greater quantifiable data to generate conclusions about the demographics of the female workforce. Employee files and applications from the 1860s were haphazardly kept and women applying often did not know what they were applying to do or what information to include in their applications, making a researcher's quantifiable determinations for this period more difficult.

With the understanding that most female clerical workers in the 1860s likely were white and middle class, delving into the narratives that fall outside of those classifications demonstrates that women's early federal employment was a more complex and diverse experience than has been previously known. Race and class status did not guarantee one a place on the federal payrolls, nor did it categorically keep one off of them. Additionally, while it is likely that applicants in the 1860s were very similar to applicants later in the century, it is also possible that a more varied group of women applied to these positions in the 1860s, when the parameters of hiring were still uncertain and looser.

Although women's employment records from the 1860s are lacking in significant quantifiable data, they are rich in anecdotal information. Replete with narratives, their employee files reveal a group of women who resist the historian's homogenizing appellations. Especially when we include manual laborers, what is striking about the women seeking federal employment during the Civil War era is their variety—if only at the margins. Female applicants were black and white. Their economic status ranged from poor to wealthy. They came from across the country and from abroad. Some were educated, others illiterate. They were single, married, separated, divorced, and widowed. Some had worked in other industries prior to applying for jobs; others had labored only in their own homes. Some, but not most, had lost brothers, husbands, fathers, and sons in the Civil War. Moreover, these classifications do not fall as neatly into clerical and manual labor divisions as one might expect. In fact, the only overriding commonality among early female federal applicants was a desire for a government salary. A few anecdotes will help demonstrate some of the variety existing among the early female federal workforce.

Not all 1860s female federal employees, including clerical workers, were white. In 1865, an Ohio newspaper printed a letter from a "friend" in Washington who described a visit to the Department of the Treasury. "Full two-thirds of the clerks are of the feminine gender," he wrote, "with complexions varying from snowy white to sooty—the tan color, which marks the mulatto, greatly predominating."[96] While his report was an exaggeration of both the sexual and racial composition of Treasury Department employees in a racist attempt to disparage the department and the state of affairs in Washington, African American women and men did work for the federal government in both clerical and manual positions in the 1860s. An 1867 city census revealed almost 250 African Americans working for the government in some capacity that year.[97] During the Civil War era, government employment became, and for decades would remain, an important means of social mobility for many African Americans.[98]

Supervisors did not typically indicate the race of female employees in the *Federal Register* during the 1860s, which has obscured the presence of African American civil servants.[99] For example, no women are noted as being African American in the *Federal Register* for the Government Hospital for the Insane, which accepted African American patients, from 1859 through 1871. The federal census for 1870, however, shows that a sixteen-year-old African American girl from Virginia, Charlotte Webster, worked as a servant at the hospital that year.[100] The *Federal Register* for the Treasury Department similarly provides no indication that messengers and laborers Sophia Holmes,[101] Susan Bruce,[102] Ruth Biggs,[103] or Caroline Davis[104] were African American. In 1865, the Register of the Treasury did note that his three messengers, Nancy White, Clara Washington, and Dorcas Freeland were "colored," though he did not indicate the race of the women in the 1867 *Federal Register*.[105] Other supervisors may not have indicated the presence of African American female employees on their staff lists. Perhaps it was because offices of the time were so small, there were few nonwhite federal employees and, to supervisors, an employee's race was so manifestly obvious that they did not feel the need to note it.[106] Whatever the reason, the silence in the record on the race of employees has hidden African American civil service employees from examination.

The press did occasionally report on the appointment of African American women (and men) to government positions.[107] In 1870, the *Evening Star*'s article entitled "Colored Girls in the Government Printing Office" reported on Superintendent Clapp's decision to hire African American women to work four new ruling-paper machines. The article succinctly noted that two African American women had already been hired and put to work.[108] Newspapers also reported on the government's employment of African American women as clerks in the late 1860s and early 1870s. In 1869, the Baltimore *Sun* ran an article entitled "Colored Female Clerks" on the employment in the Pension Office of Louise Slade and Emma V. Brown.[109] One year later, the same newspaper reported that "Kate V. Jennings, a quadroon," had been appointed to a clerkship in the Treasury Department.[110] A local newspaper refuted the *Sun*'s claim that Jennings was "the first colored appointment among the female clerks in the Treasury Department," because, "it appears [that] Eleanor J. Ketchum colored, was appointed in the Third Auditor's office on the 4th of May, 1869, this being the first appointment of that class."[111]

These early African American female employees had to withstand and overcome prejudices against both their sex and their race. It is unclear how their female colleagues received them. When Kate Jennings earned her position in the Treasury, the *Sun* claimed that "some of the ladies manifest a good deal of indignation on account of it."[112] There are other glimmers of conflict over race in the female workforce. In 1867, a Washington, D.C., newspaper reported on what it described as "A Serious Practical Joke." At lunchtime, the women who worked in the Treasury Department warmed their teapots on the building's heaters and stoves. One of the female federal employees in the Currency Bureau, reported the paper, "'just for fun,' dropped into a kettle of simmering tea, the property of a colored woman employed in the building, a small globule of green ink, which is poisonous . . . although the perpetrator of a practical joke does not seem to have been aware of that fact." The poisoned woman was rushed home "dangerously ill," but survived. The incident may be evidence of hostility between African American and white employees, or between clerical and manual laborers. The paper concludes that the woman "who so unwisely meddled with other folks tea-pots lost her situation in the Treasury."[113]

One remarkable early African American Treasury Department employee was Charlotte Pankus Gordon Carroll. Born and raised in slavery in Alexandria, Virginia, Carroll's owner sent her to schools for African American children and arranged for Carroll to be free sometime before 1846. Carroll married and was widowed before the Civil War, leaving her to raise a family of small children with the money she earned by teaching. By 1861, she had married David Carroll, a church elder and man of property, and opened a school aimed at educating children who had been slaves. Carroll ran the school with the help of her daughter until April 1865, but in 1864 she was widowed a second time.[114] By 1870, Carroll, who was now worth over $11,000 in real and personal property, was working in the Treasury Department.[115]

Women like Carroll had enough money in real and personal property to ensure a comfortable middle-class lifestyle, and for those women, income earned in the departments supplemented their finances.[116] For instance, Lucretia Kleiber, a copyist in the Third Auditor's office of the Treasury Department had assets in real estate and personal property totaling thousands of dollars both before and after the war.[117] Most of the women who applied for government work in the 1860s, however, professed to be facing acute economic crises. An 1869 newspaper tells the story of a woman whose financial situation was so dire that she drowned herself when she failed to obtain a job at the Post Office.[118]

Not surprisingly, the federal manual laborers generally appear to have come from poorer backgrounds than did federal clerical workers.[119] Defying generalization, however, not all female federal manual laborers were poor. Female manual laborers of some wealth appear across the departments in the 1860s. Harriet J. Bennett, a housekeeper at the Government Hospital for the Insane from 1865 until at least 1876, was worth $1,000 in 1870.[120] Treasury Department messengers Caroline Davis, who was African American, and Mary Hull, who was Irish, reported property worth over $1,000 and $1,500, respectively, in 1870.[121] Government Printing Office folder Kate Wright had $1,000 in personal property in 1870.[122]

Female federal employees also differed in education levels. Basic literacy was a requirement for most of the clerical positions in the government—the jobs were based on the arts of reading and writing. Literacy was not a unique skill in the late nineteenth century. In 1870, 80 percent of the total population and 88.5 percent of the white population were literate.[123] Some of the female applicants touted their schooling in their application materials, but not all the women who applied for federal clerkships were educated. The women who mentioned their educations in their letters of application during this early period were the exception.[124] Some female federal employees were clearly uneducated. The 1870 census for Washington, D.C., notes that Annie McWilliams worked as a Treasury Department clerk and also that she could neither read nor write.[125] When the Patent Office officially hired women as clerks in 1869, supervisors required them to pass the same examination given to the men. A newspaper reported that some of the women performed very well, but "one lady, upon being summoned before the examiners, frankly avowed that she could not pass the examination, and added that she had never been to school, and had married at fourteen years of age."[126] Some women used their jobs with the federal government as a way to fund their educations. In the late 1870s, for instance, two of the women on the "broom brigade" sweeping the Treasury Department were "students in Howard's University" who came "every day after school, the long way to the Treasury, to earn a part of the money which is to insure their education."[127]

Journalists and correspondents of the time often described the women working in clerical federal jobs in a way that highlighted the respectability of the women and of their families. "No one who has lived in Washington but knows that a majority of the female clerks come from the best families of the country," reported a New York newspaper in the early 1870s.[128] Most of the women who performed clerical or office work in the War Department in particular were likely middle and upper class women, which was, as observer

Ames described, "almost exclusively set apart for the widows, daughters, and sisters of officers of army or navy, killed or injured in the war."[129]

Not all female clerks came from "the best families of the country," however. Ann Szymanoskie was one such clerk. She was born in Poland around 1845; she could neither speak nor hear.[130] After coming to America as a young child, she became a ward of the state of New York and fell under the care of a man claiming to be her teacher and benefactor. In the mid-1850s, the man brought Ann and several other "deaf and dumb" children to Washington, D.C., and "exhibited them" to the citizens of the capital, asking for funds to establish an institution for their instruction. The people responded with funds to establish a school. The school's administrators soon discovered, however, that the pupils "were ill-treated by their teacher" and he was removed. Children who had come to the school from the district were returned to their parents, but there were five children, including Ann, "who had no parents who cared for them," and the city's Orphan's Court bound these children to the school. Ann remained at the College for the Deaf and Dumb until her graduation in 1864, at which she delivered in signs "a most excellent [original] composition" entitled "Florence Nightingale."[131] In 1867, Szymanoskie was one of ten women employed in the secretary's office of the Treasury Department.[132] In 1869, she was working in the Treasury Department's Library and Records room with nine other "Lady clerks" and twelve male clerks.[133]

Many divorced and separated women obtained federal employment, further complicating the narrative of a predominantly white, middle-class, female workforce.[134] In some cases, government jobs allowed women to escape violent and abusive relationships and such women were subversions of the idealized norm of the "respectable" family. Constantine Drexler was a taxidermist for the Smithsonian Institute who occasionally did side jobs, including stuffing Fire Engine No. Two's beloved dog "Tag" after the firemen accidentally ran him over.[135] Drexler was also physically, verbally, and emotionally abusive to his wife, Teresa, whom he had married in 1851. Teresa (born Rosenheimer) alleged in her reply to Constantine's suit for divorce in 1867 that he had "frequently treated her with great violence and cruelty." In October 1865, Constantine "knocked her down, cowhided her, and ordered her to leave the house" and later "threw her down and kicked her" until a female neighbor came to her assistance. When Teresa refused Constantine's demand that they separate, he allegedly offered a man $1,000 to poison her. He also threatened her with a hatchet and a knife, revealed plans to "hire a [whore] to disgrace her" and a loafer to burn her house down, and gave her sexually transmitted diseases. Constantine filed for divorce alleging that Teresa had been unfaithful, likely doing so to free himself from the financial burden of a wife. Based on Teresa's testimony and the testimony of witnesses, however, the judge denied Constantine's petition.[136] Although Constantine may have remained legally obligated to support his wife, he might not have done it. It was likely this financial situation that caused Teresa to obtain a job at the Department of Agriculture. By 1869, she was working in the department's museum. The 1870 census indicates that she worked there as a taxidermist, a trade probably learned from, if not previously performed for, her husband. By at least 1870, she was no longer living with her husband, but with a family that had come to her aid during the abuse.[137] Teresa's financial independence, enabled by her federal employment, allowed her to escape her abusive relationship.

Drexler's story was not unique. Margaret Bruce married Charles J. Ash, a harness maker, on October 16, 1862. The couple first lived in Georgetown, only for a short time when they had to move "on account of his ill treatment and drunkenness," explained Margaret Ash in her complaint for divorce. Once in 1863, Sarah Boyd was visiting Ash's home with several other ladies for tea when Charles came home inebriated. Boyd recounted to the Equity Court that Charles's "tore the gathers out of [Margaret's] dress, and after the company went away she began to cry, and spoke to [Charles] about his drinking and said it was not the first time he had mortified her. [Charles] said it would be the last" and threatened her with a knife. When the couple left Georgetown, Margaret obtained a job at the Treasury Department. At this point, Margaret began supporting the family entirely on her own, initially working as a printer's assistant in the Bureau of Engraving and Printing. She stated in her complaint for divorce: "I rented and furnished the room and paid for it. I was in the Treasury Department until 1865. During all this time the Defendant did nothing to support me, but I supported him and during all this time he was drunk whenever he could get liquor." Throughout this period, Ash reported that her husband "abused and beat me in the most unmerciful manner." Upon a promise to reform, Margaret agreed to leave her job and city and move to Philadelphia with Charles, but she later reported, "He was worse there than he had ever been." Ash endured this behavior for fifteen months, at which point she returned to Washington. Sometime around 1866, the couple had a baby girl they named Virginia. Ash, needing to support her newly expanded family, "again secured a position in the Treasury Department. I then rented a room and paid for it myself—he was with me at this time and I supported him and myself until 1870." She also endured his abuse, including one occasion on which he cut off her hair with a knife "because I would not give him 50 cents." Ash finally left her husband and moved in with her mother explaining "I could not put up with his drunkenness and cruelty." She filed her complaint for divorce on April 29, 1875 and continued to work in the Treasury Department for over fifty years.[138]

Upper-class women also sought independence from philandering and neglectful men through federal employment. Alexina Getty was President William Henry Harrison's niece.[139] By 1866, she had been "cruelly deserted by [her] faithless husband," and was attempting to support two children entirely on her own, seeking a job in the Treasury Department.[140] The preceding year, the *New York Herald* ran an article detailing the utter devastation of her life.[141] Her husband, Mr. Getty, was the son of a millionaire.[142] Alexina discovered that he was having an affair with an opera singer, and when she was unable to convince him to honor their marriage vows, she turned to her wealthy father-in-law. He "informed his son that unless he at once abandoned his intimacy with the cantatrice not one dollar of his millions should ever find its way into his pockets." The affair continued, and when the wealthy merchant died around 1862, he left his son nothing. He also left nothing to Alexina or the couple's children. Getty continued in his nefarious ways for years.[143] Alexina was not idle during this time. In 1861 she operated a boarding house in Washington for politicians.[144] She also tried to find her husband and managed to convince him to return to her and the children. He made a "promise of abiding honorably here after with his wife and family."[145] Alexina's thick file begging for work in the Treasury Department, however, indicates that he failed to keep that promise.[146] Alexina worked in the Treasury Department from 1866 to 1869, and her daughter worked there as well.[147]

The stories of Drexler, Ash, and Getty demonstrate that government employment, although perhaps intended to provide for women left destitute by the war, could also be vital to women seeking to escape and survive independently of abusive and neglectful husbands. Comparatively high government salaries allowed women to adequately provide for themselves and their children. Almost no other jobs available to women at the time could have offered a path to such autonomy. The women's stories also add color and nuance to descriptions of the female federal workforce of the 1860s.

Basic demographic details of birthplace and age further reveal a varied female federal workforce. Because Union soldiers came from across the United States, and because job opportunities were limited for women all over America, female federal employees flocked to the capital from all corners of the country. Not all states were represented equally, however. An examination of census records of 662 female federal employees reveals that over 60 percent of female federal employees in 1870 had been born in Washington, D.C., New York, Maryland, Virginia, or Pennsylvania.[148] Due to their physical proximity to the federal government, women in Washington, Maryland, and Virginia had better access to information concerning job openings, the ability to apply in person with minimal inconvenience, and a greater chance of knowing or finding people who could urge her appointment in the small town that was the nation's capital in the early 1860s.[149] Women from New York and Pennsylvania came from states with influential congressmen—an important factor in obtaining a federal job.

Although the number of women from Washington, D.C., was high in 1870–126 women, or 19 percent, of the 662 female federal employees examined in the 1870 census—the percentage of women from the district working for the federal government declined over the 1860s. In 1863, almost half of the women employed in the Treasury Department were from or had been appointed in Washington, D.C. Two years later, that percentage dropped to 37 percent, and it kept dropping over the years.[150] As time went on and more women learned of and became desirous of the opportunity, women from all states, including the Deep South, came to work in Washington, D.C.[151] Not all of the federal government's female employees were American-born, either. Female federal employees came from Africa, Switzerland, France, Spain, Germany, Prussia, England, Ireland, and the Danish West Indies.[152]

Women working for the federal government in the 1860s also spanned generations. The Lincolns' former boardinghouse keeper, Ann Sprigg, was nearly a septuagenarian in 1867 when she worked in the Treasurer's office.[153] In 1870, she lived in Georgetown with two relatives, a domestic servant, and Sophia and Harriet McCormick. The census taker noted that both McCormick women were clerks in the Treasury. Sophia was sixty-five years old. Harriet was six years old.[154] While it is questionable whether six-year-old Harriet was actually a Treasury Department employee, an examination of census records for Washington, D.C., in 1870 reveals a spectrum of ages. Women as old as seventy, Columbia Payne of Virginia in the Patent Office, and as young as ten-year-olds Sarah Teulon in the Treasury Department and Joanna Looney in the Government Hospital for the Insane worked for the federal government in the 1860s.[155]

These elderly women and young girls were the exceptions, however. Of the 662 women identified in the 1870 federal census as working for the government in the capital, the average age was thirty years old.[156] Civil service historian Cindy Aron concluded that the female clerks in Washington were "considerably younger than their male coworkers" but old "compared to women workers generally and to female clerks in other cities and situations."[157] The 1870 data confirms her findings. The majority of female federal employees (66 percent) were in their twenties or thirties.[158]

Because female federal employees of the 1860s tended to be older, many of them had had the opportunity to marry. As Aron found, however, "it is difficult, if not impossible" to calculate marital status for women at this time, because some female applicants apparently lied about being married to avoid the social stigma against married women working outside of the home and to get around departmental restrictions against nepotism, which arose late in the 1860s.[159] But restrictions regarding marriage may not have been enforced very strictly in the 1860s. Of the female federal employees identified in the 1870 census, at least twenty-one appear to have had a husband living with them. Many women who chose to seek work with the federal government were likely widowed. Washington was home to thousands of widows in the 1860s. An 1867 census taken by the commissioner of education in 1867 found over six thousand widowed women in Washington that year.[160]

WOMEN'S ENTRANCE INTO federal employment was a messy, organic affair shaped by male supervisors, female employees, and Congress, all of whom were influenced by the Civil War and public opinion. Although supervisors believed they were providing for those left destitute by the war in granting women employment, women who simply wanted or needed independence for reasons unrelated to the conflict also obtained jobs with the government. Not all of the women who applied were successful in their applications, however. Obtaining a job with the federal government was not for the faint of heart, though women often had to pretend meekness and dependence in their applications.

CHAPTER TWO

Telling Her Story to a Man
Applying for Government Work

Mary S. Sloan was busy during the Civil War. The Chicagoan was the wife of a Union Army colonel and a member of the Sanitary Commission. In early 1863, the president of the Chicago Sanitary Commission placed Sloan "in charge of stores and supplies for the wounded and sick from the late battles." Sloan traveled between Louisiana and Illinois, providing supplies for the men of the Army of the Tennessee. For her work, she received letters of appreciation from soldiers in Louisiana, Tennessee, and Pennsylvania.[1]

Sloan believed her experience in benevolent associations both before and during the war would earn her a job with the federal government. "Before the war I was one of 40 ladies who solicited the means for, and funded the Chicago 'Home for friendless children' and served 5 years as one of the managers and inspectors," Sloan wrote in an 1869 letter seeking a Congressional supporter for her federal civil service application. She continued, "during the war I served near three years in the San. Com. of Chicago [illeg.] as corresponding and recording sec. and assisted in opening and superintending hospitals and soldiers homes. . . . I have never asked for, nor received any pay for anything I have ever done or written and now that I desire to avail myself of the situation that will enable me to educate my daughter (nearly grown,) I feel that I have some claims upon government," Sloan self-advocated.[2]

Pennsylvania congressman Henry L. Cake agreed. "If any lady in the nation can be said to have a right to claim this kind of remuneration for valuable services rendered during the rebellion I believe Mrs. Sloan is the lady," Cake wrote to the secretary of the Treasury in 1869. Another of Mary Sloan's recommenders cited Sloan's postwar political activity as a reason why she should receive a federal position. Sloan worked as a "lady correspondent" and "defended Gen Grant from the charges of intemperance &c. when so violently assailed by his enemies." In yet another letter of recommendation, the president of the Chicago Sanitary Commission extolled Sloan's demonstrated patriotism, her "fine business talent and knowledge," and "unflagging energy and constant good temper." He concluded his letter: "She certainly deserves and I trust will find no difficulty in securing such position as may be pleasant to her and where her fine capacities may find employment and remuneration."[3]

Sloan did eventually obtain a position in the Treasury Department, but it was *with* difficulty. Despite her clear and proven abilities, intelligence, political work, industriousness, and multiple letters of recommendation from men of high positions, it took Sloan more than ten months to secure a position on the federal payroll. "I am of course disappointed that your [initial] efforts in my behalf were not successful, but that is what all must expect, who try even for a small bite of the Governmental loaf," Sloan wrote to Cake in May 1869.[4] Like Mary Sloan, during the Civil War era many women found that their hard work, dedication to the Union, skills, and ambition were not sufficient to earn them a "bite of the Government loaf." An examination of women's applications to clerical positions in the Treasury and War Departments in the 1860s indicates that, generally, female dependence and helplessness were rewarded over female independence and ambition. Supervisors gave jobs to women who had powerful men to advocate on their behalf, who appeared needy, and who were applying because some tragedy, often the war, had removed their male support. Women who based their applications on their skills, experience, or political work alone did not typically meet with success.

The files also reveal, however, that while many women presented themselves as helpless and dependent, their actions during the application process—including self-advocacy, working other jobs to stay fiscally solvent, and keeping abreast of developments in the departments—betrayed significant independence and ambition. Moreover, although supervisors stated their preference for hiring war widows and orphans—the preference was official policy in the War Department—an analysis of the employee files reveals that most of the women the government hired for clerical work in the 1860s were not the grieving spouses or daughters of soldiers.[5] Federal jobs were among the best a woman could hope to obtain in the 1860s. One of the government's ostensible motivations for hiring women was to reward the military service of their male relatives, but ambitious women who did not meet this criterion also found ways to secure the positions.

It was difficult for a man to obtain a federal clerkship in Washington, D.C., in the 1860s, and as the Baltimore *Sun* reported, "For young women the chances of appointment are less even . . . The places are fewer, and the applications are innumerable." The article described Washington as a place, "where so few [women] have found remunerative employment, and where so many have met with sore disappointment."[6] In a review of the employee files of 273 women in the War and Treasury Departments, 235 files contain application materials for new appointments.[7] Of these only forty-five women—or fewer than one in five new applicants—were successful in obtaining the job to which they applied.[8]

Before the passage of the Pendleton Civil Service Act (1883), politics and patronage generally trumped intellect and ability in hiring decisions for both sexes. There are important distinctions, however, between men's and women's searches for federal employment despite this commonality. Men's applications tended to be more aggressive and independent—men touted what they had done in politics, the military, or business, and what they would do in the future. Women's attempts to use this strategy failed; the women claiming to be weak and helpless earned positions over those claiming business acumen and industry. During the Civil War era, men also generally had to undergo some form of examination before appointment to demonstrate a basic level of competency. Women, save those in the Patent Office at the end of the decade, did not. Finally, at no point in the 1860s was the federal employment of men considered "an experiment." Conversely, the women hired in the 1860s comprised the test subjects of women's federal employment. The women supervisors chose to appoint to positions in their departments and the manner with which they selected them complicated women's arguments that they were as capable as their male colleagues and that they deserved the same salaries.[9] Selecting women who presented themselves as needy and dependent also reinforced over and over to supervisors and to the men, often politicians, who recommended women, that women thought of themselves as in need of male protection and assistance, and that their independence was an anomaly caused by the war or some other crisis.

"No Qualifications Are Required, Except Influential Friends": The Importance of Recommenders

Female journalist and War Department clerk Jane Swisshelm believed that the application process for women in the federal civil service suffered under "a radical error." These women were pioneers, and just as not every man was fit for the pioneer life, not every woman was suited to be in the vanguard of women's employment, "Yet such is the system, or want of system, on which this grand experiment has been inconsiderately tried. To get an appointment no qualifications are required, except influential friends."[10]

Influential friends were the most important element in any applicant's quest—male or female—to obtain federal employment.[11] Of the forty-five women in the employee files reviewed who obtained a job in the department to which she had applied, thirty-two women (71 percent) had the support of at least one congressman or senator. Of the successful applicants without congressional support, two had the support of president Andrew Johnson. Generals, police commissioners, governors, bankers, mayors, and clergymen all wrote women letters of recommendation for places in Washington, D.C. "A friend at court is better than money in the purse," Sloan closed her letter to Congressman Cake in February 1869.[12] Obtaining the support of such influential "friends," however, was difficult for women.

Denied the vote and typically relegated to the domestic sphere, nineteenth-century women did not have as many opportunities as did their male counterparts to form relationships with powerful men. Many women tried applying without them. "Having no influential friends to recommend me and hearing you were kind . . . I have taken the liberty to apply to you for employment," wrote Hettie Jacobs to secretary of the treasury Salmon P. Chase in March 1863. Even if a woman did have relationships with people in power, she may have felt uncomfortable leveraging those contacts. Maria Baker expressed some anxiety at the idea of trying to obtain influence. In her 1865 application to the War Department, she explained, "I feel too delicate to ask for [letters of recommendation], as this is quite a new position for me to be placed in." Neither of these women, or other women applying without recommenders who were listed in the files that were reviewed, received jobs.[13]

Some women tried to obtain influence by appealing personally to the president of the United States, whose support they hoped would be sufficient to earn them a place. In 1864, for instance, Lincoln wrote a recommendation stating, "I do not personally know these ladies, but very cheerfully endorse [her other recommenders], and shall be glad if the ladies can find employment in any Department or Bureau."[14] After the war, President Andrew Johnson was also subject to such appeals. In 1866, N. J. Brent wrote to him, "fearing to approach the worldly-minded Heads of the different Departments without testimonials." She described herself as "kneel[ing] in spirit at your feet—to implore your Christian pity and aid—with only God as witness to my merits." "O! pity me, your Excellency," Brent beseeched him, "pity a frail woman tempest-tossed and temptation tried! Pity my homelessness—my friendlessness and destitution."[15]

Most women quickly discovered, however, that they needed to arrive in Washington already armed with influence. In the early 1860s, some women submitted letters of recommendation for a completely different line of work, hoping that such testimonials would prove sufficient. In 1862, for example, Laura M. Hoffman sent the Treasury Department a letter recommending her as qualified to be a teacher in public school. Alexina Getty sent the Treasury

Department two letters, both dated 1861, recommending her as a boarding-house keeper.[16] But these types of recommendations would not suffice, and women had to hustle to obtain the active influence of powerful people.

The recommenders that were sought were overwhelmingly male, but certain women could also be influential. First Lady Mary Lincoln, for instance, secured positions for her psychic medium friends, Nettie Colburn and Parnie Hannum, in the Treasury Department.[17] Women likely felt more comfortable asking for assistance from women whom they did not know than from men whom they did not know. Jane Grey Swisshelm, a newspaper writer and editor, clerked in the War Department during the Civil War. She obtained the position through Secretary of War Edwin M. Stanton, whom she had met prior to the war in her capacity as a newspaper editor. During the war, she continued to write for newspapers like the *St. Cloud Democrat* in Minnesota. In one article, she expressed her disbelief at the number of applicants seeking clerkships in Washington, D.C., and especially those turning to her for assistance: "It is perfectly surprising the number of people who, generally women, who write to me even, to get them places, people I never saw, never heard of, will refer me to people I never saw, never heard of and ask as confidently as they would ask for a glass of water of one who stood by a pump—send their letters marked 'in haste' bidding me to get their places immediately and drop them a line when they will come on at once."[18]

Living in the epicenter of national political life, applicants from Washington, D.C., had an advantage in obtaining political influence. Powerful men lived, ate, and walked among them. In 1861, Abraham and Mary Lincoln wrote letters of recommendation for Ann Sprigg—their landlady during Lincoln's single term in Congress in the late 1840s.[19] When Julie Rearidan, a domestic servant in a boardinghouse, applied for a job in the Treasury Department, she turned to one of the boarders for a letter of recommendation.[20] Catherine Dodson (who later retook her maiden name, Brown), an African American woman, began working in the Senate washing drapes in 1861.[21] She moved into the ladies' retiring room as an attendant, eventually earning a promotion to supervisor. In 1863, Dodson obtained a position in the Treasury Department on the recommendation of six or seven senators—connections she had made during her work in the Senate.[22]

Women's connections to recommenders could be quite tenuous, evidencing their limited network, but also their resourcefulness. Because these contacts were so meager, however, recommenders' letters in support of the applicants were also correspondingly weak, and therefore often unsuccessful. Margaret M. Lockwood met Wisconsin senator James Doolittle once. In her letter she reminded him they had met "the day you had your ambrotype taken for your portrait." Lockwood was able to use this short, chance meeting as a wedge to successfully obtain Doolittle's influence, though not a job.[23] Henrietta B. Hewes once read a poem in front of Major General Sheridan in Albany, New York, and called upon this brief meeting to try to obtain his influence in her female friend's quest for a position in Washington, but her friend was also unsuccessful.[24] Mary E. Bennett tried to obtain a job in Washington for herself and sisters through Sam Wilkinson, a man who worked for or with the *New York Tribune* Association, and who before her birth had had a schoolboy crush on her mother. Wilkinson forwarded Bennett's long letter to the assistant secretary of the Treasury with the following explanation: "*Thirty three* years ago I had a rivalry in English composition with a bright South Carolina Union boy at a school in New Haven Connecticut. I beat him. He beat all of his class in winning the love of the beauty of the neighborhood [now] that man's and that beauty's daughters apply to me to aid them to earn their bread."[25]

Because Victorian women were so handicapped in obtaining sufficient, powerful influence, many called upon the friendships of their husbands, fathers, and brothers. Any such recommendations obtained on this basis were really requests for acknowledgments of former or future male patronage or military service to stand in for personal endorsements of the female applicants. In such letters, recommenders devoted most of their lines to recitations of the political or military contributions of men to the United States, adding, almost as a postscript, trite comments regarding the woman's "fitness" for the job and her "worthiness." Women obtained their recommendations, for instance, from men with or under whom their husbands, brothers, fathers, or sons had served. Sallie M. Madden's brother lost his leg at Gettysburg—and one of her recommenders was General George Meade. Kate Cahill's brother and brother-in-law were both killed at Petersburg. In 1865, thirty men signed a letter recommending her to a position in the Treasury Department, including generals U. S. Grant and Nathaniel P. Banks, president Andrew Johnson, and Vermont senator Solomon Foot.[26]

Women seeking manual positions with the government also had to work to obtain the favorable recommendations necessary to earn positions. A Government Printing Office (GPO) log of personnel notes the recommenders for most employees, and it reveals that women often came recommended by congressmen and senators.[27] Even the lowliest manual labor in the Treasury Department was subject to the wiles of patronage. "The office of the Superintendent of the Treasury Building was this morning thronged with persons of all sexes and colors anxious concerning the distribution of the sweeping and scrubbing patronage," reported a New York newspaper in 1869.[28]

A recommendation was vital to the success of an applicant to a government position, whether they be male or female. Simply having a letter on file from an influential person, however, was not always enough; an applicant often needed active and enthusiastic support.[29] For men there were clear methods and means by which to obtain that type of influence; for instance, by making significant contributions to a politician's election campaign. Because women were denied the vote, and could not participate as aggressively as men in politics and business due to social and economic constraints, early female federal employees had to discover the most effective ways to invest recommenders in their success. The woman and her recommenders then had to convince the man making hiring decisions that she was the best candidate for the job. While men could call on prior work experiences, women had to find other compelling justifications for their hire.

Complicating women's effort to obtain jobs were concerns about women's sexuality disrupting the workplace—fears that women's sexual power was either corruptive to, or corruptible by, men. Women's need to call upon the favor of powerful, male strangers left them vulnerable to gossip—some of it justified, most of it not—and exploitation. In order to assuage the pervasive anxiety over the propriety and wisdom of women's bodies in public, mixed-sex workplaces, women had to present themselves as nonthreatening to male power and as adhering to women's traditional gender roles.[30] Women who stepped outside of this narrative did not typically obtain the job they sought.

"The First Thing a Woman Had to Do":
Constructing a Narrative of Dependence

As Mary Clemmer Ames explained in her 1873 book about Washington, D.C., when a woman wanted to obtain a position with the federal government, "the first thing [she] had to do was go and tell her story to a man." The "story" was just as important as the "man." Ames wrote that it was vital for a woman to secure a man's interest through narrative: "If he was sufficiently interested in her story, she obtained the coveted place, no matter what her qualifications for it, or lack of them might be."[31] When a woman did obtain access to someone who could help her cause, she and her recommenders needed to construct a story that stood the best chance of getting her hired. The most common narrative focused on the woman's need to support herself or others, followed by a male relative's participation in the war, or his politics in general.

If possible, an application would often contain all of these narratives. Of only minor concern—and something that often worked against a woman if presented in isolation—were her own contributions to the war effort, politics, abilities, and education.

"It may be stated as a fact that, whereas a man by his vote or his electioneering services may secure employment under Government, a woman must attain it through her dire necessities and her bereavements," wrote Washington, D.C., guidebook author E. W. Martin in 1873. What most moved male recommenders and supervisors was a tale of poverty and suffering.[32] Although a woman's financial need was implied in every application letter and recommendation, almost 70 percent of the successful files that were reviewed were explicit that the woman needed the job for her own support.[33] In addition, 49 percent of the successful files mentioned a need to support others, typically children or parents, but also siblings, nieces, and nephews.[34]

Women's desperate financial situations are evident in their application materials, in which they emphasized their poverty and the need to provide for their dependents, most often parents and children. Applicants to the Treasury Department in the 1860s described themselves and families as quite poor. Words used to describe women in government application materials include "destitute poverty," "very poor," "indigent," in "extreme need," and "oppressed with poverty."[35] Women seeking federal work made it clear that they were applying because they needed the government salary.

This explicit and frequently cited need for remuneration as a basis for seeking a federal position by predominantly white, middle-class women stands in stark contrast to the stated motivations of Civil War nurses and aid workers. As historian Jane E. Schultz found, white middle-class women who entered the nursing profession often cited patriotism as their reason for becoming nurses, even eschewing the low wages offered by the government for their work when financially possible.[36] Additionally, while a small number of women received compensation for their services, most women performing aid work for the Union Army, including collecting and distributing supplies and funds, were also generally expected to donate their labor and resources to the cause.[37] Presenting oneself as needy, however, was critical to the success of a female applying to work for the government. The reasons for the discrepancy are not entirely clear. Recommenders explicitly and implicitly vouched for the respectability of female federal applicants, and nurses and aid workers did not, as often, have the need to produce testimonials from politically and socially prominent men. Women applying for government work, therefore, might have felt less concern over revealing their financial need since their recommenders protected their reputations. Recommenders and supervisors also needed a way to choose individual women from the multitude of applicants, and were swayed by appeals to their paternalistic benevolence. Once it was clear to women that demonstrating need was an important application feature, a statement of financial desperation became a ubiquitous feature in women's applications.

Middle-class women in the 1860s were not supposed to be "dependent upon their own exertions," as were so many of the female applicants. Nineteenth-century social norms dictated that women should be supported by their fathers, and then by their husbands.[38] But not all women enjoyed, or desired, this arrangement. The Civil War deprived thousands of women of male breadwinners through injury, death, or business reversals, and greatly increased the number of women needing to earn their own keep and feed others.[39] Other women lacked male support for reasons unrelated to the war. In their application materials women and their recommenders worked to demonstrate that female federal employee hopefuls needed work because a tragedy or aberration had deprived them of traditional support, not because they desired or wanted the independence of providing for themselves.

The prevalent narrative of need in women's application files had a clear paternalistic undertone. Most recommenders were not as overt in their paternalism as was Addie Getty's, who introduced Getty to the Treasury Department as a "beautiful curly headed little girl, alone in the world and greatly in need of protection and means of support," but many of the recommendation letters exhibit this tenor of appealing to male benevolence and female weakness and need.[40] Application files contain latent requests for the federal government to step into the shoes of an absent male breadwinner—typically the father or husband—and support the needy women.[41] An 1873 Washington, D.C., guidebook writer, recognizing this trend, included an eight-stanza verse about a Civil War widow who found a job in the Treasury Department and was thus able to move forward with her life because "the strong, benignant Government She feels about her like a lover."[42]

A number of the women requesting positions with the federal government needed the work because they had lost male support to the war, though perhaps not as many as would be expected in light of the government's repeatedly stated preference for hiring war widows and orphans and the press's preference for the narrative of war widows and orphans. Only 35 percent of the 235 applications for new employment that were reviewed contain reference to the war service of a male relative. Of the forty-five women who were successful in obtaining a job in the department to which they initially applied, the same percentage (35 percent) cited the military service of a male relative.

Grieving Civil War widows, orphans, and mothers explicitly made this request for federal protection to replace the lost male protection. In January 1863 Margaret C. Peters and Elizabeth Garretson penned a joint application to Secretary of the Treasury Chase from their hometown of Shreave in Wayne County, Ohio, to ask for jobs. The women wrote: "The war is now desolating our country has taken from us our husbands, one of whom (H. F. Peters) is now in a hospital in the enemy country—the other (John Garretson) for aught we know, may occupy a soldier's grave. The call of our country in taking our husbands, has taken our support, and want stares us and our children in the face. Now shall leave things be? Can you—nay *will* you help us?"[43] Anna Howard wrote to the War Department in December 1865 to follow up on an application she had filed in November. Had either of her eldest sons lived, she explained, she would not be seeking work in the War Department, "but under present circumstances I certainly do look for some way of a living from the government as my property and children has been sacrificed."[44] Women felt that they were entitled to government jobs as a result of the contributions of their male relatives had made to the country, sometimes citing sacrifices made as far back as the Revolution.[45]

The letters of widows and orphans detail the anatomy and geography of the war's human cost. Women lost men in terrible ways, in towns many of them never heard of. Hannah Slater wrote to the Treasury Department in 1863 that her father had been "wounded in the Battle of Fredericksburg . . . which caused amputation of the thigh." Six months in Andersonville Prison had left Mary Wanton's brother unable to support himself or his family, leading her to apply to the War Department in 1866. Lucy O. Marsh's husband returned from war "on account of a wound received at the battle of Resaca, Georgia, which permanently disabled his right arm" and necessitated that she seek a job with the War Department in 1865. Hundreds of thousands of Union soldiers did not return at all.[46] The appeals of these women demonstrate the growing conception of nationhood in America forged by the Civil War, and women's evolving relationship with the federal government.

Recommenders agreed that women whose husbands and sons had died or been wounded in service of the Union deserved the jobs they sought.[47] M. E. Lloyd's recommender described her as "possess[ing] all the qualifications" for the position she sought with the Treasury Department, "being a Lady, well educated, in health, industrious, and *above all* the widow of a brave soldier who died for his country" (emphasis added).[48] "It seems to me," mused one of Jennie Gaylord's recommenders in his letter to the Treasury Department, "that if anyone should receive favors from the Government it is the widows of those noble young men who have left their homes and perished all to maintain the institutions of their country."[49] Sarah Cahill's husband was one of eighty-eight men killed when one of the boilers on his ship, the USS *Chenango*, exploded on April 15, 1864, en route to Hampton Roads, Virginia.[50] In his 1867 letter of recommendation for Cahill, the chief of the Bureau of Steam Engineering in the Navy Department wrote that she deserved to be granted the position, "needing it most pressingly to supply that support which she lost when her husband perished in the service of his country, leaving his wife and orphaned children nothing but their claim on the government he died to defend."[51]

Supervisors and the press echoed these sentiments. No one expressed anything but support for the idea of giving war widows and orphans government work both during and after the war.[52] Some departments went so far as to announce policies that only war widows and soldiers would be hired. In 1865, a New Orleans newspaper reported that "vacancies occurring in the Government Printing Office, where women are employed, will be filled only by the widows or orphans of soldiers who have died for their country, or by the wives of soldiers now in service, who are in needy circumstances. None others need apply," though this purported policy does not appear to have been followed.[53] Surviving copies of letters to disappointed applicants in the 1860s reveal that the Quartermaster General's Office in the War Department strictly adhered to its rule of only hiring relatives of soldiers. In 1868 quartermaster General Meigs wrote to applicant Kate Mackall, "It is a rule with this office not to advise the appointment of any lady who cannot show that by the loss of relatives in the military service she has been deprived of her natural support."[54]

In 1866, an Indiana congressman offered a resolution, which was adopted, instructing the Committee of Ways and Means to codify the system of hiring women in all of the executive departments, "in every case giving precedence to the wives, daughters, mothers, and sisters of soldiers who fought to preserve the Union during the late rebellion."[55] Congress never actually enacted a government-wide policy of this type, however. In fact, almost 65 percent of the successful new, female applicants in the reviewed files from the Treasury and War Departments did not claim to have had male relatives who served for the Union in the Civil War.[56] Yet newspapers and politicians continued to stress the rightness of, and preference for, employing war widows and orphans in the government.[57]

The discrepancy between what appears in the application files and what supervisors, politicians, and newspapers claimed regarding the employment of war widows and orphans could be explained in both or either of two ways. One is that the government did seek to employ women who had suffered the loss of male breadwinners in the war, but such women, if they applied at all, were predominantly employed in manual positions for which application files do not survive or were never created. Most of the men killed in the conflict were lower-ranking soldiers, whose wives might not have had the connections, knowledge, or financial wherewithal to attempt applying to federal clerical work—jobs that commanded higher pay and were more difficult to obtain than manual jobs—especially if they did not live in the vicinity of the district. The second possible explanation is that the government and press overinflated, consciously or subconsciously, the number of widows and orphans in an effort to explain a radical practice—the employment of women in mixed-sex workplaces—in a traditional, popular way—to reward men's military service. Whatever the reason, the idea of government employment of war widows enjoyed great public favor and contributed to the idea that women held federal jobs because of what men had done, not because of what women had done, or could do.

Women who were not the relatives of soldiers exploited the opportunity of female federal employment created by this sentiment to obtain positions. Clerical hopefuls who did not have a relative who served in the military found it beneficial to frame their applications as deserving of success to reward men's political service, or the future promise thereof. "Patronage," asserted social policy historian Theda Skocpol, "was the meat and potatoes of nineteenth-century politics." Distributing offices at the local, state, and federal levels was a vital way in which politicians created and maintained networks of obligation and support.[58] Nineteenth-century women could not offer their vote or electioneering services to politicians who aided them in obtaining federal clerkships. Because of their disenfranchisement, when making a bid for a position based on patronage, women largely relied on the political activities of their fathers, brothers, grandfathers, and acquaintances, though this tactic seemed ancillary to the main thrust of their applications— women's neediness and an influential recommender.[59] For example, Colonel Forney recommended Sallie Bridges to Secretary of the Treasury Hugh McCulloch in 1865 because Henry G. Stebbins, Bridges's friend, had asked him to. Forney spent most of his letter informing or reminding McCulloch of Stebbins's contributions to the then-current administration. Forney wrote that he did not know Bridges personally, but "it is sufficient to say that she is the friend of Col. Stebbins' family."[60] Fathers of some women wrote letters of recommendation for their daughters, citing their own contributions to the country as the grounds upon which their daughters should receive the jobs they sought.[61] Ada B. Bridges's father, who assured the Treasury Department, "My daughter is one of the best girls I ever knew," asserted in his letter of recommendation, "I think I have done enough for the cause and for yourself for you to give her a place."[62] Many applications and recommendations cited vague assurances that hiring the woman in question would please her "friends," the implication being that the friends were (male) voters.[63] "I shall esteem it a personal and political favor if the Hon. Sec. will appoint Mrs. Atkinson," the governor of Georgia wrote in his letter to Secretary of the Treasury George S. Boutwell in 1870.[64] Every woman's recommender had an express or implied interest in her success, and could take the rejection of a woman they had recommended as an affront. Men hiring women knew this, and had to balance the ramifications of disappointing or offending a recommender with their desire or ability to hire the woman candidate that recommender had put forth.

The narrative women and their recommenders most often constructed in the application files in the Treasury and War Departments was one that highlighted women's neediness because of lost male support, and asked supervisors to provide the female applicant with a job as recognition of the military or political work of men. This framing was so common because it was the most successful. Most of the women in these application materials did not just want the jobs sought, they needed them because something had gone terribly wrong. For a woman to want the job simply because she desired independence was seen as disruptive, a rejection of the traditional structure of male power in nineteenth-century American society.

"Becoming Pathetic—No Office Rewards Her Persistent Demands": Straying from the Narrative of Female Dependence

Lois Bryan Adams obtained her position in the Department of Agriculture in 1863 on the recommendation of two senators and a congressman, all from Michigan.[65] Presumably, it was not only these recommendations, but also Adams's qualifications that earned her the position: she was the editor of *The Michigan Farmer*, an agricultural periodical.[66] Fitness for the position, however, was the least important qualification for female applicants to clerical positions in the 1860s, save at the Government Hospital for the Insane.[67] Qualified women did obtain positions, but they did so by adhering to the narratives of social and political conventions of female dependence and not pressing their intellectual abilities too strongly in their application materials. If the application package—letters of application and recommendations—evinced more independence than dependence, it was more likely to meet with failure than with success.

The one exception to this generalization was the Government Hospital for the Insane. Hospital Superintendent C. H. Nichols had clear criteria for applicants and would not have hired a woman simply because of her connections. He wrote one female supervisor hopeful a four-page letter explaining what type of woman he was seeking for the position: "a woman should enjoy good health and have a well-balanced, benevolent mind, of something above the average capacity; should have solid, not fashionable, educational and social advantages, be industrious and practical in her habits of life, and devoted and self-denying in the discharge of whatever duties she undertakes."[68] Nichols also required the employees to be "kind-hearted" and to have "integrity."[69] His focus on the abilities and dispositions of the woman, rather than her need or the worthiness of the men to whom she was related or the influence of her recommenders, was unique among federal supervisors.

Most of the letters in women's application files for the War and Treasury Departments contain at least some language about a woman's ability to perform the job she sought. Recommenders assured departments that they "feel confident" of the applicant's "ability to give satisfaction," or assert that the woman is "intelligent" and "educated."[70] Recommenders also endorsed the woman's moral character and loyalty.[71] The ubiquity of these comments, often made at the end of the letter of recommendation, makes clear that a woman's ability to do the job, good character, and strict loyalty were thought necessary, but not sufficient, reasons to give a woman a job. Of far more importance to supervisors and recommenders were a woman's connections, need, and the military and political service of her male relatives. Some women applying to positions with the government, however, believed that their skills and demonstrated loyalty earned them a right to government employment. Women who applied solely on their own merit met with almost universal disappointment, and in one instance national ridicule. Such women's experiences demonstrated that although some American women sought or needed financial autonomy from men, the country was not ready to deviate from the social norm of female dependence.

Women applying to clerical positions tried to demonstrate their qualifications for the position through their handwriting, as much of the office work included copying.[72] Understanding that penmanship might be critical to the job she sought, Helen Ivey sent a neatly written letter to the secretary of the treasury in 1865, stating, "You, Sir, can judge from this note of my qualifications as a writer." She also enclosed a card on which she had written in calligraphy: "Hope deterred maketh the heart sick. Washington, D.C."[73] She did not receive a job. "Of my qualifications the Commissioner will judge from the specimen here furnished," explained Laura Redden, who drafted her letter of application in four different handwriting styles, one style per paragraph.[74]

Some letters of recommendation also made reference to women's business experience or knowledge. "Jane is (as well as highly deserving) a rapid, good, and handsome writer, correct composer, and in Epistolary Correspondence view excels, and can facilitate business in an unusual degree for the sex," wrote one of Jane James's recommenders in her unsuccessful application.[75] Eliza Isams, her recommender informed the War Department in 1865, was "a skilled accountant and excellent penwoman, and knows how to use time with system and industry." Isams, "a widow with two deaf mute children" to support, did not receive the job.[76]

Women were technically excluded from battle and thus could not cite Civil War combat service as a reason they should be given a job with the government.[77] Although many men dismissed women's war activities, some recommenders recognized the importance of women's efforts and exertions in nursing the sick, delivering supplies, and transmitting intelligence. The tasks women performed demonstrated not only their patriotism, but also their intellectual and organizational capabilities. Women felt that their sacrifices and service should be considered in the distribution of jobs, as did their recommenders. Supervisors, however, did not always agree.

The most common war service cited by women, aside from the sacrifice of their husbands, sons, fathers, and brothers, was hospital work. Women typically highlighted their nursing service to demonstrate loyalty to the Union. "I have only loyalty as a plea to offer why I should receive [a position]; having been in the U. S. Hospital, as a nurse, and doing the best I could for my men while there," wrote Jane F. Adams in her letter of application to the Treasury Department, which was unsuccessful.[78] John Pierpoint wrote of Jane F. James's "large hearted and self-sacrificing devotion to the Union cause" and of how she had purchased food and drink for soldiers "from her limited means" and "with her own hands" prepared food for the sick and wounded soldiers in the makeshift hospital at a church across the street from her home. James also failed to obtain a job.[79]

Women contributed to the war effort in ways other than nursing and some women called on their service in their applications with mixed results.

S. L. Atkinson's recommender informed the Treasury that he "first met Mrs. Atkinson—then Miss Lyon,—when my Regiment was ordered into the city of Baltimore Maryland in July 1861." Atkinson "cordially welcomed and entertained" the writer and his soldiers, and "gave us a moral support we had not expected to find in the City of Baltimore." Her job application was unsuccessful.[80] Miss Wright of Winchester, Virginia, however, was the individual "on whose information Gen. Sheridan fought his famous Battle of Winchester," and received a position, and in 1867 Massachusetts newspaper reported that Wright "wears at her work a gold watch and chain with cavalry trinkets, presented her by Phil Sheridan, in acknowledgment of her services."[81]

Because application files often contained multiple justifications for hire, and because the record is silent on which among them swayed the man making the hiring decision, absolute determinations regarding what was certain to work or what was certain to fail are impossible to make. It is clear, however, that women who applied based only or predominantly on their skills or contributions to the war did not fare well. Sophia B. Gay and Dr. Mary Walker provide two good examples of women who believed that their abilities and intelligence should be rewarded, and who were sorely disappointed.

Sophia B. Gay was a teacher from Seneca Falls, New York—home of the first women's rights convention. From February to December 1863, Gay repeatedly applied for a job in the Treasury Department. She wrote five letters in her attempt and had six letters of recommendation written for her by four different people. While she and her recommenders cited her family's respectability and political connections, the main thrust of her application package was that she was smart and would be good at the job. A February 7 letter of recommendation to Secretary of the Treasury Chase described her as "a young lady of superior education," who "writes a beautiful hand, is apt and quick at business, and has had a good deal of experience in matters analogous to those in which she would be engaged in your Department." This recommender wrote a second letter the same day, to a different Treasury Department official. "It is rare that a young lady of Miss. Gay's accomplishments applies for such a situation as that now under consideration," it read.[82]

One month later, Gay had not received the job, so she contacted her recommender. She had "for some reason been so sanguine ever since I received your letter that I should be successful in obtaining a position at Washington that I cannot bear to give it up and am unwilling to believe as yet that I must do so." Gay had been reading in the newspapers that women were being appointed in Washington and was clearly frustrated since she could "see no reason why I may not expect a position equally with anyone else."[83] Gay's recommender followed up with a third recommendation in March, commenting, "I have seen some of the young ladies employed in your Department, and am sure that Miss Gay is quite the peer of any one of them." Gay also arranged for letters of recommendation from other men, including a New York postmaster, the assistant secretary of state, and a New York congressman. Gay's file ends in December 1863 and there is no indication she ever received a job with the federal government.[84]

Like Gay, Dr. Mary Walker tried to obtain a position with the government based on her own merits. Also like Gay, she failed. Walker's failure, however, was much more public. Dr. Walker was a bloomer-wearing suffragist and had tended to men on Civil War battlefields.[85] Yet Walker's 1869 attempts to obtain a job in any and all of the federal departments failed, and the press was merciless in mocking her. The papers painted her as pushy, demanding, and far too ambitious. Walker believed that her war record and qualifications should have secured her a position, and she was not shy in making her opinion on that score known to the department heads. Walker also reportedly felt that she had just as much of a right to a position as did a man. Espousing these beliefs, instead of adhering to the script of female dependence, caused her failure and public ridicule. Newspapers in at least nine different states, plus the District of Columbia, reported negatively on Walker's efforts, and their articles served as a widely disseminated cautionary tale for women applying to government work.[86]

Reporting on Walker's attempts to obtain government work, much of it laced with hyperbole, began in mid-May. On May 11, the Baltimore *Sun* reported that Walker had "been an inveterate office seeker for some weeks, carrying her importunities everywhere from the President down." The article described an encounter purported to have occurred between Walker and Postmaster John Cresswell in which Walker demanded a position, declaring, "A vacancy should be made for her even if some 'male biped' was displaced." She cited "her loyalty, her army record, &c. in support of this claim." Walker left unsuccessful: "Mrs. Walker declares, however, that she will have an office."[87] By the time the story reached the Kansas papers, it was reported that, "Mr. Cresswell showed her some female situations, but she would have a male berth or none."[88] On May 12 the *Sun* reported that Walker had attempted to obtain a position in the Internal Revenue Bureau.[89] Walker allegedly also tried to obtain a position in the Patent Office. At the end of the month, the *Boston Daily Journal* informed its readers that Walker was "demand[ing] the appointment of Secretary of Legation to Spain," and when asked if she could speak the language, "the valuable dame replied that the appointment was not a question of languages, but the recognition of the rights of women."[90]

"The Irrepressible Doctress Walker Becoming Pathetic—No Office Rewards Her Persistent Demands," read the headline of a *New York Herald* article on May 21, 1869. The article described Walker as "attacking" supervisors in the Post Office and Treasury Department. It focused on a purported conversation between Walker and the Treasury Department appointment clerk. Statements attributed to Walker suggest the frustration she must have felt. "I must fight my own way, and I think that my own persistence in my own behalf should be equally valuable with that of a politician in support of an application for clerkship," she reportedly declared. Walker complained that not only had she been slighted by officials, several reporters ridiculed her "because I am so persistent in my own support."[91]

Dr. Mary Walker failed to adhere to the conventions of female application and subsequently failed to obtain a position, but over the decade, women learned to frame their applications in ways that would get them hired. Female applicants downplayed their experience, intellect, and ambition, and paid particular attention to the feelings of men—it was what would get them hired, and once employed would help to keep them at their desks. Appointing women based on paternalistic charity, politics, and personal favor over merit, education, and intellect had consequences for female federal employment. Because federal hiring decisions were in the personal discretion of men, all female federal employees also suffered from rumors that they had earned their jobs through flirting and sexual favors. By presenting themselves as weak and in need of male protection women's employment seemed to be more charity than shrewd staffing. As women begged for paternalistic protection, however, many proved themselves quite capable of surviving without it, revealing that much of women's posturing as meek and needy in application materials was constructed fiction rather than fact.

"The Endurance of the Ancient Spartans": Female Self-Sufficiency, Ambition, and Tenacity

"Applying for a clerkship in Washington is one thing; securing it is another," reported the *Daily Morning Chronicle* in 1868.[92] The article's author addressed only men, but much of his advice and observations about federal employment applied to women as well.[93] He explained to his readers that obtaining a clerkship was a time-consuming, expensive undertaking that was likely to fail, estimating that there were between fifteen and twenty thousand applications on file in the Treasury Department alone.[94] The author commented on the "perseverance of some of these applicants," which "is most remarkable, and excites an admiration almost equal to that inspired by the story of the endurance of the ancient Spartans." He described the (male) applicants as "energetic, capable, and ambitious."[95]

Female applicants also had to be "energetic, capable, and ambitious." It was not an easy thing to obtain a government situation in the Civil War era, and although supervisors rewarded narratives of female dependence and weakness over narratives of female independence and ambition, the process of applying for a job with the government required self-sufficiency, drive, and tenacity. Even if a woman did not possess or practice these traits prior to application, she was likely to develop them in the process. Female applicants may have touted their womanly dependence and need, but they used that narrative as a weapon in their arsenal. Officials were, as the *Evening Star* reported, "besieged by lady office seekers who plead with tears, and recitals of stories of want and suffering for positions."[96] A focus on the tears has detracted from the besieging.

A November 1867 Washington, D.C., newspaper article highlighted and sensationalized the dominant paradigm of the needy, desperate woman seeking a federal job and the difficulties and dangers she encountered in her quest. It also, however, inadvertently revealed the courage, independence, and strength women had to possess to seek jobs in Washington. The article was captioned "A Sad Case." More than a year earlier, the paper reported, a young woman from rural Pennsylvania had come to Washington seeking a job with the government. The seventeen-year-old was the eldest of six children and her family was very poor. Working as a teacher, she managed to save a small amount of money to fund her trip to Washington, where she knew no one. The paper reported that the woman "tried for a long time without success, to get a place, until her money was gone; she could not go home, and alone and friendless, in a strange city, with a months' board due, the poor girl knew not what to do." A young man in the guise of a "good angel" came to her rescue: "He advanced her money to pay her board, and promised to aid her in getting a situation." A short time later, when her debts had doubled and she still had not obtained a job, it became clear to the young girl—as the common Victorian trope goes—"that Satan indeed could clothe himself in the garb of an angel of light, for the young man took advantage of the power he had gained, and the young girl, driven to desperation, fell."[97]

While "A Sad Case" was most certainly intended to be a parable to deter young women from leaving home for Washington, D.C., there are some truths at its core.[98] Women did come to Washington seeking jobs, only to exhaust their resources in the process. Like the seventeen-year-old from Pennsylvania, many women discovered that trying to obtain a job without a powerful male champion was nearly impossible and women had to be resourceful in finding a man to support their applications. Even though the young woman in the article failed in her job search, in a tragic manner that served to reinforce the gender norms, the article also reveals an important groundswell of female independence. The young Pennsylvanian had been working prior to applying for a job. She strategically saved her earnings and traveled to Washington, entirely alone and where she knew no one. She obtained boarding, and "for some time" navigated the city, visiting, presumably, multiple departments and pressing her case to numerous government officials.

Although some women applied from afar or sent someone to the departments as a proxy, going to Washington personally, as did the woman in "A Sad Case," was the preferred course. After the war, N. J. Brent moved from Richmond, Virginia, in her attempt to obtain a job, and she wrote to the secretary of the treasury, "I am in Washington but a 'stranger in the midst of strangers,'— having neither friends, nor home, nor food, nor shelter, but such as depend upon my ability to procure with money, and which means I cannot possess without employment."[99] Miss B. W. Quince was the sole support of her invalid mother and young sister. "Deprived by the late unfortunate war of *all means* of support, I came to Washington with the expectation of securing a situation that offered, disappointed in this, I am thrown on the world without *employment* and *without means*," she explained.[100] The overall tone of Brent's and Quince's application letters is one of supplication—both women beg for the help of the men to whom they are writing. Both women, however, traveled to Washington alone, found room and board, managed to obtain the ear and endorsement of President Johnson, and ultimately obtained jobs. Quince managed to do all of that work while also providing for two other people. Many more women failed to obtain the employment sought. In 1867, for example, the Sons of Temperance appropriated "$25 for the relief of a woman who came from Texas to the city expecting to obtain employment, was unsuccessful, and made her destitute circumstances known to a lady member of the division."[101]

Female applicants, like their male counterparts, demonstrated the "endurance of the ancient Spartans" in their quest for government employment. Of the 235 files reviewed containing application materials from new female applicants, forty-five women obtained jobs in the department at which they had originally applied, and nineteen obtained jobs in other departments. It took almost a third of these women more than a year of applying to obtain their jobs.[102] Eleven women applied for more than two years. Many of these women applied at multiple departments.[103] E. Jane Gay, for example, applied to the Pension Office, War Department, Patent Office, and Post Office for six years before finally securing a job in the Post Office in 1869.[104]

Women were not applying for federal jobs on a lark—they needed income. Thus, the months and years spent trying for the federal job had to also include working, and often moving. Some women gave up. Mary E. Stabler applied to the War Department in August 1865 and in May 1866 wrote again to that department, "Nine months having passed without hearing anything in relation to it, I conclude that I am ineligible to the position and respectfully desire to withdraw my application and the letters enclosed with it."[105] Other women had to resort to charity. M. K. Guthrie moved to Washington, D.C., in 1863 to seek a job in the Treasury Department, having secured the recommendation of Pennsylvania congressman Thaddeus Stevens. By October 1865, she had still not obtained a position and wrote to an army major asking for his help in securing her a position in the War Department. "Ever since I have been living in hope; but with my children, and an aged sick Mother, I have become penniless, and had not the Masonic Lodges aided me I could not have obtained sufficient to live," Guthrie explained.[106]

Despite the obstacles, women persevered, though they did not always meet with success in obtaining federal employment. Between 1866 and 1872, Fannie E. Gause lived in Virginia, South Carolina, Pennsylvania, Illinois, Delaware, and Florida. Gause, whose father died in service and whose three brothers served honorably, had supported herself by teaching in freedmen schools in Virginia and South Carolina when she began applying to the Treasury Department. After a return to her home state of Pennsylvania, she moved to Illinois where she continued teaching, work that she found "so arduous and attended with much exposure that my health has been somewhat impaired." By 1872, she was living in Gainesville, Florida, and "still very anxious to secure position in one of the Departments," but there is no evidence that she was successful in her efforts to obtain a federal position.[107] Mary F. Shockley began applying to the Treasury Department in 1864. That year, she was living in Massachusetts and working as a teacher. Her 1865 application letter noted her address as "Saratoga, NY . . . 20 degrees below zero." She wrote to Congressman Thomas Eliot of Massachusetts: "I know your good and generous heart will pardon me for bringing myself to your notice again. But if you were in these hyperborean regions, where old Boreas stalks abroad in furred garments, with his beard fringed with icicles of mercury; amid this ice and snow where the avalanche and glacier reign triumphant . . . you would have sympathy for me." By 1867, Shockley was living in Baltimore and her 1868 letter to the Treasury Department explained that she had been "teaching a colored school for nearly three years, most of the time for a mere pittance."[108] Shockley's tenacity ultimately paid off, though not exactly as she had intended. By 1869, she was one of ten undefined female employees, most likely a laborer, in the Treasury Department's Loan Division earning $2.25 per day—not the clerkship to which she had aspired.[109]

Women who remained in Washington, D.C., while their applications were pending were not passive applicants. They read newspapers for announcements or hints at job openings, maintained a network of friends who passed information about developments in the departments, and acted on the information.[110] Some women used information as a way to target their applications to positions they knew had opened. Others used the information to prod their recommenders into the most efficient action.

Female applicants Redden, Baker, and Poor all used information about recent job openings to focus their applications.[111] Redden had been an applicant for three months when she became "informed that a position in the ladies' copying room, attached to the Internal Revenue Bureau has lately been made vacant." Her application had originally been submitted to the secretary of the Treasury, but she used this new information to apply directly to the deputy commissioner of Internal Revenue.[112] Mary E. Baker applied to the War Department after "hearing from a dear friend that Miss Wallace, Copyist in the 'Recording Room' in Washington, is about to resign her position." Mary F. Poor applied to the same office after learning "that there are at present in your department, two situations recently filled by ladies, now vacant."[113]

Other women passed pieces of intelligence on to their recommenders. Mary Ream wrote to Missouri congressman James S. Rollins in December 1862, "To day I have learned that a number of female clerks are to be appointed in the Internal Revenue Bureau, and hasten to request that you will make an early application there for me."[114] Mary Sloan included as a postscript to her letter to Congressman Cake in 1869: "Since writing the above I have noticed the action of Congress increasing the number of clerks in the Treasury department, also increasing the pay. As Gen. Butler opposed of the measure, I may not do so well pecuniarily under him, as elsewhere and though I would prefer that position to all others leave the whole matter to you."[115] Tenie Sloan began applying to the Treasury Department in August 1868 and obtained a position in March 1869. She did not let her file gather dust during the seven months it took her to obtain the job. In January 1869, for example, Sloan wrote to her recommender, Senator Benjamin Wade of Ohio, "I have seen the assistant Treasurer four times since you so kindly endorsed my letter." In these conversations, the assistant treasurer had informed her that if Wade and Sloan's other recommender—New York congressman General James Garfield—would go together to see the secretary of the Treasury, they could secure a place for her. Less than three months later, Sloan had the job.[116]

African American female applicants had to overcome the racial prejudices of supervisors, as well as gender discrimination. Eleanor Ketchum's 1869 letter to Benjamin Butler illustrates some of the strategies African American women utilized in applying to the federal government. Ketchum had worked for Butler as a copyist during Andrew Johnson's impeachment trial in May 1868. At the time, Butler had endorsed a letter of recommendation for Ketchum to present to the Treasury Department. She had not used it, however, explaining, "I never presented that letter as the times were such as not to encourage a Colored woman to hope for advancement." By March 1869, the climate in Washington, D.C., had changed. Ulysses S. Grant had just been inaugurated president of the United States, and upon taking office, he signed legislation that Johnson had opposed, allowing African American men to hold office in the district. Because of this political shift, Ketchum now felt more confident that her application might be considered and timed her application accordingly. Ketchum explained to Butler that in the past year she had "never ceased to hope and to struggle," and though she "deprecate[d] the necessity of annoying" him, she felt it "necessary" to call on him once more. She signed her letter, "your ex-copyist."[117] Ketchum's attempt to secure federal work was successful. On May 4, 1869, she became the first African American female clerk appointed to the Treasury Department.[118]

Women also scoured newspapers for hints of potential jobs and pounced if they found one. On March 27, 1868, the *Evening Star*'s "Washington News and Gossip" column read: "Between this date in the first of April about thirty-five female employees in the various branches of the Treasury Department will be dismissed, and about fifteen new appointments will be made to fill some of the vacancies."[119] The next day, the paper ran a notice that the previous day's news had been "misconstrued by many of our [female] readers: in consequence of which there was a large crowd of applicants at the appointment office this morning, all of whom are disappointed, as the appointments had all been determined upon."[120] In May 1871, newspapers in Massachusetts, New York, New Hampshire, and Ohio all reported that a female clerk had died, and "two days after eighty-two women called at the department to solicit the vacancy."[121]

To improve their chances of success, women worked to obtain multiple recommendations, but these did not always prove sufficient. D. Dailey's War Department file contains recommendations from both Michigan senators, three Michigan congressmen, and a former Illinois congressman. Mary Locke obtained recommendations from both of North Carolina's senators and four of its seven congressmen for her 1869 application to the Treasury Department. Annie Gaston collected the signatures of twelve congressmen from at least six different states—New York, Illinois, Missouri, Kentucky, Indiana, and Delaware—for her 1866 application to the Treasury Department. Kate Cahill's application included a December 19, 1865, letter of recommendation signed by thirty men, including General U.S. Grant, General Nathaniel P. Banks, President Andrew Johnson, and Vermont senator Solomon Foot.[122] Women's abilities to procure the influence of multiple politicians further underscores that women were not as helpless as their application materials presented them to be.

Julia A. Wilbur's diary traces the difficult and anxiety-inducing process of applying for federal work in the late 1860s and reveals the pressure female applicants were under to adhere to Victorian gender norms. During and after the Civil War, Wilbur was an agent of the Rochester Ladies' Anti-Slavery Society, first in Alexandria, Virginia, and then in Washington, D.C. Although she worked with the Freedmen's Bureau, she did not begin working for the bureau as a paid agent until 1867. By 1869, however, Wilbur had lost her paid positions with both the Rochester Ladies' Anti-Slavery Society and the Freedmen's Bureau, and began looking for work in the federal departments.[123]

Wilbur cast a wide net, and would have been happy to secure a place in any of the departments. First, as she recorded in her diary, she wrote to Washington, D.C., mayor Sayles J. Bowen on February 14, 1869, "asking him to get me a place in one of the Departments."[124] Not much must have come of that request because a month later, Wilbur trudged through the snow to see General Oliver O. Howard, commissioner of the Freedmen's Bureau. After an hour's wait, Howard gave Wilbur two letters—one addressed to postmaster general John Cresswell and another to Jacob D. Cox, secretary of the Interior. Howard, recorded Wilbur, "was very kind, but is afraid they will do me no good, as there are hundreds of applications for every place almost." Presumably Wilbur was not seeking a job in the Treasury Department at this point because, as she noted the same day she met with Howard, there was a "great rush" for those positions.[125] On March 23 and 29, Wilbur visited the Capitol and found "Corridors thronged with men, office seekers probably, and lobbyists. Some women too." She described some of the office-seekers as "hard looking cases."[126]

On the night of April 7, Wilbur cornered Mayor Bowen at a church sociable but, she recorded, he "does not give me any encouragement. Only says he will help me in any way that he can." Her interaction with Bowen left Wilbur reconsidering whether she should apply to the departments at all, but on April 9, she wrote a letter of application to the Department of the Interior. Three days later, she went to City Hall to again press the mayor for influence, but he was at home, sick. "Things do not look encouraging for me," Wilbur lamented to her diary. On April 19, she returned to City Hall and was again unsuccessful in trying to meet with Bowen. She had no luck meeting with Bowen to garner his promised assistance the next day either, writing, "My affairs look discouraging."[127]

Wilbur was finally able to meet with Mayor Bowen on April 26. She first went to City Hall in the morning, but there were so many people vying to see the mayor that she left and returned in the afternoon. Four days earlier, Wilbur and six other women had attempted to register to vote in the First Ward of Washington, D.C. Bowen had heard of Wilbur's political activity: "He said my asking to be registered the other day would kill my chance of getting a place but he wished me to understand that he has no objections to it." Thus, although Bowen claimed indifference to Wilbur's political activity, he assumed it would be fatal to her application. Nevertheless, Bowen gave Wilbur a letter to Secretary of the Interior Cox and another to Postmaster Cresswell, though he warned her that he had heard that Cresswell was not hiring women. This was all difficult information for Wilbur to hear, but she "got through with this part bravely" and then immediately went to the Patent Office where she was told it was too late in the day to meet with Secretary Cox.[128]

Wilbur focused her efforts on gaining an audience with Secretary Cox. The day after her disappointing meeting with Bowen and her failed attempt to meet with Cox, Wilbur returned to the Patent Office—this time in the morning—but "was told 'he does not receive on Cabinet days.'" "Oh! dear," Wilbur wrote, "I will try to be patient." On April 28, Wilbur walked back to the Patent Office where she waited an hour and a half, "then was told the Sec. would receive no more to-day." Wilbur resolved to "not give it up" noting that "some 20 others were not received." The next morning she returned again to the Patent Office and "was told the Sec. wd. not receive to day, he was going down the River with the President. Well, well!" In "desperation" Wilbur went to Howard University and met with General O. O. Howard and "talked the matter over." Howard gave Wilbur a letter to Secretary of the Treasury George Boutwell, in case Wilbur was unable to gain a position in the Department of the Interior. "Told him if I failed in the Depts. I sh. come to the Bureau for a place," Wilbur wrote, "He laughed + did not say 'no.'" The next day, Wilbur again tried to meet with Secretary Cox and was for the fifth time in as many days unable to meet with him.[129]

On May 1, 1869, Wilbur walked through the rain and waited two hours in the anteroom of the Patent Office. Her tenacity was finally rewarded. Secretary Cox "was very gracious + did not talk at all discouraging," assuring her he would give her an answer as to her application in a week, when appointments were to be made. Even though Wilbur's quest to meet with Secretary Cox was frustrating, she was in a better position than many of her peers. After her meeting with Cox, the Secretary's clerk apologized profusely for not having admitted her earlier claiming that he "did not know I was Miss Wilbur," a testament to Wilbur's reputation and connections in Washington, D.C. For her part, Wilbur "smothered my resentment + even thanked him for his courtesy at the last," aware that she needed the goodwill of the secretary's clerk.[130]

When more than a week had passed with no word from Cox, Wilbur returned to the Patent Office, but was unable to see Secretary Cox. Two days later she tried again. Though she was not able to meet with Cox, he sent word that her application "had probably been referred to a Commissioner." Cox's clerk introduced Wilbur to one of the commissioners, who told her that "the female clerks wd. be discharged the 1st of July." Cox's clerk then introduced Wilbur to Commissioner Samuel Fisher "who was quite gracious, but wished me to write an application to himself. Wished to see my writing +c." Frustrated, Wilbur recorded, "Very well, I hastened home + tried an hour or two but could not produce anything satisfactory + gave it up for today. Quite discouraging!" The next day, Wilbur managed to make out her application to Commissioner Fisher. She returned to the Patent Office, but was told she could not see him. She managed to gain access to the Assistant Secretary of the Interior "but this did not amount to any thing. I feel quite discouraged of course. + had to cry."[131]

On May 14, Wilbur returned to the Patent Office and waited two hours to see Commissioner Fisher and present her application. Fisher "said he had but one minute for me. He just glanced at the paper that I had spent so much time over, but I am to go on Monday to learn the result." "This suspense is making me nervous," Wilbur wrote, "I cannot endure it much longer." The next day, Saturday, Wilbur bemoaned, "Oh! this waiting!"[132]

At 9:30 A.M. on Monday, Wilbur went to the Patent Office "for the 11th time." She was told that she could not see the commissioner until 11:00 so Wilbur waited, wandering around looking at the models on exhibit in the office. When an hour and a half had passed, she "went slowly back + waited in the Hall for nearly half an hour. Then I was ushered into the presence of Com. Fisher. He soon told me that he had concluded to recommend my name to Sec. Cox, and I asked him 'if that was equivalent to an appointment?' He said yes." "Well, the suspense is over," wrote Wilbur. She began work at the Patent Office on July 1, 1869, four and a half months after she began applying to the departments.[133]

Wilbur rose early on July 1, 1869, anxious about beginning her new job at the Patent Office. Her first day, however, included a surprise—her application process was not complete. Upon arriving, Commissioner Fisher informed her that she "must submit to an examination in various branches." At the end of the 1860s, the Patent Office began requiring that women, as well as men, pass an exam to demonstrate requisite competence—the only office at the time to do so. Wilbur was directed to a table and given a test comprised of "28 printed questions," instructions to write a letter to the commissioner, and a number of lines to copy to demonstrate how quickly and accurately she could write. At least two other women, Miss R. Elwell of Connecticut and Mrs. Murray, also took the test that morning. Wilbur recorded "we did the best we could, although we were aware we had failed in some." The writing that was to be copied, for example, was estimated to take ten minutes, but it took Wilbur 17 1/2 minutes. "I was weak + trembling + cd. do nothing well," remembered Wilbur. Fisher reassured her, however, that "it was all very credible + in the Ex's so far the women do better than the men." The office dismissed Wilbur at 1:30 P.M., telling her to return the next day. At 9:00 A.M. on July 2, Wilbur, Elwell, and Murray waited in Commissioner Fisher's room to hear the results of their exams. Fisher "said we bore a better Ex'n than most of them, but they were not absolutely the best." It was enough, however, to secure all three women their places in the Patent Office in July 1869.[134]

Competition for positions and a lack of influential connections such as those that Wilbur had forced some women to be creative. In an 1870 lecture to the YMCA, former patent commissioner Samuel S. Fisher, the man who hired Julia Wilbur, explained the methods some had used to appeal to him in their efforts to gain employment. "One lady said she had been much impressed by my remarks upon the subject of consecrating our means to Christ," and informed him that she wished to adopt his principles. "Unfortunately," she explained, "she had no means to consecrate. Would I appoint her to a clerkship in the patent office, 'so that she might be able in the future to do something in so good a cause?'"[135]

Fisher was surprised by the persistence of female applicants. He told his YMCA audience that upon assuming the position he was struck by "the great preponderance of females among the applicants for office." He found female applicants not only more numerous than he had anticipated, but also more persistent. "It was next to impossible to keep them out of one's room," he claimed, "and next to impossible to get them out when they once came in."[136] The commissioner of agriculture allegedly favored the employment of women in theory, but began to actively discourage Congress from establishing clerkships for females in his department because he could not manage the number and persistence of the applicants and their congressional supporters.[137] Such descriptions reveal that the narrative of the needy and helpless female was a strategy that women learned was in their best interest to construct. Cultivating this fiction, however, would have ramifications for women in the type of work they were permitted to do, the way they were perceived in the workplace, and the rate of pay that rewarded their labor.

EMPLOYING WOMEN WAS AN EXPERIMENT in the 1860s. In 1865, E.M. wrote to the local *Daily Morning Chronicle* in response to a rumor that government officials had deemed the experiment a failure. The writer's letter described why that might be the case: "Doubtless the evil at the root of the matter is, that appointments of women are controlled solely by influence, and that no examination is had as to their capacity for the position about to be assumed." Some of the positions to which women were appointed required "peculiar intellectual or mathematical ability" and yet these were not the bases upon which the government hired women.[138] The bulk of the positions men were willing to hire women to fill, however, required no such specific skills. Men's conceptions of what women could and could not do shaped how and where women entered the federal workforce.

CHAPTER THREE

Teapots in the Treasury of the Nation
Gendering Work and Space

Quartermaster General Montgomery C. Meigs had a problem. At the end of 1862 Meigs began to hire women to work as copyists in his office.[1] By June 1864 he confessed to Secretary of War Edwin Stanton that he had found "difficulty in placing [the female copyists] under charge of a male clerk." Meigs now wanted to segregate the women from the rest of the office, which would mean appointing a female supervisor. Unfortunately for Meigs, "No one of the ladies is willing to assume the responsibility and the labor at the rate of compensation allowed to [female] copyists," which at the time was $600 per year.[2]

Sarah F. Wainwright, however, was "willing to perform the duties if given . . . the salary of first-class clerk, $1,200 per annum"—twice what women in the federal workforce earned at that time.[3] In 1864, Wainwright, a native of Pennsylvania, was a middle-aged single mother of three children, ranging in age from eight to fourteen years old.[4] A war widow, she had joined the War Department in 1863.[5] Meigs informed Stanton that Wainwright "possesses the requisite qualification for superintendent" and recommended her appointment, in place of a recently resigned male clerk.[6] Four days after Meigs's recommendation to Stanton, Wainwright received an official letter from the Quartermaster General's Office informing her that Stanton had agreed to appoint her to a first-class clerkship, thus waiving the examination that was typically required for such an appointment.[7] Beginning in 1865, five years before Congress sanctioned appointing women to the graded class of clerks, the name "S. F. Wainwright," without the personal title "Mrs." or "Miss" that preceded her female coworkers' names, began to appear under the heading "Clerks" as a first-class clerk in the *Federal Register of Employees*—the only female name on that list.[8]

Throughout the 1860s, some supervisors endeavored to incorporate women into the federal workforce. Most took it for granted that female employees were fundamentally different from male employees, but exactly how different, and when and how those differences should matter, was contested. One important commonality, however, was the idea that the federal government employed women out of a sense of charity or connections with men which might call into question her respectability. With limited exceptions, a female federal employee did not earn her place because of her unique fitness for the work or her demonstrated intellectual capacity, but rather because she was needy and had influential benefactors. Civil War–era male federal employees also initially earned their places through patronage rather than ability, which roiled some supervisors and politicians, ultimately leading to a reorganization of the Civil Service in 1871 under President Grant.[9] The patronage that earned men their positions, however, did not carry with it the undertone of pity or a questioning of moral respectability as it did for women, and could be quickly forgotten once a man proved his worth and was promoted on his merits. Women, conversely, had to maintain the image of neediness to retain her position, and defend her respectability throughout her career with the federal government. These two ideas—female employment as charity and female federal employees as morally suspect—complicated how women were perceived in the federal workforce and the jobs supervisors allowed them to do.

Supervisors typically used gendered language to set women apart from their male colleagues. Men were clerks; women were female clerks. Appending "female" to the job title narrowly circumscribed women's roles, options, and futures in the federal workforce. Women did not always resist the female appellation or its corresponding limitations. Some embraced it, finding that it offered certain privileges and protections. A small number of women, however, favored the "clerk" half of the title "female clerk." When supervisors imposed restrictions on the female workforce those women pushed back, demanding to be treated the same as their male colleagues. As Dorothy Sue Cobble found in her study of post-Depression era labor feminists, other women, including Wainwright, tried to capitalize on the contested interstitial spaces between "female" and "clerk," attempting to exploit the benefits of both.[10] Wainwright, for instance, obtained the salary of a first-class clerk, but did not have to take the examination typically required to earn it.

No matter what her position was, a woman employed by the federal government in the 1860s experienced the Civil War and Reconstruction in a way that was unique for women of her generation. Presumably, all female federal employees had some personal connection to the war, a relative, friend, or an acquaintance in the fray. In their capacities as federal employees, however, women were also part of the Union's bureaucracy. As part of their regular work, women helped the Union prosecute the war—they were part of the workforce that instituted a national currency and they did the clerical work that allowed soldiers and their dependents to receive pensions in that currency. In the Third Auditor's Office of the Treasury Department, a woman worked as a clerk processing receipts and payments for military expenditures. In November 1869, she opened a file for adjustment and discovered that it was for her son, who had been a quartermaster. He, along with two of his brothers, died during the Civil War.[11] For many women like this clerk, the conflict shifted in and out of focus from the abstract to the deeply personal as they sat at their desks or operated their machines. This intimacy with the bureaucratic side of war was possible only because women worked for the federal government.

It is difficult to typify the work experience of all female federal employees in the 1860s. Men and women negotiated women's federal employment on a daily basis in a multitude of contexts. Still, women's labor in the federal government can be examined over three broad categories: the types of jobs women performed, how supervisors regulated and viewed female employees, and women's relationship to their coworkers and their workspaces.[12]

Women's Jobs in the Government:
"As Multifarious as Those of the Sterner Sex"?

Government employment of women was a novel enterprise in the 1860s, and one that supervisors in the executive departments undertook with little forethought or planning. Women often performed labor in which men had been engaged. Many supervisors carved out the more monotonous tasks from men's jobs and largely or exclusively assigned them to women. Others employed women in the same capacity as men, albeit with different job titles and lower pay. As women settled into these jobs, some developed prized expertise from routine and seemingly minor assignments while other women enjoyed or aspired to more challenging and varied work. No matter her position, however, a female federal employee's gender was the characteristic by which she was identified and evaluated.

Women applying for jobs with the federal government in the 1860s, and the people recommending them, often did not know precisely what the government was hiring women to do—they just knew that the government was hiring women. Although some women insisted that they would do anything, other women and their recommenders often stressed that the female applicant sought a "woman's position."[13] There were overlapping reasons for making this distinction. Some applicants or their recommenders cited gender as a way of confirming that the government was indeed hiring women. "I have heard that there is in the gift of the government situations that can be and are filled by women," Julia Richards wrote to Abraham Lincoln in 1862, a little over a week after the Union lost 13,000 men at Shiloh.[14] A number of applicants and recommenders used the gender distinction to make clear that the female applicant was qualified only so far as the job to be performed was a "woman's job."[15] While some applicants made this distinction because a job opening was for a woman to replace a departing female employee, many tied the purported gender of the position with respectability.[16] Entering wage labor was unusual for many of the middle-class female applicants.[17] Women wanted it to be clear that they were applying for jobs for *ladies*—not overstepping bounds to apply to men's jobs—and that when employed they would be working among other ladies.[18]

Many women and their recommenders found the issue important, but the idea of a government job being "female" was a fiction. There was nothing inherently "male" or "female" about any federal position.[19] For clerical jobs especially, a purported bifurcation of positions into those performed by men and those performed by women was an illusion—in many instances, men and women performed similar or even identical work. The work was sexless; the pay was gendered.

A number of federal jobs—those involving certain types of manual labor—had been from their creation assigned to females. Only women served as attendants to other women or as cooks, laundresses, and chambermaids in the Government Hospital for the Insane, and women were the rug beaters, drapery launderers, floor scrubbers, and lamp dusters of Congress and other federal buildings. Jobs such as these were seen as an extension of the labor women performed in their homes—cleaning, cooking, sewing, and laundering. As the size and scope of the federal government expanded, supervisors staffed women in positions that they deemed similarly domestic. For example, the Department of Agriculture employed women, ranging in age from children to the elderly, to fill small bags with seeds and stitch them closed so that they could be distributed across the country.[20] Women also worked as "wetters" in the Treasury Department. Lined up along a long trough in a hot attic room of the Treasury building, they saturated paper that was to be used for plate printing and pressed it between boards and cloth to obtain the desired moisture level, much as laundresses dunked soiled garments.[21]

As was the case in the private sector, although some of the work assigned to women purportedly capitalized on domestic skills and was thus seen as uncontroversial, the labor women performed for the government was far different in scale and intensity than that performed at home.[22] For instance, the Government Printing Office (GPO) employed women "in folding, sewing,

MAKING MONEY. — THE ROOM IN THE TREASURY BUILDING WHERE THE GREENBACKS ARE PRINTED

Ames, Mary Clemmer. *Ten Years in Washington: Life and Scenes in the National Capital, as a Woman Sees Them*. Hartford, CT: A. D. Worthington & Co., 1873 (page references are to the 1880 edition, which includes additional illustrations), between 318 and 319.

and stitching" reams of paper into books.[23] While touring the GPO, observer Mary Clemmer Ames found a woman in the stitching room, where folios were stitched into books, who appeared to be suffering from "the St. Vitus' dance": "Every muscle and nerve in her body flew. The very nerves in her face twitched with the quick intensity of her movement; while her fingers struck the needle and drew the thread with the persistency of a perpetual motion." The young worker explained to the concerned Ames that she had to work as furiously as she did because she was paid only thirty cents apiece and even working very rapidly could stitch only a maximum of nine pieces a day. "But I should think it would kill you to work like this all the time," responded Ames. "I've been doing it for four years, and I'm not dead yet," the young woman assured her.[24] While supervisors believed that "domestic" tasks were somehow innately female, in practice the work performed for wages bore little resemblance to the work women performed in the home.

In other manual positions, women performed the same, or very similar, work as men, sometimes laboring in close contact, although women were consistently paid less.[25] In the Treasury Department, women worked on presses alongside men, printing greenbacks and cigar stamps. A woman's job was to lay a sheet of paper, damp from its time with the wetters, in the ink-lined plate, and remove it after her male coworker had made the impression upon it.[26] Both men and women worked machines in the Government Printing Office.[27] "If there is anything that is pretty," wrote one Washington, D.C., guidebook author in 1873, "it is to see a pretty girl on an Adams' press, feeding the monster so daintily."[28] In the Government Hospital for the Insane, male and female attendants, who were required to live at the hospital, performed similar work. Some male attendants even grumbled about the sameness of their jobs, taking issue that they had to scrub floors for example, even though the Hospital consistently paid men higher salaries.[29]

In clerical positions, many of the tasks the government hired women to do also had been, and were still being, performed by men. Women entered into clerical work through the Treasury Department's clipping room, and men had clipped currency before Jennie Douglass proved that women were capable of cutting sheets into banknotes—this is also likely why the arguably "manual" job of currency cutting was at least initially considered to be clerical.[30] Once through that narrow door, women quickly spread throughout the Treasury Department and to the Post Office, Interior, War, and Agriculture Departments as well, settling behind wooden desks. Before their arrival, men had been occupying those desks.

Because supervisors had so much leeway in how they structured their departments, it is difficult to generalize about precisely what women employed in clerical labor in the executive departments did even when we know their job titles, although their gender is clear. Gender labeling of female federal employees was a common practice in the executive departments. In the *Federal Register* in 1867, 163 women worked under the job title "Ladies" in the Treasury Department, which offers no indication of what they actually did. That year, the Treasury Department also employed women as "copyists," "copyists and counters," and "female clerks."[31] During the Civil War era, all women were, with very limited exceptions, labeled as "Mrs." or "Miss" in the *Federal Register*. Although men also performed copy work as part of their jobs, supervisors never described men as "copyists," nor did they designate them as "Gentlemen" or "Mr."[32] Women's job titles were misleading as they purported to, but did not, differentiate what women did vis-à-vis men and vis-à-vis other women. In debates over female pay at the end of the decade (discussed in chapter 7), congressmen readily admitted that some men and women performed precisely the same jobs despite the men's job title of "clerk" and the women's job title of "copyist." Congressmen further agreed that the work of female "counters" was as laborious and demanding as the work of "clerks."[33] Newspapers also often described women as "clerks" who were technically "copyists" and may have been working as "counters."[34] Letters of recommendation also used the terms interchangeably.[35]

This confusion is understandable because clerical jobs were largely undifferentiated, especially in the early 1860s.[36] In one day, a clerk might perform chores such as copying or filing, but might also be tasked with more cerebral tasks such as adjusting accounts or redirecting waylaid letters. Moreover, there was no standardization as to how to title female federal employees—supervisors chose to label the women working under them in whatever way they saw fit. Because of this, we cannot determine the type of work a woman did for the federal government based solely on the job title under which her name appears on the *Federal Register*. Female federal employees performed a broad range of jobs for the government. While there was some truth to an 1870 newspaper article that reported, "The duties of the female employees in the [Treasury] department are as multifarious as those of the sterner sex," this was not the case in all federal departments.[37]

In the War Department and the Pension and Patent Offices, supervisors hired women almost exclusively to work as copyists. The tedium of such labor can be glimpsed in the December 1866 monthly report of Sarah Wainwright, the supervisor of women in the Quartermaster General's Office, on the "time and conduct" of those working under her. That month, C. L. Cowperthwaite copied "178 pages"; Miss Janney, "150 pages"; Miss Richardson, "138 pages"; Miss Sherman, "129 pages"; and Miss Wilcox, "126 pages."[38] Women in the Treasury, War, and Interior Departments all performed this same enervating drudgery day after day—rewriting the words of others, often in large, leatherbound books.[39]

The work was not only tedious, the repetitive motion of constant writing put strain on the eyes, arm, and hand, as Julia Wilbur's diary attests. On her second day at the Patent Office, Wilbur asked for work that would not require so much writing, and was told she could work as a comparer—checking the copy work of other employees against the originals. Despite her request, however, Wilbur was often assigned to copying and she found it physically demanding. A little over two weeks after she started, she noted in her diary, "My hand feels the worse for so much writing." The next day, "Arm + hand feel badly." On July 22, she recorded that she had done what she could at work "but my hand has pained me some." By August 9, her hand was "weak + lame" from all of the copying. On September 20, Wilbur wrote in her diary, "My hand + wrist pain me so much that I decided to keep away from the office today." She went back to work, but her hand, arm, and wrist continued to plague her. In the fall of 1869, her eyes also started to trouble her, and her diary is peppered with references to eye aches, the problem becoming especially acute in January 1870.[40] Wilbur's work-related physical complaints drop off, but never completely disappear from her diary, suggesting she grew accustomed to the physical demands of the job.[41]

Although comparing and copying could be tiresome, it allowed women an almost unparalleled opportunity to be privy to and engage with important political matters at a critical juncture in American history, sometimes gaining access to information before politicians and the public. This work also encouraged women to form opinions about political matters they might otherwise not have been exposed to. In January 1870, Wilbur was tasked with comparing the copywork of her coworker Miss Read in advance of the documents being sent to Congress: "All about Black Bob's Band of Shawnee Indiana. How the poor creatures have been wronged." One day the following month, Wilbur copied and compared hundreds of pages of legal documentation, recording that she found it to be a "good report."[42]

Several mundane tasks carved out of men's duties and assigned exclusively or largely to women provided women with the opportunity to develop niche expertise that gained them prestige and called them away from Washington, D.C., although their proficiency did not bring them higher salaries or opportunities for advancement. Clerical tasks assigned to women could be monotonous, but by constant practice, women were able to cultivate skills in ways men—who had performed the work only sporadically—never had. Close observers, including supervisors, frequently remarked on the value of women's work and in some instances private enterprise sought women out because of the skills they had developed.

Currency counting was one such occupation. In the Treasury Department, women worked as counters, counting bills as they ran off presses and prior to being placed into circulation. The challenges in this position were twofold: the size of the workload and the ramifications for mistakes. Female federal employees counted enormous quantities of currency. An observer estimated that one woman counted fifty thousand notes per day, or two and a half notes a second.[43] The work was not simple counting either. One 1867 newspaper article described it as "a curious, *double* mental operation."[44] After the introduction of mechanized note cutting, machines—manned by women—cut four notes out of each sheet of paper and dropped the numbered notes into one of four boxes.[45]

AMONG THE GREENBACKS.—THE CUTTING AND SEPARATING ROOM IN THE TREASURY BUILDING.—WASHINGTON.

Ames, Mary Clemmer. *Ten Years in Washington: Life and Scenes in the National Capital, as a Woman Sees Them.* Hartford, CT: A. D. Worthington & Co., 1873 (page references are to the 1880 edition, which includes additional illustrations), between 322 and 323.

As the notes were consecutively numbered, the piled notes "skipped four" so that "if the top note is 162,640, the second will be 162,644, and so on to the end." The woman counting the notes was charged with creating packages of one hundred notes each and confirming that they were properly sequenced and genuine: "while running her fingers over each note, she gives simultaneously with its count, only the final figure of its Department number, thus: '1-0, 2-4, 3-8, 4-2, 5-6, 6-0.' on through the whole hundred."[46]

The women had to perform this work rapidly, and safeguard the currency in their charge. When a counter had possession of notes, newly printed or those being redeemed, they were her responsibility. If she made a mistake and her stack was short, or if she counted and passed a counterfeit bill, the missing money came out of her small salary.[47] In 1868 Treasurer Francis Spinner informed Congress that these "female clerks . . . are subject to greater risks of loss by reason of miscounts or by passing counterfeits, for which each one is pecuniarily liable and responsible, than nine-tenths of the male clerks, whose principal occupations are books and accounts, are subject to."[48]

The work was difficult, requiring mental stamina, and counters earned respect in and out of the office for their proficiency. In 1869, Senator William P. Fessenden, formerly secretary of the Treasury, recommended that counters should be compensated equally to male clerks, as their work was laborious and required "a good deal of care and a great deal of skill also."[49] Senator Lyman Trumbull echoed Fessenden in 1870, describing the women counters as "among the most valuable class of persons in the Departments."[50] In 1869, when an accounting discrepancy arose, the Treasury Department dispatched "a dozen of the female clerks" who were "expert counters of paper and money sheets" to New York to compare the returns and figures of the American Bank Note Company to the Treasury Department's accounts.[51] The women stayed on to count the securities and gold bonds in the New York Sub-Treasury.[52] In November of that year, the secretary of the Treasury dispatched a "committee of twenty ladies" from his office to count the currency in another office.[53]

Women also developed expertise as investigators of mutilated currency—another discrete task pulled from the labor of male clerks and assigned largely to women. The Redemption Bureau employed women to identify notes that had been burned, buried, sunken, shredded, or otherwise damaged.[54] Women redeemed notes that had come from "the toes of stockings . . . from the stomachs of animals, and even of men . . . fragments of money, whose lines are often utterly obliterated, whose tissues emit the foulest smells."[55] The work required patience and tenacity. As described by Mary Clemmer Ames in 1873, the women separated "each small piece" of crumbling currency "with thin knives made for the purpose, then laying the blackened fragments on sheets of blotting-paper" they "decided by close scrutiny the value, genuineness and nature of the note" and pasted the pieces onto a sheet of paper to be returned to their respective banks or to the Treasury Department.[56]

The women of the Redemption Bureau received mutilated currency from across the country, and supervisors and the press praised their skills and professionalism.[57] In January 1869, Julia Wilbur toured the Treasury and was shown a room in which "several young women were at work" with $204,000. The steamer on which the money was being transported to New Orleans burned. The money had been "in a safe that was neither fire proof nor water proof" and sat at the bottom of the Mississippi River for two years. The female clerks worked to determine the denominations of the charred, water damaged remains. "It is a trying work for the eyes + an impossible work apparently to those who do not handle much money," remarked Wilbur in her diary.[58] In 1870, the Redemption Bureau received "a small iron safe" full of charred and blackened currency from Nashville. A Washington, D.C., newspaper reported that the notes were so badly damaged "as to make it almost impossible to recognize to what denomination they belonged." "The lady examiners" of the Bureau, however, were able to redeem the entire sum of $25,000. The article's author lauded "the wonderful expertness of the ladies in examining burnt money."[59] In 1893, a West Virginia newspaper reported that "the women detectors of burnt and counterfeit money are claimed to be the most expert in the world."[60]

Private businesses recognized female clerks' facilities in redeeming currency. The Adams' Express Company, for example, in conjunction with the government, employed women on their cases. After the Great Chicago Fire of 1871, the Treasury Department assigned six female clerks to identify over one million dollars in burned money. When a fire ravaged Boston a year later, the city sent eighty-three cases of currency to the department for the same six women to identify. One of the women, Mrs. Patterson, regularly worked on "affidavit cases" in which she had to verify the amount of mutilated money an affiant was attempting to redeem. One such case involved a trunk of money lost on the bottom of the Mississippi River for three years after a shipwreck. Mrs. Patterson managed to identify $185,000 of the $200,000 in the trunk, and the express company responsible for the trunk rewarded her with $500.[61] Thus, while some supervisors assigned women mechanical and repetitious work, women took these limited jobs and managed to develop a new niche expertise that was in demand.

Not all of the clerical work performed by females for the federal government in the 1860s was limited to or dominated by women, however. Many female employees performed the same, or very similar, jobs as their male co-workers, albeit for half the pay. Male clerks were divided into four classes, but those designations were mainly about salary rather than job descriptions.[62] As historian Cindy Sondik Aron has demonstrated, the "absence of a highly centralized, rigidly administered federal employment policy" allowed supervisors the freedom to assign women to positions that were complicated and intellectually demanding, if they chose to do so.[63]

The Post Office Department employed both men and women in the Dead Letter Office. When a piece of mail had insufficient postage, was improperly addressed, or for whatever reason was left unclaimed in post offices across America for a certain length of time, it was sent to the Dead Letter Office in Washington, D.C. The Dead Letter Office managed more than letters; all of the undeliverable flotsam and jetsam of the mail found its way to that office. The variety of materials clerks in the Dead Letter Office handled can be glimpsed in the accountings of items auctioned off during the department's "annual sale of accumulations." In 1867, such items included everything from "needles, soldiers' jackets, shoes, calicos, stencil tools, [and] spurs" to "medicines warned to cure anything or everything, pills of different manufacturers, ointments, pimple exterminators, Costar's rat exterminator, the 'Drunkard's Cure' . . . and, as an auctioneer would say, 'other articles too numerous to mention.'" In 1879, a reporter observed among articles awaiting redirection: "one half-worn gaiter-boot, two hair-nets, a rag doll-baby minus the head and one foot, a set of cheap jewelry, a small-sized frying-pan, two ambrotypes, one pair of white kid gloves, a nursing bottle, a toothbrush, a boot-jack, three yards of lace, a box of Ayers pills, a bunch of keys, six nutmegs, a toddy-stick, and no end of dress samples." Clerks had to redirect these lost missives and random pieces of property, if possible, by ascertaining each item's intended recipient or sender. This task was made difficult by unintelligible handwriting and incomplete addresses. A letter or package could be addressed simply to "Carlton in America."[64] Male and female clerks labored together using a combination of experience, teamwork, and detective skills to redirect such mail, the quantity of which was enormous. In 1868, for instance, the Dead Letter Office received over four million pieces of mail for redirection.[65]

Although the practice was limited, across departments, some supervisors likely hired women because of their particular intellect, skills, and experience. In 1871, both men and women worked as "Copyists of Drawings" in the Patent Office.[66] Only certain people were capable of the work; one observer remarked, "To do this work perfectly, a lady must be something of an artist and draughtswoman."[67] In the Treasury Department, the women of the Fifth Auditor's Office who worked on State Department accounts had to possess "a knowledge of banking, as well as of mathematics" in order to perform their jobs, an observer explained.[68] The Third Auditor's Office also employed women to adjust accounts for military expenditures.[69] Some women in the Treasury Department, including those in the Internal Revenue Bureau, worked at jobs that involved "examining, sorting, and filing the different daily communications received at the office" which required familiarity with a variety of internal revenue codes and tax regulations.[70] Lois Bryan Adams, the former editor of a Michigan agricultural periodical, began work in the Department of Agriculture in 1863.[71] Adams assisted in the museum, and an observer described her as "a woman of much intelligence, [who] has made a study of botany and natural history, which enables her to fill her present position with credit to herself."[72] Theresa Drexler, a German-born taxidermist, also worked at the Agriculture Department in her own private office.[73] In 1870, two women translated the entire foreign correspondence and kept up the accounts in various languages at the Washington, D.C., Post Office. "They are scholars in four languages," reported *The Revolution*, "German, French, Spanish, and Italian."[74]

Although a lack of centralized structure in the executive departments allowed supervisors to assign qualified women to these kinds of challenging positions, more commonly traditional notions of gender imposed limitations on what many supervisors were willing to conceive of women doing, notwithstanding the enormous (albeit unjust) potential for cost savings. In the Dead Letter Office, for instance, although both men and women redirected mail, the female clerks were banned from initially opening the mail because the letters and packages might contain something scandalous.[75] For the "merely mechanical work" of opening the envelopes, a *New York Times* article reported, some men received $1,200 to $1,400 per year, as compared to the $900 women earned for redirecting it.[76]

The law, or a supervisor's reading of it, also prevented women from assuming some jobs. In the spring of 1870, the superintendent of the census rebuked the United States marshal for the southern district of Ohio for including Lavinia Purlear and Sarah Burgoyne on his list of census-taking assistants. "These appear to be the names of women," the superintendent wrote. He explained that women were ineligible to be hired under an 1850 act and asked the marshal to make new appointments.[77] Despite women's demonstrated abilities and skills, most women in the offices of the federal government continued to be tasked only with the growing mountain of routine copying, sorting, and filing that resulted from the commission of the war.

Engrained notions about what women could or should do held many women back from positions of greater responsibility in the federal government, but some used those same prejudicial ideas to argue that women should be given greater roles in the government service. Some politicians and newspaper articles asserted that clerical work was feminine and men should be laboring in more "manly" pursuits.[78] In an 1870 Senate debate on female pay, discussed in chapter 7, Nevada Senator William M. Stewart argued that "with regard to the mere matter of copying, the mere matter of writing, that work can be done by females, and as well done; and I think it for the interest of the country that it should be done by them" because "a good many male clerks who are indifferent clerks" would be "better employed in settling up farms, if they are able to work." Stewart believed an all-female clerical workforce would be "better for the community, better for the male clerks to be sent out of the city, and better for all concerned."[79] But men were not sent to the farms. Men and women both remained in the federal service and male supervisors had to learn to manage a mixed-sex workforce.

"A Woman Can't Reason a Damn Bit":
How Supervisors Regulated Female Employees

In 1865, fourth auditor Stephen J. W. Tabor praised the labors of the seventy-five "clerks" (all male) and thirteen "ladies" in his office that had adjusted and settled a total of over $80 million in accounts in one fiscal year. Tabor reported that the women who worked under him "have discharged the duties assigned to them with intelligence, industry, and commendable zeal." He supported women's federal employment, which he believed "tends to break down that barrier which has so long debarred woman from occupations for which she was as well fitted as man, and from which she was excluded by an unjust prejudice" and also praised the "economy" of the practice, since the government could pay women far less than the men. "It should, however, be understood by ladies who enter any bureau as clerks," Tabor continued, "that as sex was disregarded in their employment, so it should not be pleaded for any relaxation or abatement of the customary rules and regulations." The fourth auditor urged women to "take a pride in showing that the department did not misjudge in considering them competent, both physically and mentally, to make efficient and acceptable clerks."[80]

Of course a woman's sex was *not* disregarded in her employment. Her sex dictated how she obtained her position, what jobs she was eligible to perform, how her work was evaluated, and how much she was paid, in addition to a myriad of other considerations. While the range of labor women performed for the federal government was wide, their pay scale was quite narrow, especially before 1870. Women's relatively flat wage schedule, combined with stereotypes concerning women's natural delicacy and the patina of charity that overlay female employment, made it difficult for some men to work with and supervise female employees. Since almost all female federal clerical workers earned the same salary, women could neither be demoted nor promoted. Confusion arose at the confluence of the deference given to ladies and the regulation of employees. Female federal employees themselves differed as to whether, when, and how their identities as females should trump their identities as employees. Although womanhood insulated them from some of the undesirable aspects of work, it also precluded female federal employees from attaining some of its benefits.

In the Treasury Department's annual reports to Congress, it is clear that women proved themselves to be capable and valued employees.[81] In 1863, the fourth auditor, Stephen Tabor, reported that the women employed as copyists in his office had "given entire satisfaction."[82] In 1865, the second comptroller, J. M. Broadhead, reported that a number of the women in his office "have been found fully competent to examine accounts and settle claims of the heirs of deceased officers and soldiers." Broadhead continued that the new female employees "report as large a number of accounts adjusted as their male co-laborers engaged on the same class of work, and they have been found, almost without exception, assiduous in the discharge of their several duties, and uniformly observant of the rules and regulations of the department."[83] In 1866, Treasurer F. E. Spinner declared the employment of females to be a "success."[84] Spinner was so pleased with his female employees, he began that year to push for a reorganization of his office that would result in it being predominantly female.[85] In 1868, Alexander Delmar, the director of the Bureau of Statistics, wrote that the women he employed, who were "mostly engaged in compiling the warehouse accounts, and in the preparation of statistical tables connected therewith . . . have exhibited clerical abilities of a high order" and that they had proven themselves capable "of performing equally arduous and difficult services" as the male clerks.[86] Third auditor R. W. Clarke wrote in his 1869 report that the women of his office "are prompt to duty, and attentive and industrious in its performance, and above reproach."[87]

While supervisors recognized women's value as employees, some of their praise had prejudicial undertones. Women's work as counterfeit detectors provides a good example of this duality. Counterfeit detection was an art consisting "of subtle perception, of fine, keen vision, and of exquisite sensitiveness of touch," noted one observer. Both men and women worked as counterfeit detectors in the 1860s, but supervisors—most notably treasurer Francis Spinner—preferred women for this work.

Women were "better" at counterfeit detection than men, the press averred. A Washington, D.C., observer commended one female counterfeit detector who had "detected spurious notes in many instances which have passed in the hands of skillful bank officers and been considered genuine."[88] Treasurer Spinner informed Congress in 1868 that for currency counting, redemption, and counterfeit detection, women "excel, and, in my opinion, are to be preferred to male clerks."[89] In 1869, "In order to test the difference between two kinds of clerks, on [counting and counterfeit detection] more thoroughly, the female clerks were required to review and recount the work of the male clerks." The experiment revealed that women not only found mistakes in the men's counts, they also detected counterfeits that had "been overlooked by the male clerks in the offices where they were originally received, and by those in this office, who had counted them."[90] Spinner did not attribute a woman's adeptness at counterfeit detection to her assiduity or intelligence.

COUNTING WORN AND DEFACED GREENBACKS, AND DETECTING COUNTERFEITS.
This room is in the Redemption Bureau, Treasury Building. Over One Hundred Thousand Dollars worth of Fractional Currency alone is here daily received for redemption; out of which about $350 dollars' worth of counterfeit money is detected, stamped and returned.

Ames, Mary Clemmer. *Ten Years in Washington: Life and Scenes in the National Capital, as a Woman Sees Them.* Hartford, CT: A. D. Worthington & Co., 1873 (page references are to the 1880 edition, which includes additional illustrations), between 354 and 355.

Instead, Spinner contended: "She cannot tell you *why* it is counterfeit because a Woman Can't Reason a d___m bit, but her perceptions are quicker than those of a man."[91]

By concluding that women could excel at tasks such as counterfeit detection simply because of some innate quality they possessed by virtue of being women, supervisors like Spinner ignored and negated women's critical thinking abilities and hard-earned skills, often crippling their careers. In a response to a survey sent to workforce supervisors at the end of 1867, for example, several men indicated their perceived limitations of women's abilities, despite the success women were having in other offices. N. Sargent, commissioner of customs, who had no female employees, wrote that he would be "unwilling" to trust his work to women. The duties of his clerks included "the revising and settling long and intricate accounts, involving innumerable questions of law and practice, and not unfrequently the unraveling of confused and erroneous statements," and he had "never yet seen the woman equal to such a task."[92] The assessor of the 29th district of New York, J. P. Murphy, who also had no women working for him, wrote, "I doubt whether any female could be found in this district, or in any other, possessing the requisite qualifications to make a good assistant assessor."[93]

Even when supervisors were willing to hire women to do clerical work men had been or were still doing, they did not pay them as much as men. Not only was the structure of women's pay unfair, however, it was also flat. With very limited exceptions, the best female clerk received the same salary as the worst female clerk, and supervisors felt unable to correct that imbalance. The horizontal structure of women's salaries created two intertwined problems for female federal employees and their supervisors. First, it did not incentivize women to work harder; and second, women who did excel at their jobs lacked a clear channel by which they could advance.

In his annual reports to Congress, Treasurer F. E. Spinner argued for the gradation of women's salaries. He first raised the point in 1865, but as time passed and Congress failed to take action, he became adamant on the issue.[94] In 1866 he complained that women's flat pay scale was "unjust and pernicious. It pays the merely tolerable as much as the very best." He asked for a graded pay scale so that women's "ambition should be stimulated by the prize of promotion for well-doing." As it stood, "instead of inciting a poorer to emulate the best clerks, it tends to demoralize them, and brings them down to the level of the poorer class."[95] In fact, the flat pay scale may have punished those women who worked the hardest. Spinner explained to Congress in 1868 that supervisors were more likely to grant leave to mediocre clerks because they could be spared and less likely to grant leave to good clerks, because they were needed.[96]

The horizontal pay scale also provided women no clear opportunities for promotion and limited options for transfers. While currency counters were respected, once a woman learned that skill, it applied to no other job in the federal department. Achieving proficiency only at the mundane work that was assigned cemented women in place. Supervisors had no incentive to move quick and neat copiers and rapid and accurate counters to more intellectually challenging work in their departments.[97]

Other obstacles to women's advancement were a serious lack of training and a hiring practice that favored the neediest and best connected over the most qualified. Representative Thomas Jenckes, an early and devoted proponent of civil service reform, included women in his reform aspirations. In a speech to the House on the reorganization of the civil service, Jenckes explained that by appointing women without clearly defining their duties, tenure of office, or method of advancement, female federal employees were professionally handicapped. To Jenckes, the problems surrounding the government's employment of women were institutional. "They are thrust without previous training into places sought for them, and are retained under lax discipline," he argued. Because of the manner in which the government employed women, "the result is what might be expected of persons, who have no hope of the recognition of merit or of the reward of promotion, and who are continually admonished that they may be dismissed at any time without notice and without cause." Jenckes was confident that if the government regulated female employment in the same way it regulated male employment, women would thrive.[98] Even if, despite these obstacles, a supervisor wanted to promote a female federal employee, they were on shaky legal ground in doing so until 1870, when Congress legislated that women could be appointed to the graded class of clerkships.[99] This was likely why, for example, the War Department dropped the "Mrs." from Wainwright's name in the *Federal Register* after Meigs and Stanton somewhat surreptitiously began paying her the salary of a first-class clerk.

Because they were the most poorly paid, laborers and messengers were the two classes of female employees that did at least have some advancement path prior to 1870. Treasurer Spinner promoted women, including Sophia Holmes, an African American woman. In 1860, Holmes was a washerwoman with $100 of property supporting five children. By 1870, she was a messenger in the Treasury Department with $2,800 in real and personal property, a large sum for a woman at the time. Holmes first appeared in the pages of the *Federal Register* for the Treasury in 1863, when she was listed as a "Female Temporarily Employed." She earned $216 per year. By 1865, she was one of seven female laborers under Treasurer Spinner, and her compensation was $288 per year. In 1867, she was a messenger and her salary jumped to $720 per year, the same salary the three white female messengers received.[100] In 1892, *The Woman's Journal* ran an article explaining how Holmes obtained her promotion. The article claimed that one night, when Holmes was sweeping up, she discovered a box containing $50,000 in greenbacks that had been accidentally left out. Instead of calling the watchmen, who she feared "would be tempted beyond resistance," Holmes "sat down upon the box and quietly waited for the hours to go by," despite "her four small children at home alone." When she heard Spinner in the corridor, Holmes gave him the box. The next night, reported the *Journal*, Spinner "placed in her hand her appointment papers, given for honesty."[101]

Other female laborers and messengers were able to advance in the Treasury Department under Spinner as well. By 1869, Spinner had promoted Ruth Biggs, an African American woman; Caroline Davis, a "mulatto" woman; and

Delia Foley, an Irish woman; from laborers to messengers.[102] Irish-born Catherine Maroney worked her way entirely up the short ladder of female federal employment. In 1865, Maroney was working as a laborer earning $24 per month. By 1867, she was a "messenger" in the Treasurer's Office, earning $720 per year. In 1869, the last year Maroney's name appears on the *Federal Register* in the time period under examination, she was earning $900 as a "Lady Clerk" in Spinner's office.[103] For most women like Maroney, however, a clerkship was as far as they could advance in the government in the 1860s.

A small number of women, including Sarah Wainwright of the War Department, however, managed to advance from a female clerkship position prior to 1870 by becoming supervisors of other women. The Patent Office, Post Office, and Government Hospital for the Insane also employed female supervisors.[104] While female supervisors had greater responsibilities than the women working under them, they were not always paid more. In the early 1870s, an observer remarked upon a woman in charge of a division in the Internal Revenue Bureau who had held her position for seven years. She supervised the work of forty-five women and was "highly spoken of by all who have business dealings with her, as possessing every qualification necessary to the discharge of her duties." Her salary remained at $900 per year while male supervisors in that division earned at least twice that amount. The observer informed his readers that "every man who entered the office at the same time as herself has been gradually promoted to the highest salaries, or found a better employment outside, while she remains."[105]

Moreover, female supervisors had only limited authority. Wainwright, for instance, could only suggest to Quartermaster General Meigs how to assign work to the women working under her; she could not change the women's assignments herself.[106] She sometimes signed her letters to Meigs as "Lady in Charge," but Meigs was the person who made decisions regarding sick leave and work assignments for the women.[107] In August 1866, Wainwright made several suggestions to Meigs, but he made only one minor assignment change and it lasted a mere month.[108] Thus, female supervisors served only as intermediaries through whom men's authority flowed to the wider female workforce.

The handicaps placed on women's advancement meant that the most well qualified and best performing employees could be taken advantage of by supervisors and colleagues. Women could supervise men who earned significantly more than they did, and could be tasked with men's work in addition to their own.[109] An observer described one woman who prepared statistical tables for congressional reports for the Treasury Department as a "mathematical genius" and "one of the best practical mathematicians in the Treasury Department." This female mathematician's male coworker became such a terrible alcoholic that his friends committed him to an "inebriate asylum" and she assumed his job duties as well as her own, performing the work of two $1,800 a year clerks for $900.[110]

In addition to navigating how to staff their departments and promote their female employees, supervisors also sometimes had to discipline women working under them. Some found reprimanding women to whom they were not related to be awkward, especially when women became emotional. In their defense, women often invoked the protection of the powerful men who had aided their appointments, adding difficulty to supervisors' efforts to discipline their female workers. Supervisors' reluctance to correct female employees' work habits would have made it difficult for women to improve their job performance. It also may have given some supervisors pause when considering whether to incorporate women into their offices.

Employee records reveal that at least some supervisors felt that their female employees had to be shown some degree of deference because they were women. Helen C. Briggs of New York came to the Treasury Department well recommended. She was a widow supporting two sons and had worked as a teacher. Briggs received a position in the Treasury Department in 1863, and in October 1867 she was transferred to the departmental library, "and there has not been a week's tranquility in my Division since that time," reported her supervisor in a February 1868 request to have her transferred out. The librarian, Mr. Atlee, found no fault with Briggs's "punctuality, industry, or accuracy," and though her handwriting was "not suitable for the records" it was at least legible and "this deficiency might be passed over." "But she has an ungoverned temper and an unruly tongue," Atlee continued, "and these infirmities have made her universally unpopular amongst her colleagues." He explained that he had "endeavored to get along with her," but had become "wearied out with her." Atlee's chief complaint was that Briggs had "taken a prejudice to [the] chief assistant Mr. Kimball" and instead of coming to him to discuss the matter, Briggs had enlisted the support of a male colleague and created a feud between the two men. Atlee found this behavior "subversive of all discipline," and did "not think that it should be tolerated." Had Briggs been a man, it seems, Atlee would have terminated her, but, "as she is a woman and a widow" he stated that he "should be sorry to see her taught discretion by dismissal and have therefore asked a transfer."[111]

A similar kind of delicacy with regard to supervising women occurred in the Post Office and War Departments as well. In an 1871 article about the workings of the Dead Letter Office, a New York newspaper explained that occasionally the male supervisor had to follow up with the female clerks on a mistake in their work and in doing so, had to be careful, as "each and every lady" was "very sensitive . . . to the slightest reproach or reprimand."[112] War Department employee Jane Swisshelm reported that male coworkers and supervisors had a difficult time conceiving of women as workers rather than as women. Not one in twenty men could "go into a room where women are employed, and transact business with one of them without in some way reminding her of her womanhood," she claimed. According to Swisshelm, "The idea of treating them as copyists and clerks, simply this and nothing more, is beyond the mental caliber of almost any man with whom they are brought into personal relations." She argued that men's patronizing behavior was damaging, and since men behaved as if women were not respected as employees, some women had to resort to personal favoritism to maintain their positions, giving credence to the negative stereotypes of female federal employees.[113]

While some supervisors seemed to be solicitous toward female employees, however, appearances could be deceiving. Most women who obtained their positions through the recommendation and support of powerful and influential men and women could leverage those relationships to thwart supervisors' efforts to discipline them. Reprimanding or firing a female employee could have negative consequences for the supervisor if a woman's recommender took her case personally. Mary A. Brennan circumvented the normal chain of command when an issue arose with her work. In the summer of 1863 Brennan received a notice of transfer. Seemingly due to her poor performance, she was to be moved from the position she occupied to the counting room of the Treasury Department. Rather than discuss the transfer with her supervisor, Brennan approached Maine senator (and future secretary of the Treasury) William P. Fessenden, who had helped her obtain the position. Fessenden in turn wrote to Brennan's supervisor. He was clearly concerned with Brennan's feelings, and expected her supervisor to be as well. Fessenden explained that Brennan "is evidently laboring under a misapprehension as to the satisfactory character of her work, and, for some reason or other seems to have a strong aversion to the counting room." Fessenden asked that her supervisor allow her a further trial, "as she seems very sensitive on the subject, perhaps because her pride is troubled at the idea of not succeeding."[114] It is unclear from her employee file if Brennan retained the job, but Brennan likely knew that her supervisor would be more receptive to Senator Fessenden's request on her behalf than to her own entreaties.[115]

Although many supervisors held some notions about what women were and were not capable of doing in the federal departments, the novelty of women's federal employment in the 1860s allowed women some latitude to negotiate the terms of their labor. For example, women did not simply accept the standard hours of the workday. Like so many other aspects of federal clerical work, supervisors dictated the length of the workday in their individual departments.[116] Typically, in the executive departments the workday began at 9:00 A.M. and ended at 3:00 or 4:00 P.M., with a half-hour break for lunch, and could vary by the season.[117] Women, who likely desired an earlier dismissal time to tend to family duties and domestic burdens, negotiated with supervisors to adjust work hours. The women of the Dead Letter Office had found the seven-hour day (9:00 A.M. until 4:00 P.M.) overlong, and arranged with their supervisor to end the workday at 3:00 P.M. In exchange, they worked industriously and did not leave for lunch, "nor did they waste much time in discussing the lunch they have brought," reported an observer.[118] In the Patent Office, the workday also began at 9:00 A.M. and ended at 4:00 P.M.[119] In November 1869, the women of the Patent Office also traded their half-hour lunch break for an earlier dismissal, but their success must have been short lived because in May 1870 a local newspaper reported, "A deputation from the lady employés of the Patent Office yesterday waited upon Secretary Cox for the purpose of having the working hours reduced from 4 to 3 o'clock."[120] Cox "praised the manner and faithfulness with which the ladies did their work," but he was not as impressed with the work of the *men* in the office, "for whose special benefit the extra hour had been added." The article noted that if Cox did agree to shorten the workday, something he promised to consider and the paper believed he would do, the "gentleman will be indebted to the enterprise of the ladies who presented the petition and their eloquent pleading."[121]

Female federal employees tried to modify other regulations to fit their desires. In 1869, the secretary of the Treasury issued a circular to the clerks in his Department containing nineteen questions that they were ordered to answer. The questions ranged from personal demographic information to queries regarding at whose recommendation they had received their appointments.[122] The female clerks raised an outcry over one question in particular: "What is your age?" A Kansas newspaper informed its readers that the female clerks were "highly indignant" about this question, which they found offensive.[123] A Texas newspaper explained that some of the women "insisted that it is their secret."[124] Nine days after the *Daily Morning Chronicle* reported that the interrogatories had been issued, it reported in a follow-up article that "the lady clerks are relieved by the Secretary from the requirement of affixing their ages to the list."[125] The following month the *Albany Journal* in New York reported that the female clerks "greatly rejoiced" in their success.[126]

Women also successfully rejected certain workplace norms that they found oppressive. In a long, front-page article concerning the introduction of women into federal offices in the Washington, D.C., *Evening Star*, the author included a discussion of supervisors' inability to curb women's chitchat. The article's author claimed that "repeated efforts have been made by the officials to put a stop to the chatter of the female employees" but "nothing has been accomplished toward stopping their tongues during office hours, and all hopes of breaking up this practice have long since been abandoned." Supervisors apparently tried to encourage female employees to behave like their more laconic male coworkers, but "talk to each other [the women] will, in spite of all threats, coaxing, and promises." The article noted, however, that despite their chattiness, "as a general thing, [the female employees] are attentive to their business and prompt in their attendance."[127]

"Fifteen Ladies in a Room, / Dark and Cold and Dreary, / Ask to Have a Carpet, New, / Bright and Warm and Cheery,": Accommodating Spaces and Working with Men

Supervisors had different opinions regarding not only about what jobs women should do, but also where they should do them. Gender segregation in the workplace ranged from an attempt at entire separation of the sexes to men and women laboring as a team on the same machine. Separation provided women with greater freedom to govern their workspaces, but deprived them of being part of the larger workforce. It also marked female workers as distinct and different from male workers. Integration gave women greater opportunities to learn the business of the department and to form camaraderie with male coworkers, but women also found that their presence was not always welcome.

The quartermaster general and the patent commissioner attempted to entirely segregate women from the male workforce (save their male supervisors) and from the public. In 1873, an observer described the offices of the female copyists in the War Department as "three comfortable rooms . . . not so handsome as those in the Treasury, but are much less public. No male clerks are in these rooms."[128] Women in the Patent Office worked in the "ladies' department," located in the basement of the building. A former patent commissioner described that space as "entirely removed from the rooms of other clerks. No gentleman occupies any portion of their rooms or halls, and male clerks or visitors are not allowed to appear upon the floor of the building unless upon business."[129] Women's segregation in these offices limited their interactions with coworkers and reduced women's ability to learn departmental business to what they could glean in the materials they were tasked with copying. Separation did, however, give women a degree of autonomy, and perhaps security, that they did not enjoy in other departments. The women in both the Patent Office and the War Department worked under female supervisors and seem to have had greater control over their physical workspaces.

The women in the War Department's Quartermaster General's Office worked under Sarah F. Wainwright. The quartermaster general (QMG) never employed more than thirty-one women during the 1860s, and all the women employed in that office, save Wainwright, were copyists. As part of her job, Wainwright, along with other supervisors in the War Department, submitted a monthly report of "the time and conduct" of the women working under her. Twenty-nine of her thirty-six monthly reports for the period between January 1865 and December 1867 survive in the records of the Quartermaster General's Office.[130] In these reports, Wainwright noted the average arrival and departure times of each employee, as well as the number of days, if any, a woman was absent.[131] Women may have felt more comfortable explaining reasons for absence to a female supervisor than to a male supervisor. For example, when Augusta Brown had to miss one day of work in May 1866 "on account of sick child," it may have been easier for her to explain her predicament to another mother.[132]

The office experienced little turnover under Wainwright. Only forty-three different names appear on the monthly reports. Although Mrs. Gurney lasted only one month, the average length of employ was twenty of the twenty-nine months for which reports survive. This was longer than the average female job tenure in the 1860s, which, based on analysis of almost three thousand female federal employees, may have been only one year or less.[133] Twenty of the forty-three women appear in all twenty-nine reports.[134] The women of the War Department seemed to have felt secure in their jobs. The market for female government employment was tight, even cutthroat, in some departments and employment terms tended to be short. Yet three women in the War Department—Emma D. Sedgwick, Eliza Barstow, and Garaphelia Howard—attempted to get jobs for friends while they were still working there, suggesting that they did not fear for their own jobs and felt uniquely confident enough in their own work to believe they were in a position to recommend other employees.[135]

In the War Department, at least, the segregation of the sexes was not absolute. Despite Meigs's insistence that the men and women in his department remain separated there was certainly interaction between male and female clerks. In fact, men and women managed to form serious relationships. From the statements of War Department clerk Swisshelm noted above, it was clear men were allowed in the women's workspace.[136] In the late 1860s, Jane D. Baldwin, a copyist in the War Department from Louisiana, loaned money to a male coworker.[137] Angie Emery, who joined the War Department in February 1866, had to resign a year later because her affair with a married male coworker, Edwin Phillips, came to light.[138] The barriers claimed to isolate women in other offices may have been similarly porous.

The Patent Office also took pains to separate men and women employees. Women, including Clara Barton, had worked in the Patent Office in the late 1850s. Sometime in the early 1860s, women began to perform their Patent Office copy work exclusively at home, transporting the work by messenger.[139] Women returned to the Patent Office in 1869, and the female copyists worked under Mary Capen, of Massachusetts.[140] Like Wainwright, Capen commanded a higher salary than the copyists she supervised, earning $1,200 per year in 1869 to their annual salary of $700. Capen, whom an observer in 1873 declared was "a woman of remarkable business capacity," was, like Wainwright, hidden in the *Federal Register* by her first initial and surrounded by male names, since prior to 1870, women were not technically permitted to be classed as clerks or to be paid more than $900 per year.[141] In April 1870, "D. P.," a correspondent for the *Cincinnati Commercial Tribune*, toured the office with Capen, whom the correspondent described as "a hand some woman, yet on the winning side of thirty, with an admirable figure, erect and well proportioned" and with a face that "told the story of organization and command." D. P. explained that it was Capen's "business to superintend these workers and direct their work. She turned over her books and exhibited the time tables, where opposite each name was the hour and minute of arrival and departure, the time lost and the work done."[142]

Although some female employees may have been more comfortable working directly under another woman, Julia Wilbur, who for years had worked somewhat autonomously as an agent for the Rochester Ladies' Anti-Slavery Society and later the Freedmen's Bureau, initially chafed under Capen and her diary suggests that other women did as well. The women's difficulty with Capen does not appear to have been with the woman personally, but because she was the female employees' disciplinarian and taskmaster, and the female clerks were adjusting to their realities as salaried employees.

On her first full day of work at the Patent Office, Commissioner Samuel S. Fisher led Wilbur to the basement, where fifty-three women labored in six rooms. Fisher told Wilbur that two men were in charge of the division and that Miss Capen assigned the work. Wilbur asked to be made a comparer (comparing copied work to the original, rather than performing the copy work), and her request was granted. Increasingly, however, her work involved copying, and on July 20, 1869, she complained in her diary that this was "unjust" and that she had been "constrained to speak to Miss Capen about it." Her conversation with Capen does not seem to have resolved her concerns because two days later, Wilbur, whose hand and arm were bothering her, recorded, "Wonder if I had better see Mr. Fisher + tell him how it is!"[143]

Wilbur met with Fisher on July 24, but it did not go as she had intended. After explaining what she felt had been an injustice done to her, Fisher "said it was left with Miss C. to assign the work." Fisher's point to Wilbur, as she understood it, "amounted to this, 'Govt. pair a certain sum for having a certain amount of work done + if I could not do it, why, then I could not expect to be employed by the Govt, even though I might be deserving.'" Fisher made clear to Wilbur that there was a job attached to her salary determined by Capen, and if she couldn't do it, they could find another woman to take her place. Wilbur received that salary for the first time on July 29, noting that while most clerks received $58.97 per month (or approximately $720 per year), Capen received $1,200 per year. In early August, Wilbur tried again to go around Capen's authority in the assignment of work. She noted that Mr. Upperman "spoke to Miss C. about my work. She will show me no favor."[144]

At the end of the month, while Capen was away from the office, Commissioner Fisher came to the basement and addressed the female clerks, a number of whom appear to have been unhappy with Capen's assignment of work and had been, like Wilbur, trying to circumvent her authority by appealing to a man. Fisher, according to Wilbur, told the women that he "approves of every thing Miss C. does. Says Mr. Upperman has nothing to do with the ladies. (Must not go into their rooms) he is Chief of the Copying Division + will send the work to Miss C. + see that it is right when done." Wilbur, who believed "Miss C. has the ill will of the ladies generally," interpreted this lecture not as support for Capen's authority, but as an undermining of Upperman's: "Mr. U. must feel indignant + humiliated." The next day, new rules were handed down in the department and it was Wilbur's turn to feel humiliation, "Reins are being drawn very tight. It is really humiliating to submit to such tyranny without daring to say a word."[145]

September, however, brought a thawing between Wilbur and Capen. On September 4, Wilbur noted that she "Talked with Miss Capen. She is a little more reasonable now." A few days later, Wilbur and Capen went together to view the body of the late Secretary of War John Aaron Rawlins. Wilbur's complaints about her hand, arm, and eyes continued, but rancor toward Capen for her assignments fell away. Wilbur instead began to have some sympathy for Capen. On May 2, 1870, Wilbur noted that Miss Capen was struggling with the female staff as "a few ladies are disposed to be insubordinate."[146]

Capen's responsibilities and authority did not appear to extend to controlling the physical workspace, however. When the women in the Patent Office wanted to alter their workspace, they petitioned the patent commissioner, not Capen.[147] The women did so in a unique manner that at the time would have been considered appropriate for ladies. Speaking to a YMCA meeting in Ohio, S. S. Fisher explained to his audience that his female employees requested a new carpet for their offices. The women's petition was as follows:

Fifteen ladies in a room,
Dark and cold and dreary,
Ask to have a carpet, new,
Bright and warm and cheery,
Not with little whirli-gigs
Of yellow, red or green;
But roses bright, and lilies fair,
And violets in between.
Or else, a cornucopia full
Of nature's choicest flowers,
So that their eyes may be made glad
Through all their business hours.
And this they ask the powers that be,
Commissioner and chief clerk,
And promise, faithfully through *all*
Their business hours to work.
Nay, more, henceforth in business hours
They hope to take the van
In promptitude and rapid work,
And *carpets—if they can.*
We signed our names, we all are one,
We all have got the floor;

And if we fail in this, we won't
Petition any more.
But, if we get the whirligigs
We hope the present *"Moses"*
(The leading carpet dealer in Washington)
May, when he spies the promised land,
See *them* instead of *roses*.[148]

In the form of a deferential and light-hearted poem, the petition demonstrated the women's efforts to feminize their "dark and cold and dreary" workspace. The women were particular. They did not want a rug with a design of "whirli-gigs," which perhaps was the design of other federal office rugs; they wanted one with a floral pattern. Moreover, these petitioners demonstrated solidarity ("we all are one") and workplace activism in their attempt to procure a new rug. Women's segregation from men in the Patent Office allowed them greater confidence and more freedom to attempt to alter their workspace to fit their wants and desires. There is evidence their petition may have been successful. On October 31, 1870, Julia Wilbur remarked in her diary that the women of the office were dismissed early, noting "putting down carpet."[149]

Women were segregated, but not entirely separated, from men in the Post Office Department's Dead Letter Offices, where they performed the same work. Women entered their workspace through a special door located near the Ladies' Delivery window of the Post Office. Once they entered, the women ascended a staircase to their section of the office, located in a crowded gallery that ringed a spacious room in which the men labored.

The women of the Post Office were not happy with their workspace.[150] Mary Clemmer Ames wrote that the women working there reported to her that "their little gallery is the escape valve to all the poisoned air below; that their heads are so near the roof there is no chance for ventilation."[151] In 1873, another observer described the room in which the men labored as "an extremely imposing-looking room, large and well ventilated," whereas the gallery ring in which the women worked was "the receptacle of all the foul air from the room below."[152] In trying to "protect" women's respectability by separating them from men, the Post Office Department relegated them to the least desirable, most physically uncomfortable, workspace in the office.

Most women who worked for the federal government in the 1860s were employed in either the Government Printing Office or the Treasury Department, both of which contained more integrated and heterogeneous work-

DEAD LETTER OFFICE, U. S. GENERAL POST OFFICE — WASHINGTON

Ames, Mary Clemmer. *Ten Years in Washington: Life and Scenes in the National Capital, as a Woman Sees Them.* Hartford, CT: A. D. Worthington & Co., 1873 (page references are to the 1880 edition, which includes additional illustrations), between 398 and 399.

spaces than the Patent Office or Post Office.[153] In some offices, men and women worked not only in the same rooms, but on the same machines. This commingling allowed women to learn more about the workings of the office and also allowed for greater camaraderie between male and female coworkers. Women had less control over their workspaces, however, and men did evidence some resistance to what they perceived as a feminization of the office.

In 1864, the head of the Treasury Department's National Currency Bureau, Spencer M. Clark, responded to a request from the assistant secretary of the Treasury to "report the number of Ladies employed in this Bureau—their compensation, and general character of their duties" and "to report how many rooms are specifically assigned to them, and if, in any case, clerks occupy desks in such rooms."[154] Clark reported that he had thirty rooms occupied by 477 employees and that many of the rooms were "crowded to a degree very prejudicial" to the health of the workers. Although Clark reported 477 employees, his tabular listing of the employees by room includes only 457 employees. Of these, 214 were male and 243 were female. In some cases, it is clear that men and women worked in the same room. The employees in other rooms were obviously all male or all female. In other cases, it is unclear. Clark divided his table into "uses," but each use occupied anywhere from one to sixteen rooms, so it is not always possible to determine if women and men worked in the same space. For example, 104 men and 95 women worked in seven "Printing" rooms. Of the twenty-five "uses" Clark enumerated, twelve were jobs performed by both men and women across multiple rooms. The descriptions of some tasks, however, indicate a sexually integrated workforce. For example, eleven men and eight women worked in "Pressing" in two rooms. Clark described the work as: "The girls count and place in and out of press board—the men work the presses."[155]

Sexual integration of workspaces gave male and female employees opportunities to socialize. Coworker interaction is evident in newspaper accounts of events that occurred at the departments. For instance, a local newspaper reported "quite a little flutter amongst the busy clerks and clerkesses of the Internal Revenue Bureau" when the men and women mistakenly believed Brigham Young had come to visit with a bevy of this wives. A "waggish clerk suggested to one of the messengers" that the man was Brigham Young. "That was enough!" the paper exclaimed. The speed with which word spread and people gathered indicate that male and female employees were working in close proximity and were in regular communication. "In the shaking of a lamb's tail desks were vacated," the article reported. "From down stairs and up stairs came the clerks, and in less time than it takes to write the sentence the halls and corridors of the office were filled with the curious throng of both sexes," the article continued. The paper included a sampling of comments by and between male and female employees—including an African American female messenger—that evidence a community of coworkers that enjoyed a degree of sociability.[156] The misapprehension of a more serious event in the Government Printing Office reveals similarly friendly relations between male and female coworkers. In 1865, hot water pipes burst in the GPO. Female employees took the sound to mean the imminent explosion of the steam boiler, panicked, and "stampeded" in an effort to escape. The sound of the women's exodus panicked the men working near them, and they joined in flight. Fearing the worst, "many were the embraces and farewells between young and old, male and female."[157]

Coworker camaraderie among men and women working together is also evident in the presentation of gifts to supervisors. Men and women occasionally presented supervisors with tokens of appreciation as a same-sex group of employees.[158] On November 10, 1870, the women of the Patent Office presented retiring Commissioner Fisher with "a gold headed cane ($50)." (Not everyone participated in the gift giving, however. Wilbur, who received her position from Fisher, confided to her diary, "I gave nothing. I do not believe in making presents to officials. It comes hard on the poorest ones for they do not like to refuse," noting that one woman gave her last fifty cents to the gift fund, and another had to borrow the fifty cents to be able to contribute.)[159] In the Treasury Department and Government Printing Office where men and women often worked together, male and female employees often made such presentations jointly.[160] These gifts required forethought, funds, and cooperation among colleagues. In the fall of 1867, the men and women of the Second Comptroller's Office assembled in the office of Dr. Brodhead and surprised him with "a large photograph, being a picture of all the employees of the office, (over 100,) with Dr. B. in the center."[161]

Coworkers also came together in times of need demonstrating the formation of camaraderie among colleagues. In all-female workspaces, assistance came from other women. Women who worked in the Treasury Department as counters were personally liable for any mistakes in their counting or if they inadvertently counted a counterfeit note as genuine.[162] This rule could impose a crippling fine on a woman for a careless error or reasonable oversight. Treasurer Spinner explained to Congress that "restitution for these errors sometimes takes, during a month, more than one-half of the month's salary," because of the huge quantity of money women counted relative to their salaries.[163] In order to mitigate these risks, the women came to each other's aid. "It not unfrequently happens that a number unite to make up the loss of the unfortunate ones," Spinner reported, "thus detracting something from the salaries of each."[164] In the Patent Office, women developed friendships with coworkers, would come to each other's assistance when needed. On June 16, 1870, Julia Wilbur fell ill at work, and was too sick to even leave the office. At 4:00 P.M., when the office was dismissed, one of her colleagues, Miss Reed, accompanied her home "+ stayed till dark."[165]

In offices in which men and women worked together, men joined women in providing assistance to female coworkers. In the summer of 1869, disaster befell Mrs. Lang of the Government Printing Office. Lang, the widow of a soldier, supported two small children and her invalid mother on the money she earned in the folding room of the GPO.[166] Sometime in June 1869, Lang's mother and youngest child became severely ill, and Lang was "compelled to remain at home." When she had not returned to work by August, a "lady friend in the folding-room, becoming uneasy because of Mrs. Lang's long continued absence, went to see her at her house." The friend discovered Lang, her mother, and children had been evicted, and were homeless, sick, and starving. The coworker gave Lang the little money she had and reported her situation to the (male) supervisor of the folding room, who provided further aid. Coworkers then circulated a newspaper article reporting on Lang's situation through the entire Government Printing Office, and collected $206.65 for their coworker's support.[167] Men also defended the honor of their female coworkers. In 1866, Mr. Nadal, a messenger in the Interior Department, accused a female copyist who worked there "with expressing language that can come forth only from the lewdest heart."[168] Nadal told his father of this female copyist's alleged lewd language and the father contacted the secretary of the Interior, "who, after a rigid examination, pronounced the young lady perfectly innocent of the charge against her." Other men in the office confronted Nadal in defense of their female coworker.[169]

While there is evidence of cooperation and camaraderie between male and female federal employees, there is also evidence of antagonism and animosity.[170] Men were especially resentful when they felt that women were taking over a workspace. Secretary of the Treasury Hugh McCulloch was displeased to discover women's teapots appearing in the windowsills of the Treasury Department. A local newspaper explained that the "female employees of the Treasury Department are accustomed to take tea with their lunches, and to warm the cheering beverage over the heaters and stoves in the building."[171] McCulloch was reportedly vexed with "the accumulation of teapots in the Treasury of the nation." Observer Ames claimed that the teapot was seen as evidence that women were "unfit for Government service," since they implied that women could not do their jobs without the stimulating beverage. (Ames questioned, however, why no one took issue with the cigars men used to help them through the workday.)[172] Men's aversions to the teapots probably had less to do with what the "accumulation of teapots" said about their female coworkers as what it said about men themselves. Historians Brian P. Luskey and Carole Srole argue that male clerks struggled with suggestions that clerical work was unmanly.[173] Men may have felt that dozens of teapots dotting the stoves and sills of the Treasury Department feminized their workspace.

Teapots were not the only evidence of women in the federal buildings. In 1864 a woman working in the Treasury Department had her dress tangled in a machine "and was rapidly drawn towards the revolving wheel." Her screams attracted some coworkers, who managed to pull her away from the machine, though her dress was "completely torn to shreds."[174] This incident prompted a new rule in the Treasury Department. In 1867, a New York newspaper described placards posted in all the rooms containing steam-powered machinery that read: " 'Ladies Must Not Wear Full Skirts in This Room.' " The article's author noted "through working hours limp skirts hang upon forlorn figures. But in passing the dressing-rooms and alcoves we notice that each, with its long rows of nails, is a museum of hoops, all waiting to be donned at the close of the day when the Bureau is still."[175] Teapots, hooked hoopskirts, and signage about dresses were all reminders to clerks that they worked in mixed-sex workspaces, and suggested a permanency to the practice of employing females in the government.

A FEMALE FEDERAL EMPLOYEE's gender limited her options in government employment. Supervisors' prejudices concerning women's intelligence and abilities and the institutional regulations of female federal employment, including hiring, promotion, and pay, drastically narrowed the positions to which women could aspire. Yet, when possible, women modified employment practices to fit their needs and desires. Although they may have hidden away their teapots and hung up their skirts during work hours, women were undeniably present in the federal workforce in the 1860s. Despite institutional obstacles and gender prejudice, women quickly adjusted to work life, excelled at their jobs, and claimed control over their workspaces and positions. They would need to call upon the resourcefulness and independence shown in their work to navigate the city of Washington, D.C.

CHAPTER FOUR

A Strange Time to Seek a Residence in Washington
Perils and Possibilities of Life for Female Federal Clerks

Near the end of 1862, Mary F. Holmes wrote a letter to Abraham Lincoln's vice president, Hannibal Hamlin, from her home in Norway, Maine. After introductory pleasantries, Holmes came to the point of her letter. "This may seem a strange time to seek a residence in Washington," Holmes wrote, "but I am very anxious to spend the coming winter there." Holmes needed a government job in Washington, D.C., she informed Hamlin (who was a friend of her father), because she needed to support herself and her family.[1]

The Civil War era was indeed "a strange time to seek a residence in Washington."[2] From 1861 to 1865 America was at war and the city of Washington, D.C., was perilously close to the front lines of the conflict.[3] Washingtonians lived with constant risk of enemy attack or subversion. Sixty forts, 93 batteries, 837 guns, and 25,000 soldiers ringed the Capital by the end of 1863.[4] Inside the perimeter of defenses was a chaotic city full of transients, drenched in blood and wrenched by conflict. The marital dangers abated after the war, but Washingtonians continued to endure crime, overcrowding, housing shortages, infrastructure inadequacies, disease, and inflation.

Washington, D.C., however, was also a city that was hiring. Over the course of the decade, this sleepy, southern town of magnificent distances morphed into a bustling, overcrowded, decidedly northern city. Men and women, black and white, young and old, flocked to the City of Washington to nurse broken bodies, embalm corpses, pour drinks, cook food, wash shirts, stitch cloth, bang nails, shoe horses, lie with lonely men, take pictures, act in plays, pick pockets, lobby congressmen, and write newspaper articles. Into this bustle, thousands of men and women came to work for the quickly waxing, and never to wane, federal government. As more applicants began to pour into Washington, these jobs became increasingly difficult to obtain and retain. The salaries they commanded also became increasingly difficult to live on as the government moved from gold to greenbacks and inflation mounted. Paying exorbitant rates for the necessities of life was hard for male federal employees. It was much harder for their underpaid female counterparts. Yet women not only survived; many thrived in this tough city. In the chaos, they managed to find places to sleep in a tight housing market that was suspicious of single women, care for families on limited budgets, and navigate the uniquely irksome and sometimes dangerous city streets.

In doing so, the female federal employees of the 1860s experienced the Civil War and Reconstruction intimately and holistically. Female federal employees not only lived among the blood, disease, and stench of war; the war happened under their fingertips as they copied requisitions in the Quartermaster General's Office for ammunition and beeves for undersupplied forts, laundered the bloody garments of wounded men at the Government Hospital for the Insane, and redirected wayward mail between soldiers and their families in the Dead Letter Office. While the entire nation experienced the social and economic turbulence and upheavals wrought by the Civil War and Reconstruction, the female federal workforce lived and labored at the political and economic epicenter of those national spasms.

Civil War–era female federal employees earned women a foothold, not only in federal employment, but also in the public life of the nation's capital. Female federal clerks joined in social, philanthropic, and intellectual activities with their male and female coworkers and boardinghouse mates. As the number of female federal employees grew, they became a recognizable market, and shops and schools catered to them. For those who chose to do so, female federal employees' salaries, newly acquired political knowledge, and personal associations provided them with the financial and practical wherewithal to participate in political movements, including the suffrage movement. Female federal employees were visible all over the city of Washington, D.C.—riding on omnibuses, walking in the streets, gathering in the galleries of Congress, shopping in the markets, chatting outside of boardinghouses, enjoying pleasure cruises, and assembling in meeting halls—helping to normalize the presence of middle-class women in the streets of the nation's capital slightly earlier than occurred in other cities. In forming this new, conspicuous community of independent women in full view of the nation's politicians, early female federal employees became a part of the struggle for women's rights, whether they intended to or not.[5]

"There Are Some Sad Stories I Could Tell You about the Woman-Clerk Life in Washington": Challenges of Life in D.C.

Civil War–era Washington was not an easy place to live. The city presented serious challenges to the women who came to work for the government. It was crowded, expensive, and poorly planned. Other cities of the nineteenth century shared these difficulties, but the capital had additional and unique hazards and obstacles, not the least of which was that for the first half of the 1860s, it was the vulnerable command center for an active and hard-fought war.[6]

The fratricidal conflict between the states immediately generated a strong gravitational pull to the District of Columbia. The population of Washington City increased by over 75 percent between 1860 and 1870, rising from 75,080 to 131,700.[7] Those figures belie the even more astounding population surge in the war years. In 1864, the superintendent of the Metropolitan Police estimated in a report to Congress that there were 160,000 souls residing in the city.[8] Historians estimate that there were more than 200,000 people in the District of Columbia during the Civil War.[9] Overcrowding did not end with the surrender of General Robert E. Lee; it continued through Reconstruction. In 1867, the local *Daily Morning Chronicle* reported, "Washington city is crowded—crammed almost to suffocation."[10]

The crowds were diverse as well as large. Thousands of the new arrivals were African Americans. In 1860, the federal census reported 10,983 African Americans in Washington. Ten years later, that figure was 35,392.[11] Journalist and Department of Agriculture employee Lois Bryan Adams opined in 1863 that "no other city ever presented such a conglomeration of humanity as may be found in Washington just now. The shades of color are indescribable."[12] Tens of thousands of newcomers were transients. Many came only to plead a case or find a lost loved one and had no intention of remaining beyond the time it took them to do so.[13] Soldiers crowded the streets of Washington, D.C., as well, noted Adams, "singly and in squads, on foot and on horseback, lounging on the walks, swarming at the doors of restaurants and liquor shops."[14]

While many newcomers to the city were only visitors, others had long-term ambitions. Throughout the 1860s men and women arrived with letters of recommendation addressed to executive department heads folded neatly and carefully stowed in pockets and purses. For every person who obtained the position sought, however, many more failed and were obliged to return home.[15] Even if one was successful in finding a job, it did not mean that he or she would retain it. A federal clerk wrote of clerk life in 1867, "Everything is temporarily here, sir. There is a wind in Dante's Hell that, by fits and starts, sweeps certain lovers away—they cannot pause and rest. That dreadful wind blows in Washington."[16]

When a woman arrived in Washington, D.C., to seek or start a federal position, her first order of business was to secure a place to sleep in the midst of this movement and disorder. Due to overcrowding, beds were scarce and dear.

"Rents are very high and not a house to be got," declared Jane Swisshelm in the summer of 1863.[17] One month later, she reported the same, "There are but two trades in Washington that are zealously followed just now, office hunting and house hunting. . . . It is a mystery where people are going to stay when Congress meets, for the houses are all full now."[18] Federal employee and journalist Lois Bryan Adams described to her readers how "every available nook and corner, from cellar to garret, is put in requisition" as sleeping spaces.[19]

This limited housing was not cheaply had, and male clerks found expenses to be impossibly high. In 1863, one group of male clerks formed a committee to investigate the feasibility of moving to Baltimore, where the cost of living was lower, and commuting to Washington for work.[20] One agitating male clerk suggested that the "Government build 200 or 300 cottages, located on its 'reservations,' to be rented to its Clerks only, at a low rent."[21] "The $1,200 allowed [first-class male clerks] is just adequate to meet the urgent demands of boarding-house keepers, and nothing more," asserted the *Daily Constitutional Union* in August 1866.[22]

Male clerks earned salaries two to three times greater than the salaries of female clerks.[23] If men found difficulty affording housing on their federal salaries, women must have struggled mightily on their significantly smaller incomes.[24] A widely run article in 1866 estimated that female clerks spent forty dollars a month, more than half their salaries, on room and board.[25] Another article published two years later described a soldier's widow spending "$40 per month for an attic room and board for herself and youngest child, while the board and schooling of the other does not cost less than $20 per month, leaving a margin of $15 per month for clothing and other necessaries."[26]

The housing women did manage to secure could also be less than desirable. War Department clerk and newspaper correspondent Jane Grey Swisshelm complained to her readers about the inadequate heating in her rooms when her fireplace failed to warm her space on an April night.[27] A "young lady clerk" in the Treasury Department discovered that she shared her rooms with rodents when a mouse crawled out of her hairdo one Monday morning while she was at work.[28] Women who worked as government laborers or messengers earned even less than female clerks—in 1873, for instance, a federal charwoman's salary was $180 a year—and would have had correspondingly worse accommodations.[29]

In summer 1871, Patent Office clerk Julia Wilbur filled her diary with complaints about her boarding room at 476 Pennsylvania Avenue—the third room she had rented since she started work in the Patent Office two years before. She moved into the room on June 1, 1871. The next day she wrote in her diary, "Think I cannot stay here. Dirty bad smelling. No parlor. Miserable fare. Course, low-lived boarders. Breakfast late." Wilbur found the meals so distasteful that she split her room and board, taking meals at another boardinghouse. The insects with which she shared her room and the smells that assaulted her in it vexed Wilbur most acutely. Wilbur's bed housed a bedbug population that cleaning could not cure, and mosquitoes joined in to keep her awake at night. She began to sleep on the floor in an effort to evade the bugs that robbed her of her sleep. By July 4, "*creeping things*" on the floor sent her back to the bed "but oh! too much walking over my face + head. It was fearful." In the middle of the night she set herself up in a large chair and napped until the morning. "I think I could not stay in this room another night. Can't sleep on bed, + am afraid to sleep on floor," she wrote, and indeed she did not. That night she left for a visit to New York, and when she returned she relocated to a new boarding house.[30]

The women employed at the Government Hospital for the Insane were exempt from the trials of house hunting, though their living situation presented its own challenges. The hospital's superintendent required that attendants, male and female, live on the premises.[31] As attendants were the primary caregivers for mentally ill patients, the work at St. Elizabeths was ceaseless. Attendants ate with the patients, and slept in the same rooms as patients or in adjoining rooms with only a lattice wall separating them.[32] This work wore on employees, especially as patients, male and female, could be dangerous. Female patients were often "hysterical" and sometimes violent.[33] For the women who worked at the Government Hospital for the Insane, finding housing in Washington, D.C., was not an issue but their lives consisted of little more than work.

Other female federal employees had to secure housing in the crowded market. An examination of the 1870 census provides some insight into the differing living arrangements of female federal employees. I have identified 662 women as female federal employees in the 1870 census. Of these, 325, or 49 percent, did not live with anyone of the same last name.[34] The balance of women lived with various permutations of family members: 21 percent (141 women) lived with parents; 19 percent (124 women) appear to have supported children; 3 percent (21 women) lived with a man of similar age and the same last name, probably husbands but perhaps brothers, and 28 percent (186 women) lived with siblings, nieces, nephews, or grandparents. In Civil War–era Washington, D.C., hundreds, if not thousands, of women were entirely supporting themselves and living on their own.

Single women in most cities in the mid-nineteenth century faced challenges finding lodging. "There is, I believe, a natural antagonism between boarding house keepers and single women," wrote Margaret Campbell to *The Woman's Journal* in 1870. Describing her experience house hunting in Boston, she explained that boardinghouse keepers looked at single women "as though they would bring upon them and their houses all the plagues of Egypt."[35] Concerns about single women's respectability complicated female federal employees' quest for housing, especially as the reputation of female federal clerks specifically was constantly in question. In cities around the country, working women seeking independent lodgings were at risk of being assumed prostitutes.[36] This was especially true in Washington, D.C. During the Civil War, the number of prostitutes in the capital ballooned to better serve the number of potential clients. In 1862, Washington's *Evening Star* reported "an unusually large number of strumpets" had come to the city to serve the thousands of soldiers encamped there.[37] Newspapers around the country, especially those run by Democratic editors, charged that brothels had overrun the city.[38] Prostitution in Washington was not confined to any one area; bawdy houses could be found practically everywhere in the city.[39] The result was that every single woman searching for a house in any neighborhood of Washington was at risk of being mistaken for a prostitute.

A *Daily Morning Chronicle* article from the summer of 1866 suggests that female clerks encountered difficulty searching for boardinghouses because of this stigma accorded to single women. On August 10, the newspaper published a short piece warning boardinghouse keepers "that many of our residents who have rooms to let are being sadly imposed on by vile and abandoned women, who engage and occupy their rooms, use them for illicit purposes, and finally leave without paying their rent." A person with a room to let might think twice about renting to a female stranger after reading in the paper that "Some of our best families have been caught in this manner, and more than once the police have been called on to oust them from the premises."[40] Moreover, the lines between a boarding clerk and a boarding prostitute were not always distinct. In 1870, for example, twenty-eight-year-old Emma Forsyth, a female clerk in the Treasury Department from New York, boarded in Maggie Brown's boarding house in the second ward. Her boardinghouse mates included twenty-three-year-old Molly Smith and nineteen-year-old Nettie Hamilton, both of whom listed their occupation as "prostitute."[41]

Even if a potential landlord understood that a female federal employee was not a prostitute, she could still encounter resistance. In an article that ran in

Texas, New York, California, and Utah between July and September 1866, the author, whose clear intent was to dissuade women from seeking federal clerical work, claimed that boardinghouse keepers in the capital were "unfriendly to female clerks." The author asserted that the main reason was that "they are unprofitable, and are too poor to pay the most exorbitant prices." Another "aggravating" fault was that "they are often very pretty; they attract gentlemen, perhaps to the neglect of the landlady or her daughters." Female clerks also allegedly "burn gas late, or they stay out late; are deemed universally trouble-some and not to be desired."[42] While this author was likely exaggerating the difficulty in his or her quest to keep young women in their hometowns, it is clear that a woman's gender was a liability in searching for lodgings in Washington.

At least some enterprising boardinghouse keepers began to realize, however, that there was a market in these female federal employees, indicating that such women were becoming more visible and accepted. Female federal employees were beginning to reshape what people thought of young women living on their own. On October 27, 1865, the *Daily Morning Chronicle* ran an article entitled "A Good Idea." It was directed to "Ladies in the Departments" and described the "novel enterprise of a boarding-house where gentlemen are not admitted, which has just been started in the city by lady of the highest respectability."[43] On the preceding page, an advertisement for the rooms announced: "Ladies of the Departments preferred."[44] One month later, the same landlord advertised, "Two or Three Ladies Engaged in the Departments can be accommodated with BOARD, by applying immediately."[45] Later that year, another "Respectable Lady" sought "two or three young ladies" to board in "a respectable neighborhood."[46] Because of female federal employees, unattached women coming to the city were now being recognized as "respectable" and desirable potential tenants.

Female federal employees who lived with their families in Washington, D.C., faced different challenges. Although parents or male relatives may have assisted in securing housing, women living within families were often dependent upon and beholden to them. Historians of laboring women have found that working women shouldered a far greater portion of domestic responsibilities and chores than did working men. Employed sons were more apt to spend their free time at the saloon or in self-improvement pursuits, whereas working daughters were expected to return home to assist in child care, food preparation, and cleaning.[47]

Working single mothers would have experienced significant domestic burdens. Of the 662 women identified as female federal employees in the 1870 census, 124 (19 percent) appear to have cared for children. Of these 124, 98 appear to have cared for children entirely on their own.[48] Eliza Boston was one such mother. The twenty-eight-year-old illiterate African American woman was employed in the Treasury Department as a sweeper or scrubber. In 1870, she was the head of household, living in Washington's second ward with her five young children. Her eleven-year-old daughter, Ida, and her nine-year-old son, Richard, attended school and her six-, four-, and one-year-old sons remained at home.[49] Because of cost, many single mothers rented rooms, but others lived with their children in boarding houses.[50] Thirty-seven-year-old white Treasury Department clerk Mary Royston from Maryland, for example, lived in a boardinghouse in the second ward with her four sons, ages six to fifteen.[51]

Even if mothers appeared to have help in the form of an adult relative, that appearance could be deceptive. Working women could simultaneously be caring for both children and parents, or children and grandchildren. In 1873, Edward Winslow Martin described a widowed woman taking care of her widowed daughter and two grandchildren. He observed, "The outside life of women like these can well be imagined. The six hours passed in the office are probably the least fatiguing of the day."[52] If a woman rented rooms instead of boarding, explained *The Revolution* to its readers, she must "buy, and cook her own food, pay for her washing, or do it at night and neglect the mending; (making—poor thing she is not much troubled with), and all this before nine in the morning [*sic*], or after 4 P.M. when weary with a hard day's work she returns to a comfortless home, and work again."[53]

In addition to the high cost of shelter, dining out, which could be necessary when living in a rented room, was expensive.[54] Options were also limited. Restaurants, first established in the 1830s in America, were often male spaces, especially in the evenings when unescorted women or groups of women were not typically welcome or even permitted.[55] During the workday, most women appear to have brought their lunches or purchased them from a stand in the workplace—likely because lunchroom options for women were few.[56] One observer described strolling through the Treasury Department and seeing "a number of pretty female clerks, who were busily engaged in demolishing sandwiches."[57]

To spare their purses, female federal employees likely dined at their boardinghouses or prepared their own food outside of work. Boarders could also split room and board, sleeping in one boardinghouse and eating in another, as Wilbur did for a time in 1871. Women who sought to cook for themselves faced high prices at the market—one 1873 guidebook author claimed higher than in New York or Baltimore.[58] "Boarding is enormous, as provisions are mostly brought from a distance and there appears to be no city regulations to restrain pedlars who buy up and retail, at their own prices, completely controlling the market," Swisshelm informed her readers back in Minnesota.[59] Male clerks petitioned Congress for "subsistence stores at Government rates" to allow them to survive on their (much higher) salaries.[60] Observer Edward Winslow Martin described many of the female clerks as having to live "in attics or in shabbily furnished rooms in remote corners of the city, and prepare their food, of the plainest description, by means of a gas stove."[61]

To defray the high cost of housing and boarding, some female clerks ran boardinghouses concurrent with their federal employment. In 1869, a Massachusetts newspaper reporting on female clerks in Washington, D.C., profiled one Dead Letter Office clerk, the widow of a Union army officer, supporting four children and her mother and father. She had "established one of the best boarding house [sic] in Washington, and presides over it and attends daily to her clerical duties."[62] Virginia Brewster, a divorced single mother, also kept a boardinghouse.[63] In September 1868, two and a half years after she filed for divorce, Virginia obtained a job with the Treasury Department and was still working there in 1871. She switched jobs at the department at least once.[64] While working as a federal clerk, Brewster was the sole caregiver for her two daughters, sixteen-year-old Mary and seven-year-old Ida. Brewster also continued to run her boardinghouse in the second ward. In 1870, it housed her and her daughters, seven male clerks, and two female domestic servants.[65]

Once a female federal employee secured housing and sustenance, she needed to sort out how she was going to get to work. A woman's travel between home and work was a dirty, malodorous, and somewhat dangerous twice-daily event. Washington was a city wholly unprepared for rapid expansion it experienced, controlled by only a small number of speculative landowners, and run by an inexperienced municipal government that had been butting heads with Congress over responsibility and finances since the city's birth.[66] Antebellum Washington's defining characteristic was its unfinishedness.[67] On August 3, 1861, Department of the Interior employee Annie G. Dudley recorded her first impression of the city: "feel quite *disappointed*; falls far short of my expectations. Everything seems to be in such an *unfinished* condition and the streets so filthy."[68] In the early 1860s, a correspondent for the *London Telegraph* described Washington as a city that did not "precisely languish, but it wallows in the dust like an eel in a sand-basket . . . slightly repulsive to the sight before it is skinned and cooked."[69]

Female federal employees did not all have the luxury of living near their jobs, though a significant portion managed to do so. For example, approximately half of the female federal employees identified in the 1870 census as working for the Treasury Department, Post Office, and Patent Office lived in close proximity to their work.[70] The rest had to travel further through the city each day. The women of the Government Printing Office were the most likely to have longer commutes—only 9 of the 110 female GPO employees identified in the 1870 census lived in the fourth ward, where the GPO was located.

The distances could be significant. In 1870, two female Treasury Department clerks lived in Tenleytown, approximately four miles away.[71] One female federal employee who supported an "aged husband" and an "invalid" stepdaughter boarded in Alexandria, Virginia, across the Potomac River and approximately seven miles away, as her salary did "not permit her to pay the exorbitant rent in Washington."[72] Julia Wilbur was very excited about her new boarding situation in the summer of 1870 at 1925 I Street: "there is a home like atmosphere wh. is worth everything." But the difficulty of the commute— which required her to take horse drawn streetcars—quickly became apparent. Two weeks after moving in she noted in her diary, "Only objection now is being so far from office that I have to ride." In September, she complained that "the walk + the ride in cars both tire me." On September 24, worn out from the commute, Wilbur went to the pharmacy for assistance: "Bought 'Balm of Life.' Will see if there is any virtue in it." Wilbur began to consider finding another living situation, even though she enjoyed the other aspects of 1925 I Street, including her room and the company there. On September 28, she wrote "very tired. Must try to find boarding place nearer office."[73]

As Wilbur's diary suggests, travelling through Washington to work could be an unpleasant undertaking. On a still day, when the temperature was high, 1860s Washington stank of garbage, sewage, and rotting animal flesh.[74] The city government, underfunded and overextended, had never provided adequate infrastructure, even for the needs of its prewar inhabitants. People disposed of garbage and sewage in unpaved and unlit streets where pigs rutted and roamed. Standing water, a cocktail of rain, urine, excrement, and slop water, formed fertile breeding grounds for disease-carrying mosquitoes.[75] The city's sewage, drainage, street, and sanitation problems only worsened with the enormous surge of more inhabitants.[76] Lack of adequate sewers was a major problem in 1860s Washington.[77] Frustrated, the Superintendent of the Metropolitan Police complained in his 1868 report to Congress "that these unsightly and pestiferous channels for filth should be permitted to poison the atmosphere for years unmolested, on the very borders of the pleasure grounds of the national Capitol, and within full view of the Capitol building and our principal streets, is surprising to say the least."[78]

The principal receptacle of a great deal of the city's filth was the Washington Canal. Begun in 1810 by local businessmen, the canal stretched from Tiber Creek to the Eastern Branch. Its purpose had been to provide an inland passage across the city for merchants to gain access to seafaring boats in the Eastern Branch. The canal opened in 1815, but silt choked the channel.[79] It became the city's dumping ground and main sewer line. Lifetime Washington resident Joseph Kelly recalled that in walking over bridges spanning the canal, one "encountered all sights and smells that came from muddy flats . . . and occasionally a human derelict who had stumbled to his death or drink."[80] Some female federal employees had to cross the canal twice a day. Twenty-eight women who worked in the Treasury Department, for instance, lived in the seventh ward, and the canal was directly in their path to work. The concern was not merely an olfactory one. In 1869, the sanitary force of the Metropolitan Police wrote in its report to Congress, "Suffice it to say that serious apprehensions are now felt by scientific and other experienced men, that at no distant day some dreadful epidemic may be produced from its gangrenous bed, which shall make victims of many valuable lives."[81]

Even if women could avoid the canal, they could not avoid Washington's crowded streets, which were also fetid and potential sources of disease.[82] Because of the city's poor drainage, the roads over which female federal employees had to travel were often mired in filthy muck.[83] "The streets, avenues and alleys must continue to be dirty and insalubrious as long as very great amounts of garbage and offal are deposited on the surface, either to be removed after a lapse of time, or in many instances, to decay where they lie," the superintendent of the Metropolitan Police reported in 1863.[84] Jane Grey Swisshelm described the streets to her readers as "plentifully besprinkled with dead horses, dead dogs, cats, rats, rubbish and refuse of all kinds."[85]

Unsurprisingly, disease flourished in Washington during the Civil War era. Smallpox, typhoid, cholera, malaria, and measles ripped through the city. Historian Kenneth Winkle notes, in his history of Washington, D.C., during the Civil War, that "life in Washington was so precarious that the British Foreign Office designated the city a hardship posting."[86] Disease did not discriminate based on gender. In March 1863, Interior Department clerk Annie Dudley recorded in her diary that "one of the young ladies in the house was taken sick and died within one week. She was from Maine and her name was Annie [illeg.], a very amiable and lovely girl," noting, "A sad blow indeed to her parents to have her die away from home."[87]

Dirty streets were annoying, as well as dangerous.[88] Washington's muddy streets, although not uncommon in nineteenth-century cities, posed a particular problem to women, who wore floor-sweeping skirts. An 1865 newspaper article described how the city's mud left strangers visiting Washington "amazed and horror-stricken."[89] Two years later, the *Daily Morning Chronicle* implored the city to "come to the rescue of the ladies" and "furnish some means of crossing streets without getting into mud at least shoe-deep." The article described the crossings "in nearly every part of the city" as "almost impassable for ladies."[90] The following year, the newspaper insisted on the "adoption of some method by which pedestrians may be able to traverse the streets without being obliged to wade, often ankle-deep, through thick tenacious mud which defiles polished boots and snowy skirts in a manner decidedly unpleasant to contemplate."[91] When the streets weren't muddy, they were often dusty; dust was a common complaint in Julia Wilbur's diary. Dust even infiltrated the federal offices. December 6, 1870, was, reported Wilbur, "Uncomfortable in office. dust sifted in through closed windows + room close, stifling."[92]

Female federal employees had to guard their personal safety while traversing these streets. Hack drivers did not always obey the law that pedestrians had the right of way in crosswalks and women were among the people hit by these early taxis.[93] Women also faced concerns of crime. Not all of the newcomers to Washington, D.C., during the war were green soldiers, grieving parents, or federal clerkship hopefuls. In 1862, the superintendent of police informed Congress that the increased population of the city was "not only transient in its character, but largely composed of the very worst and most disorderly class of residents from other cities."[94] This rogue element did not leave when the war ended.[95]

The small Washington, D.C., police force was unable to cope with the huge population surge brought about by the Civil War and Congress had to create an entirely new department—the Metropolitan Police—in 1861.[96] The Metropolitan Police superintendent repeatedly asserted in his annual reports to Congress that there was a dangerous criminal population in the city.[97] During the war, criminals had largely focused their attentions on soldiers, and after "now that this occupation is taken from them by the close of the war, they prey upon our citizens," he wrote in 1865.[98] Although the superintendent's reports may have been exaggerated to create a stronger case for a bigger budget, local newspapers complained of crime as well.[99] An October 1865 newspaper article on the "frequent and nightly increasing cases of burglary," recounted to readers tales of a man garroted on the street and of boarders chloroformed and robbed in their rented beds. The paper warned readers that, "with a town necessarily filled with strangers, and whose population is constantly changing, it behooves every citizen to be on his guard."[100]

Women were among the victims of this crime. In April 1863, Treasury Department clerk Mary A. Mason had money stolen from a trunk in her room where she lived with her stepfather.[101] Annie Dudley had a close call in May 1864. She recorded that her "boarding house was visited by a robber last night, and succeeded in getting over a hundred dollars, my door (fortunately for me) was locked and probably saved my watch and some money thereby."[102] Fellow current or former female federal employees also committed some of the crimes perpetrated against women. Mary A. Gatewood worked for the Treasury Department in 1865 on the recommendation of President Andrew Johnson. The next year, she was arrested for a string of thefts.[103] In December 1869, Julia Wilbur had her umbrella stolen from the Patent Office.[104]

Although women could be victims in their homes and offices, they were more vulnerable to victimization on the bustle and commotion of the city streets, especially at night. The *Evening Star* cautioned readers away from the Smithsonian grounds where "roughs" were "daily and nightly congregated." The Smithsonian lay in the center of the city, near the executive departments. The paper explained, "It is common for ladies to be insulted daily, men to be robbed, and even worse crimes perpetrated in these grounds."[105] "It is becoming quite dangerous for any person to be found on our streets late at night," reported the *Daily Constitutional Union* in February 1865. The paper described the city as "infested with a gang of thieves and robbers who are nightly committing all sorts of depredations . . . on some of our most public thoroughfares" and advised its readers to "be on their guard, and when business called them out during the night."[106]

The *Daily Constitutional Union* may not have considered its admonition applicable to women, but, like men, female federal employees did have "business" that required them to be "out during the night." The length of the workday for female federal clerical workers varied among the departments, but was typically from 9:00 A.M. until 4:00 P.M. In the winter months, this work schedule could have required some women to return to their homes in the dark, depending on how far they lived from work. In 1867, the *Evening Star* appealed to departments to let their employees leave work at 3:00 P.M. in the winter, since by leaving at 4:00 P.M., the employees "find darkness upon them before they have dined, and if they are called upon to shop or market or attend to any business away from their places of residence, they are obliged to do it under discomforts and disadvantages" of the dark in the poorly lit city.[107] Women who worked in the currency bureau of the Treasury Department and at the Government Printing Office faced late hours at work requiring traveling at night more frequently and year-round. In the early 1860s, women in the currency bureau worked at night, in addition to or in lieu of day shifts. These night shifts began at 4:00 P.M. and ended at midnight.[108] In the GPO, a day's work was ten hours long, meaning women left work later, and one observer noted that the building was often "lighted up and machinery in motion until 12 and 1 o'clock at night."[109] The GPO was also located in a dangerous neighborhood known as "Swampoodle," which experienced racial violence between Irish-born inhabitants and newly arrived African Americans.[110]

As a woman deeply involved in philanthropic and political activities, and one with a number of friends throughout the city, Julia Wilbur found herself walking at night, sometimes alone. Some nights, the walk was tolerable. In January 1871, Wilbur left the lecture hall after hearing a women's rights lecture at 9:30 P.M. She waited for public transportation for an hour before giving up and walking home. Though it was "very hard walking" on the snowy sidewalks, Wilbur recorded that she "was not in the least afraid" because "many people were going to + fro" from the theaters. One journey home on the night of November 17, 1871, however, was a "Dark walk [and] a little skeery."[111]

Female federal employees faced harassment on the streets and in the public spaces of their work.[112] These women were regularly in the streets during times of high traffic and worked in government buildings that were indiscriminately accessible to the public. In 1869 the *Evening Star* reported with disgust the "disgraceful habit which has so long prevailed without restriction, that of young men (and old men too,) locating themselves in positions at the foot of the many stairways in and about [the Capitol] much to the embarrassment of the lady visitors." It was not the men's mere presence that caused "embarrassment"; the paper reported that the men were in the practice of "annoy[ing]" the ladies, "not only by their imprudent staring, but often with vulgar remarks loud enough to be overheard by the objects of their impertinence."[113] The article referred to "lady visitors," but the ladies most commonly and regularly going into and out of public buildings were federal employees. Women's employment in the federal government thus incrementally changed the use of space in the nation's capital. Whereas it had once previously been appropriate for men to lounge on the stairs of public buildings, women's increased presence made such behavior "disgraceful." Public buildings had become mixed-sex spaces.

To avoid or at least minimize the inconveniences and dangers of the streets, or because the trip to work was long, some women, like Wilbur, traveled to work on horse drawn passenger vehicles known as omnibuses or streetcars.[114] These forms of conveyance posed their own challenges. The omnibus lines were limited and did not cover as much of the city as the citizenry desired.[115] Moreover, women traveling to work made many of the complaints we hear still today—for example, slow cars and frozen feet waiting for them in winter.[116] Women may also have been more exposed to crime and harassment on the public conveyances than they were in the streets.[117] Travel on public transportation could mean close contact with strangers—including men.[118] In 1866, a blacksmith from the Navy Yard harassed "several respectable young ladies" on the streetcar.[119] In 1870, another local newspaper reported a man harassing four women on the omnibus.[120] Crowded conditions were also perfect for those picking pockets. An 1866 newspaper article described the streetcars as "infested with pickpockets."[121] In January 1869, a man on a streetcar stole Julia Wilbur's purse, containing $6 and four tickets to an upcoming lecture by Frederick Doulgass.[122]

By whatever means women traveled to and from work, between 1861 and 1865 they traversed a city at war. Washington, D.C., was the seat, not only of the government, but also of the Union Army. Situated between seceded Virginia and hostile Maryland, the residents had reason to be wary. The capitals of the Union and the Confederacy, lying only one hundred miles apart, were each other's targets. Lee's thrusts into Pennsylvania and Maryland terrified the people of Washington, prompting Lincoln to order the arming of all (male) government employees.[123] In July 1864, Confederate troops came close to invading Washington during General Jubal Early's raid.[124] The war was omnipresent in Washington, which was flooded by war materiel, including horses, guns, uniforms, food, mules, hay, and firewood. Green soldiers descended upon Washington, many returning wounded and sick. Trains, carts, and boats brought hundreds of thousands of ill, injured, or dead soldiers into the city during the Civil War to occupy the dozens of hospitals that were created or constructed to meet the demand and female federal employees volunteered at the hospitals.[125] Many men did not survive their wounds or succumbed to disease, and embalming businesses sprouted up in the city to cater to families mourning fallen soldiers. Female federal employees may likely have had to pass by shops advertising "Embalming of the Dead," and smell the corpses that lay inside those shops awaiting the procedure, some of which had been on the field for days before being transported into the city.[126] Being surrounded by such tangible fear, gore, and grief, as opposed to reading about them in newspapers from the comfort and distance afforded to residents of other major cities in the Union, gave female federal employees a visceral wartime experience. After the war, the city remained chaotic and in flux. Women lived through the racial equality "experiments" of Reconstruction taking place in Washington, D.C., and efforts to stitch back together the nation that had been torn asunder by war.[127]

Despite obstacles and hardships, female federal employees successfully managed to navigate the city of Washington, D.C., and did so with little apparent complaint. This was no small accomplishment. Other cities of the period shared many of the same dangers and annoyances of overcrowding and crime, but Washington had been uniquely designed for a seasonal and masculine population.[128] Female federal employees challenged the character of the city, and carved paths through it, expanding the number and variety of places in which it was acceptable for women to be, and importantly, did so under the gaze of the men retaining and creating laws and regulations which affected women's positions in society.

"Women, Women, Everywhere Women": Female Federal Employees in Washington, D.C.[129]

Washington, D.C., was dirty and dangerous, yet people continued to flock there because, as Department of Agriculture employee Lois Bryan Adams explained to her readers, the opportunities and excitement of the "freedom of the pavement" outweighed any superficial negatives that detractors could cite.[130] There was a great vitality in Washington in the 1860s that can be glimpsed through the words of Adams as she chronicled the diverse and vibrant street life to her readers back in Michigan: "rich and poor, young and old, foul with rags, and decked with gold, the nabob and his dusky brother, once a slave, now pass each other on the freeman's level and all together conspire to make lively times in Washington."[131] Adams and her female coworkers were part of these "lively times in Washington." The city rewarded those women who could tolerate her noxious sewers, overcrowded and overpriced housing market, and rampant pickpockets with unparalleled access to social, educational, philanthropic, and political activities. By capitalizing on these varied opportunities, women not only enriched their own lives, but also increased the public presence and acceptance of women on the streets and in the meeting halls of Washington.

A writer to the suffrage newspaper *The Revolution* was amazed at the prevalence of women in the public buildings in Washington, D.C., in 1870. She reported to the newspaper that she had expected to be "an isolated member of my sex," when she visited the Capitol, but discovered to her great surprise that the reception room was "filled with women of every rank in life, from the humble war-widow to the elegantly-dressed lady." As she continued her tour of public buildings, she found "women, women, everywhere women." The writer applauded the female presence in the government buildings noting, optimistically, "The nation, by a happy premonition, has made its capitol ready for woman law-makers."[132]

Many of the women the writer observed were likely female federal employees or applicants to federal positions. These women played a key role in transforming the masculine character of the nation's capital to one more accepting of women's presence and receptive to their wants and needs.[133] In the summer of 1867, for instance, the Washington, D.C. Post Office closed the "separate apartment in which ladies applied for their letters" and opened a window in the general area "exclusively for the use of the ladies," and staffed by two female window clerks.[134] Three years later, in the summer of 1870, Mary Green of Ohio became the Government Printing Office's first female compositor and was quickly thereafter the first woman accepted into the Columbia Typographical Union, by an almost unanimous vote.[135] During the Civil War era, women began to change the composition of the city's streets.

It is not surprising that women flocked to Washington, D.C., during the Civil War era despite its dangers and annoyances. The *Cincinnati Commercial* reported in 1869, "Washington, by virtue of its being *the* capital, necessarily draws to it a great variety of character. There are a singular set of men and women here." The author of that article had noticed that "ladies—those connected with the better class of Government clerks; the brighter, more self-reliant women from New England perhaps . . . are all pleased with this city." The author suggested a few reasons why despite the difficulties of living in Washington, women might be so pleased to be there, including the weather and the architecture, but concluded, "perhaps more than all, the very unconventional social freedom which really exists, offer to intelligent, spirited women an irresistible charm."[136] Julia Wilbur, originally from New York, thought of Washington as "the city of all cities to live in." Wilbur appreciated the "wide diversity in the circumstances of human beings in the narrow boundaries of a city," offering scenes which "cd. not be seen in any but the National Capital," and recognized that living in Washington and having access to the opportunities the city provided was a "privilege." To Wilbur, the "only drawback" was that her friends living elsewhere "cannot have my privileges."[137] Government employment provided many women with the time, money, and possibility to expand their social and political lives in ways few other opportunities did.

Moving to Washington, D.C., to work for the federal government gained hundreds of women significant independence and a heterogeneous peer group of coworkers. As noted, almost half of the 662 women identified in the 1870 census as federal employees appear to have been living away from family. This type of female independence was anomalous at the time.[138] Even if they lived with family members, most female federal employees also lived with at least one person to whom they do not appear to have been related. Eighty percent of female federal employees lived with people having different last names from themselves. There were several reasons why female federal employees were more likely to live independently than working women of other cities, and for it to be so common for them to live with persons unrelated to them. First, jobs with the federal government were highly sought after and women were willing and financially able to relocate to work there and to live independently. Second, Washington was a boardinghouse city built to accommodate (male) clerks and politicians away from their families and when women came they had to find room in that housing infrastructure. Finally, the high cost of living and impermanence of federal positions made it a dubious financial proposition for even higher-paid male clerks to move their families to Washington.[139] Unlike other cities, such as New York, the transience of Washington meant that young women lacked even the community control imposed upon their sisters in other urban neighborhoods.[140]

It was more common than not for any female federal employee, regardless of whether she lived on her own or with family, to reside with at least one other person who worked for the federal government. A majority of female federal employees (455, or 69 percent) lived with another federal employee; 131 women lived with at least one other female federal employee; 144 lived with at least one other male federal employee; and 180 lived with at least one male and one female federal employee. Work and home were thus intermingled for female federal employees. Although many women lived with unrelated fellow government workers, for some, federal work was the family business.[141] Fifty-four-year-old single mother Cecelia McKenna of Ireland, for example, began working in the Treasurer's Office around 1865.[142] In 1870, she had stopped working and was living in Georgetown. Her twenty-four-year-old son, Bernard, was working as a laborer in the Post Office, her twenty-two-year-old daughter, also named Cecelia, was now working in the Treasury Department, and her twenty-one-year-old son, Jason, worked in the Government Printing Office.[143]

Some women who lived with persons unrelated to them likely found their living situations through relationships formed at work. Charles Russell, a Post

Office Department clerk, lived with his wife, son, and daughter in the fifth ward. The 1870 census shows that they employed a house servant, and took in boarders: fifty-seven-year-old Rowena Whitman of Maine and twenty-three-year-old Fannie Gilbert of New Hampshire. Both women were clerks in the Treasury Department. Rowena Whitman had known Russell's daughter, Louisa Russell, since at least 1865, when the women clerked together in the Second Comptroller's Office. Fannie Gilbert was only a year younger than Russell, and they may have met in the Treasury as well.[144] Another household in the first ward consisted of Semour Shidley, a twenty-nine-year-old from New York, Ennestina Becker, a twenty-nine-year-old from Saxony, and Amelia Tenner, a sixteen-year-old from New Jersey. Aside from the age similarity of Semour and Ennestina, the only thing the roommates apparently had in common was that all were clerks in the Treasury Department.[145] These work connections may have helped to replace at least some of the sense of community such women (and men) relocating to Washington, D.C., would have found in neighborhoods in other cities.

More than a quarter (186, or 28 percent) of female federal employees identified in the 1870 census lived in large mixed-sex boarding houses.[146] Sixty-five of these women lived in these boardinghouses with family members, and the remaining 121 boarded in these large houses on their own. Treasury Department clerk Sophia Harrison, age twenty-nine, for instance, lived in a second-ward boardinghouse with thirty other people, including two male Post Office Department clerks, one male War Department clerk, three male Treasury Department clerks and two other female Treasury Department clerks, Sarah Wheeler and Fanny M. Roberts, both twenty-five years old.[147] This type of living situation provided women with a significant degree of mixed-sex peer interaction.

If one didn't like one's boardinghouse or housemates, one had the freedom to move. Annie G. Dudley kept a journal between 1861 and 1868. During much of this time, she lived in Washington, D.C., and worked for the Department of the Interior in the Bureau of Indian Affairs, sometimes taking her work home, but not always. In January 1863, she recorded in her diary, "I changed my boarding place on the first day of the month from H St. to Vermont Avenue." In May 1864, she and a friend went to Georgetown to look for a place to board for the summer, "but found it to be too far from the horse cars and price too high to suit us." In March 1867, she recorded, "I don't like our boarding house very well, think I shall change in the Spring or next month rather," and then in September that she had "changed my boarding place and like much better. The people are very pleasant and have a very pleasant room with a darling little roommate from Maine."[148] Patent Office clerk Julia Wilbur lived in six different boardinghouses between 1869 and the end of 1871. Many young women lived on their own in other cities, including New York, although as historian Christine Stansell found, "Admittedly, few girls lived altogether free of family authority, which diffused itself through other modes of community control," typically through ethnically homogeneous neighborhoods or tenement buildings.[149] The overwhelming transience of Washington, D.C., meant many women lived with more freedom from this type of family or community control of their everyday home life.

In these varied living arrangements, women forged peer relationships with fellow female federal employees. Mary A. Mason, the female Treasury Department clerk whose house had been robbed in 1863, worked as a kind of accountant for Jane Swisshelm who worked in the War Department. The two knew each other because, as Swisshelm noted, Mason "resides at my boarding house."[150] This formation of a peer group was important for women who were likely to be living on their own for the first time. Separated from parental influence, female federal employees would have turned to each other to determine how best to navigate their new independence in the strange and challenging urban environment.[151] Women also formed relationships with men who lived in or visited their boardinghouses. Female War Department clerk Angie Emery, for example, had an affair with Edwin Phillips, a male coworker who boarded with his wife at the same boardinghouse as Emery.[152] Boardinghouse life also granted women the freedom to entertain male guests. "In the evening, received calls from some officers from the Forts across the river. Think I shall like my new home very much," recorded Dudley in her diary in January 1863.[153]

Boardinghouse life not only afforded women freedom in their homes, but freedom from the home as well.[154] Some observers did not believe this to be a good thing. One woman who wrote a memoir of her time in Washington opined that hotel and boardinghouse life was dangerous: "There are no home duties to be performed, no parlors to dust, no treasured china and silver to be washed after a cosey [sic] breakfast, no dainty cake or dessert to be prepared . . . how are people to kill the time of which they have such an abundant supply?" Female federal employees happily found a multitude of ways to occupy themselves.[155]

As did working women in other mid-nineteenth-century American cities, women of Washington, D.C., socialized in crowded city streets with neighbors.[156] In the summer of 1864, Lois Bryan Adams painted a picture of the end of a woman's workday. She described Washington in the twilight time between work and sleep. Children played in the streets while women sat on porches or chairs brought from inside, sitting with each other, "often knitting, sewing, crocheting, or reading by the light of gas in the window, chatting the while, and making the streets cheery with their gossip and gay dresses." She described "young girls, and older ones too, who have been bound all day to the copying desk," who "put off their weary faces with their working dresses, and come out now with pleasant smiles and pretty muslin toilettes to be happy in the moonlight."[157]

Women also attended parties and dinners held in the city. Between March 1869 and February 1871, Julia Wilbur attended ten receptions at the White House, including President Andrew Johnson's last reception and First Lady Julia Grant's first one. Wilbur actually began to grow bored of these affairs, writing after a White House reception on February 24, 1870: "I came away saying I had got about enough of Receptions."[158] Annie Dudley's wartime diary is also peppered with entries about social activities. She attended Presidential receptions, parties thrown by politicians, numerous dinners, and sometimes had soirees of her own, "dancing in the parlor occasionally." In February 1869, she attended a gymnastic "exhibition & Birthday hop." Occasionally, she stayed out very late, underscoring that her life in Washington, D.C., afforded her the freedom to do so. In May 1864, she attended a ball "given in honor of the Ladies of the Patent Office Fair," and "enjoyed the evening very much, did not get home till day-light." That February, she attended a party given by officers in Arlington, Virginia. They encountered some trouble coming back over the bridge into the District that night, and "did not get home till seven o'clock in the morning."[159] As is further discussed in the following chapter on the reputation of female federal employees, this freedom helped to feed the rumor mill that called their reputations into question.

Women also took advantage of the myriad intellectual and religious activities offered in the capital. Female federal employees enjoyed the use of, and helped to cultivate, clerk libraries.[160] In 1869, the *Daily Morning Chronicle* reported on a "movement for the organization of the female literary society in the city."[161] Reading was one of Julia Wilbur's favorite pastimes. In addition to newspapers and periodicals, between April 1, 1869, and October 26, 1871, Wilbur noted at least twenty different books by name that she was reading, ranging from familiar authors like Charles Dickens and Louisa May Alcott to the feminist writers Tennessee Celeste Claflin and Anna Dickinson.[162] Women also joined associations such as the Social Science Association, which opened its membership to women and held lecture series.[163]

Judging from the diaries of Julia Wilbur and Annie Dudley, female federal employees spent a good deal of their free time listening to debates in the House and Senate. Dudley was present when the Senate voted to abolish slavery in the Capital. In April 1864, she witnessed the signing of a treaty between the U.S. government and a delegation from the Chippewa tribe in Minnesota.[164] Julia Wilbur was a frequent visitor to the galleries of Congress going to either the House or the Senate at least thirty-seven times between March 1869 and January 1871. During that period, she was an engaged and critical listener to debate on a wide range of topics including the repeal of the Civil Tenure of Office bill ("interesting"), naturalization laws ("Very interesting"), a dispute between Great Britain and the United States over damages incurred by British-built, Confederate-operated ships ("more interesting to me than any thing I saw"), over readmitting Virginia, Mississippi, and Georgia to the Union (there "will be great rejoicing in Va. especially among rebels"), multiple debates on whether to annex Santo Domingo ("Came away a little disgusted"; "A remarkable day in my calendar. One that I am grateful for . . . sat 5 hrs. in close attention + with nerves strained to their utmost tension"), the swearing in of four African American congressmen, over the removal of Charles Sumner as chairman of the Senate Committee on Foreign Relations ("It is done to make the Annexation of San Domingo certain + easy. . . . It was painful at times to hear the words that were spoken. . . . . It will rupture the Repub. party +c. It will no doubt divide the party + the Democrats are well pleased over it"), the civil rights bill ("I enjoyed it"), appropriations distribution ("So it will be again that that the old folks will get little help"), and alleged outrages in the southern states and the Ku Klux Klan Act.[165] When Wilbur was unable to be present at Congress for debate over an issue in which she was particularly interested, she would go to the office of the *Congressional Globe* and acquire transcripts that she could read at home.[166] Living in Washington, D.C., provided politically minded women like Wilbur easily accessible and current information about important developments in foreign and domestic policy issues of the day.

Life in Washington also provided women with the ability to participate in the civic events of the city, which, by nature of it being the capital, also had a nationalistic flavor. Some events were fairly common and familiar to other nineteenth-century urban residents. Wilbur enjoyed the concerts performed on the White House lawn, building dedications, school commencements and graduations, and cultural festivals. Alongside other Washington residents, Wilbur also observed the passing of politicians, although in a few instances she clearly did not mourn. When Secretary of War John Rawlins died in September 1869, Wilbur attended his funeral "which was expected to be something remarkable." It was not, but she appreciated having the day off since the federal departments closed in observation. When former president Franklin Pierce died, Wilbur similarly "Hoped we should have the holiday + the Depts. wd. be closed"; unfortunately, however, the funeral was scheduled for Sunday, "so we shall make nothing by it. Too bad!"[167]

Other events and celebrations Wilbur witnessed and participated in were of greater national significance. In March 1869, Wilbur and four female friends braved the rain and crowds to attend General Grant's inauguration. Standing on an iron chair near a statue of George Washington, the women watched Chief Justice Salmon Chase swear in Grant on a platform "decorated with flags," "a beautiful sight." Wilbur, a staunch advocate of African American rights, also attended an anniversary celebration the emancipation of slavery in Washington. Wilbur "put out flags" on the morning of April 16, 1869, and watched the procession from a friend's house. Although a city-specific event, Wilbur also understood its significance for the country: "Not wishing to waste the inspiration wh [*sic*] our Flag always gives, I transferred it from the quiet of our house . . . and threw it to the breeze from Miss Evans window; and many were the cheers and bows which greeted us on its ascent." Wilbur, who had been in Washington since the war, found on this day "the whole atmosphere of the White House . . . changed." To the Patent Office clerk, women's rights activist, and advocate for the freedmen, Washington, D.C., felt more egalitarian: "The Conservatory was open and ladies and gentlemen, white and colored and boys and girls just from the street found their way in and were shown all alike through the rooms." On the train on the way home from the day's events, Wilbur and her female friends (white and African American) interacted with a number of senators leaving them star struck, "Just think of the notables we have seen today!" On April 1, 1870, she, along with many others in Washington, celebrated the ratification of the Fifteenth Amendment by listening to speeches by President Grant, Vice President Schuyler Colfax, and African American Mississippi senator Hiram Rhodes Revels.[168] Decoration Day, the precursor to today's Memorial Day, was also an important holiday to Wilbur, other Washingtonians, and the nation. In May 1870, Wilbur gathered all the roses from her yard, rented a carriage and horses (the frugal Wilbur noting in her diary, "$8 for his carriage + balky horses. $1.65 apiece"), picked up friends, and headed to Arlington National Cemetery for the observance. Her party "stopped where colored soldiers are buried + left our flowers, putting one flower on each of nearly 200 graves. + wished to make sure of so much, as sometimes these have been neglected." She estimated that 20,000 people were at Arlington, including President Grant and his cabinet. Only five years since the end of the Civil War, tensions remained: "A watchmen at the rebel graves prevented the rebels from putting flowers thereon. They were very indignant. I am glad there is spirit enough left with us to not allow this on the days that Union Soldier's graves are decorated."[169] Through such observances, Wilbur and her peers reaffirmed their commitment to and connection with the nation, binding them even more tightly to the federal government for which they worked.

Although there are more entries in her diary chastising herself for not attending church than entries recording her presence there, Annie Dudley did go to church and occasionally attended sermons at night.[170] Julia Wilbur's diary is also full of references to attending, and not attending, church. Wilbur was a Unitarian, but seemingly for social reasons she also attended the Methodist Metropolitan Church where President Ulysses Grant and his family worshipped, the Catholic St. Stephens for at least one Good Friday observance ("expected something more than usual. But there was nothing but a prosey sermon by a big fat priest"), the Congregationalist First Congregational Church (after a reverend who had been resisting integration left—"I hope it will now be a free Church in reality as well as in name"), Episcopal St. Johns Church for a funeral, and the predominantly African American Fifteenth Street Presbyterian Church where Sojourner Truth and Elizabeth Keckley worshipped. Wilbur also attended church-affiliated events, such as sermons at City Hall and church socials (one on March 25, 1869, she found "duller than usual" but they did have "very nice refreshments").[171]

Washington, D.C., also afforded women the opportunity to hear lectures given by famous, sometimes controversial, speakers. During her time in Washington, Annie Dudley heard lectures on topics such as "Civil War as viewed from Great Britain" and "The Perils of Honor," the latter of the two being delivered by antislavery and woman's rights orator Anna Dickinson.[172] Attending lectures was one of Julia Wilbur's most significant and frequent pastimes. She went to lectures so often that in September 1870 she bought a season pass to the lectures at Lincoln Hall.[173] Wilbur's interests varied. Some lectures were educational, with topics including the "Washington Territory," the Franco-Prussian War, what is was like to visit Spain, Wendell Phillip's famous "The Lost Arts" speech, and a lecture given by a black South African who had spent time with the missionary and explorer Dr. David Livingstone. Others were political, including multiple lectures given by Fredrick Douglass who addressed topics including whether the United States should annex the present-day Dominican Republic, and a lecture by a doctor from New York City on the "Social Evil question."[174] Wilbur attended many lectures given by women. In March 1869, she heard Julia Ward Howe read some of her poems and attended a lecture by spiritualist Cora Tappan. In February 1871, she attended a woman's lecture on kindergartens and another Tappan lecture.[175]

The most common topic of the lectures Wilbur attended, however, was women's rights. Although most female federal employees were not actively involved in the women's rights movement, a select number, including Wilbur, were heavily involved, and their federal salaries and schedules afforded them this opportunity. Wilbur attended multiple lectures by famed orator Anna Dickinson. She heard speeches by female labor reformer Jennie Collins and feminist crusaders Elizabeth Cady Stanton and Susan B. Anthony (the latter of whom Wilbur considered a friend).[176] She also attended talks made by speakers whose names are lesser known today, including some who spoke against women's rights—though she disagreed vehemently with their arguments (describing one such lecture as: "untrue, absurd—muddled,—behind the age—but very *orthodox*, 'aujience' delighted, generally, of course").[177] Wilbur supported all women who spoke on behalf of women's rights, and was distressed when lecturers would speak ill of other reformers. In October 1871, Wilbur attended a lecture given by a Mrs. Joseph Ames entitled, "Women Who Work vs. Women Who Talk." Wilbur had expected Ames to speak in opposition to women's rights, but "instead, of this she goes for the entire Emancipation of Women." Wilbur enjoyed the lecture but did not enjoy Ames's remarks about "the leading W. R. Women," whom she called "would be reformers + fanatics," remarking "I was sorry to hear this!"[178]

Many of the women who came to the capital to work for the government were not from Washington, D.C., so sightseeing was another common activity—one that bound them to the city of Washington as well as the larger nation it represented and increased the presence of women in the streets and in public. There was much to see. "The city abounds with places of interest to the sojourner or tourist, and one may while away days and even weeks and not begin to exhaust their treasures. And then, too, all these places are free!" gushed Washington memoirist Jane W. Gemmill.[179] A Wisconsin girl who traveled to the capital to nurse her wounded soldier brother remembered that "after I came home from the hospital and [Treasury Department clerk] Miss Sweeney was through with her day's work," the pair would go to "many places of interest in and around Washington. We went to Georgetown and Alexandria, where we went into the church which President Washington used to attend, and sat in his square box pew."[180] After the war, female federal employees toured what were now the new relics of the old Confederacy. In May 1870, Julia Wilbur and friends went to Alexandria and viewed the old "Slave Pen. part of it [illeg.] torn down."[181]

The offices of female federal employees were themselves sightseeing desti-nations, underscoring the importance and prestige of their positions. Julia Wilbur showed five sets of visitors around the Model Room of the Patent Office between February 1870 and February 1871.[182] In 1873, one observer de-scribed that room: "Amongst nearly a hundred thousand models stored in the splendid galleries of that institution, one may wander in hopeless bewilder-ment, feeling that ever model, however small, is the work of some patient year, lifetime, and often of many lifetimes, so that the entire contribution, if achieved by one mind, would have extended far into a human conception of an eternity of labor."[183] Visitors also specifically wanted to see the work the women performed. In February 1870, Mr. and Mrs. Curtis and their family "visited the ladies' rooms + examined the work" and in May 1870, Mr. Angle "called at office . . . was shown the ladies' books, +c."[184] Presumably it was the frequency of this practice that led supervisors in the Patent Office to issue a "New Order" in June 1871, which included the rule, "No visitors."[185]

Although the city offered women unique pleasures and pastimes, female federal employees could also get away from the city. General Spinner, trea-surer of the United States, had a personal summer camp at High Island, on the upper Potomac, to which he invited his clerks, both male and female.[186] *The Revolution* wrote of the camp in 1870, and described to readers that on High Island, "the kindly Secretary entertains batches of the young women connected with his department, giving them those opportunities for out-door air and exercise in the midst of beautiful scenery which these sedentary occupations render so essential to health during the sultry dog-days, and which, perhaps, in many cases, their limited purses would not allow them to secure for themselves."[187] When at High Island, clerks slept in tents and Spin-ner believed the break from work did them well, remembering in an 1875 newspaper interview, "The girls and the boys used to come down and stay with me, for they needed rest as well as I, and I always found they worked a great deal better for it."[188] As is discussed in the next chapter, this type of un-supervised heterogeneous mingling of peers raised concerns about the repu-tation and propriety of female clerks. Female federal employees may also have organized (or at least fantasized about) trips themselves, taking them far outside the City of Washington. In December 1871, Julia Wilbur recorded in her diary that the "Ladies talk of going on Excursion to Geo. + Florida."[189]

The federal government employed thousands of people in the 1860s, and businesspeople took advantage of the economy of scale to organize formal outings and activities marketed to federal employees—both male and female. At the end of June 1866, the *Daily Constitutional Union* reported, "The ladies and gentlemen employed in the various departments are about having an excursion to Mount Vernon" and described a planned trip on the steamer *Wawassett.*[190] A few days later, the *Daily Morning Chronicle* announced a "Fourth of July excursion down the Potomac" explicitly "for the accommodation of the employees of the several departments and their friends."[191] In the winter of 1866–1867, entrepreneurs built an ice-skating rink in Washington. They ran various promotions, advertising masquerades and contests in local newspapers and reported the attendance of a large number of women.[192]

At least one shop saw a market in female clerks, and advertised to them directly. Between April 28 and May 6, 1870, the "Cottage Gallery," a shop selling cartes de visite and "Pearls, Ambrotypes, and Gems," ran eight advertisements in the *Evening Star* directed at "The Ladies Employed in the Treasury Department." The advertisement urged female federal clerks to visit the store, "(but 1 1/2 squares from the Treasury)."[193] By recognizing female clerks as a class of consumers, businesses acknowledged and reinforced the financial and social autonomy of female federal employees.

Of course, while women earned more working for the federal government than they could earn in other lines of work, they were still paid far less than their male counterparts and thus only had a limited amount of disposable income. Tight purse strings are evident throughout Patent Office clerk Julia Wilbur's diary. In September 1869, Wilbur was relieved to have found her spectacles at a friend's home. "I feared I had lost them," she jotted in her diary, "If that had been the case I should have been 'done broke.'" A few months later, she had to replace her umbrella, which had been stolen from the office and so "feel to [*sic*] poor to pay 50 cts. to hear" a lecture on Shakespeare. In April the following year, her male travel companion took a sleeping car on their trip from Washington to upstate New York, but Wilbur "cd. not afford that luxury," and spent the long trip in a "smoky—gassy—fishy—too cold—too hot—light glaring—noisy" train car. Still, female federal employees did have independent resources that they could spend as they saw fit. After work on one "Indian summer" Saturday in October 1870, Wilbur confessed to her diary: "Made some silly purchases at *the 25 cent store.*"[194]

Private business schools also capitalized on this new class of potential students, further demonstrating the conspicuousness of female federal employees. The Consolidated Business College advertised directly to women employed, or previously employed, by the government.[195] In 1868, the school ran an advertisement in the *Daily Morning Chronicle's* local news section. It began, "What Will They Do?—Fifty-three young ladies were thrown out of employment at the Government Printing Office on Tuesday last. The majority of these are dependent upon their own exertions, and many have relatives looking to them for daily bread." The ad mused that those women who had "a rapid and legible style of penmanship and a familiar acquaintance with business affairs, may find remunerative situations elsewhere; but alas! For those who have not!" The school encouraged "young persons, and all whose early education has been neglected" to attend classes at the Consolidated Business College where presumably they would gain the skills that would keep them employed.[196]

Commercial business schools were not new, nor was it new for them to admit women.[197] What was significant for Washington, D.C., business schools in the 1860s was that they recognized the potential client base in female federal employees, indicating a long-term acceptance of women performing clerical work for the government and more broadly in the private sector. In 1869, 20 percent of the student body at the Union Business College was female.[198] Two years later, Wilbur assisted in teaching at a Business College. For a period of about a week in October 1871, Wilbur would leave work and assist the teacher—"Mrs. Spencer"—in teaching, a task Wilbur enjoyed.[199] Also important were the dialogues happening at these schools. Men and women not only learned how to keep books and write a fine hand. Students also engaged in debates about women's role in education and business.[200]

Women's success in government work helped to expand public perception of the possibilities of female education and employment. In October 1869, a letter to the editor of the *Daily Morning Chronicle* urged the establishment of a "law school for young ladies." The idea was prompted in part by the refusal of the Columbian Law College to admit a Washingtonian female applicant. The letter writer claimed "some of our most wealthy and influential citizens" had expressed interest in "supply[ing] a deficiency in our system of public education which has long been felt by the community at large." Although the need was pervasive throughout the country, the writer thought the capital was the best place for such an institution, citing, "hundreds of young women employed in the several departments of the Government who do not intend to fill clerkships all their days, and who would gladly avail themselves of an opportunity to prepare for more responsible duties."[201] Some female clerks actively pursued a legal degree. A Cincinnati newspaper reported in 1871 that seventy-two-year-old Treasury Department clerk Mrs. Harris was "studying law, in the hope of being admitted to practice next spring or the following fall."[202] Later that year, *The Revolution* printed a short biography of Lydia S. Hall, "acting Assistant United States Treasurer during the recent absence of Treasurer Spinner," who was "at the same time studying law."[203]

In addition to socializing, sightseeing, shopping, and learning, female federal employees also engaged in philanthropy and aid work. During the war, the city was full of hospitals and injured men. After the war, freed people, destitute women, and wounded soldiers still needed assistance. Female federal clerks participated in helping to put the country back together. Women like Clara Barton permanently left the office for the field.[204] Most, however, contributed what time and money they were able to spare outside of work to various causes.[205]

Some female federal employees directed their philanthropy locally. In late 1869, a few women of the Treasury Department tried to leverage their earnings in a way to help other women earn a living. These women pooled resources to purchase a $48 sewing machine. They gave, or lent, the machine to Mrs. H. T. Trumbull, allegedly "with the understanding that she should own it, if she conducted herself properly." When Trumbull went to the workhouse for vagrancy, another woman obtained possession of the machine and Trumbull charged her with theft. The result was a trial that spanned several days and was labeled by the *Daily Morning Chronicle* as "The Sewing Machine Case."[206] Although the female clerks' actions reveal their attempts to force middle-class norms on working-class women, they also demonstrate an understanding that women like themselves and Mrs. Trumbull had to work to survive and provide evidence of women forming significant relationships with female coworkers outside of work.

The names of female federal employees pepper newspaper articles on various fundraisers and events. Women did not always engage in this charitable work at the same time the government employed them. For example, Lizzie Lester ran a table at the St. Vincent Female Orphan Asylum fair in October 1867 and four years later became a Treasury Department clerk.[207] Others seem to have worked in charity efforts while working for the government. Olive Freeman of Maine began to work in the Treasury in 1870. That year she also served as a "Visitor to the Poor" for the third ward, in which she lived.[208] In addition to basic altruism, some felt that female clerks had a special responsibility to serve the nation that employed them. In February 1865, a group of women formed a sewing association "whose operations are to enure to the benefit of women and children, colored or white . . . rendered destitute by the rebellion." The newspaper article announcing an upcoming meeting

noted that, "The attendance of ladies who are clerks in the different departments of the Government is specially requested."[209]

Several women were involved with the Ladies National Union Relief Association. Mary A. Mason served as secretary.[210] Jane Swisshelm, Mason's
boardinghouse mate, also worked with the group.[211] As of March 1865, the
Association enjoyed a large attendance at its weekly evening meetings at Cavalry Church. A newspaper article reporting on the association noted that its
members enjoyed more than the satisfaction of doing the good work of aiding destitute women and children. The meetings were "made the means of
pleasant social and intellectual culture." They brought together "the humane
and patriotic of both sexes in a common and in enobling cause. It gives agreeable occasion for strangers to become acquainted, and thus benefit each
other, as well as to extend help to the poor."[212]

Josephine S. Griffing was a woman deeply involved in woman suffrage,
equal rights, and the peace movement in the 1860s. Serving variously and
sometimes simultaneously as founder, vice president, chairperson, speaker,
moderator, and committee person of groups including the Washington, D.C.,
Equal Right's Association, the Universal Peace Union, and the Universal
Franchise Association, Griffing delivered addresses in Washington and New
York, petitioned congressmen, organized and administered meetings.[213]
Griffing was able to engage in this work in part because her and her daughters'
government salaries kept the family solvent. Griffing began work with the
federal government aiding former slaves in 1864 and was appointed the position of "special advisor to the assistant commissioner" of the National Freedmen's Relief Association of the District of Columbia in June 1865.[214] Bureau
officials dismissed Griffing in June 1865 for making contentious remarks about
the condition of freedmen in Washington, but rehired her in March 1867.[215]
She continued to be a controversial employee, flouting regulations when she
believed it was in the best interest of those she was trying to help.[216] It is not
clear when Griffing cut ties with the federal agency, though in 1869, she un-
successfully petitioned for the position of Postmaster of Washington.[217]
Griffing's daughters also worked for the government at different points in the
1860s and early 1870s. Her daughter Helen (age twenty-two in 1870) appears
in the *Federal Register* in the Treasury Department in 1867 and 1869. In 1869,
Helen was one of only four female clerks in the Tonnage and Navigation division.[218] Griffing's older daughter, Josephine E. Griffing (age twenty-six in
1870), worked in the Pension Office in 1871.[219] Griffing was able to accomplish her important work, in part, because of the federal salaries she and her
daughters earned.

Prior to becoming a Patent Office clerk, Julia Wilbur was an agent for the Rochester Ladies Anti-Slavery Society. During her time as a clerk, she continued to work for freedmen's relief, including visiting the poor and coordinating supply distribution with Josephine Griffing and aid societies.[220] She was also involved with the National Association for the Relief of Destitute Colored Women and Children of which she was on the Board of Managers and for which she was responsible for auditing accounts of the treasurer.[221] Wilbur audited the accounts of the Colored Orphan's Home in Washington and attended the meetings of organizations such as the Colored National Labor Union convention.[222]

Through her involvement with an organization Wilbur referred to as the "Women's Club" in Washington, D.C., Wilbur and her fellow activists became invested in the plight of "fallen women" in the fall of 1871, facing "oppos[ition] + ridicule" from most of the public for their efforts. In the face of this resistance the Women's Club and Wilbur pushed forward in their goal to "provide a *home* for all the women who desire to leave their present mode of life. + earn an honest living.—a place of refuge until employment can be found them" with each woman personally pledging "a home to *one at least* of these women until she can do better." By September 30, 1871, the Women's Club had secured rooms and furniture to accommodate women escaping prostitution. "The Club is a success," recorded Wilbur in her diary that day, "although it is terribly misrepresented." The success, however, was short lived as by mid-November Wilbur reported that the club was running low on funds and that she had heard "they will not be forthcoming." The following month the club was hoping to get federal funds to aid them in their efforts, and despite turnover in the club's executive team, Wilbur was happy to record in her diary that "20 women have been helped more or less. A good work has been done + *it must not stop now.*"[223]

Patent clerk Wilbur and the Women's Club also had smaller victories. In December 1871, the women convinced Martin "Reddy" Welch, "a rowdy, a rough, a bruiser" and the proprietor of a "saloon-dance house" that was, as Wilbur described it, a "Rendezvous for the vile + the vicious of W. of both sexes- girls + men" to "shut up his place + promise to marry the girl he has lived with 3 years." Members of the YMCA had been beseeching Welch to reform, but it was the ladies of the Women's Club who persuaded him. On December 3, 1871, Wilbur was among "about 30 persons," comprised of members of the club as well as friends of the bride and groom, who traveled through the cold wind and rain to witness Welch's marriage to his bride, whom Wilbur found to be "a mere girl—pretty—innocent-looking." Wilbur, a woman long accustomed to philanthropy work that involved engaging directly with the people whom she was trying to help, worried about Welch's chances for permanent reform: "But how much that man will have to contend with! how much he will need encouragement + kind counsel + instruction." After the ceremony, Wilbur attended a YMCA meeting, and was disappointed that "all that was said + prayed + sung at this meeting was not calculated to benefit such as 'Reddy.'"[224]

In their postwar multivolume history of the woman suffrage movement, Elizabeth Cady Stanton and Susan B. Anthony described women's entrance into the civil service and expressed their belief that the Civil War attracted "many bright, earnest women to Washington, led thither by patriotism, ambition, or the necessity of finding some new employment" and that "this new vital force, this purer element, infused into the society at the capitol, has been slowly introducing more liberal ideas into that community."[225] One "liberal" idea was that women should have the right to vote, and a handful of important participants in the woman's suffrage movement had themselves been or still were female federal employees, or were supported by female federal employees.[226] As Stanton and Anthony noted, however, the liberal ideas were introduced "slowly"; female federal clerks were not overwhelmingly in favor of female suffrage and suffragists expressed frustration that they were not more involved in the movement.

The suffrage movement benefited from the participation of any female federal employees. Women's suffrage associations in the mid-nineteenth century suffered from a lack of resources.[227] Social movements require funding and women's historic and consistent financial subjugation hamstrung the woman's rights crusade. Historian Faye E. Dudden, who has written on the suffrage movement during Reconstruction, describes suffragists as being in a "Catch-22": "to campaign for their rights, women needed resources, yet in the absence of those rights, women could not acquire many resources from their most ardent supporters—other women."[228] When the government began hiring women as clerks, some became able to both support themselves and the movement. Although the pay was a fraction of men's pay and the city was expensive, it was more than women could make in other lines of work, and the hours allowed women the free time to participate in activism, if the meetings were held outside of the workday.

Some women were heavily involved in the movement. In addition to her soldier relief efforts and founding of the American Red Cross, former Patent Office employee Clara Barton delivered addresses at women's rights conventions and was elected to a vice presidency of the Universal Suffrage

Association.[229] War Department clerk Jane Grey Swisshelm was also involved in the women's rights movement.[230] Mary E. Gage worked for the Post Office until 1869 and obtained a job in the Treasury Department by 1871.[231] In 1870, she was appointed to a standing committee of the Universal Suffrage Association.[232] Treasury Department clerk Lydia Hall was also on the Board of Managers for the Universal Franchise Association.[233]

Federal employment influenced women's advocacy. Julia Holmes and her husband were both federal employees and involved in the women's rights movement.[234] Julia spoke in local woman's rights meetings, served as the corresponding secretary of the American Equal Rights Association, and was on the Board of Managers of the Universal Franchise Association.[235] Newspaper records of her remarks show that she believed in the importance of labor to women's rights—an issue she likely learned while working for the Treasury Department. In September 1867, she cited "the manner in which [women] had filled Government clerkships" as evidence of women's equality with men.[236] Similarly, Eliza H. Stanton specifically called upon her former work in the Loan Branch of the Treasury Department in advocating for women's rights. Stanton worked for the department from 1865 until 1867.[237] In January 1870, she spoke at a large women's rights meeting at which she argued for equal pay for equal work and defended the reputations of female employees.[238]

There is also evidence of lower-level participation by female federal employees in the women's rights movement. In 1869, *The Revolution* reported "large numbers of women from the several departments" were present at "the first National Woman's Suffrage Convention ever held in Washington," and that they were "attentive listeners."[239] Two years later, in April 1871, approximately seventy women attempted to vote in Washington, D.C., claiming the right to do so under the Fourteenth Amendment. Of these, at least thirteen of these women were, or had been, female federal employees.[240]

Julia Wilbur actively and consistently participated in the women's suffrage movement. Her diary allows us to see the opportunities available to politically minded women, but also provides evidence that participation in the movement was not encouraged, nor was it especially popular among female federal clerks. On April 22, 1869, Wilbur—not yet a federal employee—was one of seven women who attempted to register to vote in the first ward of Washington, D.C., signing a letter to the Judges of the Election of the City of Washington stating that she and the other women "believe ourselves entitled to the franchise" and if there was a law forbidding their registration "we hereby solemnly protest against an exclusion from the highest privilege of American citizenship to which our consent has never been asked." Wilbur and her peers' efforts were an early example of what was known in the women's rights movement as the "New Departure" strategy—arguing that the Constitution already provided women with the right to vote.[241] Wilbur personally presented the letter to the man representing the Board of Elections at the Hibernia Engine House, recording in her diary that day that she "hoped that ladies in every Ward will do the same" as she was "convinced that when a sufficient number ask for suffrage they will get it." As we saw in chapter 2, the mayor of Washington chided Wilbur for these actions, admonishing her that in attempting to register to vote she likely had "kill[ed her] chance of getting a place" on the federal payroll.[242] Although Wilbur did secure a position in the Patent Office despite her advocacy, she failed to join women who went to City Hall two years later attempting to register to vote, though she noted the event in her diary. Fear of reprisal may have been to blame.[243]

Although she did not join the hopeful voters in April 1871, Wilbur did continue her involvement with the suffrage and women's rights movement during her tenure as a federal employee. While "Julia A. Wilbur" may not be commonly recalled among the names of important nineteenth-century women's rights activists, she was friends with key figures in the movement and shared their political visions. In January 1869, she accompanied Elizabeth Cady Stanton and Susan B. Anthony to the studio of Vinnie Reams (a former federal employee) to view her in-progress sculpture of President Lincoln.[244] In 1871, Reverend Olympia Brown came home with Wilbur after a women's rights meeting and shared her bed, and Wilbur also became friendly with Victoria Woodhull.[245] Like the women she so admired, Patent Office clerk Wilbur wanted women to have their say at the ballot boxes and in meeting halls. Numerous diary entries bemoan meetings of women being dominated by the voices of men.[246]

Wilbur attended multiple women's rights meetings and events. To attend her political meetings, she sometimes had to take leaves of absence from the Patent Office or use overtime she had accrued. In January 1870, Wilbur left work at 11:00 A.M. to attend a meeting, returning to the office at 1:00 P.M.: "First time I have asked to be excused. + Miss C. objected. After this I shall leave without asking permission, I think."[247] On January 11, 1871, Wilbur left work at 9:30 A.M. so that she could be at the Capitol by 10:00 A.M. and witness the historic event of Victoria Woodhull addressing the House Judiciary Committee (the first woman to address a Congressional committee) to argue that, as Wilbur paraphrased it, "the Constitution gives equal suffrage to all," including women. Wilbur "thought it a great privilege to be present on such an occasion." She went back to work from 12:30 P.M. and left again at 3:00 P.M. so that she could attend the opening session of a women's rights convention at Lincoln Hall, later recording in her diary: "Several office ladies went. Quite encouraging." Wilbur had mixed results in her attempts to convince her co-workers to join the movement for women's suffrage. The next day, Wilbur "called at office to leave tickets," presumably for her coworkers to attend the afternoon or evening session of the convention. Wilbur recorded that night that there had been "great enthusiasm" at the evening session, "Many have been interested who never were before." One such woman was her coworker, Mrs. F. C. Thompson of Virginia, as well as Thompson's niece, both of whom "had never heard any thing of the kind before. They were delighted." The following day, however, Wilbur noted that, "Office ladies interested, mostly against the movement."[248]

The National Woman Suffrage and Educational Committee was born out of this January 1871 women's rights convention. Susan B. Anthony, Paulina Wright Davis, Josephine S. Griffing, Wilbur and other women attended the meetings, held in the room of the House of Education and Labor Committee with the permission of Republican congressman and chairman of the committee Samuel Mayes Arnell.[249] Although Anthony suspected the Republicans' arrangement for the women to use the room in the Capitol was a "Republican dodge," Wilbur was optimistic.[250] "These ladies *mean* work, no mistake," recorded Wilbur after a meeting on January 25. The next day, Wilbur brought two coworkers, Miss Read (a woman with whom she often socialized) and Mrs. Thompson, directly from the office to the committee room, which was "Filled with ladies."[251] While Wilbur may have been able to spark some interest among the women with whom she worked, she did not record the presence of coworkers at subsequent meetings.

Wilbur remained positive. On February 15, 1871, Wilbur "distributed tickets to ladies for meeting to-morrow evening" at Lincoln Hall to hear Victoria Woodhull lecture on constitutional equality.[252] She distributed tickets again the next day as well, with her friend Josephine Griffing even dropping by with more tickets. "All supplied," reported Wilbur. That night the hall was "filled in every part," she recorded. Wilbur found Woodhull to be "very able—wonderful indeed . . . splendid." "Oh, it was a great occasion! Something to be remembered. It will be an era in history," Wilbur predicted. The next day at the Patent Office, Wilbur found the "ladies in rapture over Mrs. Woodhull."[253]

Wilbur was proud of the women who spoke and petitioned for women's rights. In December 1871, after hearing Mary Livermore speak, Wilbur recorded in her diary: "Have no words to express my admiration of the woman, So sincere—wise—earnest—eloquent. Worth living in this age merely to see + hear such woman." Referencing all of the women at the Masonic Hall that day Wilbur wrote, "I am so proud of them."[254] At the women's rights convention on January 10, 1872, Wilbur had a chance to join the women whom she respected so deeply. After chatting with Victoria Woodhull, recorded Wilbur, "she told me to sit on the platform + I did so."[255]

Although a handful of women made important contributions to the cause and women like Wilbur encouraged their coworkers to participate, national leaders of the women's suffrage movement seemed frustrated that most female federal employees did not advocate for suffrage. In 1868, Elizabeth Cady Stanton reported to readers of *The Revolution* that she had toured the Bureau of Statistics and met the women who worked there, "of course we talked suffrage to them all," but she only "found here and there one who saw the connection between bread and the ballot."[256] "You who are in the departments especially, why will you persist in being afraid or ashamed of this Suffrage question? When the Negroes, Indians, and Chinamen vote, what chance will you have to earn an honest livelihood, as things go?" *The Revolution* asked the following year.[257]

Female federal employees would likely have considered such criticisms to be unfair. Involvement with the women's rights movement could be difficult for women employed by the government. As was evident in Wilbur's diary, meetings were often held in the middle of the day, when female federal employees could not attend.[258] On Wednesday, November 24, 1869, for example, a "pleasant and intellectual company of ladies" assembled at Union League Hall at 1:30 P.M. to discuss "the elevation of woman; the liberty of the ballot; a fair share in the educational and labor movements of the day." At the end of the meeting, the group resolved to hold their weekly meetings on Wednesdays at 2:00 P.M.[259] There is anecdotal evidence that female federal employees wanted to attend such meetings and were frustrated that they could not. At the very next assembly of the women meeting Wednesdays at Union League Hall, "A motion was made to commence the meeting for women at 5 o'clock P.M. of each Wednesday hereafter; which was carried."[260] In 1870, a San Francisco paper reported that a female clerk in the Treasury threatened to break "$20,000 worth of looking-glasses" over Grant's head if he "refused to allow the girls any leave of absence to attend a woman's suffrage convention."[261]

Larger meetings had both day and evening sessions, however, and women would have been out of work in time to participate in the evening sessions.[262] In 1870, the Woman's Suffrage Convention met at 10:00 A.M., 2:00 P.M., and 7:30 P.M.[263] The Equal Rights Association, which desired "to secure equal rights to all American citizens, without regard to race, color or sex" also held evening meetings.[264] As noted, however, traveling through the city at night could be a dangerous undertaking. Some of these meetings let out very late. On April 1, 1869, a meeting held to discuss women's suffrage began sometime in the evening and lasted for three hours, the newspaper reporting on the meeting noting it "adjourned at a late hour."[265]

As Wilbur's diary suggests, female federal employees may have also feared employer reprisal for their suffrage agitation. Retaining a job with the government was a constant challenge and women would have hesitated to be seen as too radical. The risk was more than theoretical. During an 1871 women's rights meeting, "several cases of political proscription were reported as having been exercised toward women who had signified their intention to unite with these parties in securing to herself the ballot." One woman was "an employee in one of the departments, who was threatened with the official guillotine" if she joined a women's suffrage group.[266] In the late winter of 1869, meetings of the Washington Suffrage Movement and the Equal Franchise Association were repeatedly interrupted and broken up by "rowdies," to the point of requiring police presence.[267] *The Revolution* alleged that the young men disturbing the meetings "are most of them clerks in the Government Departments here," and that their "ringleader" was a Treasury Department clerk.[268] Female federal employees may have felt uncomfortable in meetings knowing that they might face hostility at work the following day. Whatever the reason, female federal employees' lack of overwhelming participation in the suffrage movement, and conversely the suffrage movement's lack of concentrated involvement in the plight of female federal employees, was to, as we will see, injure the interests of both.

INDEPENDENT WOMEN CAME TO Washington, D.C., to work, and life in the city reified and amplified the freedom and liberty many of them felt. The more political and civic-minded female federal employees channeled this independence and freedom into philanthropic, political, and self-improvement activities. Other female employees, freed from the watchful eyes of parents, influenced by peers, and surrounded by strangers of the opposite sex, gravitated to and relished in the social activities the city offered. These unaccompanied women traversing the streets day and night and living and working among male strangers caused some observers a degree of cognitive dissonance—women were believed to be in need of male protection, support, and guidance. The independence women brought to and cultivated in the city of Washington did not go unnoticed by the nation at large in this turbulent decade.

CHAPTER FIVE

The Picked Prostitutes of the Land

Reputations of Female Federal Employees

Early in May 1864, a Washington, D.C., newspaper printed the obituary of a young woman named Maggie Duvall who had died "of typhoid pneumonia, after a lingering illness of 9 weeks, which she bore with great resignation."[1] Duvall had been a "beautiful and attractive young lady, with auburn hair, somewhat freckled," another Washington newspaper recalled.[2] Her funeral was scheduled to take place at her father's home in the city the day after her death.[3] Newspapers further reminisced that Miss Duvall "had a petite, pleasing figure, and . . . this, with her suavity and charms of conversation made her an agreeable as well as captivating companion."[4] Colonel Lafayette C. Baker suspected that she had been much too captivating. The morning of her funeral, as the bloody Battle of the Wilderness commenced in Virginia, Baker, known to many in Washington by his cold, gray eyes, visited Duvall's father's house and informed her family that he believed she had died from a botched abortion, and that her death had to be investigated.[5]

The family was "horror struck."[6] Despite protests from Duvall's family and physician, Colonel Baker's hastily convened coroner's jury insisted that they perform an autopsy. After removing Maggie's hysterical sister from the room "by force," four physicians performed a postmortem examination on the girl in her father's home, on the day that was to have been her funeral.[7] Baker instigated the coroner's inquest because testimony from a local actress led him to believe that Duvall's death had been caused by medicine taken to produce an abortion, and that the unwanted pregnancy had resulted from a sexual affair between Duvall and a coworker or supervisor in the Treasury Department.[8]

Rumors whispered in the parlors of Washington, D.C., about the local curiosity of the government employing women exploded into vitriolic national debate after the Treasury Department Scandal of 1864 involving Maggie Duvall and her coworkers. In light of the more pressing news of the Civil War, female federal employment had not been much remarked upon in the national press. After the scandal, however, the public became fascinated in the topic. As employees of the United States government, the "experiment" of employing women, especially potentially sexually immoral women, became a matter of national interest, discussed in newspapers from Maine to Hawaii. Simply by taking a job with the federal government, middle-class white women challenged nineteenth-century societal norms. Not only were these women working for wages, some were engaged in jobs that had been, and in certain cases still were, performed by men. Often in mixed-sex workplaces, women carried out important affairs of the nation including creating, verifying, and shepherding enormous amounts of U.S. currency. And, allegedly, many of them were also engaged in some form of prostitution.

In his investigation of the scandal, historian Michael Thomas Smith notes, "Civil War–era Northerners . . . conceptualized civic virtue and personal virtue as one and the same," and argues that the scandal reveals "the critical connection that republicanism insisted existed between the moral character of individuals and the political health of the nation."[9] Smith's primary focus is on the men in the scandal and how northerners understood their transgressions, but the attack on female Treasury employees also had implications far beyond the scandal and the Civil War era. As public servants, female federal employees were accessible and beholden to the nation's citizenry in a way middle-class white women had not been previously—they worked in public spaces open to the indiscriminate public, they performed work of national importance, their salaries were paid with public funds, and matters relating to their employment were nationally debated. The pall cast over the entire female federal labor force as a result of the scandal was damaging to the public's trust in its government and called into question the employment of women. Politicians, the press, and the public appropriated the reputations of female federal employees. Politicians variously reduced female federal employees to whores or war widows to garner public support. The press printed salacious stories about and images of female federal workers to slander political parties and to sell newspapers.[10] People seeking to repress women's newfound freedom also used allegations of wanton behavior to try to control women. Smith argues that: "To Civil War–era Northerners, there was a clear and direct correlation between public and private virtue, and therefore one could not trust a man who would carry on an extramarital affair to serve the public interest."[11] The scandal also raised doubts in the minds of Civil War–era northerners about the ability of women to serve the public interest—and not simply the women involved. The scandal threatened the entire experiment of female federal employment.

While reports of female federal employees' dissolute behavior were greatly exaggerated, some of the thousands of women employed by the government during the 1860s did conduct themselves in ways that ran counter to the sexual mores of most mid-nineteenth century middle class Americans. Such behavior, or the perception of it, was partially a symptom of how women obtained and retained their government jobs; women's employment was at the discretion of men, and flattering and pleasing men was the primary career strategy available to women. Additionally, young, single, adventurous women came to Washington, D.C., and, like their male counterparts, some of them engaged in relationships with members of the opposite sex that society deemed improper. When these liaisons were discovered, however, women were punished more harshly than men, and the behavior of one female federal employee called into question the virtue and worthiness of all.

As the stereotype of the female federal employee as prostitute circulated in the national press, women employed by the government went about their daily lives in Washington, D.C. Women had to safeguard their reputations against allegations of sexual promiscuity that arose from efforts to exploitatively politicize their perceived transgressions of norms or to restrain women's behavior. Like female workers in other cities, female federal employees had to assert their physical respectability against sexual harassment as they moved through the streets of the city and labored in mixed-sex workspaces, some of which were open to the public. Depicting female federal employees as either depraved whores or noble widows complicated women's entrance into the federal workforce by obscuring their identities as employees. Although supervisors were pleased with their new female employees and praised them in annual reports to Congress, this negative, national conversation led many Americans to question whether women should be working for the government at all, and likely caused psychological angst for the women who had to endure public libel and slander.

"Nothing More Nor Less Than a House of Ill-Fame": The Treasury Department Scandal of 1864

Women's entrance into the federal workforce was not a topic that initially generated many lines of print in newspapers. "The demand for Treasury notes is so great that additional clerks, including some ladies, have been employed to cut and fill them up," succinctly reported a Philadelphia paper in September 1861.[12] Other early articles were equally brief, though some were glib and flippant, highlighting the novelty of the development.[13] In April 1863, for instance, a Boston paper reporting on the innovation of women clipping Treasury notes quipped, "What better could be than that the tender sex should prepare the legal tender."[14]

Prior to the events of spring 1864, most newspapers reserved judgment on women's entrance into the federal workforce, although there were some glimpses of approval for the practice. A local paper declared of Fanny Steele's appointment to the Post Office Department in 1863 that it was "gratifying to see worthy women appointed to such positions as they can fill under Government, especially in these times of war, when the young men are wanted for the sterner duties of the field."[15] "'Woman's rights' to perform labor which they can do as well as men we go for," awkwardly proclaimed a Maine newspaper reporting on women's employment in the Treasury Department in 1863.[16] While newspapers were largely silent on the subject, there is some evidence that the new female federal employees set tongues wagging in Washington, D.C.[17] It would be surprising if the government's employment of women did not serve as grist for the rumor mill. By 1863, hundreds of women regularly traveled on city streets to their government jobs in publicly accessible buildings—a new sight in the traditionally masculine city.

While it is unclear how much notice the public initially took of women's governmental employment, it is certain that citizens in the North were very interested in other Treasury Department affairs. To help finance the Union war effort, Secretary of the Treasury Salmon P. Chase and Republicans in Congress instituted a new, uniform currency of questionable constitutionality in early 1862: the greenback.[18] Greenbacks were not backed by specie; their value was based solely on the integrity of the nation. Smith has noted "a remarkably potent cluster of political, economic, and even religious concepts . . . worked together to raise public fears about paper money." Democrats were especially opposed to this new currency.[19]

Spencer M. Clark was the man in charge of creating greenbacks. In the early 1860s, Clark suggested a variety of innovations to Secretary Chase related to the printing of America's new currency. Clark proposed the use of official seals, different modes of note manufacture, and printing of all government securities in-house, as opposed to using New York vendors, as had been the practice.[20] Chase adopted many of Clark's ideas, and beginning in the fall of 1862, engraving, printing, sealing, separating, and trimming of Treasury notes began in the attic of the north wing and basement of the Treasury Department under Clark.[21] To find the hands to perform much of this work, Clark turned to John Defrees, Superintendent of Public Printing at the Government Printing Office, who supplied the new operation with male and female employees.[22] Clark also contracted with Dr. Stuart Gwynn of Boston to manufacture a new "membrane" paper to use as counterfeit-proof currency sheets.[23]

With a new currency of questionable constitutionality, printed in large denominations on experimental paper in a newly created bureau, rumors about the Treasury Department began to swirl around Washington charging fraud, theft, and immorality.[24] Neither Chase nor the Republican-dominated federal government could afford doubts about the integrity of the Treasury Department or the nation's financial system—the value of the dollar was tied to the nation's confidence in the currency. To quash the negative rumors, Chase ordered Colonel Lafayette C. Baker to investigate the Treasury Department in December 1863.[25]

Once on the case, Baker immediately arrested an embezzling (male) Treasury employee.[26] Baker next arrested Dr. Stuart Gwynn, the maker of the "membrane paper" meant to foil counterfeiters.[27] The solicitor of the Treasury, Edward Jordan, granted Baker's request to imprison Gwynn based on the detective's assertion that he had discovered undeniable evidence of Gwynn's guilt, but Baker's evidence proved to be less than compelling.[28] Understandably angry, Gwynn filed three suits against the detective, charging unwarrantable arrest, trespass, and libel.[29] Jordan alleged Baker threatened that "if the Treasury Department did not defend him [against Gwynn's suits] he would be compelled to defend himself, and intimated that it was in his power to bring to light facts very damaging to the department."[30] Jordan called Baker's bluff, and Baker immediately set about gathering evidence concerning another immorality he believed to be festering in the Treasury Department: that S. M. Clark was a morally corrupt man, and "that among the hundreds of females employed [in the Treasury], some were not virtuous."[31] This shift in focus—from fraud to females—would have long-lasting negative implications for all of the women working for the federal government for decades.

Baker claimed that rumors swirling around the city made him aware of the problem of sexual immorality in the Treasury Department. In a letter to Solicitor Jordan, Baker alleged that Clark and his female employees had "been the subject of street and barroom gossip of this city."[32] Baker obtained incriminating testimony from three current or former female Treasury Department employees.[33] To obtain these statements, the detective enlisted the assistance of "a female attaché of one of the theatres in town," Ada Thompson.[34] Thompson lodged in No. 276 Pennsylvania Avenue, as did Ella Jackson, an eighteen-year-old employed in the Treasury Department, a girl later described by the press as "a pleasing ladylike personage . . . [who] dresses in black with exceedingly good taste" and who, in addition to working in the Treasury Department, was "known to theatrical fame" in Washington, D.C.[35]

Ella Jackson [created between 1855 and 1865]. Library of Congress Prints and Photographs Division, Brady-Handy Collection.

Jackson's friend Laura Duvall,[36] also eighteen and also employed as a Treasury Department employee, appears to have occasionally stayed with her.[37] On April 9, 1864, when Jackson was out, Baker and Thompson broke into Jackson's room, and went through her private papers, diary, and notes. When Jackson returned, they told the girl that her roommate had confessed to certain immoralities and wrongdoings, and that she too must confess, or be sent to the Old Capitol prison.[38] Jackson allegedly confessed, signing "a statement written by the detective."[39] When Duvall returned, they played a "similar ruse" and obtained her signed statement. Jennie Germon, another young Treasury Department employee who had been implicated in Jackson's and Thompson's statements, gave a corroborating statement. All three women's testimonies "concluded with the statement that the disclosures were made voluntarily, without fear, duress or fee"—an assertion that begs credulity in light of Baker's threats and Thompson's collusion.[40]

The statements of the women and the diary, notes, and letters allegedly confiscated from Ella Jackson disclosed a series of trysts between Jackson, Germon, and Duvall, their supervisor, S. M. Clark, and G. A. Henderson, another Treasury Department employee. According to Jackson's testimony and diary, Clark "very often" asked her and Duvall to "drink ale in his private office," usually at night.[41] Thompson alleged that Jackson once told her that Clark and Henderson had been in her room late at night, and that they had all been drunk.[42] Jennie Germon stated that "Mr. Clark has paid me as high as forty dollars . . . independent of my wages earned in the Department," intimating that he had engaged her as a prostitute.[43] She claimed that Clark once told her that his wife "believed that the Treasury Department was nothing more nor less than a house of ill-fame," and that she had spent the night with Clark in his marital bed when his wife was out of town.[44] Baker gathered other testimonies to corroborate these statements.[45]

On April 19, 1864, Jordan sent Baker's report and the statements and material confiscated from Jackson's room to Secretary Chase. On Chase's request, Solicitor Jordan interviewed the men and women who had given statements, and reported back to Chase that he had "an entire conviction that the most material of those statements are true, particularly those contained in the affidavits of Ella Jackson, Jennie Germon, and Laura Duvall."[46] Jordan twice gave the women a chance to recant their testimony.[47] On Jordan's second meeting with the women, Jackson only made "a few, not very material, corrections in regard to dates and some minor circumstances" to her statement. He remembered: "I said, 'You are acting under no duress or apprehension or inducement to represent this case.' They said, 'Certainly not.' 'Now,'

I said, 'what do you say, is this affidavit, as I have corrected it, true or false?' The maker of it paused a moment and said, 'Mr. Jordan, I cannot tell you a lie. It is true.' "[48]

Baker's investigation of the Treasury Department in the winter and spring of 1864 eventually came to the attention of James Brooks, a Democrat representing New York in the House of Representatives, and the internal investigation exploded into a Congressional inquest.[49] The House committee began its investigations on May 3, 1864. It focused on two lines of inquiry: (1) "the printing of the national securities in the Treasury Department," and (2) "the alleged immoralities of persons employed therein."[50] The committee investigated the introduction of Gwynn's membrane paper and printing presses. Committee members toured the Treasury Department, speaking with male and female employees. The men tried to ascertain both the efficiency of the new technology and the system's security from theft and fraud. Testimony and opinions on these issues ranged wildly. The committee also investigated the charges of sexual immorality. They interviewed women who worked in the Treasury Department, as well as witnesses who claimed to have observed immoral behavior among the employees.

During the investigation, Maggie Duvall, the freckled, auburn-haired young woman introduced at the beginning of this chapter, died. The *Daily Constitutional Union* reported that she had become "the victim of Mr. Clark, and in consequence of which, to hide her shame, which was becoming very apparent, went to Philadelphia . . . for the purpose of having [an abortion.]"[51] Baker instigated the coroner's inquest into Duvall's death.[52] The *Evening Star*, another local Washington newspaper, devoted a significant amount of ink to the Duvall case, reporting that it, "promises to be one of the celebrated ones of history."[53] However, even the *Star* had to tear itself away from Duvall and Jackson at times as they were "unavoidably crowded out . . . by the pressure of war news."[54] Outside Washington, D.C., the Civil War continued to rage. Militarily, the Union was suffering enormous casualties. From early May to early July, Grant's army lost 64,000 men.[55] Because of these losses, and the blood-weariness of the North, Lincoln and his Republican administration were suffering politically.[56] On June 18, 1864, a Michigan newspaper observed, "Lincoln stock is not worth any more in this community, than Chase's Greenbacks, which is now about fifty cents on the dollar."[57]

On June 30, 1864, the House Committee presented its 418-page report on the Treasury Department investigation. The Republican majority report was penned by future president James A. Garfield of Ohio, and signed by three fellow Republicans.[58] A fourth Republican submitted a brief statement concurring with the majority report in all respects save one, thus giving the Republicans the majority.[59] Democrat James Brooks wrote the minority report, which was signed by three other Democratic committee members.[60] The minority and majority differed widely in their conclusions on nearly every aspect of the investigation.[61]

In regard to the charges of sexual immorality, Garfield and the majority determined that Baker and Thompson had coerced Germon, Jackson, and Duvall's statements.[62] The Republican majority concluded that the charges of sexual immorality were: "[partly] the result of an effort . . . to break up the plan of printing in the Treasury Department, and partly the result of a conspiracy on the part of Colonel Baker and the female prostitutes associated with him, by the aid of coerced testimony, to destroy the reputation of Mr. Clark, and, by the odium thus raised against the Treasury Department, shield himself and justify his unauthorized arrest of [Gwynn]."[63]

Brooks and the minority did not dismiss the charges so easily, finding that the statements of Jackson, Germon, Duvall, and Thompson "disclose a mass of immorality and profligacy, the more atrocious as these women were employees of Clark, hired and paid by him with the public money." The minority continued, "Neither the laws of God nor of man, the institution of the Sabbath, nor the common decencies of life, seem to have been respected by Clark in his conduct with these women. A Treasury bureau—there, where is printed the money representative . . . of all the property and of all the industry of the country—there . . . upon the faith and good conduct of which depends, more or less, every man's prosperity—is converted into a place for debauchery and drinking, the very recital of which is impossible without violating decency."[64]

In reviewing the scandal in its entirety, it is clear that it did not begin as a sex scandal, although to this day, that is typically how it is remembered.[65] The initial charges concerned fraud, theft, counterfeiting, and questions about the sagacity of the move to a national currency, not sexual immorality.[66] While the scandal did not begin as a sex scandal, it is undeniable that it ended as a sex scandal.[67] In part, the sexual accusations arose from Baker's vindictive investigation of Clark and female Treasury employees. Baker's decision to take the investigation in this direction was probably motivated by his desire to see Clark punished for what Baker perceived as his various misdeeds, and thereby to punish Treasury Department officials for not giving Baker's report its due credit. Once Baker had produced the women's testimonies, whether they were real or false, the sexual aspect of the scandal took on a life of its own and did not confine itself to Washington, D.C.[68] Even if one cannot cite the scandal as the point of origin for rumors of immorality of female clerks, it is clear that the scandal popularized them and made it acceptable to discuss the sexuality of female clerks in the national press.

"Are Not the Treasury Clerks Ladies?":
Birth of a National Stereotype

After the events in the spring of 1864, all women who worked in the Treasury Department fell under open suspicion of being sexually promiscuous. It was a suspicion that proved hard to shake. In 1869 Dr. John Ellis published a guidebook to Washington. Ellis remembered standing outside a theater and hearing "a young snob exclaim to his companion, 'Let us go now, Tom! We've seen all the ladies! The rest of these women are only Treasury Clerks!'" Ellis recalled that he asked himself, "Are not the Treasury Clerks ladies?" He reported that "the majority of them are, but it is a melancholy fact that many of them are either suspected of immoral practices, or looked down up on by the Washingtonians as being of a lower order."[69] Specifically referencing the scandal as shaping the reputation of these women, he quoted Brooks's minority report and explained, "These disclosures attracted considerable attention at the time, and, unfortunately, had the effect of causing every female employee of the Treasury to be suspected, and was, doubtless, the original cause of the suspicion attaching to the position to-day.... The suspicion which rests upon these clerks as a class, is most unjust and unfounded."[70] The problem, Ellis explained, was one of counterfeit detection. Ellis claimed that it was "impossible to tell how many of these female clerks are pure women, or how many impure." He continued, "all are outwardly virtuous, and each would indignantly repel any charges brought against her. The black sheep are greatly in the minority, but are still believed to be numerous."[71] Four years later, another guidebook writer warned his readers, "It is not doubted that in some of the departments, stained women hide," indicating that the rumors about women in the Treasury had also blemished the reputations of women in other federal offices.[72]

The idea of sexually promiscuous women working in the government, especially in the Treasury Department, gained and held traction partially because politicians and newspapers exploited it for political gain.[73] After the allegations of sexual immorality and impropriety came to light, Republicans used the young women involved as scapegoats to protect or promote individual political careers, political parties, and the integrity of the Treasury Department.[74] The powers that be—the older, more powerful, upper-class

men—shoved the blame and public opprobrium for the Treasury Department Scandal onto three young women, and in doing so, cast a pall on the
entire female federal workforce for decades, threatening the practice of female employment entirely. As historian Christine Stansell found in her study
of women in New York City from 1789 to 1860: "The equation of prostitution
with any form of women's public life was not new."[75] What is new here are the
national scope of the charges, and that the allegations were implicitly and
explicitly leveled against thousands of women at a critical juncture in women's
labor history.

Democrats immediately used the sexuality of female federal employees as
anti-Republican fodder. By the spring and summer of 1864, when the Treasury Department Scandal occurred, the Copperheads had reached the apex
of their power and Lincoln's reelection was in serious jeopardy.[76] Democrats
cited the scandal as one of many instances of corruption and dishonor in the
Republican administration.[77] News of the scandal spread quickly. At the end
of April 1864—after Baker had acquired the women's testimonies but before
the congressional committee met—J. Henry Mullford wrote to Lincoln from
New York declaring his disgust that "the Treasury has been converted into
the most extensive *Whorehouse* in the nation." He asked Lincoln, "Do you
suppose that you can permit such things to continue, without bringing on
yourself dishonor and disgrace" and advised him that if it was "necessary to
have a *National Whorehouse*," that it at least "be placed *a little out of town*."[78]

An 1864 Democratic political cartoon entitled "Behind the Scenes" contains several jabs at the Lincoln administration, including an image of Lincoln in blackface and an inebriated Secretary of State William Seward. On the
left side of the cartoon, five scantily dressed women mill around under a sign
announcing, "Treasury Department: A New Way to Pay Old Debts." A man
standing in front of the women appears to be appraising them—suggesting
that he is deciding which woman to select and that all women who worked in
the Treasury Department were prostitutes.[79]

Newspaper accounts of the scandal further spread the harmful stereotype.
In Washington, D.C., the Democratic *Daily Constitutional Union* printed the
statements of Jackson, Duvall, and Germon almost in their entireties.[80] It
apologized to its readers for doing so, claiming that its sense of duty impelled
it to print the "disgusting" material. Suspicion that the public's prurient interest would sell more papers probably also contributed to the paper's decision.
The *Daily Constitutional Union* claimed it believed that it needed to expose
how the Treasury Department was run, and how "corrupt men" in the Republican administration distributed their patronage "to corrupt women and

Behind the Scenes [ca. 1864]. Library of Congress Prints and Photographs Division.

for the corruption of virtuous young girls." The paper did not, however, make the claim that all women employed by the government were immoral. Insisting that it printed the women's testimonies as information, not entertainment, the newspaper added, "there are very many highly respectable young ladies employed in the Treasury building whose characters should not suffer by any concealment of the damning guilt of this man Clark."[81]

Outside of the capital, newspapers of both parties were not as careful to draw a line between Germon, Jackson, and Duvall and the hundreds of other women employed by the federal government. In New York and New Hampshire newspapers declared that "a regular system of prostitution is carried on in the female bureau of the Treasury."[82] The *Chicago Times* portrayed the Treasury Department as "a seraglio ablaze with jewels and musical with wanton laughter" and claimed that other offices employing women were similarly debauched.[83] The Massachusetts *Springfield Republican* described female clerks as "vile women, and known to be such, who have been links in a chain of vice and corruption, reaching up and down, and polluting even the chambers of the capitol."[84] An Ohio newspaper characterized women employed in the Treasury Department as "women of easy virtue," and claimed that the department "has a few rooms fitted up in oriental style of splendor, and that a regular harem is kept . . . for the benefit of persons high in the confidence of the President."[85] In New Orleans, a newspaper declared, "Whatever may be the result of these investigations, the employment of female clerks will not henceforth be popular here."[86] As the federal employment of females was still an "experiment" in 1864, such statements would have been of concern to women and their supporters.

Female federal employment became a political tool for newspapers to either support or denigrate the Republicans in power. The *Houston Union* ignored the negative rumors, and applauded the Republicans in March 1869 for hiring women to work in Washington, D.C., thus showing the party's commitment to "equal rights to all." The paper remarked that it was doubtful that Democrats would have been so noble, and rejoiced "to know that a large majority of the educated females of the United States are thorough Republicans."[87] Democrats, conversely, railed against the Republican Party for filling the executive departments with prostitutes. The *New Hampshire Patriot* complained that ever since the Radicals rose to power and employed women, the Treasury Department had become "a scandalously immoral place, even for Washington."[88] In discussing the rumors that congressmen used the executive departments as "berths for mistresses," a Democratic Chicago newspaper exclaimed that since the Republicans' majority, Washington was "more rotten, corrupt, indecent, and morally diseased than any other city upon the face of the globe; lower in its depravity and open-handed profligacy then ever was Sodom and Gomorrah."[89]

Because of allegations against women—some perhaps containing degrees of truth, many others exaggerated or entirely false—"Treasury girl" became a national slur or an insult largely synonymous with "prostitute." A Massachusetts newspaper reported in 1866 that one woman in the heat of verbal altercation called another "'a villainous Copperhead Treasury Clerk woman.'"[90] In 1871, a Chicago newspaper claimed that two men were murdered in a "house of ill fame at Washington by a female clerk in the Treasury Department, assisted by *another prostitute*" (emphasis added).[91] Women working in the Treasury Department had to fend off these assaults to their reputations for decades.[92]

During the 1860s, newspapers from Philadelphia to San Francisco firmly maintained the allegation that women working in the Treasury were the kept mistresses of government officials. There were two theories underpinning this claim—either the women gained their jobs by virtue of having already been prostitutes or mistresses, or the atmosphere of government service, the city of Washington, and the methods for retaining jobs caused otherwise virtuous ladies to fall into sexual immorality. Since, as Smith has argued, many northerners believed in the "inseparability of public and private virtue," both theories were damaging to the "experiment" of the federal employment of women—either women were corrupted or easily corruptible.[93]

Some newspapers charged that members of Congress staffed the executive departments with their mistresses and concubines.[94] A Texas newspaper described the "Hon. Mr. Buttonhole" insisting to the secretary of the Treasury that "Miss Pretty Ankles shall have a snug place and a nice salary" even though "the young lady has no other qualifications."[95] A Chicago paper asserted that "the female clerks in Washington are but the picked prostitutes of the land, chosen on account of their beauty, well-developed legs, beautifully rounded chests, sweet faces, and gushing gushes, and winning ways."[96] In 1870, a New York newspaper declared that one senator had "stocked no less than six of his mistresses on the civil service as clerks" and "adds to the number every season," while another "foisted his mistress on the Treasury Department last year, and was influential enough to have her salary continued while he sent her onto New York to undergo an abortion."[97] "That Senators and members maintain women who are clerks in the Treasury, in the Postoffice and in sundry other departments, is as notorious here as the coming of Christmas but once a year. These things are true," declared a San Francisco newspaper.[98]

Other articles, those aimed at dissuading young women from seeking careers in government employment, proclaimed that to move to the capital was to damn oneself.[99] A Utah newspaper in 1867 asserted that women obtained jobs with the government either because they were prostitutes or "with the intention and understanding on the part of those who had them appointed to make them such."[100] A guidebook claimed that many of the women who worked in the Treasury Department were "young girls with dangerous attractions for public atmospheres or public individuals."[101] In an article that ran in substantially similar form in Utah, San Francisco, Texas, and New York in 1866, the writer counseled young women against seeking a federal position. The author described a young girl from the country naively traveling to Washington, D.C., to secure a position, "unwitting that she is walking into the very clutch of temptation if not vice."[102] A Washington correspondent for a Georgia newspaper conceded that some female Treasury Department employees led "pure and virtuous lives." "But they move in a tainted atmosphere, exposed to baleful influences, and many will live to rue the day they entered the portals of the Treasury building," he explained, claiming, "I would rather a sister of mine should go into a blameless grave . . . than step foot within its granite walls."[103] Federal employment was among the highest paying and intellectually satisfying work available to women of the Civil War era. Articles such as these, claiming that it would be better for a woman to be dead than to be a federal clerk, would have given women and their families pause in considering federal work.

Clearly, such statements were more than political jabs at the incumbent Republicans. The overblown accounts and hyperbole in some of the newspaper articles indicate an almost hysterical discomfort and eroticized preoccupation with women working in the government. In her study of the women in Davenport, Iowa, in the 1870s and 1880s historian Sharon E. Wood found that middle-class women working for wages made people deeply uncomfortable because "When a woman earned an income of her own, she placed herself—at least symbolically—outside the reciprocal obligations of marriage," and "having no need of a breadwinner, she no longer owed her sexuality to one man alone."[104] Allegations born in the scandal grew through the decade fed not only by political wrangling as Smith explains in his analysis of the scandal, but also a fear of women's newfound independence. Social conservatives used these slanders against female federal employees to try to keep women from working for the government and to malign those that did.[105]

A colorful example of the nation's salacious interest in and fears of female federal employees is an 1871 Chicago newspaper article, allegedly written by a female Treasury Department clerk named "Selina Tewksbury." The article's author, most likely a male editor or reporter, claimed that a group of the younger, prettier female Treasury Department clerks had banded together to form a club in response to an attempted curtailment of their behavior by their responsible female coworkers. They called themselves the "Jolly Independents." The author provided the paper with what "she" alleged were the "rules" of the group:

> Whereas, Certain straight-laced and puritanical females, who, being
> devoid of the natural passions and desires of the fair sexes, are not sus-
> ceptible to pleasurable emotions, and whose beauty being of the mind,
> useless, and not of the body, attractive, and whose conduct is far more in
> consonance with that of Pilgrim Fathers than of fun-loving youth, and,
> furthermore, as the said staid and serious damsels are endeavoring by
> looks of disgust, words of reproach, exhortation, deeply-drawn sighs
> (of enormous size) and sundry sneers, groans and looks of despair to
> cause the dismissal or ejection of all those who "would live while they
> live," is considered necessary to organize for the defense of our rights, and
> it is hereby resolved:

. . . .

Second. All ladies between the ages of fifteen and twenty-four, of good health, fair complexion and lively dispositions, whose consciences are not wrung by outlandish and abnormal sentiments, born of Sunday-schools and prayer-meetings, are eligible to membership; and, therefore, office, for all are equal in all respects, each candidate for admission merely being required to take the following oath: [I] . . . agree to become an active member of the Jolly Independents, swearing to do as my inclinations shall prompt, taking no heed of conscience or other warnings—ever striving to assert and maintain my independence. So help me G—eorge Washington.

Third. There shall be no stated place of meeting, no officers, no fees and dues, and no limit as to dress or undress.[106]

The female federal employees depicted in this article were young, free spirited girls and women, "striving to assert and maintain [their] independence." They were depicted as sexual beings, "susceptible to pleasurable emotions," and possessing "natural passions." This kind of female eroticism and independence was emblematic of Victorian fears of unrestrained and unleashed female sexuality.[107] Female federal clerks, like the women of the "Jolly Independents," were portrayed as sexually available, predatory, and destructive of morality, and, as such, clearly unfit for government service.[108]

In addition to being sexually immoral, newspapers also alleged that female employees did not actually work, caring more about dresses and hair ribbons than counting or transcribing. An article in the Hawaiian *Pacific Commercial Advertiser* in 1866 declared that the experiment of employing women in the federal departments was failing partially because of women's "over-fondness for dress."[109] An 1869 political cartoon depicted Secretary of the Treasury George S. Boutwell entering the Treasury only to find it full of women engaging in a variety of activities, none of which were related to their jobs. One woman lounged in a chair reading, another gazed out the window, women chatted in groups and admired each other's hair and dresses while ink spilled across the floor.[110] These images of female federal employees in the nation's press conveyed that women were at best disinterested and lackadaisical employees and at worst dangerous prostitutes.

While much of the reporting about female federal employees was overwrought and inaccurate, there was some truth to criticisms of women's work and behavior. Julia Wilbur, who at age fifty-five in 1869 was older than the average female federal clerk, found some of her female coworkers in the Patent

Office irksome. She recorded her annoyances with her "chattering" and "gab-bing" colleagues in her private diary. "I do wish ladies had more respect for themselves + had some regard for the credit of the Division," she wrote in November 1870. There is also evidence in Wilbur's diary that her female co-workers were less than ideal employees. Wilbur noted women's insubordina-tion to the female supervisor and "shirking" work. In August 1871, the women of the Patent Office were informed of new rules, including one that appar-ently made sick leave unpaid: "Nobody will *play sick* now, if the pay stops. Can't afford it," Wilbur predicted, revealing that some women had been "playing sick."[111]

Another female clerk lent some credence to the claims. Jane Swisshelm was a staunch advocate of women's rights who argued for dress reform and married women's property reform, and had compared women's political posi-tion in America to slavery.[112] In 1865, Swisshelm wrote a scathing description of her female coworkers for the Minnesota *St. Cloud Democrat*.[113] She di-vided female federal employees into five "types." Four of the "types" are de-fined by either their sexuality or ignorance. The first was "a little piece of painted impertinence" who obtained her position by being a "female friend" of a congressman. Next, there was the New England woman who picks up knitting between work projects and gives credence to allegations that women clerks "do nothing but knit." The third type of female employee was a lazy, entitled woman who manages to avoid doing any work and distracts the people around her with constant prattle. Swisshelm next described the office flirt. When a male coworker comes to speak with her, she "draws her lips to a 'prunes, prism, and potato' pucker ... [and] tells the unfortunate man that she dreamed last night that she was married to *him*." Finally, Swisshelm de-scribed "perhaps a majority of female clerks ... working like horses, scarcely taking time for lunch." Swisshelm's article ultimately argued that honorable women—who were the majority—deserved and could do the work, but by using the greater part of her article to substantiate, in detail, the rumors against female federal employees, she did herself and her coworkers a disservice. The reader comes away remembering not her argument for jus-tice for the majority of female federal employees, but the credibility she gave to allegations of morally loose and incompetent employees who were only a minority of the workforce.[114]

The revelations of one purported female Treasury Department clerk cap-tured the attention of the nation at the end of the decade. In spring 1869, "Hannah Tyler" filled newspaper columns around the country with scathing critique of her fellow female federal clerks, accusing them of being sexually immoral prostitutes. Tyler wrote a disparaging letter to a New York newspaper, alleging that her coworkers possessed "scarcely education enough to tell the day of the week by a counting-house calendar, and they owe their appointments and continuance in office to their personal advantages."[115] "Altogether, this is one of the most remarkable disclosures ever made from Washington. It is getting a wide circulation through the press, and cannot be without its effect," opined Parker Pillsbury for *The Revolution*.[116]

While at least one antiadministration newspaper took Tyler's statements at face value, however, other news outlets pushed back, defending the reputation of female federal employees and claiming that there was no Hannah Tyler.[117] A Massachusetts newspaper carried an article in April 1869 that tried to shift the conversation from women's sexuality to women's abilities as employees.[118] The author quoted one female clerk, Mrs. Ingersoll, at length:[119] "The result of my experience and observation in the departments would lead me to say that, instead of there being 'crowded' with women worthless as workers, there are but few such; that, instead of 'scores' who do not do 'an hour's work per diem,' there are perhaps, on an average, two such in each bureau; that, instead of respectable women being insulted by being placed by the side of the disreputable, not one in fifty deserves that reproach. . . . I believe the majority of [the] ladies are sensible, educated women, and superior in every sense of the word. That there are some shirks, some rebels, and some objectionable characters in the departments, among the 1,500 women, is, of course true; but the large majority are far, far otherwise."[120]

"More Than One Romeo Has . . . Found His Juliet": Liaisons in the Executive Departments

While accounts of the lascivious female clerks were certainly overblown, as Ingersoll indicated there was some truth to the allegations that women engaged in sexual relationships with men in power, with coworkers, or with other men to whom they were not married. Some of these rumors stemmed from the manner with which women gained jobs with the federal government—at the discretion and favor of men. Affairs with coworkers or other men could result from men and women working or living in close proximity.[121] When such liaisons came to light, however, the double standard of morality punished the woman implicated far more harshly than the man. Affairs, and rumors of affairs, also called into question the respectability of all women employed by the government and the wisdom of female federal employment.

A woman obtained her government appointment through the actions of a man. In 1868, *The Revolution* alleged that William E. Chandler, who had been the assistant secretary of the Treasury from 1865 to 1867, frequently tried to solicit sex from women who sought work in the Treasury Department. "Poor enough these women were, and needing employment, God only knows how much; but they refused to pay the price demanded of them, and they were not appointed. Particular instances might be mentioned, and facts proved, but women are not willing to have their sorrows and degradations dragged before the public," reported the newspaper. Chandler may not have been the only man who abused his power in this way, either. "It is well known that many other men of power and influence in departments have used, and are still using, their power and their influence in the attempt to debase women who have desired appointments," the paper claimed.[122]

Historian Cindy Aron found that some female federal employees may have used their sexuality in the workplace as a means of securing advancement, although "only a small minority" likely engaged in such practices.[123] Of more pressing concern than advancement in the 1860s was job retention. Discussed in more detail in the following chapter, retaining one's position was a constant battle and the matter was largely in the hands of a woman's supervisor. Since many women performed routine jobs that required little training, women could be easily replaced. This meant that a woman's relationship with her supervisor was often essential to retaining her position. In 1870, *The Revolution* described women having a "*painful* consciousness of total dependence on masculine favor—*dependent on those who held the power to do or undo*" (emphasis in original). An attempt to remain in a supervisor's favor may have been misinterpreted as something more scandalous than it was, and perhaps that was the intent of some women, for whom *The Revolution* found "a desire to court that favor" which "exposed them to just criticism."[124] Even if criticism of the women who engaged in flirtatious behavior to obtain or retain a position was "just," however, that is not how a majority of women obtained their positions and "if a few unworthy women have been appointed through the influence of certain Senators and Representatives of . . . low moral status, are the majority of women-clerks to be despised, jeered and scoffed at for this?" asked *The Revolution*.[125]

Some young women, many of who were for the first time living on their own without strict supervision in a tremendously exciting city populated and visited by the most important and powerful men of the day, likely did hope to make romantic connections with men of influence. Young women, a number of who were living independently of their families and at least somewhat liberated from community control, socialized with men inside and outside of work.[126] Emily Edson Briggs, a newspaper correspondent living in Washington, D.C., who frequently wrote articles describing politics and Washington society occasionally inserted references to female federal employees into her observations. She found their amorous aspirations naive.[127] On March 5, 1869, Briggs described the Senate chamber during President Grant's inauguration as filled with "aristocratic assembly, and yet an occasional pretty Treasury girl's face peeked out, proving some great man's exquisite taste." One year later, recounting a reception at the home of the Speaker of the House, Briggs proclaimed, "If there is one sight in this wicked world, more pitiful than another, it is to see . . . an innocent young Treasury employee in her simple robes of muslin, apparently raised for a brief time to the social platform of wealth and power."[128]

Consensual, if improper, office liaisons occurred. When touring the Treasury Department and meeting employees, Mary Clemmer Ames observed, "Here and there may be seen a young man and maiden . . . loitering in the shadow of pillar or alcove, lingering by stair or doorway, saying very pleasant things to each other."[129] Another Washington, D.C., observer, Jane W. Gemmill, remarked that "more than one Romeo has . . . found his Juliet" in the executive departments. She continued, "Youthful couples thrown so constantly together frequently become interested in each other, and before they are aware the dangerous little god has marked them for his own." The process of the workplace affair proceeded along a predictable course, she explained, "The other clerks enjoy watching the progress of the *affair du coeur*, while the love-stricken parties innocently imagine it is known only to themselves. After a time . . . the lady bids adieu to those around her, and quietly remarks she is not coming back anymore."[130]

Not all workplace liaisons proceeded so smoothly, however, and scandalous affairs gave credence to negative rumors. Angie G. Emery, a soldier's widow, worked for the War Department in Elmira, New York, for two years. When that office closed in November 1864, she sought employment in Washington. Her recommenders from the New York office were effusive in their praise of Emery's "zeal, efficiency, and uniform attention to duty." One of her recommenders wrote that he found her to be "reliable, intelligent and capable, and in all respects a worthy woman," and assured the reader that Emery would "acquit herself with credit, and to the entire satisfaction of the offices of the Department in which she might be employed." She obtained a position in the War Department in February 1866.[131]

Sometime later, Emery began an affair with Edwin Phillips, a married coworker who lived in her boardinghouse with his wife. Phillips's wife discovered three love letters from Emery to her husband in his clothes. The letters were addressed to "Dear dear Eddie" and "My Darling Eddie" and were laden with outpourings of love and requests that Eddie leave his wife, but also some mundane coworker banter ("Mrs. Wainwright [supervisor of female employees in the War Department] is sick"). When Mrs. Phillips became unable to locate her husband, she brought the letters and her marriage certificate to the acting quartermaster general (QMG). He questioned Emery about the letters, and she acknowledged "having written the three notes and says in examination that Mrs. Phillips is a bad woman and that Mr. P. is about to get divorced from her." The acting QMG noted in his report that "one of the notes dated 9 A.M. bears evidence of having been written in the office." He concluded that "Mr. Phillips and Mrs. Emery are in criminal correspondence." Emery was forced to resign; Phillips's fate is unknown.[132]

The local *Evening Star* contained further evidence of the occasional sexual indiscretions of female federal employees inside and outside work.[133] The editor did not typically highlight or emphasize a woman's employment in their articles, however. Instead, the paper tended to note a woman's job as a biographical fact. This was likely due to the fact that a substantial portion of the local newspaper's readership was comprised of clerks, politicians, and their families who would not have been happy to see the moral character of federal workplaces denigrated in print. It also suggests, perhaps, a growing acceptance and degree of comfort with the concept of female federal employment in Washington. The local paper could recognize the scandalous behavior of individual women without devolving into hysterical fears about all of them.[134]

In 1867, for instance, the *Evening Star* reported on "A Divorce Case," which involved a wife claiming her husband had been having an affair with Margaret Kavender. Kavender was "a clerk in the redemption bureau of the Treasury Department" and she "denied having committed adultery."[135] Other witnesses to the case included Isaac Williams "colored" who testified that Kavender was married to a man in Philadelphia, from whom she was separated and that she "was always fond of men, and frequently had three or four about her." Williams further testified that he "had access to [Kavender's] bedroom," had watched her have sex with the subject of the divorce case from her bedroom's verandah, had had sex with her himself "in Philadelphia at her husband's house, and also at his own" and that "he keeps her."[136]

Later that year the newspaper reported on the death of the infant of Miss S. E. Harrison at the Columbia Lying-in Hospital, "the circumstances being of such a peculiar character as to excite suspicion that there had been foul play."

The article described "evidence of strangulation" including "discoloration of the face and neck" and claimed that the mother "refused to give any account of the matter, nor did she seem to feel the slightest distress." Harrison, a native of Mississippi, had been in Washington for over a year and the *Evening Star* explained that part of that time was "employed as a clerk in the Interior Department."[137]

Although some of the facts in the stories above may have been in dispute, Treasury Department employee Anna Kendrick readily admitted she lived and had had a baby with a male coworker to whom she was not married. In 1869, the *Evening Star* reported on a custody battle between Kendrick, "a young woman employed in the Currency Bureau of the Treasury Department," and Tyler V. Durham, also employed in the department. Durham was the father of Kendrick's three-year-old illegitimate child. Kendrick and Durham had been living together until a year or so prior to this dispute, "when he left her, and shortly afterwards, she alleges, he abducted the child" and married another woman. Kendrick testified that she went to Durham's home to attempt to reclaim her child and he tore her dress and punched her in the face.[138]

When affairs in the federal departments came to light, women often shouldered more of the blame. This was not unique to female federal employees, though their shame could be far more public.[139] Returning to the Treasury Department Scandal, Baker testified that Treasury Department officials "insisted" that Jackson and Duvall "not be discharged until Mr. Clark was."[140] A week after the solicitor of the Treasury instructed Clark not to discharge the women, they were fired.[141] Clark, however, remained at the Treasury Department until 1869.[142] Not only was Clark retained in his position, he was completely unchastened by the events of the spring of 1864, as evidenced by his decision to have his own portrait placed on a new five-cent note in 1866.[143] Similarly, when Angie Emery's affair with Edwin Phillips was discovered, the QMG recommended Emery's dismissal, and Emery resigned on July 6, 1867. Phillips's fate is unknown. While he does not appear in the 1869 *Federal Register*, the report and evidence were filed in Emery's file, suggesting that she bore the brunt of the punishment for the couple's illicit affair.[144] Treasury Department employee Anna Kendrick did not regain custody of her baby.[145]

It is not surprising that among the thousands of women who were hired based predominantly on the strength of recommenders they were able to secure and the tales of woe they were able to construct, were those who "played sick," shirked work, and engaged in extramarital sexual relationships. Claims in the press concerning the sexual immorality of female federal employees was, however, out of proportion to what was actually occurring and overshadowed the good work most women were doing during the critically nascent phase of female federal employment.

"When Rose Is Near . . .": Daily Realities of Bodily and Reputational Exploitation

The effect of the reputational assaults against female federal employees on their daily lives is difficult to judge. Victorian women rarely left written accounts of matters relating to sex. Most of the negative articles appeared in other states, and thus women may not have read many of the articles branding them prostitutes or incompetent, but some negative out-of-town articles did make their way into women's workspaces. Almost all female federal employees worked out of necessity, rather than desire, and their everyday concerns could have helped to crowd out contemplation of how they were being maligned in the national press. It affected them, however, as supervisors and the public allowed negative stereotypes to overshadow women's capabilities as employees. Female federal employees had more immediate concerns with regard to their bodies in the public offices than the distorted national caricature. Women had to contend with unwanted attention from coworkers and the general population milling around Washington, D.C., men likely emboldened to approach female federal employees because of the conversations happening about their sexual availability. This assault on women's reputations could have been traumatic, and likely dissuaded women from applying to government positions.

Wood found that when women began clerking in Davenport, Iowa, in the 1870s and 1880s: "middle-class workers discovered what poor and working-class women had known all along: when women intruded into streets considered men's territory, they compromised their safety and respectability."[146] Even before the Treasury Department Scandal and the resultant gossip, female federal employees faced unwanted male advances just by virtue of being so publicly accessible. Women working for the government regularly came into contact with male strangers.[147] Female federal employees not only mingled with male coworkers, but the indiscriminate male population now also had access to them. A young Treasury Department employee named Rose Bielaski experienced the dangers of accessibility. In May 1863, a Treasury Department official wrote to Secretary of War Stanton, complaining that a man named Richmond, a chaplain in the army, "has annoyed one of the ladies engaged as a copyist in this office," noting that "his behavior has been very scandalous."[148] Stanton dispatched J. Hertford to investigate and Hertford sent back a report of his findings. He explained that Richmond "was in the habit of visiting the Treasury Department almost daily and writing [letters] at one of the tables at which doorkeepers usually sit and requesting one of the messengers to deliver them to the ladies."[149]

The letters, directed to Rose J. Bielaski, were dense ravings, often vulgar and occasionally with accompanying illustrations. Bielaski began work in the Internal Revenue Office on January 22, 1863.[150] James Cook Richmond was a chaplain for a Wisconsin regiment and was in his late fifties.[151] How the two met is unknown, although one of Richmond's letters suggests that they met at Armory Square Hospital—perhaps Bielaski was visiting the hospital and Richmond was there in his capacity as a chaplain.[152]

Richmond, a graduate of Harvard College, began sending Bielaski graphic letters as early as April 4, 1863—prose interlaid with poetry and written in small, scratchy print with comments between lines and written up the sides of the pages.[153] He included illustrations in one letter, depicting his flaccid penis, with the notation "This is the state of Prick when at quiet & ease when Rose is not near" and then underneath it, an erect penis with "9 inches long" marked down the shaft, and the notation: "*His length above* is about 3 inches—in presence of the sweetest girls mine is 8. When Rose is near he measures full *nine long inches*." Richmond also included illustrations of Bielaski's genitals.[154] In another letter, Richmond describes performing oral sex on Bielaski.[155] In his letters Richmond alternates between praising her virginity and excusing her for any past lovers.[156] To what extent Bielaski invited Richmond's advances, if at all, is unknown. Richmond referenced one walk the two took together and claimed Bielaski stated that she loved him, but also alluded to a different man being Bielaski's "beau."[157] At some point in late April, however, Bielaski stopped communicating with Richmond, and he became demanding and unhinged.

The public nature of Bielaski's workplace allowed Richmond access to her. The War Department investigator detailed how Richmond used the infrastructure of the Treasury Department—the building, the desks, and the messengers—to deliver his missives to Bielaski.[158] Had Bielaski been a domestic servant or a seamstress, Richmond would not have had the freedom or right to squat in her workplace or co-opt a private business's infrastructure as a means to harass her. Richmond also used the geography of the Treasury Department in his plans for assignations. On May 1, 1863, Richmond sent a letter to Bielaski asking to meet her and telling her to "Send me word or come & tell me (at head of great stair case) whether you will look for me, at P.M. at the open gate, South of Treasury."[159] In an undated note, Richmond demands that Bielaski come down to see him, writing, "I am waiting at the entrance to the grounds South of the Treasury." He threatened that if she failed to do so he would send a copy of one of his graphic letters to her mother.[160] Richmond begged Bielaski to know when he could "see [her] when at leisure," suggesting that he was only otherwise able to gain access to her when she was at work.[161]

The War Department investigator, Hertford, observed Richmond writing one of his letters in the Treasury Department and called upon the superintendent of the Metropolitan Police, Mr. Webb, to assist him, "as [he] feared there was no law in the District to reach such cases." Webb ordered Richmond's arrest, but Hertford did not state on what grounds.[162] Hertford and a Metropolitan Police official implicitly exonerated Bielaski determining that Richmond was insane and banishing him from Washington, D.C.[163]

As investigator Hertford noted, the law did not technically protect women like Rose Bielaski from the unwanted sexual advances of men. Even if Richmond had also been a Treasury Department employee, the law would still not have protected her. Workplace sexual harassment was not a crime in the 1860s. In fact, such behavior did not begin to be criminalized until 1879, when Missouri passed a state statute protecting only a limited set of female domestic servants from the sexual harassment of their employers.[164] Early female federal employees had to navigate these newly heterogeneous workspaces protected only by cultural conventions against sexually harassing women, and such societal proscriptions were not always effective.

As is still the case today, sexual harassment was an underreported crime in the nineteenth century. Such harassment did, however, occur in the federal departments.[165] Clara Barton's biographer found that Barton had experienced malicious sexual harassment as a very early employee of the Patent Office in the 1850s.[166] Barton's supervisor apparently put an end to her abuse, but harassment continued in other offices. In addition to the women allegedly involved with S. M. Clark in the Treasury Department Scandal, other female employees reported harassment to the investigating congressional committee. Sixteen-year-old Sarah Lulley testified that her supervisor, Mr. Gray, propositioned her to do "night work." When asked by the committee: "At the time did you think he meant anything improper?" She replied in the affirmative and added that Gray would sometimes "shake his head and wink his eyes" at her.[167] Her father, Mano Lulley, corroborated her testimony.[168] Mrs. Beattie Pumphrey testified that an African American woman who kept a confectionary stand in the Treasury building brought her messages from S. M. Clark that included veiled offers of sex for money.[169]

While men's accessibility to female federal employees exposed women to greater potential for sexual harassment than they would have otherwise experienced, their status as public employees offered at least a slight degree of protection from such behavior. A private employer could more easily conceal harassment; women working as domestic servants had little or no recourse if their boss or other member of the household harassed them. Female federal employees, however, may have had more freedom to bring charges against harassers. Moreover, supervisors became incentivized to proscribe harassing behavior for fear of public reprisal. Probably in response to allegations made during the Treasury Department Scandal, for example, Chase's successor, Secretary of the Treasury William Pitt Fessenden, drafted an order to all employees of Clark's Currency Bureau in November 1864 which created a system for any employees, "whether males or females," to report "any real personal grievance or . . . any reasonable and just complaint against any other person in the division, growing out of his, or her conduct."[170] Due to the nature of the allegations in the Treasury Department Scandal, this order was likely one of the first attempts in America to curb workplace sexual harassment.

Harassment continued, however. Jessie Tyrrel's sister Addie reported in 1868 that Jessie endured "persecution" as an employee in the Treasury Department. Addie Tyrrel wrote that Jessie had been made "a hopeless maniac . . . by the vile slander of the clerks in your Department," likely of a sexual nature.[171] Ann Douglass allegedly lost her job in the Treasury Department in the mid-1870s because, as reported a friend, she "had incurred the enmity of a man who had sufficient influence with [her supervisor] to cause her discharge, simply because she would not consent to, but refused, an improper proposal."[172] Harassment also occurred in other federal workplaces. In 1870, a local newspaper reported that a male printer at the Government Printing Office made an insulting remark to a female coworker. The paper described how the "spunky female employee . . . slapped him in the face, and then chased him all over the building, belaboring him constantly with an umbrella."[173]

Newspapers also ran stories that revealed that the bodies of female federal employees could be subject to intense public scrutiny. Women were most vulnerable to having their bodies described and examined in print—in intimate detail—post mortem. Newspapers provided their readers with grotesque portraits of women's corpses, including Maggie Duvall, who opened this chapter, and the federal employees who died in an explosion at the Washington, D.C., Arsenal in 1864. In the reporting of these events, there is a sense that the public had a right to inspect—and thereby control—the bodies of female federal employees.

Lafayette Baker pulled Maggie Duvall's body off of her funeral procession and ordered that physicians examine the former Treasury Department employee for evidence of an abortion. Prior to Maggie Duvall's autopsy, Dr. Barrows told the coroner's jury that he had been caring for her in the months before she died, and that her lungs were tubercular.[174] Although Dr. Barrows insisted "there was no medicine that could be administered to produce an abortion that could possibly bring on a violent and acute pulmonary disease," the postmortem proceeded anyway.[175] The four physicians performing the autopsy found, and newspapers subsequently reported, that Duvall's "left lung was so strongly adhered to the chest that it was with the greatest difficulty that the doctor, with his assistants, succeeded in separating it from the chest."[176] The young lady clearly had died of pulmonary disease, yet they then inspected her uterus, which showed no signs of pregnancy. One doctor observed and newspapers publicized that Duvall's "womb appeared to be that of a virgin and the uterus had the softness, whiteness, and cleanliness only found about a womb into which extraneous matter had never been deposited."[177] Finally, after inspecting the woman's reproductive organs, the doctors opined that her death had been caused by pulmonary consumption.[178]

A little over two weeks after Congress released its report on the Treasury Department Scandal, an explosion rocked the U.S. Arsenal, resulting in the death of twenty-one women who had been employed packing cartridges for the Union Army.[179] The *Daily Morning Chronicle* described the female Arsenal employees as "worthy young women" who had "died stainlessly, in the midst of youth and beauty."[180] Thousands of people attended the funeral of the victims, including President Lincoln and Secretary of War Stanton.[181] Newspapers reporting on the accident included gruesome descriptions of the corpses. A San Francisco paper recounted "seething bodies and limbs, mangled, scorched and charred beyond the possibility of identification."[182] Local papers reported in grim detail the state of the bodies of the women killed. The "charred remains" of seventeen victims "lay scattered about, some in boxes, some on pieces of boards, and some in large tin pans. . . . In nearly every case only the trunk of the body remained, the arms and legs being missing or detached." Another paper described the "beautiful forms" of three of the young women who were "in pieces."[183] The *Evening Star* wrote of a box in which "was collected together a large number of feet, hands, arms and legs, and portions of the bones of the head."[184]

There is a tension in these articles. To some extent, descriptions of the deceased and their ravaged bodies are reminiscent of accounts of dead and wounded soldiers.[185] Since the victims of the arsenal explosion died in the commission of fabricating weapons of war, this is not surprising. But there is also a salacious and gratuitous element to the newspaper accounts. An *Evening Star* article details one body as "that of a young girl, every shred of dress had been burned from her but her gaiter shoes." Another body only "bore some vestiges of clothing about the loins."[186] This undertone of eroticism served to remind readers that these war deaths were different because the victims were women.

Living female federal employees were also at risk of having their bodies sexualized by the press. Late in 1869, for instance, $750 in fractional currency went missing from the currency printing bureau of the Treasury Department. The bureau's Superintendent "ordered that each person in the separating room [where the money was supposed to have gone missing] should be examined." The "persons" working in that room included or were exclusively women, and "two ladies were employed to search all the females, and they were compelled to undergo a rigid overhauling."[187] "The young girls were literally obliged to take themselves apart. Dresses, petticoats, waterfalls, and every article of their attire were stripped off," reported a local paper. *The Critic* chastised the Superintendent for his decision to subject the women to "the humiliation of being searched."[188] Yet the paper, by describing the "young girls" being "stripped" of "every article of their attire," contributed to the women's likely humiliation and invited the general public to imagine the women's "rigid overhauling."

The sexualization of female federal employees put additional stress on women who may already have been struggling with the move into the federal workforce. Job seeking could be uncomfortable in an atmosphere that might include improper propositioning by supervisors or recommenders, "For every woman feels degraded and debased by the fact of a man having dared to propose to her dishonorable bargains," explained *The Revolution*.[189] In response to a series of negative rumors about female federal employees an editor of *The Revolution* proclaimed, "Why [a] decent woman should seek or desire a clerkship in Washington, is past all comprehension."[190] Sallie Bridges applied to the Treasury Department over a year after the scandal, and her application reveals that some women felt trepidation regarding how federal employment would reflect on them as women. In her September 1865 application, Bridges considered the pall cast over the female employees in the Treasury Department and preemptively defended her own respectability. "I know that the ill-reputation and conduct of former attaches of this Department have cast a certain odium upon its female employees as a class," Bridges wrote, but added that she also knew that virtuous women like herself worked there.[191]

Heightened concerns over the general reputation of female federal employees resulted in some supervisors demanding strict propriety from the women in their workforce.[192] Since individual supervisors had wide latitude regarding personnel decisions, women could be fired from one office for behavior that may have been acceptable in another.[193] As noted, supervisors and the public also held women to a higher standard of behavior than men.[194] Women had to be careful to monitor their behavior out of, as well as in, the office. On August 21, 1872, a policeman discovered Charles Forbes lying in the street with several open head wounds. He told the policeman that a woman who worked in the Treasury Department, Minnie Brien, had been beaten with a bottle.[195] Brien had been working at the Treasury Department for over three years, and as a result of this incident was fired that day. She defended her actions in a letter to the editor of the *Chronicle*, explaining that Forbes was her uncle and she had forbidden him from visiting herself or her sisters. Forbes had arrived at Brien's residence with another man, and when Brien asked him to leave, Forbes "became most boisterous and assaulted me, where on my sister and myself drove them both from the house, but not with the bottle, as reported, but some tea-cups." Her sister also wrote a letter further explaining that when Forbes refused to leave, Brien "started to look for the police," and to stop her, Forbes grabbed her and "hurt her face severely." Brien begged the editor to correct the mistaken points in the original article about the incident. Both women's letters to the press appear as clippings in Brien's file, but she was not reinstated.[196]

Other supervisors were not as aware of concerns about propriety, though the women who worked under them were hyper-aware. General Spinner, treasurer of the United States, had a personal summer camp on an island in the Potomac River to which he invited both male and female employees.[197] In September 1869, a Chicago newspaper reported on the camp, describing Spinner as playing "the gently-piping shepherd to perfection" while he "entertains the fair Helens of the Treasury."[198] A few days later, a New Orleans newspaper reported that the article "fell into the Department like a bombshell . . . and the indignation of the fair Helens therein described, was terrible to behold." The women first took the offending newspaper to their female supervisor, "who held the obnoxious sheet at arm's length, as if it had been a 'red-hot' poker." Spinner himself finally "calmed the tumult, and with a 'tut, tut,' 'pooh, pooh,' silenced the threats of vengeance dire which were freely uttered." The article indicates that Spinner did not recognize why the women were so upset, describing him as "fond of a good joke" and seeing "in the description of his tent life only a playful and laughable squib."[199]

To women, it was not a "laughable squib." Many of the women employed in Washington, D.C., were of, or had been raised by, a generation that believed that a woman's name should only appear in the pages of a newspaper twice—when she married and when she died.[200] *The Revolution* bemoaned the "many reports detrimental to the reputation" of female federal employees that had "been rife in our Congressional Halls and through the columns of the press" because "to many of those women a fair name was an only inheritance, and once stolen could never be wholly regained."[201] Although most female employees' specific names were not in the press, they now belonged to and were identified with a group that was being maligned in national newspapers. "Such targets for newspapers and Congressional abuse have these clerks been made, that each seems to feel herself responsible for the honor of the whole," explained Edward Winslow Martin.[202]

Rumors of the sexual immorality of female federal employees in the 1860s were especially damaging because many considered the government's employment of females to be experimental, if not temporary. Negative publicity overshadowed the success women were having in their new employment. Annual departmental reports to Congress contain glowing praise of women as employees, but the caricature of women created by the press threatened women's positions.[203] Calls in the press to abolish the practice of employing women in the executive departments began after the Treasury Department Scandal.[204] Even years after the scandal, the events of 1864 were still cited by those opposed to the government's employment of women. In congressional debates over women's pay in 1867, Democratic senator Thomas A. Hendricks of Indiana described the employment of women as of "doubtful propriety" and "the subject of very much scandal."[205] "It is not clear, when a man looks into some of the congressional investigations," said Hendricks, "that the system is promotive of advantage in the several Departments."[206]

Even when the scandal was not explicitly mentioned, the reputation of sexual immorality that attached to women served to call into question the wisdom of women's employment. At the end of 1866, there was a pronounced movement to end the employment of women in the Treasury.[207] Newspapers claimed that Secretary of the Treasury McCulloch was seriously considering replacing all of the women employees with men.[208] San Francisco's *Evening Bulletin* provided four reasons why McCulloch would be right to dismiss all of the women. Three of the four reasons related to the women's suspect or weak morality: (1) "the complement of the female clerks (as has frequently been stated and commented on) is made up of those of all sorts and conditions; of various shades of morality and immorality"; (2) "hopeful applicants

without number are continually pouring into the Capital, only to be grievously disappointed [since] after all, only a very few hundred can be accommodated with places"; (3) "the extravagance and temptations of a city like
Washington (not to speak of comparatively meagre salaries)"; and (4) the cor-
rupting influence "generated in subordinate positions in the departments."[209]

Women and their supporters fought negative stereotypes, but the main argument offered in favor of women's employment still failed to support them
as employees.[210] The common counternarrative to the prostitute stereotype was that female federal employees were the noble wives and orphans
of soldiers. In the investigation of the Treasury Department Scandal, for
instance, the majority report declared that the charges of sexual immorality
were "exceedingly unjust and cruel [because] they have to some extent compromised the reputation of the three hundred females employed in the printing division," most of whom were "wives or sisters of soldiers who have fallen
in the field."[211] Newspaper also reported that the women employed in the
Treasury Department were "mostly the wives and widows of our soldiers."[212]

The widows and orphans defense was problematic because it vested a
woman's worth in her relationship to a man. Not all, perhaps not even a majority of, federal female employees were related to Union soldiers and that left
this class exposed and suspect.[213] The defense suggested that women had no
right to be respected as employees, per se. According to this line of reasoning,
the government should only hire and retain female employees based on their
relationship to a Union soldier, regardless of her individual abilities or merit.
Such an argument did not offer a good long-term prospect for female federal
employment.

The characterization of female federal employees as poor widows and orphans also placed women in a perpetual childlike position in the federal government. Supervisors became proxy fathers or husbands and women became
employees of whom little was expected. The *Evening Star* depicted Treasurer
Spinner in this pseudo-parent, pseudo-lover role in 1870. The paper described
the treasurer as being "much esteemed by all of his lady employees" who daily
brought him "fragrant bouquets arranged by delicate hands [and] luscious
fruit in season." The paper intimated that "younger men" should envy Spinner who was often surrounded by "a bevy of girls." The "girls" in question reportedly spent their lunch recess "propounding dozens of questions" to the
general, who "pleasantly answers," and "never allows talk to interfere with his
business."[214] As portrayed by the *Evening Star*, a group of "girls" annoy the
avuncular and hard-working general with questions so inane and meaning-
less that he can easily continue to labor on with the difficult and important

work of overseeing the finances of the nation while responding to them. Yet the scene could have been painted very differently. Female federal employees, denied any job training or clear avenues of promotion, had to spend their lunch period clarifying work issues, learning more about the operations of the Treasury Department, and building a relationship with the man in whose discretion their continued employment lay.

THE STEREOTYPES ATTACHED to female federal employees evidence a struggle to align nineteenth-century conceptions of womanhood with this new avenue of employment. Negative rumors of female federal employees contributed to the country's perception of women's movement into this previously male enclave of employment and deprecated women's contributions to the labors of government during a time that was critical to the women's movement. In 1871, Carrie Tweed wrote to the Boston *Chronicle*, proclaiming: "Two months in the Treasury Department has made me feel proud that I hold a position there. I know whereof I affirm when I say that no better, more intelligent, or refined class of women can be found in any circle of life."[215] Despite all of the negative press, the rumors, and the constant threat to a woman's reputation, many female federal employees still gained a sense of pride and empowerment from their positions. Unfortunately, retaining those positions was almost as difficult as was obtaining them.

CHAPTER SIX

I Am Now Exerting All My Thinking Powers

Women's Struggle to Retain and to Regain Federal Positions

In 1869, the Baltimore *Sun* printed what it characterized as an "Amusing Dilemma of a Female Clerk." A recently dismissed Treasury Department clerk inquired at the department "to ascertain if the demand of a Congressman that she should be reinstated would be successful. 'I must know at once,' said she, 'for I have received an offer of marriage, and, although I don't fancy the man, if I can't get reinstated I must accept.'"[1]

The "experiment" of employing women in the federal government was successful in that women became a permanent component of the federal workforce. Even as newspapers around the country ran dozens of articles announcing federal workforce reductions, the number of persons employed in the executive departments in Washington, D.C., generally increased, and the percentage of females employed by the federal government continued to grow. As a group, women never left federal employ after the 1860s, but individual women like the "female clerk" did struggle to retain their jobs, especially at the end of the decade when the work generated by the Civil War began to dwindle.

Insecurity and volatility plagued the federal workforce of the 1860s. Positions with the federal government were hard to get and easy to lose as workloads and budgets increased and decreased and political fortunes rose and fell. Historian Cindy Sondik Aron found a higher degree of employment permanence in the later period. She calculated that two-thirds of the men and almost half of the women working in the Treasury Department in 1871 remained at that department for at least ten years.[2] This long employment was not the case in the 1860s. During the war and the immediate postwar period, departments coped with volatile workloads through unsystematic, nonuniform, rapid expansion and contraction of their workforces that resulted in short employment periods for both men and women. Records reveal that over half of the women working for the federal government during the 1860s may have been employed for only one year or less.

The female clerks who fought to keep their jobs displayed more aggressiveness than they had when they were new applicants. Like the "female clerk," women turned again to politicians to pressure departments to retain or rehire them. Women fell back on tactics that had helped them to obtain their jobs—narratives of female dependency and stories of men lost or wounded on the fields of battle. They wielded these constructs more force-fully, however, in their attempts to regain their jobs. Many women needed the work to support themselves and their families. The loss of a woman's federal job could be catastrophic for an entire family that had become reliant on her salary.

Dismissed female clerks had also developed civil service acumen from which they could draw in their attempts to keep or regain their jobs. Women monitored rumors of layoffs and marshaled preemptive support. They learned the rules and language of federal employment, instructing their rec-ommenders on exactly what to say and to whom to say it. Some women also became cutthroat, singling out other women who should be fired to create room for themselves or friends. Not all women lost their jobs in the 1860s. Some went on to long careers with the federal government. Others left fed-eral employ, either voluntarily or because they were not rehired, and pursued different careers or kept homes. In their attempts to remain federal employ-ees, women demonstrated that they had quickly come to view their positions with a sense of ownership, many evincing a strength and self-confidence that seemed to have been gained through their employment as civil servants.

"Note of Dismissal in a Yellow Envelope": Postbellum Job Losses

Letitia Arnold began applying for a job in the Treasury Department in Febru-ary 1862, when she was in her early thirties. Between 1862 and 1868, Arnold sent at least two letters of application and caused to be sent at least ten letters of recommendation to that department. She was finally successful in Febru-ary 1868, six years after her initial application. She held the job for only ten months. In November 1868, Arnold was let go as part of a reduction in the force.[3] Letitia Arnold might have received the news of her dismissal in a yellow envelope, the sight of which, reported one newspaper, "is awful to a government employee. It tells the sad tale before it is opened."[4]

The size of the federal bureaucracy exploded during the Civil War. Soon after the war's end, newspapers began to report on the ramifications of re-turning to a peacetime economy, including "clerks discharged from govern-ment offices" because of a reduction in the amount of federal work to be done.[5] Initially, the federal departments still had an enormous backlog of work to attend to, but eventually clerks caught up with workloads and em-ployee reductions—of both male and female employees—became necessary.

Articles regarding layoffs of federal employees began in late 1865 and continued through 1866.[6] News of the dismissal of federal employees became more frequent in 1867 when a lack of work resulted in sweeping dismissals of both men and women.[7] By 1868, understanding that the executive departments were overstaffed, Congress cut appropriations to departments necessitating the firings of hundreds of male and female employees.[8] In November 1868, the *New York Herald* informed its readers that recent dismissals in the Treasury Department were merely the beginning: "there are indications that the official guillotine will be busily at work throughout the whole of the coming winter . . . there are dim foreshadowings that several other bureaus will soon receive a visit from it."[9] Indeed, reports of dismissals continued in 1869. Congress pressed departments to slash their payrolls and departments tried to comply.[10] At the end of 1869, the *Public Ledger* in Philadelphia provided a summary of the dismissals in the executive departments for the previous eight months. The paper reported that more than six hundred employees had been dismissed from the Treasury Department, two hundred had been dismissed from the War Department, and enough people had been fired from the Post Office Department to result in an annual savings of $2 million.[11]

Contrary to the plethora of newspaper articles in the late 1860s concerning the reduction of the federal workforce in Washington, D.C., the number of federal employees listed in the *Federal Register* actually grew during that period, with the exception of a slight dip in 1869. Even though Congress attempted to trim payrolls in a retrenchment effort, the federal bureaucracy never returned to anything close to its prewar size. The number of employees listed on the *Federal Register* as working in the Patent Office, Post Office, Pension Office, Treasury Department, Agriculture Department, War Department, and Government Hospital for the Insane in Washington, D.C., grew 392 percent, increasing from 850 in 1859 to 4,181 in 1871.[12]

More significantly for present purposes, the number of female employees grew steadily throughout the period under examination. In 1859, the *Federal Register* listed 18 women in the executive offices and departments. In 1871, that figure had grown to 922, and the *Federal Register* was a source that significantly underreported federal employees. For example, in 1867, a local newspaper reported that 700 women were employed in the printing bureau of the Treasury Department alone. Those women do not appear in the *Federal Register*, nor do the hundreds of women employed at the Government Printing Office.[13] The percentage of female employees in the federal departments in Washington, D.C., also consistently increased. The Treasury Department, which employed the largest number of women during the period under consideration, had no female employees in 1859. In 1871, the Treasury Department's workforce, as listed in the *Federal Register*, was almost 28 percent women.

Because supervisors could pay women less than men to perform the same work and because Congress was cutting department appropriations, the government had an economic incentive to keep women on its payrolls. Supervisors also faced unrelenting pressure from female applicants, even in the midst of announcements of large-scale layoffs. In the summer of 1868, a local newspaper reported that between three and four hundred employees, mostly women, were to be dismissed because of an appropriation reduction. The newspaper continued, "Notwithstanding the reductions in Treasury Department, about one thousand applications for positions are received weekly."[14] An April 1869 newspaper article noted both that "removals in the [Treasury Department] are constantly going on" and that "at noon about a hundred men and women were waiting there to see the appointment clerk [of the Treasury]," including "newcomers."[15]

Thus, although women as a group maintained employment, individual women were justified in fearing for their jobs. Because much of the basic work women did for the federal government could be adequately done with relatively little training some supervisors saw female employees as interchangeable. Even if a woman was not removed in one of the many sweeps of reductions announced in the newspapers, the enormous competition for jobs meant that she could be removed to make room for another woman that someone in power believed to be more deserving. A woman could also be removed from her job because of her politics or because of poor job performance.

In the 1860s, a woman's tenure in the federal government was likely to be brief. Of the almost three thousand female federal employees profiled, over 58 percent appear to have worked for the government for only one year or less. Almost 80 percent appear to have worked for the government for only three years or less.[16] This was not necessarily by choice. Of 273 files of employees from the Treasury and War Departments reviewed, one hundred women worked for the federal government for some period of time. At least forty-three of these women sought reinstatement, and as the records were spottily kept, that number was likely higher.

Competition for places was intense. In many instances, in order for a woman to get a place, another woman had to lose hers. Newspapers printed articles announcing the appointment of a woman to a place from which another woman had resigned.[17] Internal files show a similar one in, one out adjustment.[18] A woman with more powerful friends or a more "deserving" story could knock a woman out of her place despite her good job performance. In March 1868, a local paper reported that a spate of reductions of the female force in the Treasury Department was "partly for the purpose of giving place to more meritorious persons."[19] In 1866, for instance, General U. S. Grant wrote to Secretary of the Treasury Hugh McCulloch recommending Sophie Curtis for a job. She was the widow of Captain George Curtis, who had served during the entire duration of the Civil War and died a few days after he was discharged. Her father and brother also died in the service.[20] Three days after the date of Grant's letter, the assistant secretary of the Treasury instructed one of his supervisors to "dismiss Miss Mary Middleton now employed in the 4th Auditor's Office, and whose father is a Fourth Class Clerk in 2d Auditors Office, and has not served in the Army, and appoint Mrs Curtis, the widow of a Union soldier and the daughter of the Naval Hero Comr. Cassin."[21] Mary Middleton, a former schoolteacher, had been employed in the Treasury since 1865 and had assisted in soldier relief efforts in the city.[22] In the Patent Office, Julia Wilbur reported "excitement + disturbances in Office" when "Mrs. Van Anden got her dismissal + a new lady, Miss Burgess, was seated at her desk. Quite unexpected to all of us," causing "constant interruption + noise."[23] Such sudden and unexplained dismissals and replacements would have been unnerving to women who were desperate to retain their positions.

Supervisors and recommenders treated female employees as fungible. In 1868, George Woodward, a Pennsylvania congressman, wrote a letter to McCulloch recommending two women for employment in the Treasury Department. He included a list of women employed in the department from Pennsylvania, on which he "indicated four names by underscoring them, two of whom might I think with propriety be displaced to make room for the above named friends." He believed that the two women he had noted had "been in the office long enough to have laid up something for the future, and two of them can afford to give my applicants a chance."[24] The women whose removals he had suggested would very likely have disagreed with his assessment.

Although women could neither hold office nor vote, like men, they could lose their jobs because of their politics. Women could be fired for their own political activities.[25] Jane Swisshelm lost her position with the War Department in early 1866 despite her political connections when she began to publish the *Reconstructionist*, a newspaper that was hostile to President Andrew Johnson's reconstruction policies.[26] In February 1866, *The Reconstructionist* reprinted a letter from the *Delaware County Republican* reviewing the paper, which noted, "Mrs. Swisshelm, we believe, holds a position in one of the Departments, but that does not prevent her from expressing her honest convictions on all subjects connected with the Government."[27] Swisshelm perhaps should not have been so cavalier. On March 1, the *Daily Constitutional Union* informed its readers of "the prompt removal of one Jane Swisshelm from her clerkship in the Quartermaster's Department, by order of the Secretary of War."[28]

Just as women could gain jobs because of the politics of their male relatives and recommenders, they could lose them for the same reason. In the spring of 1870, a D.C. Common Council member campaigned for the removal of fifteen-year-old Maggie Fenton from her position as a folder in the GPO because her "father had always been opposed to the Republican Party."[29] Men and women usually depended on a high-powered recommender, often a congressmen or senator, to keep their places. If an employee's recommender failed to gain reelection or fell into political disfavor, that employee could lose his or her position.[30] Julia Wilbur's diary reveals that in November 1870, the women in the Patent Office were thrown into "a flutter of apprehension + excitement—fear of losing places," when Patent Commissioner S. S. Fisher resigned—an occurrence over which the women had no control, but the ramifications of which could be dire. "A day of confusion," Wilbur described the day following Fisher's resignation. In April, rumored "changes in the cabinet" caused the "political pot" to "boi[l] furiously" stirring up "quite a breeze in [the Patent] office" as "some dismissals are anticipated," Wilbur recorded.[31] Such political vagaries could have affected women more dramatically than men, who had a better chance of having additional support to draw from in an attempt to keep their jobs, including their own political activities or connections.

Departments also fired women for their behavior at work or absence from it. Some women simply failed to be good employees. Sallie Madden began working at the Treasury Department in July 1864 and was fired on the last day of 1865 for being "remiss in her duties."[32] A female attendant at the Government Hospital for the Insane lost her job after striking a patient.[33] Other women lost their positions because of absenteeism. The Treasury Department fired Ella Ladde in December 1866 after she failed to return from her leave.[34] In September 1866, General Meigs recommended the dismissal of Emma C. Duncanson from the Quartermaster General's Office because he found her "unfitted by ill health for the duties of the office she now holds."[35]

Ineptitude or absence did not always result in women being fired, however, revealing that a woman's connections, perceived helplessness, or personal charms could trump negative reviews of her work. Failure to fire a woman for poor performance further reinforced the notion of women's employment as paternalistic benevolence, rather than deserved and respected employment. This was especially true in the War Department, which aimed to hire only those women who lost close male relatives in the Civil War. In March 1866, for example, Sarah F. Wainwright, the woman in charge of female copyists in the Quartermaster General's Office, informed Quartermaster General Meigs that Mrs. Morris was "not capable or industrious" and in December 1867 that she was "not fond of work." The same month, she noted that new hire Mrs. Tardy was "inefficient."[36] Despite these observations, both women kept their jobs in the War Department. Annie W. Morris did eventually lose her job in the Quartermaster General's Office, but only after being absent from her desk for 430 days between 1866 and 1869.[37]

Unlike what occurred in factories after soldiers returned home from World War II, there was not a strong public sentiment after the Civil War to eject women from federal employment when the Minié balls stopped flying, although a small number of women may have lost their jobs to returning soldiers.[38] Perhaps some people believed, as did Quartermaster General Meigs, that the widows and orphans of soldiers had equal claims on the government as the men who fought.[39] In 1868, the *New York Herald* assured its readers that the Register of the Treasury "has been careful to retain the widows and daughters of soldiers and others who have no means of support apart from employment in his bureau."[40] Women were also somewhat protected from losing their jobs to returning soldiers because some performed the same job for far less money than a man would command, an important consideration as supervisors' budgets continued to contract throughout the decade, and others, such as counters, performed jobs that became "feminized" by virtue of women having performed them.

Whatever the reasons for female job loss and employment volatility, reporting on the issues resulted in an anxious female workforce.[41] Many of the female federal employees needed their jobs to support not only themselves, but also their families. A Texas newspaper explained the toll the uncertainty took on women, depicted a female clerk's life as "anxious," living "in constant fear of being summoned to the chief of the department, and told that she is one of a number dismissed."[42] An observer in 1869 described the consternation of the female clerks as "actually painful to witness."[43] Newspapers recognized that reductions to the civil service "will unfortunately create a great deal of distress by throwing out of employment many utterly hopeless females, as well as male clerks."[44] Female federal employees were so clearly vulnerable and desperate to keep their jobs that at least two separate men created blackmailing schemes, one in 1869 and one in 1871, to capitalize on women's fear of dismissal.[45]

A local paper, the *Daily Morning Chronicle*, acknowledged, "It will bear hard on many a young man and woman, after long and peculiar service in the departments, to be thrust out in the world." The paper advised the fired employees to "buckle on the armor of honest ambition, and seek in other and far more independent, manly, and womanly spheres a life of industry and usefulness."[46] But that was precisely the problem for discharged female federal employees. Male and female federal employees were all vulnerable to outside pressures, and the whims of supervisors. While men had almost every avenue of employment open to them, however, the jobs of "industry and usefulness" available to females paid only a fraction of what they had been earning in the government. Mary Arnold was about to lose her job in the Treasury when she wrote to senator Henry B. Anthony on Treasury Department letterhead asking that he assist her to retain her position he had helped her to obtain five years earlier. Arnold wrote, "I am now exerting all my thinking powers to discover how I shall be able to maintain my mother (a lady of seventy five years) and myself—when U. S. Government no longer employs me."[47] For a female federal employee, the loss of her job was not an "amusing dilemma." Women had fought hard to obtain their jobs—these positions were at the pinnacle of what women could achieve in employment at the time. Their employee files reveal they fought even harder to keep them.

"She Is Poor Enough But I Think Is Insane": Retaining and Regaining Government Work

Clara G. Scott worked for the Treasury Department for just seven months in 1865 as a temporary employee in the currency room. She spent the next fifteen years trying to get her job back. In her crusade, Scott utilized practically every method other female federal employees would employ in their efforts to regain their jobs. While Scott presents an extreme example of the lengths to which women would go to keep their jobs, her effort illustrates the passion and aggression of women attempting to regain the positions they so badly wanted and needed.

First, Scott tried to preemptively prevent her dismissal. Departments paid temporary employees, male and female, from specific funds and when those funds were exhausted, they let the employees go. Scott, who was such a temporary employee, appealed to President Andrew Johnson asking that she be brought on as a permanent clerk in October 1865.[48] Her bid failed and she was terminated later that fall. Scott then devoted herself to regaining her job. She obtained letters of recommendation from senators, congressmen, and generals and sent application letters to the Treasury Department. A note in the file indicates that she sent or caused to be sent to the Treasury Department at least sixteen letters between 1866 and 1870. She sought out the wife of Secretary of the Treasury Hugh McCulloch and handed her letters to pass on to her husband. She visited with President Andrew Johnson. She pressed her case in person at the Treasury Department, perhaps as often as monthly. By 1869, she had also applied to the War Department.[49]

Scott very much believed that the government owed her a job and was incensed that it had been taken from her. In November she insisted to Johnson that she had "been *wronged out* of my *just rights* [to] employment in the Treasury." Scott based her claim on a number of factors. She had been immediately and unflinchingly loyal to the Union during the Civil War. She had cared for sick and wounded soldiers. She lost male relatives in the conflict. Scott described her destitute circumstances, stemming, she claimed, from her benevolence in caring for children orphaned by the war. Scott frequently complained that women obtained and retained jobs who were disloyal or did not need the salary as much as she did. Scott named specific women who should be fired to make room for her. In the fall of 1866, only one year into her fifteen-year attempt to regain her job, the assistant secretary of the Treasury Department passed a message to Johnson, who had written a recommendation for Scott, that stated: "I have carefully investigated the case. Mrs. Scott is poor enough but I think is *insane* & I do not see how we can employ her."[50] Women's aggression in trying to retain or regain positions could be seen as insanity, rather than ambition.

Scott would not be deterred. Simultaneous with her attempts to regain her job, she demanded back pay from the time she had been "unjustly" let go—an audacious claim no other civil servant appears to have attempted in this time period. In September 1866, Scott wrote to Johnson, "If you expect God's *blessing* to rest on your efforts to *restore* this *union* you will order me *paid in full* every dollar that has been given to other females." Ten days later she wrote to the Secretary of the Treasury that she desired "one years and one month's salary including the hundred dollars paid other female clerks and reinstated next month. Are you willing to award me that?" He was not—the assistant secretary of the Treasury informed her on October 10, 1866, "the Secretary decides that neither by law or usage can you be allowed the claim." Less than a week after receiving the rejection of her request for back pay, she elevated her claim to Congress. Scott petitioned the Committee on Ways and Means multiple times through 1867 for back pay and reinstatement. It was not until February 1880 that Scott finally withdrew her application from the Treasury Department, never having received back pay or regaining her position in the government.[51]

Scott's spectacular efforts failed to regain her a position, but her tactics and arguments were not anomalous. Maintaining a job with the federal government was a job in itself; successful job performance did not ensure a long career. A female federal employee had to be relentlessly aggressive—far from the helpless suppliant persona she presented in her initial application. Her efforts to maintain her position typically involved a combination of tactics, and while women reapplying appear to have had a higher success rate than initial applicants, success was far from guaranteed.[52] The struggle was constant. A woman could gain and lose and regain her job multiple times over even a short career with the government. Jennie Tall provides an example of the complexity of the experience. A document in Tall's file, typed on Treasury Department stationery, summed up her staccato career with the Treasury Department:[53]

> Appointed January 5, 1865, in the office of the Secretary of the Treasury, at $600, per annum.
>
> December 15, 1865, removed. February 26, 1866, removal revoked.
>
> Removed July 31, 1870. April 1, 1875, appointed in Bureau Statistics, temporary, at $720 per annum.
>
> March 1, 1876, transferred and promoted a clerk at $900, in the office of Internal Revenue. Removed June 15, 1877.[54]

Keeping a job with the government required a woman to be ambitious and enterprising. Women freely reused earlier narratives of female dependence and reliance on a male relative's service record in their bids for retention and reinstatement, but they honed these narratives to a sharper edge. They now had more in their arsenals. Female federal employees had created their own work records and had learned a bit more about how the federal workforce operated. Women marshaled support preemptive of termination, stayed abreast of department news, offered supervisors solutions as to how they could retain them, and moved laterally within and between departments. Because of the enormous pressure for jobs, some women also tried to have female coworkers fired to create room for them to regain or retain their positions.

Traditional notions of women as dependent, helpless creatures had helped women gain their jobs with the government, stirring supervisors' paternalistic benevolence. When faced with dismissal, women resurrected their sad tales of poverty and bereavement, but now brandished them as shield and sword. Women cloaked themselves in sadness in an effort to reawaken the protective and altruistic feelings in supervisors, but also thrust their losses and needs at them, daring supervisors to be the type of men who would inflict further injury by taking away a poor woman's job. During their federal employment, many of these women had become breadwinners for their families, so when asking to retain or regain their jobs, female federal employees were both appealing to men as women in need of male protection and as trying to fulfill their responsibilities as heads of households. In her bid for retention, for example, Alexina Getty appealed to the secretary of the Treasury as both "a delicate woman with only one lung" and as a person with "two children and niece dependent upon me for a support."[55] "Few persons realize the difficulty of discharging a hundred ladies, all depending upon clerkships for subsistence," the Baltimore *Sun* informed its readers in 1868. The article described "tear-inspiring, mirth-provoking and temper-rising exhibitions . . . freely indulged by those clamoring for reinstatement." The scene was "the perfect pandemonium." Women delivered "spontaneous, impromptu opinions . . . in all sorts of voices, from the faint, hesitating whispers the loud tones of the angry strong-minded, who expresses her views on the discharge question generally, and herself individually, in no measured terms."[56]

Women's retention and reapplication materials are saturated in stories of the deep misfortune and distress the loss of a federal position would create for a woman and her family. Such stories were intended to sway decision makers regarding her retention or rehiring. They also reveal how fully women had assumed the position of breadwinner in their families and the anxiety they felt over not being able to provide. Hester Peters worked in the Treasury Department from 1865 to 1869, when she was let go as part of a reduction in the force. Soon after she lost her job, she wrote to the secretary of the Treasury, explaining, "My family, consisting of four children are entirely dependent at present, on my efforts. My husband with enfeebled health unable to assist—chiefly owing to overexertion in the Quarter-Masters Dept during the war." The family eventually managed to survive on the salary earned by Peters's daughter in the printing bureau of the Treasury Department. Between 1869 and 1873, Peters sent and caused to be sent on her behalf seventeen letters in an attempt to regain her job. In one of the last letters Peters sent, she wrote, "I am growing impatient, while at the same time I am endeavoring to obey the injunction, 'not to be importunate—.' " "But, I am so embarrassed!" she exclaimed, to have the entire five member family depending on her "young daughter" for support. Peters ended her letter, "Do not take this as a specimen of my handwriting—I am distressed."[57]

Women and their recommenders again waved veterans' bloody shirts at supervisors. In her letter for reappointment to the Bureau of Statistics, Jennie H. Tall included her husband's military record. In 1877, when Tall attempted to regain her lost job, she wrote: "I desire the position of a first-class clerk to support the soldier . . . whose days are numbered. I desire it to enable me to provide necessary medicines, to defray doctors' bills, and, above all, for the purpose of making the last days of the gallant and honorable Union officer as bearable as possible."[58] It took Maude A. Reddick years to obtain her job in the Treasury Department. When she lost it in 1869, her recommender begged for a reconsideration of her termination. He explained that though Maude's father and brothers had returned from war, the father was too old to work, and the younger brother, "though not wounded by bullets . . . was otherwise injured so as to disable him."[59]

Women also pressured recommenders to encourage supervisors to retain them. As had been the case in initially securing the position, successfully motivating a recommender to plead her case may have been a woman's greatest tool. Former Patent Commissioner Samuel S. Fisher explained that a woman who had been removed would "assault you with such an array of 'influence' that you seriously began to ask yourself the question whether your retention in office or hers was of greater importance to the nation."[60] The local *Evening Star* reported in 1866 that the Secretary of the Treasury could not reduce his staff of female employees, "discharge being impossible, in the face of importunities without number, made from all influential sources."[61] The *New York Daily Tribune* claimed department heads timed layoffs to occur when congressmen had departed the city for the year "because the Secretaries had no desire to be importuned by them to reinstate clerks once dismissed."[62]

Alexina Getty used the female construct of helplessness to ably maneuver General Ulysses S. Grant into ensuring that she was restored to her position. In 1866, Grant recommended a woman for a place in the Treasury Department. The woman received the place, but Getty, whom he had earlier recommended, was fired to make room for her. General Grant wrote to the Secretary of the Treasury expressing "regret that any one should be removed to make place for any one recommended by me, unless there be other cause for removal.— however deserving any one may be who receives a recommendation from me." Grant had learned of this situation from Getty who wrote to him beseeching him to save her job: "My hope is that you who have so nobly defended, and saved our beloved country, will save from misery and want a poor woman." Grant followed up with the secretary of the Treasury two days after his initial letter, repeating, "I regret exceedingly that Mrs. Getty was unmanned to make place for anyone recommended by me," and assuring the secretary, "I promise in future to make no more recommendations unless there are extraordinary grounds for doing so and then I will state them." Getty also wrote to the assistant secretary of the Treasury, begging him to "grant the request of our noble General Grant, who has asked for my retention in office, conditioning himself to ask no more appointments." Getty was restored to her place on January 2, 1866.[63]

Historian Cindy S. Aron found that federal departments in the 1860s "functioned, in many ways, according to informal, personal, irregular rules," making holding on to a job a complicated affair for men and women.[64] It would have been in the best interest of any federal employee to cultivate a good relationship with his or her supervisor. For women, any closeness with their male supervisors and recommenders may have been misconstrued and likely contributed to rumors of female federal employees' improper relationships with men. By the nature of the way jobs were acquired and retained, most female federal employees presented themselves to recommenders as helpless women in need of a man's friendship, sometimes at congressmen's or recommender's homes.[65] During the 1860s, hundreds of women convinced men of power, including congressmen and senators, to use their influence to obtain and retain their positions.

Occasionally, close relationships can be assumed by a woman's retention in office, despite a clear reason to dismiss her. On May 23, 1867, Secretary of the Treasury Hugh McCulloch made inquiries to Alex Delmar, director of the Bureau of Labor Statistics as to Mrs. M. Aubrey's long absence. She had been gone since at least April 1. Delmar likely could have terminated Aubrey, but instead he explained to McCulloch that "Mrs. Aubrey's absence was due to her having been obliged to submit to a surgical operation (the removal of a tumor)" and that Aubrey was an "attentive and assiduous clerk and performs a valuable service in this Bureau." Delmar further wrote that he "has had no cause to find fault with her, but on the contrary would rather have her services retained." Aubrey's retention may likely have been due to her relationship with Delmar, who had recommended her for the position in September 1866.[66]

In other cases, favoritism was clearer. In 1875, for example, Treasurer Spinner described meeting Sarita Brady, who was employed under him in 1871. Spinner said of Brady, "She's a bright girl. I love her very much. I didn't know her very well when she first came into my department, but something happened that sort of attracted me to her, and I have liked her ever since." Spinner recalled that one day Brady had "done something that made Mr. G.____ mad—he had charge of her division—and he dragged her into my room by the arm." Mr. G. reportedly asked Spinner, " 'What shall I do to this girl. She has been'—and he told me something she had been doing—I don't remember what it was." Spinner does remember his response. He told Mr. G., " 'You take her back and set her at work.' She was so lady-like, and had such a bright, frank, and open face, I knew she hadn't done anything wrong intentionally.' "[67] Such decisions contributed to the stereotype of morally questionable or overly flirtatious women working in the departments.

In addition to appealing to supervisors and recommenders, female federal employees also tried to garner general public support for the retention of women in government employment through pleas in local newspapers. In 1867 "an employee" wrote to the editor of the *Evening Star* to "beg" him "to call the attention of heads of Departments to the justice and humanity of retaining in employment those single [women] or widows who have helpless relatives depending on them for support." The paper also published a letter from "H," who had read that the commissioner of Agriculture planned to dismiss most of the employees in the department's seed room, mostly women, and that the Treasury Department was also going to dismiss female employees. "H" wrote that this was "unjust and terribly severe upon a class of persons who have and are rendering efficient and faithful services . . . to be 'discharged' and thrown in absolute destitution upon the world is terribly hard and undeserved, and, what is more, unnecessary." She asked for a protector for the female employees, and specifically called upon the editor of the paper to "hear us, and plead for the widows and orphans. God help them, if this thing is to be done."[68] Supervisors would not have relished being seen by their community as the men who sent Christian, Civil War widows and orphans onto the streets.

When women originally applied to the federal government, these constructs of female dependency and the influence of powerful men had been their primary tools to obtain work, but during stints as federal employees they gained knowledge, experience, and confidence. Dismissed women put these forces to work in their attempts to retain or regain their jobs. Retention and reapplication materials show growth in women who now saw themselves as valuable employees and who adroitly navigated the civil service system.

Female federal employees knew that a powerful recommender was an invaluable tool, and they coached their recommenders using inside knowledge they had gained in federal employment to better their chances of remaining in it. When Maria Linton lost her job in 1875, she instructed her recommenders in several letters how they should proceed in assisting her to regain her position. She provided specific information and reminders on to whom to talk to ("Capt. Adams (appointment clerk)"), when they should go ("to-morrow (Wednesday)"), and what they should say. Linton had a clear understanding as to how the system of appropriations and appointments worked. On January 12, 1875, for example, she explained to one of her recommenders, Mr. White, that "there is no vacancy [in the 5th Auditor's Office] now, and my hope is that I may be appointed to some other office, where there is one—and detailed to the 5th Auditor. Mr. Steel is paid from the 5th Aud's office—and on their rolls and it could be arranged to put me on the Secretary's Roll." She again wrote to White on January 21 that she had gone to the Fifth Auditor's Office to see if they wanted her back ("of course they did"), but they did not have a vacancy. "If I could be appointed to some other office and be detailed there, it would be agreeable to them. I then told the chief clerk and Mr. [illeg.] I thought if they would see the appointment clerk and say so to him he would arrange matters without much delay," she explained. Linton's information was based on her meticulous reconnaissance. Linton went to the Treasury Department to speak to officials and learned information from a network of female friends. She devoted herself to regaining her job, staying current on information regarding when and where vacancies were occurring and who was filling them.[69]

Women discussed the jobs they were trying to retain with a language of ownership. Jennie Tall asked to be returned to "my old place in the Bureau of Statistics." In 1875, Maria L. Linton asked White to help her regain "my old desk in the 5th Auditor's office," explaining that she was "familiar with the work in my old office, where I served faithfully eleven years nearly." Linton wrote White again nine days later, asking again about "my old desk."[70] In the Patent Office, Wilbur describes two women who, after being fired, refused to leave their desks. In May 1870, the women of the Patent Office were in a state of agitation, having heard that "several dismissals will take place the 1st of July." On May 23, in advance of that round of layoffs, a "rebel clerk," for whom Wilbur had no sympathy, was dismissed, and, Wilbur reported, "She has kept the rooms disturbed all day. She will leave no means untried to get back." Then, on June 30 of the following year, "Mrs T____," likely thirty-year-old Theodotia Tolcott, single mother of five children ranging in age from eleven years old to three years old and caretaker to her "lame and hopeless" mother, was "asked to resign" but she "refuse[d]." Talcott, a widow, had been seeking federal work since 1867, when she began applications to the Treasury Department. "I beg leave, most respectfully, to call your attention to the application of Mrs. Talcott, under the belief that a case of such helplessness will address itself to your kind feelings and consideration with more force than any mere political recommendation," wrote one of Talcott's recommenders in 1868. Talcott failed to secure a job in the Treasury Department, but found a place in the Patent Office by 1869. The day after she was dismissed in 1871, Talcott came to work. "Her friends tell her not to resign," noted Wilbur, continuing, "She sent note to [then commissioner of Patents Mortimer Dormer Leggett] saying that she does not intend to resign. He sends note back informing her that her services are dispensed with." Talcott "left at once saying she must give that to the President," but the outcome is unknown. "What unreasonable people there are in this world," Wilbur quipped.[71]

Wilbur was wrong to consider her dismissed coworkers unreasonable. Women felt a sense of ownership of their jobs and rights to them because they had performed them well and faithfully. Talcott, for example, occasionally acted as substitute supervisor, according to Wilbur's diary, suggesting that the Patent Office supervisors were pleased with her work.[72] In the forty-three employees' files containing reapplication materials, twenty-three contained an argument for rehire based on women's work records. Mary Arnold argued in her letter for retention, "I have constantly applied myself to the business since [being appointed], with the exception of attendance upon my Father's death bed." In 1872, three years after losing her job, Hester Peters wrote several letters to the secretary of the Treasury citing her prior work record. She argued that she filled her appointment in the Office of the Comptroller of the Currency "satisfactorily and credibly until the year 1869, when with others I was removed [as part of a reduction in the force]," and later that year referred him to letters from her supervisors on file in his office.[73]

Recommenders also cited women's work records, demonstrating that some men did not view women as interchangeable employees. Peters's recommender described her as "an efficient faithful and industrious clerk—worthy of confidence and employment." Maria Linton had beautiful penmanship and "no superior in clinical qualifications" assured her recommender. Jane Little's recommenders wrote of her in 1870 that she was "a capable and efficient clerk." The Commissioner of Customs helped Alexina Getty retain her position in his office in 1866 writing to Secretary of the Treasury McCulloch and "bear[ing] testimony to the faithful services rendered by Mrs. Getty while employed in this Bureau, as well as to her capacity as a clerk."[74]

Performing one's job well, however, was not sufficient grounds for a woman to retain her position as the *Troy Weekly Times* pointed out in December 1866. The paper explained that "while many of [the women employed in the Treasury] are capable and earn their salaries," dismissals still had to occur. Some women tried to preempt their termination. To do so, female federal employees listened for rumors of layoffs, and acted in advance to try to secure their jobs.

To stave off job loss, women had to be vigilant and aggressive. Sylvia S. Bemis of the Register's Office in the Treasury Department "learned from a reliable source, that there are a *great many dismissals to be made*, after the adjournment of Congress."[75] Bemis, a widow from Massachusetts, wrote to Congressman N. P. Banks in April 1869 after her "several attempts" to see him in person had failed. She asked Banks to use his influence with the secretary of the Treasury "to enable me still to hold my place as a clerk."[76] When Jane W. Little feared that she might be terminated in March 1870, she marshaled the support of twenty-six men of her home county in New York, including a Supreme Court justice, former assembly members, bankers, and a postmaster to ask that she be retained. In 1875, hearing of another rumor of layoffs, she had twenty-four men write a letter to the commissioner of Internal Revenue.[77] At the end of July 1866, F. T. Pillsbury feared a reduction of the force of the Quartermaster General's Department, where she worked. She obtained the support of General Howe, who wrote to Quartermaster General Meigs that "should any such reduction of employees be made you will much oblige me if you can retain Miss Pillsbury on your list of lady clerks in some branch of your department."[78] When whispers portending yet another round of dismissals unnerved the women of the Patent Office in 1871, even Julia Wilbur, who had been heretofore fairly calm in the face of such rumors, scrambled to marshal support. One warm June day that year there was "some excitement about dismissals" in the Patent Office. This led Wilbur to travel to Howard University after work, in search of her friend, General O. O. Howard, but he was not there, so later that evening she went to his house. "He will do what he can to make me secure in my place," she wrote in her diary that night, adding with what must have been relief, "Gen. Leggett served under him. + they are good friends."[79]

Female federal employees had to become politically savvy and well informed, learning the relevant rules and regulations of the civil service system.

When Emma A. McCully's mother faced termination because of a new rule prohibiting two members of one family being employed in the Treasury Department, McCully sent a letter to a supervisor asking them to reconsider as "heretofore a situation in Mr. Jewell's Department [where her mother was employed] has not been considered as an appointment, they work as any day laborers and only receive pay for the time actually employed" and "besides South Carolina from which State she came is entitled to 45 appointments and only has I think 15 employés in the Treasury Dept."[80]

As McCully's letter indicates, women were well aware of the patronage regulations that governed federal employment. Because each department and office had a great deal of autonomy, it is difficult to now determine how geography dictated the number of appointments in the executive departments in the Civil War era, but female federal employees knew. Women often manipulated these systems, shifting the state from which they were appointed.[81] Several women's reapplication materials make reference to the states to which they could be charged. Annie E. Byus, originally appointed to the Treasury Department in 1868, wrote in her 1877 reapplication, "I really have no home. Have been in Washington eight years, and in other Cities in the [illeg.] Before the death of my Father, lived for a time in Madison, Wisconsin, which my friends thought I should have mentioned to you."[82] Helen Briggs, originally appointed to the Treasury Department in 1863, wrote to the assistant secretary of the Treasury in 1878 to "ask the correction of the mistake which I find has been made in your Department by charging me to the 'District of Columbia' instead of New York City, where *I belong*, from *whence I was appointed*." Briggs was attempting to regain her position in the Fourth Auditor's Office, and likely thought she had a better chance as a New Yorker than a Washingtonian as there were a disproportionate number of federal employees from Washington.[83]

Once a woman obtained a job in the federal government, she did not necessarily remain in that specific job. Moving within or between departments also demonstrated women's resilience and resourcefulness.[84] Some women moved within one department. Amanda Dodd joined the Treasury Department in 1863 as a counter, but by 1865 had moved to the Fourth Auditor's Office, where she worked as a copyist until at least 1869. Delia Stack began in the press room of the GPO, but transferred to the bindery. Maria Vanentina was working as the chief cook in the Government Hospital for the Insane in 1865 and successfully applied to the hospital's superintendent for the situation of chief laundress.[85] Women moved between the departments as well.[86] Several women moved from the GPO to the Treasury Department.[87] Flora V. Dobson moved in the opposite direction. Dobson worked in the Treasury Department in 1867 and 1869, but by 1870 was working in the press room of the GPO.[88] Many others moved out of the Treasury Department. Frances Richardson, H. M. Barnard, and Frances Plummer all transferred from the Treasury Department to the Pension Office by 1871.[89] Mary V. Ward worked in the Treasury Department in 1867, but in 1870 the Baltimore *Sun* reported that the secretary of the interior had appointed her a copyist in the Patent Office.[90] Some female employees, including S. P. King, Alice Martin, and Mary White, moved out of the Treasury Department and into the Post Office.[91] C. V. Millar moved from the Post Office into the Treasury Department.[92] Miss E. A. Koones moved from the Post Office to the Department of Agriculture.[93]

Fannie Kemp Breedin had to cobble together short-term government positions.[94] Breedin's pluck shines through her application materials. She was on her own, having lost her father when she was eighteen years old and her mother when she was twenty-two. In response to a question in a Treasury Department circular inquiring as to her legal residence, Breedin replied: "I have no legal residence. I am a cosmopolite—have lived in Virginia, South Carolina, Washington, D.C. and Illinois." In a different circular, she responded to the question "Are you married?" writing, "No, I am an 'old maid.'" Breedin had a long and varied career in federal work. In her July 1872 letter to the Treasury Department applying for "for a Clerkship (Class I) in the Sixth Auditor's Office, Money-Order Bureau," thirty-four-year-old Breedin succinctly recounted her employment history to Secretary of the Treasury Boutwell: "I was engaged as a Copyist for the Patent Office and War Department from October 1868 until June 1869–when my services being no longer needed, I was employed in the Surgeon General's Office, where I remained 14 months, and was discharged solely on account of legislation which prevented any further payment for my services Early in December, 1870, I was engaged by Hon. B. V. Abbott to assist in the 'Revision of the Laws'—which work lasted only seven weeks. Since then I have been Teaching."[95] Breedin's use of the passive voice ("was engaged as a Copyist"; "was employed in the Surgeon General's Office"; "was engaged by [Abbot]") obscures the tremendous effort she likely had to expend to remain in the federal employ.

Perhaps because the federal job market was so tight, women did not typically come together to pool knowledge and resources about job retention, except in small clusters of friendly coworkers. Instead, competing women used knowledge and rumor against each other. Some women explicitly singled out specific women that should be fired to make room for themselves or others, believing their claims on the government trumped those of women occupying their former desks. When Jennie Tall was let go from the Treasury Department in the spring of 1877, she asked to be reinstated in the job then occupied by Nancy D. Bishop.[96] Tall wrote to the secretary of the Treasury on April 28, 1877, charging Bishop's brother-in-law Edward Young, the chief clerk of the Bureau of Statistics, with nepotism in appointing Bishop to her place and arguing that neither person deserved the job because they were not Americans. Tall also argued that her husband's war record was more impressive than was the war record of Young's husband. Tall asserted that her claims—which consisted of her Treasury Department employee file and her husband's service record—were "unquestioned and unquestionable. . . . But what are the precise claims of the lady who now fills my place . . . or of her brother the chief of this office?" Tall concluded another letter to the Treasury Department that officials would not want it to "be said that those ladies in the Treasury Department who spend large portions of their liberal salaries annually in Canada on finery are well provided for, while the American lady who desires to labor hard and intelligently for herself and shattered soldier husband finds no suitable reward."[97]

The women whose jobs were under siege from female coworkers defended their places. When Clara Barton put down her pen to help the soldiers in the Civil War, her male coworker and friend, Edward Shaw, saved her job at the Patent Office, working late to complete her work.[98] When it was clear that her soldier relief efforts would take all of her time, Barton and her supervisor, Commissioner Holloway, entered an arrangement whereby a coworker, Mr. Upperman, worked as Barton's substitute. Upperman drew half of her salary and Barton drew the other half.[99] In the winter of 1863, Clara Barton learned from Upperman that Holloway was terminating their arrangement because her female coworkers had complained that she was getting paid to perform a job she was not performing. The women further believed that Barton was receiving a salary for her soldier relief work on top of her Patent Office salary.[100] Barton was indignant. She immediately fired off a letter to Holloway arguing that the "twenty or more" ladies who had complained about her were misrepresenting the situation. Barton explained that she received no money from the government for her soldier relief work, and declared the allegations of the women "willfully and maliciously false." If Holloway were to acquiesce to the complaints of the women, Barton told him she would lose her rented room in Washington. Although she could dispense of the "little contents" of the room to the poor of the city and perhaps stay at a soldiers' hospital if she fell ill, Barton stated that: "My chief regret will consist in the loss of the few dollars to the needy soldiers I meet in my rounds, but if the ladies who write for you need it more than our troops in the field, I have nothing to say in opposition to the transfer.... It has been a fact of the work of my lifetime to aid in opening every avenue to honorable employment for my own sex. I hope these ladies are equally generous with me."[101] Scarce appointments and intense competition meant, however, that female federal employees did not always have the luxury of generosity.

"I Never Get Tired of My Work": Long Careers and Life after Civil Service

Although women fought to retain their positions, not all women wished to remain in the government's employment. Some resigned of their own accord.[102] Women left their jobs when they married or when their husbands came back from the war. Mrs. C. Bloor, for example, worked in the Treasury Department from 1863 to 1865. In 1870, she was "keeping house" for Jno D. Bloor, a department clerk.[103] L. G. Plunkett, who had been born in Africa, worked in the Treasury Department from 1865 to 1867. In 1870, she was keeping house for William A. Plunkett, a Treasury clerk, and their six-year-old son, Charles.[104]

Some women tried to exercise control over their jobs even in their resignations. Mary Ream resigned her job in the Internal Revenue Office of the Treasury Department on April 27, 1865. In her letter to secretary of the Treasury McCulloch, Ream requested "that my sister, Miss. Vinnie Ream, be appointed to fill my place."[105] At the time, Vinnie was working in the Post Office Department, and had been since 1863. Vinnie, an artist, did not get the job in the Treasury Department, but in 1866, Congress commissioned her to sculpt a statue of the late President Lincoln.[106]

Like Vinnie Ream, other women went on to new careers after their time working for the federal government. Angie Kinney worked in the War Department for several years. When she was discharged, she returned to her father's home in Pennsylvania. Though reportedly depressed by her job loss, Kinney learned accounting and telegraphy. She then applied to be a telegraph operator in Elmira, New York, using "abundant recommendation[s]" from her work with the government to secure the position.[107] Julia Gove was able to move into a different type of clerical position from her work at the Treasury Department, becoming a clerk in a grocery in 1870.[108] Catherine Maroney joined the Treasury Department as a laborer in 1865, advanced to a messenger position in 1867, and advanced again to a "Lady Clerk" position in 1869. In

1870, Maroney was working at a grocery in Washington with her fourteen-year-old son, Thomas.[109] Other women, like Ream, were able to capitalize on artistic or literary talents. Mary Stoops worked in the Treasury Department from 1865 to 1867, but in 1870 was an "embalmer of flowers."[110] Miss Snead moved to Washington with her widowed mother in the 1860s to obtain positions in the government. Her mother worked in the Treasury Department and she worked in the Department of the Interior. When she was discharged, reported a California newspaper, "she began at once to consider the necessity of turning her attention to some new work." Bolstered by the encouragement of friends, Snead began a successful career as a society reporter.[111] One woman leveraged her experiences working for the federal government into a state position. M. E. Hartwell resigned her job with the Register's Office in the Treasury Department in 1869 to accept a position with the State of Kentucky.[112]

More commonly, women went back to the limited employment options available to them: teaching, sewing, and domestic work. After losing her job, Kate Cain asked for her letters of recommendation on file with Treasury Department so that she could use them to obtain a teaching position.[113] Like Cain, Mary V. Heath worked in the Treasury Department in 1867 and 1869, but in 1870 was teaching.[114] Elizabeth McLeod, worked in the Treasury Department from 1865 to 1869, but was working as a teacher in 1870.[115] Annie York, who was one of the first women to join the Treasury Department on the recommendation of General Spinner, worked there until at least 1870, but by 1880 worked as a dressmaker.[116] Emma Richmond worked in the Treasury Department from 1865 to 1867, but in 1870 was a domestic servant at the Ebbitt House hotel.[117] Mary McVay was employed at the Government Printing Office in 1864 and 1865, but in 1870 was a domestic servant.[118]

Of the almost three thousand women analyzed who had been employed between 1859 and 1871, only 20 percent appear to have worked for the government for longer than three years. There is still evidence, however, of long careers begun by women in the 1860s despite the numerous obstacles they had to overcome. Mary Lyons was appointed to the Bureau of Engraving and Printing in the Treasury Department in 1868. She earned four promotions over the years and died on June 25, 1906, still an employee of the federal government.[119] Elizabeth Stoner worked for the Treasury Department for thirty-two years (1862–1894) and stated of her work record that it "means so much to me."[120] Jane Little joined the Treasury Department on December 27, 1862, at the approximate age of fifty. She worked there for over fifteen years, until her retirement in June 1878.[121] Margaret Ash began working in the Treasury

Department in November 1863 and after a career full of fits and starts—including a break for a divorce and the birth of a child—she retired at the end of August 1921. She was quoted in the *Fitchburg Sentinel* in 1917 as stating of her career, "I never get tired of my work. On the contrary, I am lonesome and dissatisfied whenever I am obliged to stay away from the Bureau."[122] Plucky Fannie Kemp Breedin began working for the federal government in the fall of 1868 and worked there, on and off, until she retired at age eighty-four on August 20, 1922.[123]

THE FEMALE FEDERAL EMPLOYEES of the 1860s worked in an irregular environment, largely dictated by the political and personal motivations of a small number of supervisors.[124] This employment structure made for a highly insecure and competitive work environment, which did not encourage group action. Individual women had to find their own ways to keep their jobs. As time went on, women gained knowledge of how the civil service—and politics—operated and began to use this information to help safeguard their places. From the seemingly meek and supplicant women who had joined the federal workforce in the early months of the Civil War had emerged strong, capable, and intelligent workers who would force Congress into the first federal debate over equal pay for women.

CHAPTER SEVEN

What Makes Us to Differ from Them?
The Argument for Equal Pay in the Nation's Capital

Walt Whitman did not earn enough money. The "Good Gray Poet," who was a bachelor, found it, "impossible, with the most rigid economy, to meet the demands" of life on the annual $1,600 salary he earned as a clerk in the Attorney General's office.[1] Whitman's male colleagues agreed. The male federal clerk salary—ranging from $1,200 to $1,800 per year—was, as Third Auditor John Wilson argued to Congress in 1868: "wholly inadequate in many cases to the most meager support of [clerk's] helpless families."[2] Female clerks, who earned at most (with limited exceptions) $900 per year in 1868, or only 56 percent of Whitman's salary, also believed that their salaries were too low.[3] One such woman, Mrs. A. R. Benedict, lived in the same house as Walt Whitman, in Washington's second ward, and like Whitman, agitated for higher pay, signing her name on a "Petition of Female Employees in the Treasury Department Praying An Increase of Salary."[4] Benedict was not alone. Although women were still new to their jobs and retaining them somewhat precariously, between late 1864 and early 1870, Congress received at least 740 female federal employee signatures on eleven separate petitions asking for greater pay.[5] Some of these women argued that since they performed the same work as men, they should be paid the same.

The efforts of these early female federal employees and labor feminists engendered a precocious debate in Congress about gender equality that came remarkably close to achieving pay parity for women. In three debates in the Senate and one in the House of Representatives between 1867 and 1870, congressmen engaged in dialogues about fiscal pragmatism, justice, gender equality, and the responsibility of Washington, D.C., to set an example for the nation. Although both houses passed legislation providing for equal pay for women and the public expressed support of it, the movement ultimately failed.

That women were underpaid was nothing new. Women had been underpaid in America since they entered wage labor and, when possible, protested the injustice.[6] Previously, however, many of the wage-paying jobs held by women were segregated to their sex and job distinctions had provided a tacit justification for low pay.[7] In the executive departments, women often performed the same work as men. More important, Congress set the salaries of clerks and only Congress could modify them. By assuming men's jobs, performing them as well or better than men, and demanding equal pay for doing so, early female federal employees forced Congress to publicly rationalize wage discrimination. Many congressmen found they could not. Those that struggled to justify unequal pay offered rudimentary arguments that opponents of equal pay would refine over the decades and into the next century.

Conventional understanding of the equal pay movement holds that it did not gain momentum until World War I or even World War II, but these early postbellum debates reveal that generations earlier, women and their advocates in Congress fought passionately for wage justice.[8] The defeat of the 1860s equal pay movement had consequences that far outlived the agitating female civil servants. By failing to equalize wages in the federal workforce, the government set a national standard devaluing female labor. Women's continued performance of men's jobs for a fraction of their salaries gradually depressed the wages of male federal employees in the last decades of the nineteenth century. This provided validation of the arguments of many opponents of equal pay who claimed that women's presence in the wage labor force undercut male wages.[9] The federal government did not enact a law requiring equal pay for women until 1963. Today, women still have not achieved pay parity with men.

Congress's receptivity to this early equal pay movement was partially due to the unique time and place of Civil War– and Reconstruction-era Washington, D.C. Although historian Christine Stansell argued that after the Civil War, "the air would be too thick with pronouncements on women's proper place for working-class women to speak much for themselves" on issues of pay, as historian Kate Masur has noted, there was an "unusually unadulterated debate about the meanings of equality" going on in the capital in the 1860s.[10] It was a time and place sparking with the ideology of equal rights and chest-swelling proclamations of justice. Federal attempts at legislating and protecting justice and equality were on the rise: in 1864, Congress granted equal pay to African American troops, who previously had only received a fraction of white soldiers' pay, and in 1869, Congress passed the Fifteenth Amendment, granting African American men the right to vote.[11] Moreover, Republicans, the political party in power, had a closer relationship with women—especially middle-class white women, which most of the female clerks were—than had other political parties in the past. Women worked directly with Republican politicians in the antislavery movement, and the Republican Party (the "Grand Old Party," or GOP) hired women to speak at campaign events. Through the

1862 pension law, the GOP also had demonstrated a desire to care for women in need.[12] It seemed very possible, therefore, that the political party that had been so friendly to women would provide female federal employees with the justice of increased, and perhaps even equal, compensation.

The equal pay movement owed its near success to the early labor feminists who wrote and signed petitions and formed committees to press upon Congress the injustice of their comparatively meager remuneration. Hundreds of women, many signing multiple petitions, believed that Congress, and by extension the nation, should fairly value their labor. The resoluteness and confidence women displayed in pursuing greater pay demonstrates that although women may have projected an aura of helplessness and dependence to obtain their jobs, they were capable and self-reliant. Women and their supporters, however, ultimately could not overcome the custom and cost savings of underpaying women. The equal pay debate also called into question, for some, the experiment of female employment, demonstrating that although this moment was pregnant with possibility, women were still far from achieving true employment equality. While it was a woman's fight, many of the records we are left with contain the words of men. This archival fact underscores the handicapped position from which women fought: disenfranchised, shut out of most occupations, and restricted in movement and speech by Victorian social norms. In light of these barriers, it is all the more remarkable how close they came to achieving their goal.

"The Vast Disproportion Existing between the Salaries of the Male and Female Clerks": 1861–1866

When women entered the executive departments, supervisors set their salaries at one-half of the amount paid to men for the same work—$600 per year, compared to $1,200 per year to the lowest-paid male clerk.[13] Initially, women's employment was informal and temporary, but over the 1860s, Congress legitimized the practice in appropriations bills and deficiency acts. Congress also institutionalized the salary discrimination, capping women's annual salaries at $600 in the Deficiency Act of March 1864.[14] Despite the pay inequality, many working women were excited by the opportunity to work for the federal government, since these salaries were far higher than the pay women could earn in other professions.[15] Male clerks' efforts to secure greater wages, however, reveal that women's salaries were thought too low to maintain a middle-class lifestyle in Washington, D.C.[16] The cost of living in the nation's capital skyrocketed during the war and stayed high throughout the decade.[17]

Every year, the annual report of the secretary of the Treasury was laden with supervisors' begging for more money with which to pay their (male) clerks, who routinely left for higher-paying private-sector jobs.[18] During the mid-1860s, thousands of male government employees requested their salaries be raised, some singly, some in petitions signed by hundreds.[19] All cited stagnant salaries and increased costs of living, and all of the male clerks were earning far more than their female coworkers.

Women quickly set themselves to correcting that problem. The earliest, most well-publicized push for greater female federal employee pay came in 1863 at the Government Printing Office which employed hundreds of women to feed printing presses and fold sheets into books for binding.[20] On February 19, the *Daily Morning Chronicle* reported that the female press feeders were demanding an increase of their five-dollar-per-week salary to one dollar per day. When they did not receive it, "these females, to the number of nearly twenty-five, refused to go to work, and appeared ready to oust out of the building any person who should dare to attempt to take their places." The newspaper explained that the strike prevented the printing of a Senate Finance Committee bill, and as a result, "the girls were informed that their wages should be increased as much as demanded. This satisfied them, and they went to work as usual."[21] Some of the female press feeders, perhaps a bit heady with success, mocked their male coworkers for their inaction. One male printer had prevented a strike among his fellow journeymen and may have tried to prevent the women from striking as well. The *Daily Morning Chronicle* reported that when the women had learned they would gain their raise: "One of the most beautiful of the fair 'strikers,' with the consent of the rest, sent a petticoat up stairs, and presented it to [the printer], with a request that he should wear it; and further, that by so doing, the printers might be able to obtain what they had just secured by virtue of courage and independence—an increased pay."[22]

Female clerks also demonstrated "courage and independence"—traits that were not rewarded when seeking to obtain federal work—in asking for higher salaries. While some, including six women in the Department of the Interior and three women in the War Department, joined forces with their male coworkers, adding their signatures to general petitions for increased pay, others argued their case to Congress independently.[23] Forty-two women in the Treasury Department petitioned Congress in January 1865 "for an increase of salary commensurate with the increased price of living in this City." The women argued that "the majority of us have Mothers and others dependent upon us, whilst others are widows with families to support and educate," and noted that "many of us are employed upon works such as commands for Gentlemen $1,200 and $1,400 per annum, and they complain of their inability to provide for their families."[24]

Congress referred the women's petition to the Committee on Finances on January 30, 1865, the day before it approved the Thirteenth Amendment, abolishing slavery. That year, Congress raised women's pay to $720 per year. While $720 was preferable to $600, it was still not what men earned for performing the same work. It was also less than some women and congressmen had been pushing for in 1865.[25] According to the arguments of male clerks, it was also not nearly enough on which to live in the capital.

The debate on female clerks' pay was not only happening in Washington, D.C. Federal civil servants were a national concern. In April 1866, a Texas newspaper ran an article satirizing the inequality of male and female clerks' pay for performing identical work. *Flake's Bulletin* reported that women in the Treasury Department asked to be provided with penknives to do their jobs, "alleging the smallness of their salaries." The article jested that the Treasury's stationery clerk estimated that the cost of a penknife for a gentleman clerk was two dollars, but for a female clerk, the same penknife cost only one dollar and twenty-five cents.[26]

A little over a week after the *Flake's Bulletin* article ran in Texas, fifty-nine female Treasury Department employees petitioned Congress for a salary increase.[27] They began by expressing gratitude for their positions with the government, "enabling us by honorable industry to provide for our families, who are in most instances the families of those who have lost their lives in defense of their country." "Yet," continued these early labor feminists, "we would most respectfully present to your consideration the vast disproportion existing between the salaries of the Male and Female clerks of this department." The petitioners continued: "While we do not grudge our male friends one iota of the success which falls to their share, yet when they by whose side we sit day after day, whose labors and duties are identical with our own and whose home responsibilities in most instances are not so great—whose salaries commence with $1200 per annum—when they are promoted from first to second and from second to third class clerkships. The question forces itself upon us,—What makes us to differ from them?"[28] Here was the crux of the female petitioners' grievance. The female clerks asked, "If women can perform the same clerical duties as men, should not their salaries approximate in some degree to theirs"? They requested either a salary increase or that, "the Female clerks of this Department [who uniformly received the same pay and were not eligible for promotion] be classified in the same order with the Male clerks, and thereby become liable to the same promotion which is awarded to their fellow-laborers."[29]

The female employees of the Post Office Department also petitioned for a pay increase. On May 11, 1866, one month after the women of the Treasury Department asked for equal pay with their male colleagues, twenty-seven female postal clerks submitted a petition to Congress.[30] The "Ladies of the Post Office Department, having *always* received one hundred dollars less than the Ladies in the Treasury and other Dept's and believing that we are honestly entitled to the same," asked that Congress make their salaries equal to whatever they determined to pay the women of the Treasury.[31]

In the General Appropriation Bill of July 1866 Congress at least partially acknowledged the requests of these female petitioners. Women could now be classified as "clerks," not just "copyists" or "Ladies." The bill also fixed their salaries at $900 per year.[32] Although the additional salary was undoubtedly welcome, the conversation about female clerical pay was just beginning.

"We Are Not Playthings":
Demands for Wage Justice in Civil Service

Hundreds of women from the Treasury, Post Office, Interior, and War Departments and the Government Printing Office wrote petitions to Congress stating that they wanted and deserved higher pay. The eleven petitions for higher pay signed by women contain more than 700 female signatures, but many women signed at least two petitions. At least 608 women signed petitions. Of these, 121 signed two petitions, and one woman—Carrie Dice of the Government Printing Office—signed three of the eleven petitions.

Of the eleven petitions examined, eight were exclusively female. In these all-female petitions, women reverted to the narratives that had originally helped to secure them their jobs, including reference to male relatives' war service, cited in four of the eight petitions. In six of the eight all-female petitions, women, like male civil service petitioners, referred to the need to support relatives. Women also appealed to men's paternalism. Kate F. Keene, who had worked in the Loan Branch of the Treasury since 1865, sent a letter dripping in religion, deference, and pathos to the Committee on Appropriations in 1867 asking that women receive a pay increase as God's will, and begging the congressmen to *"give us the crumbs that have fallen from the table."*[33] Although most of the petitioners were middle-class women, in May 1870, seventy-one female "sweepers and scrubers in the Treasury Dept." who earned fifteen dollars per month ($180 per year) told Congress "the *amt* we receive is so small that it is impossible for us to maintain our *Families* and keep up the necessities of life." They asked "in the name of *Justice* and *humanity*," that Congress grant them "more pay so that we can live with oure families without being compeled to beg as manny of us have to do."[34]

Despite narratives of helplessness, women asserted themselves and acted in a manner that was autonomous of men and determined. In addition to petitioning for equal pay, women crowded alongside their male coworkers in the galleries when the Senate debated federal pay.[35] Female federal employees also formed small committees to press their cause, an unusual strategy in the federal work culture, which discouraged employee collective action. A letter to the editor of the *New York Times* in 1867 described "a self-appointed committee of two strong-minded women" lobbying "every Senator and member of Congress" regarding equal pay for "the past year."[36] L. A. Corbin, A. E. Carver, and M. E. Collier signed the 1867 petition from the female folders in the Post Office under the title, "Committee of Three including all."[37]

Women demonstrated knowledge of the operations of the federal workforce in their petitions. Four of the eight petitions referred to the pay and labor of women working in other departments to argue that their pay should be higher. In December 1868, for example, 285 women in the Government Printing Office argued to Congress "that our labor is more arduous, we are required to devote more hours to the same and our salaries are far less than that of ladies employed, in a similar capacity in any other branch of the public service in this City."[38] The petitions also reveal that women stayed abreast of congressional action on federal workforce matters.[39]

Female federal employees and their supporters also expressed themselves in the pages of newspapers.[40] Their frustration is evident. In 1867 the *Evening Star* opined that male and female federal employees should receive a contemplated 20 percent pay increase.[41] Initially, men received the bonus, but women did not. Cloaked by the anonymity of the signature, "A Woman," one female federal employee wrote to the editor of the *Daily Morning Chronicle* asserting that it was "well-known that a majority of the employees in the Printing Bureau are ladies who deserve for their industry a better compensation than that which has been heretofore allowed them." "Had they been *men* whose influence would have told upon the arena of public life," she argued, "the decision of the Comptroller [denying them the 20 percent] might have been different. But they are women." "A Woman" demanded to know, "Why such partiality between individuals whose qualifications are the same, and whose services are equally necessary to the good credit of the department?"[42]

"Laura" claimed not to be a federal clerk, but she did "deeply sympathize" with "this much abused class . . . in their grievances." She wrote to the editors of the *Evening Star* in February 1868 and the *Daily Morning Chronicle* in March 1868 to encourage Congress to increase the pay of female clerks.[43] She saw no reason why Congress should fail to make the increase. "Have they not discharged their duties faithfully, and done the same work if not more than has been done by the male clerks?" she asked. Laura had heard it "whispered" that female clerks "consider it a pastime to work in the Treasury" and countered, "Do the male clerks consider it a 'pastime' to work in the 'treasury'?" She pushed for Congress to affirm *"the rights of the female clerks and of all the women who toil for their daily bread,* (no matter in what capacity,) to be properly remunerated, according to their ability and services."[44]

"What is our work? Is it brain work? Does work have sex?" asked Gertrude, who wrote to the pro–women's suffrage newspaper *The Revolution* in December 1869, continuing, "What difference is there in value to the government between *my* work and that done by the *pantaloons* standing near me? We have performed the same amount and the same kind in the same time, and who can discover the sex of the same after it shall have passed from our hands?" Gertrude, who explained that she had been a clerk in the Treasury Department for almost four years, informed the readers of *The Revolution,* "We do not want to be petted. We want simply justice. . . . We are not playthings. We are not dolls. We are human beings, responsible alike with males to the God who made us of flesh and blood, bone, brain and muscle—to nourish and sustain which, it requires just as much 'bread and butter' as it does the 'lords of creation.'"[45]

Other women who wrote to newspapers in support of female clerks' quest for higher pay cited only the smallness of their salaries and avoided any comparison to male compensation, perhaps cautious to overreach. "J. H. R." wrote to the editor of the *Evening Star* in January 1868. Congressman Rufus P. Spalding of Ohio had introduced a resolution to increase clerical compensation, but as it was drafted the lower grades of employees—porters, watchmen, laborers, and all female employees—would not receive the increase.[46] In a letter in favor of including these omitted classes, J. H. R. focused on the female employees, perhaps because they were the most sympathetic. "How they ever manage to pay board and lodging with [their small salaries] is a mystery to me," J. H. R. declared. He or she described the female employees as "Department girls [who] help to support, out of their meagre wages, their mothers and their little brothers and sisters" and argued that this "great nation" should "pay a premium upon devotion like this."[47]

Around the country, letters appeared expressing support for women to receive pay equal to men. An anonymous contributor wrote to the *New York Times* in February 1869, "Very few persons deny the justice of the principle that equal work should demand equal pay without regard to the sex of the laborer." The writer continued, "An example of justice by our National Government in placing the labor of woman upon an equal footing with that of the man in the Departments, could not fail to exert a wholesome influence upon individual employers and the country at large."[48] A correspondent for the *Cincinnati Commercial Tribune* toured the Patent Office and expressed dismay at the discovery that the hard-working women working there earned only $900 per year and that for the same job, a man earned $1,200 to $1,800 per year. "This matter of compensation is a burning shame to our Government," the writer declared, emphasizing, "a sin and a shame."[49] Even one newspaper that tended to be hostile to civil servants supported equal pay for female clerks. In November 1869, the local *Evening Star* quoted a *New York Tribune* article in favor of equal pay, noting that the *Tribune* "is not apt to say overkind things in regard to the Department clerks, and therefore the following paragraph, doing justice to one class of them, has the weight of favorable testimony from an adverse witness." After a group of female clerks from Washington ("General Spinner's cleverer accountants") had traveled to New York to count the funds in the Sub-Treasury, the *Tribune* mused: "It would be a curious commentary upon an injustice which has too long prevailed if these women, who do their work so much better, as this and many previous facts have attested, than men can do it, should be paid less wages, merely because they are women."[50]

"Stupid Men Ask": The Absence of Women's Rights Organizations in the Struggle for Equal Pay

Female federal employees and their supporters petitioned Congress, expressed their opinions on the pay issue in letters to newspaper editors, and personally solicited the support of legislators. Around the nation, groups of women met to urge Congress to equalize male and female salaries. Yet while the female suffrage movement desired that Congress codify equal pay for women, it did not devote substantial resources—time, energy, or money—to the cause of female federal employees, and the female clerks were disadvantaged by the absence of their organizational experience and political acumen.[51] Women's rights activists, including Susan B. Anthony and Elizabeth Cady Stanton, believed in the justice of equal pay, but thought the best way to achieve that goal was by gaining the vote, and on that goal they focused their limited means. In April 1869, Anthony and Stanton's *The Revolution* published an article explaining this strategy: "Much is said, written, printed of woman's work and wages. And stupid men ask, why not dwell on this theme altogether, and mend the matter, instead of talking forever about Woman's Suffrage? And no form of answer, argument nor illustration can ding it into such skulls that the surest way to remedy the work and wages evil, is to get hold of the ballot for woman."[52]

To suffragists, equal pay was a laudable, but ancillary, goal. In January 1868, the inaugural issue of *The Revolution* included in its platform "Equal Pay to Women for Equal Work."[53] Participants at women's rights meetings discussed the justice of equal pay and women's rights associations passed resolutions urging Congress and the public to support equal pay measures.[54] Their focus was clearly on the vote, however. For example, at the January 1869 Convention of the National Woman Suffrage Association in Washington, D.C., Susan B. Anthony proposed four resolutions to present to Congress, all of which were adopted. The first urged the passage of a Sixteenth Amendment, forbidding discrimination in voting based on sex. The second asked that women be allowed to vote in District elections. The third requested that Congress grant women in Utah the right to vote as a way to end polygamy. Finally, the fourth asked Congress "to amend the laws of the United States so that women shall receive the same pay as men for services rendered the government." Later, when a Washington, D.C., woman raised the equal pay issue again in a slightly different context, Anthony abruptly told her the matter had been addressed and then dropped the subject.[55]

The suffragists elevated suffrage over salary for two reasons. First, they genuinely believed that achieving the vote was possible and that the ballot was the surest way to secure equal pay. Second, Susan B. Anthony, a leader in the movement, had had a failed foray into labor issues during the time of the equal pay debates in Congress, and from that experience she and her compatriots determined to streamline their approach and focus on the ballot.[56]

Female suffrage seemed a real possibility in the late 1860s.[57] Women had worked closely with Republicans on antislavery matters before the conflict, and during the Civil War put aside the suffrage issue to support the Union war effort and Republican campaigns. When the South surrendered, and Congress debated the meaning of citizenship in the newly reconstituted and free United States, women's rights activists justifiably hoped that the Republicans in power, their friends and allies, would recognize their rights as citizens.[58] Even after the woman's suffrage movement fractured over the Fourteenth and

Fifteenth Amendments, which, respectively, introduced the word "male" into the Constitution and granted African American men the right to vote but ignored women, suffragists still believed they could ultimately prevail and focused their efforts on achieving that goal.[59]

Susan B. Anthony had also had an experience working with female laborers that caused her to not be overly eager to again direct her energies squarely on wage issues. In September 1868, Anthony and a group of female wage earners founded the Working Women's Association.[60] The association was short lived. Although it was intended to be inclusive to all workingwomen, female typesetters—a skilled, well-paid minority of women in the private workforce—dominated.[61] Suffragists and the typesetters clashed over the importance that agitating for female suffrage should play in the organization. Suffragists believed it to be paramount, and the typesetters disagreed, not wanting to be seen as too radical and not believing that the vote would solve all of their workplace grievances.[62] The Working Women's Association also struggled to meld the middle-class suffragists' idealized and romanticized notions of the poor with the real-life needs of wage-earning women. In the spring of 1869, the female typesetters joined forces with the National Typographical Union, Susan B. Anthony was expelled from the National Labor Congress, and the Working Women's Association crumbled.[63]

As the Working Women's Association was collapsing, Congress revived debates on suffrage with discussions regarding the Fifteenth Amendment, reinvigorating woman's rights associations' commitment to achieving female suffrage.[64] Then, in late 1869 and early 1870, Congress decided to reorganize the government of Washington, D.C., providing the movement an opportunity to press Congress to grant women voting rights in the nation's capital.[65] During this time, which seemed ripe for success, suffragists turned away from the economic issues they had dabbled in and recommitted themselves to gaining the vote. Again and again, in the pages of *The Revolution*, and also, but to a lesser extent, in the competing suffrage organization's newspaper, *The Woman's Journal*, suffragists reiterated that the surest way for female federal employees to obtain better wages and employment was by securing the ballot.[66] In April 1869, *The Revolution* warned that unless the women of Washington, D.C., had the right to vote, "we shall soon see their places filled by black men, at higher salaries too."[67] "The women who work in the Treasury Department in Washington, at half the salary of the men . . . could not be so employed if they held the ballot in their right hand when they asked for work," proclaimed Paulina W. Davis in October 1869.[68] In December, the editors of *The Revolution* agreed that the civil service system needed to be reformed, but contended that such reform must "come by introducing Woman into equal, active participation in all the affairs of the government. Wherever woman goes, reform is sure to follow.... Seek first the ballot for woman, and its righteousness, and be sure that all other necessary things will be added thereunto."[69]

The disagreement over which goal to preference—wages or the ballot—also engendered a degree of hostility between the movements. In 1870, *The Revolution* chided the working women's movement for not acknowledging the debt it owed to the suffrage movement: "Without the initiative of the so-called agitators on the woman question no voice would have been raised to demand equal pay for men and women. They are too short-sighted, perhaps, to see that the ballot and woman's work and wages go hand in hand together; but while they are just entering the field on their war-path of reform they ought not to fling a stone at the friends who have heretofore done their work for them."[70]

For their part, female federal employees seem to have done little to court the support of the woman's rights movement. This is unsurprising. Women who worked for, or wanted to work for, the government were discouraged from participating in the movement. Agitating for higher pay was already a progressive undertaking for women and they would not have wanted to jeopardize the backing of Republican politicians in their quest for equal pay by mixing up the issue with the far more radical request for the vote. The diary of Julia Wilbur, Patent Office clerk and women's rights advocate, is entirely silent on the equal pay issue, suggesting that even suffragists who were federal clerks believed pay equality to be a secondary goal. Because suffragists' chosen strategy was to direct their efforts on achieving the vote, and because female federal employees did not align their cause with that of the suffrage movement, the women who worked for the federal government lost a potentially vital ally in their fight for equal pay, a fight that would drag on for years in both houses of Congress, with surprising results.

"Why Should Not the Compensation Be the Same?": Congress Debates Equal Pay, 1867–1870

When a popular bill providing a 20 percent pay increase for all federal clerks reached the Senate in 1867, it snagged on the issue of whether female clerks would share in the largess.[71] The conversation soon expanded beyond the bounds of the bill and Senators engaged in a heated debate concerning equal pay for equal work.[72] Women received the 20 percent bonus, but the equality issue remained unresolved—but not forgotten. On December 16, 1868, Thomas L. Jones, a Democrat from Kentucky, submitted to the House, "by unanimous consent," the following resolution: "Resolved, That all females in the employment of the Government be allowed equal pay where they perform like service with males."[73] Baltimore's *Sun* applauded this action, reporting that the female employees "have been asking for this all session, but unfortunately they, it seems, could not obtain a champion until this late day."[74]

From 1867 to 1870, women and their advocates in Congress fought to have female salaries brought into parity with the male salaries. The issue was argued in the Senate in 1867, 1869, and 1870 and the House in 1870. The prevailing spirit in the debates and newspaper articles reporting on them seemed to be for equality of pay. Both houses of Congress passed bills effecting this change, but for reasons congressmen themselves claimed not to understand, the change did not come. The arguments in the four debates were very similar and as no changes were effectuated until the conclusion of the last debate, they can be analyzed as one long conversation. There were three positions on the issue of women's wages: in favor of equal pay, in favor of pay dictated by the market, and in favor of fair pay. Some men also used the equal pay issue to question whether the government should employ women at all.

In 1869, Senator Samuel Pomeroy asked, "Where labor is performed the compensation should be according to the capacity and character of the labor; and if the same labor is performed by one person as by another, and the same amount of time in the day bestowed on it, why should not the compensation be the same?"[75] Radical Republicans including Pomeroy led the charge for equal pay, but they were not alone. Some Democrats, including former slavery supporters, also argued that women should be paid the same salary as a man if she performed the same work. The arguments for equality were straightforward and imbued with the ideological rhetoric of equality permeating the nation's capital.[76] The men ascribing to this position expressed embarrassment that the government would discriminate against women in pay and wanted Congress to set an example for the nation by choosing the justice of equal pay over the cost savings of discrimination.

Republican senators Richard Yates of Illinois,[77] Lyman Trumbull of Illinois,[78] and Samuel Pomeroy of Kansas,[79] all supporters of female suffrage, spearheaded the equal pay campaign in Congress. They were incredulous that anyone could argue against them.[80] "I can see no reason, in fact I have wondered what reason could exist, why we should discriminate against a female employee where she does the same work, where she works as many hours, where she accomplishes as much as a male employee of the same class," Pomeroy argued in May 1870.[81] To Senator Trumbull the matter was "so eminently just and proper that females employed in the public service should have the same pay, the same compensation for doing the same work, that males receive," that he could not conceive how others could contend otherwise.[82] "No reason given, none has been given, and none can be given," he declared.[83]

While Pomeroy and Trumbull were the most vocal in their sentiments, they were not alone. Advocating equal pay for female clerks was not a fringe position.[84] Senator William Stewart, a Republican from Nevada, professed: "I cannot see why a female should not have the same compensation for the same labor as a male. I never could understand it."[85] Nebraska's Republican Senator John M. Thayer opined that paying a woman less than a man for the same work was "utterly indefensible on any rule of justice or right."[86] Irish-born Senator John Conness of California could not understand how his fellow senators could admit that "the value of the services of the female are equal to those of the male" and still propose to pay women less.[87]

Republican Florida Senator Adonijah Strong Welch went the furthest of all in his assertions for equality between the sexes. Calling the pay inequality "the sheerest prejudice, unfounded in any genuine philosophy," he expressed high hopes of gender equality for the nation: "I believe the time is coming when all men and all women will have free access to the higher walks of learning and literature and art and the higher professions, and it is an ignoble prejudice for men of high standing that Senators have obtained to here to make any distinction in the payment of labor simply because the laborer is a female. I would have all treated alike, and I am sorry that the word 'male' or 'female' has to be introduced into any bill whatever."[88]

As suggested by Welch's optimistically egalitarian dream of the future, supporters of equal pay did not limit themselves to ending sex discrimination in salaries. Representative Samuel M. Arnell, Republican from Tennessee, introduced a bill to the House in 1870 that would not only require that government employees be paid based on the "character and amount of service performed by them" and "irrespective of sex" but also forbid discrimination in hiring decisions and examinations, explicitly opening all civil service positions to women, including "chief clerk" and "head of section."[89]

Even some men who had supported slavery argued in favor of equal pay for women.[90] Representative Daniel W. Voorhees, a Democrat from Indiana who had been proslavery, argued in the House in 1870 that the issue was one of simple justice: "as honest men we should pay everybody that we employ according to the work they do for us." It was not a question of sympathy or soft hearts, he asserted, but "a claim for exact, absolute justice. If we employ two hands and one head to do the work of any other two hands and one head we should pay the same wages"—an odd assertion for a former supporter of slavery.[91] Senator Garrett Davis of Kentucky, also a former supporter of slavery, claimed to not subscribe to the "dreamy theories" of perfect equality and justice, but to instead "take a common sense, practical, and just view of the subject," which in effect was identical to the "dreamy theories" he rejected. His view was that "the laborer is worthy of his hire or her hire, and that where a female clerk or employee does as much service as a male clerk or employé as a general principle of justice she ought to receive the same compensation."[92]

Many of these men claimed embarrassment that the government discriminated against women in regard to pay. In March 1869, Pomeroy characterized the government's unequal pay of female clerks as "perfectly disgraceful."[93] He was, he said, "mortified and ashamed that we made an invidious distinction between males and females in paying for the services they render."[94] Senator Trumbull believed the practice was "discreditable to the age [and] discreditable to the Government."[95] Republican Representative John F. Farnsworth proclaimed that it was "a shame and disgrace" that women earned $900 a year, "while some stripling, who half his time is smoking his cigar with his heels on his table, receives $1,200, $1,400, or $1,600."[96]

The men who advocated for equal pay believed that the government should be a force for social change, and their position is understandable, as the government had just wrought dramatic changes in bringing about the demise of slavery, and would soon enfranchise African American men.[97] In 1867, Senator Yates argued that Congress should establish the principle of equal pay for equal work. He called upon his fellow senators to "let an example go out from the American Congress that labor performed by everyone shall have its fair reward, and that there shall be perfect equality between all American citizens, without reference to color, race, or sex."[98] Other congressmen shared Yates's vision. Pomeroy understood that women were paid less in other lines of work, "but why should we work that misfortune when they come to perform labor for the Government into discrimination against them?"[99] Senator Stewart understood that women's labor was undervalued in America but when the government acted as employer it "should not follow this unjust practice."[100] Republican Job E. Stevenson of Ohio argued that Congress should work to remedy the discrimination in society, even if only gradually. When the amendment to raise female laborers' salaries from $240 to $720 failed, he introduced an amendment to raise their salaries to $300 a year, which would at least "indicate a disposition to take a step in the right direction."[101]

Not every congressman, or even every Republican congressman, shared this ideological view, and several men had a different conception of the role of government in American society. Such men viewed the government as a business and believed that as congressmen they had a responsibility to the people of America to guard the coffers. The government could pay women less because female labor was worth less than male labor the nation over. There was also a seemingly limitless supply of it. In the March 1869 Senate debate, Timothy O. Howe, Republican senator from Wisconsin, explained: "The simple truth is that female labor, as society is constituted, does not command so high a price as male labor."[102] Senator Roscoe Conkling, a Republican from New York who believed in government frugality, argued the pay question was a straightforward matter of supply and demand.[103] The supply was vast. Women all over the country were begging for government jobs.[104] Because women were willing to work at $900, Conkling argued, "[it] is not true as a business proposition that more money to need be appropriated in order to command the services."[105] Conkling could not "vote that the funds which we administer as trustees here shall be paid in greater sums than are necessary to obtain, and abundantly and certainly obtain, the service required."[106] Republican South Carolina senator Frederick A. Sawyer concurred. He argued that when the government was acting as an employer, it should try to obtain "the best labor at the lowest compensation which it is practicable to get it for."[107]

These arguments failed to sway equal pay advocates.[108] When Representative Arnell, for example, took issue that female laborers in the Treasury Department were paid only one-third of what male laborers earned, Massachusetts Republican congressman Henry L. Dawes explained to him that it was because "there is an abundance of female labor at that price throughout the city." Arnell responded: "I would ask the gentleman if male laborers are not equally plentiful? It does not seem to me that his argument holds good." Dawes admitted he had not looked into the matter.[109] Senator Trumbull was of a similar mind—just because you could pay women less did not mean that you should. He pointed out to his colleagues, "we could find plenty of persons willing to occupy these seats for less than $5,000 a year."[110]

Men advocating for market-controlled pay believed that the government should not be used to effect social change. New Hampshire Republican senator Aaron Harrison Cragin believed that it would be "bad policy" to pay women more. "We all know that there is a distinction between the compensation paid to females and males in all the departments of life," he stated. While Cragin was "not saying that this is right," it was the case, and to try to change society by paying women more would be unnecessarily expensive.[111] Senator Sawyer did not believe that government should be ahead of society on the issue of female pay. He thought equal pay for equal work was "a perfectly sound proposition," but argued that "it is a very different question whether the Government should put itself in the attitude of upsetting all the existing theories of wages and labor for the purpose of carrying out abstract justice when everybody else is working on the existing basis."[112]

The argument against equal pay that appeared to have had the most resonance among congressmen was based on the market, but cloaked in purported altruism and clear paternalism.[113] Senator Morrill of Vermont argued in 1869 that equalizing wages would "end in the abandonment of the employment of female clerks."[114] This demise would come in three ways. First, heads of departments would no longer hire women, as the only reason they had been hired was because they were cheaper. Second, men would use their status as voters to crowd women out of the jobs. Finally, increasing female salaries, which were already so far above the salaries women could earn in any other line of work, would cause the hordes of female job seekers to grow to such an extent it would crush the system of female federal employment, or in the alternative, underpaid women would rise up against it in jealousy-driven destruction.[115]

Republican Senator James Harlan of Iowa claimed that department heads would "in all human probability" fail to hire women at $1,200 a year.[116] Senator Stewart agreed with Harlan, asserting, "There is not a head of a Department nor head of a bureau who would not rather have a male clerk in the bureau than a female clerk doing precisely the same work."[117] The result of raising women's salaries, he contended, "will be to drive the females from the Departments and substitute for them male clerks."[118] Sawyer claimed he had spoken with "three or four of the sensible female clerks on this very point," and they had all asked that they not be given $1,200 salaries because "there is a disposition to have as few female clerks as possible."[119] He was confident that a poll taken of female clerks would reveal that three-fourths of them "would say, 'Vote it down;' and it is because those who reflect on this matter will anticipate that if it is passed they will be turned out of the Departments sooner or later, and probably soon."[120] Working women have a sad history of accepting low pay for work because of their desperation for any pay. In 1830, one observer of female labor explained why needlewomen did not complain when their wages were gouged by clothing manufacturers: "Their numbers and their wants are so great, and the competition so urgent, that they are wholly at the mercy of their employers."[121] Female federal workers were similarly "at the mercy" of their government employer. Miss A. E. Fithian of the Loans Division of the Treasury Department, "one of the Ladies interested in the matter of an increased salary," wrote that she believed women deserved more money, but "any amount over $1200 would be superfluous if not pernicious."[122]

Senator Thayer inquired, given Sawyer's confidence that women would be replaced by men, whether Sawyer had discussed this matter with the department heads. Sawyer answered that he had not.[123] Yet supervisors had not been mum on the subject of female clerks. Beginning in 1863, for example, female clerks were discussed, in varying levels of detail, in the Treasury Department's annual reports to Congress.[124] These reports were never explicitly mentioned in the equal pay debates, nor did anyone reference a recent circular sent by a congressional committee to principal officers in the federal workforce across the country that included a question regarding female clerks.[125] If congressmen truly wanted to know supervisors' opinions on the subject of female pay, they had dozens of typed pages to which they could refer.[126]

Every year, supervisors in the Treasury Department complained, emphatically, that their male clerks were underpaid and that they were losing valuable men to the private sector. Supervisors also generally agreed that their female employees were underpaid, but whether and how much their salaries should rise was a source of disagreement. Several supervisors praised the "economy" of employing women, who quickly proved capable of doing all of the work at half of the pay, suggesting that these men did not desire a female clerk pay raise.[127] Other men argued that women were unfairly underpaid and the situation needed rectification. E. A. Rollins, Commissioner of Internal Revenue, informed Congress in 1865, for example, that the women employed in his office "should be remembered in this organization, and receive compensation more commensurate with their services. There is no reason why they should not be recognized."[128] In 1868, the Director of the Bureau of Statistics, Alexander Delmar, made an unambiguous argument for the "justice" of equal pay for female employees. The women he employed were "mostly engaged in compiling the warehouse accounts, and in the preparation of statistical tables connected therewith" and had "exhibited clerical abilities of a high order." Nonetheless, they were paid only half the salaries of the higher classed male clerks. "There does not appear to me to be any sound reason why, as government clerks, if they prove capable of performing equally arduous and difficult services, they should not be equally remunerated," Delmar wrote.[129]

Overall, however, there was ambivalence on the subject of female pay among executive department supervisors. Like many congressmen, supervisors struggled to square the obvious injustice of paying women less for the same amount of work with the entrenched notion that they simply should be paid less. In 1865, for instance, register of the Treasury S. B. Colby described women's success in his office, but observed "there are very many of these in this bureau receiving a salary of only sixty dollars per month, who are as capable in every way as male clerks who receive $1,200 per annum." "It is not easy to justify this discrimination," Colby mused; "The just expenses of ladies are as great as those of single men. Their sacrifices for the country have gone beyond all recompense." Despite his inability to "justify this discrimination," his recommendation to Congress was not equal pay: "I therefore believe it to be due from Congress to authorize by law a classification of female clerks into three or four classes, with salaries graded from $600 to $1,000 per year."[130]

Treasurer F. E. Spinner was particularly torn over the issue of female pay. In 1864, he praised his female employees, who had saved his office from drowning in work. "But for the employment of females whose compensation is low, and in most cases too low," he wrote, "it would have been impossible to have carried on the business of the office."[131] In 1865, he called for an increase in female compensation, but in proportion to male compensation rather than equal to it.[132] Beginning in 1866 and throughout the remainder of the decade, Spinner began to call for an entire reorganization of his department that would involve its becoming approximately 50 percent female. This proposed reorganization had two apparent driving motivations: cost savings to the office and recognizing the work of the female employees. Spinner tried to accomplish these twin goals in a structure that would employ more women at higher wages than they were currently receiving, but still less than men, and would pay them on a scale similar to the male salary scale. In making his claim, Spinner praised the work of women and highlighted the need to distinguish among them in pay.[133]

In his annual reports, Spinner lauded the abilities and accomplishments of women in his office, emphatically stating that in certain tasks they were superior to men. He used words like "justice" and "right and fair dealing," and the press repeatedly reported he was in favor of pay equality for women.[134] Yet he did not call for Congress to equalize women's wages with men. His purported reasoning aligned with the cost savings arguments of congressmen opposed to equal pay. Although Spinner consistently bemoaned the hemorrhaging of qualified and talented male employees to the private sector, he acknowledged in his 1869 annual report that the situation was different with regard to female clerks. "Nearly all other avenues to obtain an honorable livelihood being closed against their sex," he wrote, "they flock to Washington to seek employment as clerks in the various departments of the government. So there is little difficulty in procuring the services of any number of female clerks that may be required, and that, too, at the present uniform rate of compensation." Spinner's argument was thus that women did not have to be paid more because qualified women would work for so much less, though he acknowledged that "many who are now employed in his office in the handling of money have, by long practice and close application, become experts, and do as good, and in many cases better, official service than male clerks who receive double their compensation."[135]

In addition to relying on unsubstantiated claims that supervisors would fail to hire female clerks at "male" salaries, congressional opponents of equal pay argued that if women were to receive the same pay as men, men would crowd them out of their jobs. This line of argument brought the issue of suffrage into the congressional debates on equal pay in different ways.[136] Some congressmen used it as a bogeyman, warning their colleagues that by devaluing female labor they were strengthening the argument for female suffrage. In the May 1870 Senate debate, Pomeroy cited this devaluation of labor as the main reason why women should be enfranchised, warning, "if these persons had the ballot you could not pass over their claims with impunity."[137] Senator Stewart agreed: "Among the arguments I've heard in favor of female suffrage, the strongest has been the fact that performing the same service in various departments of life women were not equally compensated."[138] These senators suggested that if their colleagues continued to block equal pay as too radical a change, they might be faced with an even greater change—female suffrage—as a result.

Equal pay advocates also argued that if Congress was not going to give women the right to vote, giving them equal pay was a reasonable concession, highlighting the tension between the equal pay movement and the suffrage movement. During the May 13, 1870 debate, Senator Pomeroy informed the Senate that a group was organizing in Boston, "not to secure the ballot for women, but to secure equal wages and equal pay." According to Pomeroy, the group was opposed to female suffrage, "but they do insist and do urge that she should be paid for labor, performed for the Government or for individuals, the same that is paid to men for performing the same work." He urged senators who were opposed to granting women the right to vote "to at least come up to the position of this organization, and give equal pay for equal work."[139]

Others used women's disenfranchisement paternalistically, citing it as a reason to continue to pay them less. Congressman William Kelley of Pennsylvania was, "satisfied that if you make the pay equal[,] the ballot and political maneuvering will exclude women from Government employment."[140] Massachusetts congressman Henry Dawes agreed. If the government paid women and men equally, "these positions will be open to all the political influence brought to bear upon members in reference to their conventions at home and in other respects, so as to secure these places for their male friends," and women would be "entirely crowded out." Dawes contended that women would be fired "to make way for those who have done the dirty work in political conventions," continuing, "While they have no other reliance than abstract justice they are powerless, but when they have the ballot they will stand on an equality with the men, and will be able to protect themselves."[141] Such men were, in essence, arguing that rather than elevating vulnerable women, Congress should keep them underpaid so as to make them less attractive targets.

Female suffrage advocates agreed with Dawes's reasoning. Parker Pillsbury wrote to *The Revolution* in March 1870, specifically citing Dawes's comments. He conceded that, "Intelligent females, both in and out of the Departments," believed Dawes was correct in fearing that if the government paid men and women equally, women would be turned out in favor of politicking men, and this was precisely why women needed the vote.[142] In light of Dawes's comments, a correspondent to *The Revolution* personally interviewed female clerks about the proposed equalization of wages, and "much to our astonishment find a majority of them opposed to it. When asked why they felt thus, they replied: 'Now we are sure of our positions; we do our work as well as men, and we do it for less pay, therefore it is to the interest of the government to employ us. But raise our salary to the male standard, and you at once rob us of every advantage. Men are, *politically*, more available than we, and will naturally supplant us.'"[143] Correspondent H. C. I. also wrote to the *Evening Star* on this issue in June 1870. She claimed that she had been opposed to female suffrage but was becoming convinced it might be necessary because of arguments made by some congressmen that men would take women's places if pay was made equal. She asked, "Do the friends of women in Congress . . . really believe that the excellent work done by excellent women for government in departments here, will be taken from them, if they are justly paid, unless they have a vote wherewith to protect themselves?"[144]

A few congressmen attempted the bizarre argument that raising the salaries of the female federal employees would be generally unfair to the women of America, showing the contortions men attempted to justify the unjustifiable. Senator Cragin contended that if Congress were to "single out a few women in this city, less than a thousand in number, and give them $1,200 a year, whereas at home these same persons as a general thing could not make a quarter part of that sum, those at home will feel it," and it would cause dissatisfaction.[145] Senator Morrill of Vermont believed that to increase the salaries of the female clerks, "we make all the ladies that are equal in ability to perform the duties at home discontented; we create an aristocracy here for the benefit of female employees of the Treasury Department."[146] Senator Howe, taking a slightly different tack, claimed that in increasing the pay of the female federal employees, Congress would be "doing injustice to all the rest of the sex" by "taxing all the rest of the sex to confer a special benefit on the few who are thus employed."[147] Some congressmen also claimed that if salaries were raised, women would destroy the system in a crushing avalanche of applications.[148] Representative Jacob Benton of New Hampshire told his colleagues, "There is now the greatest rivalry going on for a purpose of securing these employments at the rates which are now paid," and increasing salaries would exacerbate the pressure.[149]

Finally, some politicians took a middle-ground view, advocating not equal pay, or pay dictated by the market, but fair pay or pay based on need. This idea of fair pay was the least developed of the arguments in these debates. The concept was founded on the idea that a woman's pay merely supplemented a male family member's salary and therefore could appropriately be less than the pay of men.[150] In these debates, the fair pay argument was a tentative idea raised by men who may have been uncomfortable with, or seeking to justify, pay based solely on the market. What constituted fair pay was contested.

Senator Hendricks, who in 1867 had questioned whether the government should employ women at all, argued in 1869 that the initial salary of $600 paid to women was "a very handsome compensation for female labor" and had been twice raised. Raising it again was unnecessary and gratuitous.[151] Other men argued that women bore less financial responsibility than men and therefore did not need so large a salary. Senator George Williams acknowledged that some female clerks supported themselves or relatives, but "as a general rule, men support their families or relatives and the women support nobody but themselves."[152] Senator Roscoe Conkling agreed that female heads of households were "the exception to the rule, and legislation proceeds not for the sake of the exception, but for the sake of the rule to which the exceptions exists."[153]

Congressmen advocating equal pay pointed out that women could not live more cheaply than men and dismissed arguments that women had fewer financial responsibilities.[154] Pomeroy implored his fellow congressmen to realize that "no female can in Washington get board and clothing any cheaper than a male clerk. No avenues are open to them to lessen their expenses."[155] All female clerks "have to live; they have mouths to feed; they must wear clothing; there is no house in Washington open to them any cheaper than to males."[156] He disagreed with the argument that women who supported themselves or families were anomalous.[157] "The question for us," Pomeroy argued, "is what is a reasonable compensation, in view of the expenses of living in Washington, for persons employed in Government service?"[158]

Perhaps not surprisingly, the debate over women's pay caused some men to question their employment altogether.[159] In the February 1870 House of Representatives debate, Democrat Anthony A. C. Rogers of Arkansas announced that he was opposed to the government's employment of women. "These ladies should go somewhere else they can gain a living in a manner better calculated to elevate them and the race to which they belong," Rogers declared.[160] He was opposed to hiring women even to sweep rooms and wash drapery. When asked who he would have perform this work, Rogers responded, "There are plenty of men in the city who would do it; colored men, white men, and for aught I know, yellow men; plenty of them." If it were up to him, Rogers exclaimed, he "would send these women home and give them husbands if I could, and let them go to doing something for their country . . . instead of being about the public buildings here," a rant that received "great laughter" in the House.[161] Rogers's tirade and his colleagues' response demonstrate how long the road to employment equality for women would be, despite the sentiments of justice expressed in Congress.

"If I live to be a month older I intend to introduce a bill . . . abolishing this whole business of female clerks in the Departments," Rogers threatened. Suggesting that the female clerks were actually prostitutes, Rogers continued that it was "degrading to the people of this country that we should have congregated here year after year, around this Hall and in our lobbies, a parcel of women, hired, it is pretended, for the purposes of the Government, but in many instances, I believe, for other purposes altogether." What most offended Rogers was the "sight of these ladies running about the streets and lobbying with members to get their salaries raised every session of Congress."[162] Rogers did not "want to hear the sound of their rustling silks giving warning of their approach on any such errand."[163] He had very specific ideas with regard to women's proper place: it was in the home, serving men, as God intended.[164]

Representatives Kelley and Stevenson were quick to defend the women Rogers had so casually maligned. Although Stevenson claimed to wish Rogers no harm, he hoped Rogers would not live the thirty days he had stated he needed to draft the proposed bill, abolishing female employment.[165] Rogers accused Pennsylvania representative William D. Kelley of being a "woman's rights man" because of Kelley's defense of the reputation of female employees.[166] "I had a mother, and I have a daughter, and I respect women," Kelley retorted.[167] Rogers did live thirty more days, and he kept his promise. On March 14, 1870, he introduced House Resolution No. 1516 to "abolish female clerks in the Departments of Government."[168] The women he sought to displace responded. Four days after Rogers introduced the bill, the *Jamestown Journal* reported that "the girls in the Treasury clubbed their resources and sent him a leather medal," a symbol of derision.[169] The women's action was a play on the practice of government employees, male and female, of bestowing group gifts upon supervisors as tokens of esteem.[170] Using a custom they had adopted in their identities as employees, these women sent Rogers a public message of contempt and defiance. They were still angry with Rogers in January 1871. In a speech at a Washington woman suffrage convention, one of the speakers described H.R. 1516 as "a law too infamous to mention." The bill did not pass.[171]

"I Do Not Know How": Failure of the Equal Pay Movement

The movement for equal pay for female clerks enjoyed significant support and a strong majority in Congress, and yet it still failed. This failure was unexpected by the press, politicians, and women, creating a good deal of confusion. Newspapers repeatedly announced that an equal pay measure had passed. In December 1868, the *Daily Morning Chronicle* reported that the House had passed the equal pay resolution, describing equal pay as "the child of common sense and justice" that "undoubtedly reflects the opinion of the mass of the American people."[172] On March 15, 1869, the *Houston Union* praised Congress, believing it had equalized male and female federal salaries.[173] In June 1870, *The Revolution* declared that "Congress has decided to pay the women employed in the government departments the same salaries as are given to men."[174] A couple of months later, it reiterated, "Congress did one good thing at least, during its last session, by awarding to female clerks in the various departments of the national government the same compensation as is paid to the male clerks for doing the same style and quantity of labor."[175] Yet Congress had not.

Congressmen themselves professed to be confounded about how that could be. The House and Senate did pass bills raising female pay only to see them die in committee. In 1868, for example, the House passed Jones's resolution that women and men should be paid equally by a margin of 123 to 27.[176] In the February 1870 House debate, Representative William Holman claimed the 1869 bill failed because it was sent to a committee of conference late in the session, "and by one of the most extraordinary instances of legislation this provision, which had been concurred in by both branches of Congress was stricken out 'after full and free conference.'" Representative Farnsworth believed the bill "was not carried out because by reason of its phraseology it would not be construed by the officers of the Department to give the female clerks the pay which it was intended by Congress they should receive."[177] Senator Trumbull thought they had equalized pay in 1869 "by a very decided vote ... but somehow or other in a committee of conference the provision was lost, I do not know how."[178] Senator Pomeroy was similarly mystified as to how this failure had occurred since the Senate had passed an amendment "without a division," but he acknowledged that it "finally fell through in some way."[179] It is worth considering whether the active participation of women adept in politics, such as suffragists Anthony or Stanton, could have helped to successfully shepherd these bills through committee.[180]

Everyone, it seemed, was confused about the outcome of the March 1869 debates on female pay. In June 1869, the *Daily Morning Chronicle* reported, "Many of the lady clerks of the Treasury Department have been under the impression that a recent act of Congress provides that they shall receive the same salaries as the male clerks of the same grade."[181] That month the assistant secretary of the Treasury had to ask First Comptroller Tayler whether the Appropriations Act should be construed as equaling wages since he had been allocated enough money to give the women the additional pay. Tayler responded that the Act of July 12, 1866, set female pay at $900 per year, and though Congress had allocated additional funds, that allocation was not enough to supersede the 1866 Act. Tayler laid out the movement of the bill through the House. Several amendments had been made increasing the salaries of specific groups of female clerks. Then "another member moved that all female clerks should be paid $1200, and this was adopted with a further amendment that they should be paid the salaries of the higher classes when they performed the duties of those classes," and so the appropriation was increased. All of the multiple amendments increasing the salaries of female clerks, however, "were rejected or stricken from it" during "subsequent process of the bill toward its final passage," reported Tayler. The increased appropriation was therefore an oversight, and women's salaries were to remain at $900 per year.[182]

Congressmen advocating equal pay in 1870 were frustrated that their intent had not been carried out the year before. Their efforts were more successful in theory in 1870, but failed in practice yet again. In the May 1870 debate, Senator Trumbull proposed an amendment which stated that "the compensation of the female clerks, copyists, and counters employed in several Departments and bureaus . . . shall . . . be the same as male clerks performing the like or similar services."[183] The Senate did not adopt his amendment. Instead, it adopted an amendment giving the department heads the discretion to appoint females to the graded classes of clerks.[184] Trumbull opposed this change, arguing that department heads could so appoint females as the law stood.[185] He predicted that the practical effect of the amendment would be "simply that the Departments would do nothing."[186]

Trumbull was right. It is clear from the *Federal Register* for 1871 that department heads did not begin promoting women in any appreciable way. The practice was rare enough that Quartermaster General Meigs felt compelled to write the secretary of war a letter of thanks on November 6, 1871, for promoting Emma P. Sedgwick of Connecticut. Sedgwick joined the War Department in 1863 at $600 per year. She appeared on the *Federal Register* as a "copyist" in 1865, 1867, 1869, and 1871. In November 1871, she was appointed to a first-class clerkship.[187] Meigs wrote, "It is an acknowledgment of and incentive to faithful service and is executing a law of Congress which has not, I fear, been as generally useful as was intended by Congress itself—because it has not yet been sufficiently acted on." He closed that he believed that the law would "work its way into general recognition."[188]

It did not do so for many years. With tight budgets, no congressional mandate, and a seemingly endless supply of female applicants, department heads were agonizingly slow in promoting women, although there was a small flurry of promotions in 1870 and 1871, indicating that some had been awaiting the opportunity to do so.[189] Ten years later in 1881, 79 percent of female Treasury clerks were still earning $900 per year or less. The highest salary women earned that year was $1,400, and only 2 percent of women, or 11 out of 569 female Treasury clerks, earned that much. By contrast, 67 percent of the male Treasury clerks that year earned $1,400 per year or higher. In 1901, more than thirty years after Representative Welch declared that it was "an ignoble prejudice . . . to make any distinction in the payment of labor simply because the labor is a female," 43 percent of women in the Treasury Department still earned only $900 per year or less.[190] That year, 53 percent of male Treasury clerks earned $1,400 per year or more, as compared to only 17 percent of women.[191] In 1943, bookbinders at the Government Printing Office received thirty to fifty-two cents an hour less than men received for performing the same work.[192]

Although women's salaries rose slowly in the decades following the debates, they did rise. Conversely, men's salaries started to fall as men moved into positions that paid the lower "female" salaries.[193] By the end of the nineteenth century and into the twentieth, a frequent argument against equal pay was that it would devalue the labor of men.[194] Thus, in failing to equalize wages in the debates of the 1860s, Congress not only reified and legitimized unequal pay, but also created a system that strengthened the arguments for maintaining this injustice in private industry.

Congress and the country expressed support for pay equality, and yet equality did not come. The multiple failures wore on the women. A female correspondent described the Congressional debates as degrading. "Nothing could be more humiliating to a high-spirited, intelligent, honorable woman, than to . . . be compelled to listen to a debate on woman's work and wages," she wrote.[195] A male Washington observer wrote that after their multiple failures, "it seems preferable to bear with the glaring injustice than, by endeavoring to be righted, endure the humiliation of another debate in Congress."[196]

The equal pay debates of 1867–1870 reveal Congress struggling to justify a practice that many realized was logically indefensible. In their discussions, congressmen used nascent rationalizations for paying women less that became more formalized and gained power with time. Some, including ideas that women's financial needs were less than those of men because women did not independently support families, had predated these discussions and would continue to be used as a justification for wage discrimination.[197] Others, including the much-touted argument of cost savings to the government and the claim that women would be made too jealous if female clerks were to receive higher salaries, began to fall away after these debates, replaced by more carefully developed arguments regarding women's place in the family and men's place in the workforce.

IN THE LATE 1860S, the U.S. government missed a crucial early opportunity to elevate female labor. Women's introduction into the federal civil service encouraged private employers to hire women to perform clerical work.[198] Although imagining alternative history is a tricky undertaking, it is at least worth considering whether a firm stance by Congress establishing that the federal government valued men's and women's labor equally might have influenced and encouraged private employers to be of similar mind. *The Revolution* thought this was possible. In misreporting that Congress had equalized wages, the newspaper declared its belief that now "women in other occupations should and will push their claim for equality in the matter of wages."[199] Equal pay would have been a difficult policy to retreat from once adopted, and could have accelerated women's civil rights battles in other areas, including suffrage. Instead, Congress sent a clear message to the nation's employers that it was acceptable to treat women as exploitable and marginal employees and to women that they were somehow fundamentally inferior to men in matters of employment. The fifty-nine female Treasury Department employees who, in 1866, rhetorically asked, "What makes us to differ from them?" never received an answer. The answer, of course, was that they were women.

Epilogue
We Do Not Intend to Give Up

In 1908, a bronze statue collected dust among moldering lumber in the dark and rarely visited basement of the Corcoran Art Gallery in Washington, D.C. It had languished there for well over a decade, but had not been forgotten. Women of America, led by a handful of Civil War–era female Treasury Department clerks, had been working since 1891 to commission and erect the statue of General Francis Elias Spinner. The women sought to have it erected on the grounds of the Treasury Department in honor of his decision to bring women into federal employment.[1]

The movement for the memorial began just after Spinner's death in 1890. Elizabeth Stoner, Frances I. Hoey, and Nellie Devendorf, who had joined the Treasury Department in 1862, 1864, and 1865, respectively, founded the Spinner Memorial Association in January 1891. Stoner served as the association's president and Hoey as its secretary.[2] The bulk of the money raised for the memorial came from women employed in the federal offices in Washington, D.C., but working women across the country recognized the debt owed to Spinner. "Donations for the proposed memorial came pouring in, for nearly every woman in the country, holding a position in the work-a-day world, was and is anxious to do what she can to show her appreciation of the man who first fought for her rights in government offices," reported a Philadelphia newspaper.[3] With the funds that were collected, the group commissioned sculptor Henry Elliot, who created the statue, a "work of art," that a congressional committee declared "worthy of a conspicuous place in our city."[4]

Secretary of the Treasury John G. Carlisle refused the initial application of the women to place the statue on the grounds of the Treasury Department because he was not sure he had the authority to allow it.[5] Due to his refusal, the women of the General Spinner Memorial Association petitioned Congress in 1896 to erect the statue "upon one of the approaches to the Treasury Department, or . . . upon one of the buttresses of the large flight of steps at the north entrance to the building." The "grateful women" who had contributed to the statue's creation could "conceive of no location more suitable than the Treasury building" at which to honor Spinner's memory. The association asked that action be taken as soon as practicable so that "those of us who knew and revered General Spinner, and who honor his memory, are able to participate in this grateful and loving duty."[6] Despite a favorable committee report on the proposed bill, the House of Representatives never voted on the issue, and subsequent secretaries of the Treasury did not overturn Carlisle's refusal.

There were echoes of the frustration of the equal pay struggle in women's quest to have the Spinner statue placed on the grounds of the Treasury. In September 1901, the *Philadelphia Inquirer* reported that the women were still fighting to have the statue erected, "but for unexplained reasons success constantly eludes them," and added that the statue seemed "doomed to remain in seclusion," hidden in the Corcoran Art Gallery, where it had been deposited after the sculptor's death. The ladies of the association, however, remained "determined and courageous; they are fixed in their purpose to carry out their plan and set the memorial in a conspicuous place, despite all opposition." "Although we have met with so many failures, we do not intend to give up," proclaimed Frances I. Hoey, "in fact, the opposition with which we have met, unfair as it seems to us, has only made the association the more determined."[7]

Newspapers across the nation agreed with the women that the statue was a fitting tribute to Spinner and his work in introducing women into the Treasury Department. "If any man deserves the gratitude of the 'new' woman," declared an Iowa paper in 1896, "it is the man to whom the sex is indebted for one of the greatest advantages which women enjoy at the present day—that of holding office under Uncle Sam."[8] The papers expressed confusion and disappointment over the reticence of Congress and officials to place the statue on Treasury Department grounds. One paper claimed that the statue remained hidden in Corcoran's gallery because of sheer misogyny. The *Springfield Republican* asserted in 1908 that it was *because* Spinner's legacy was that of introducing women into the executive departments that Congress failed to approve the request to place the statue on Treasury Department grounds. "Man's jealousy of woman is a very petty thing," the paper concluded.[9]

Despite Hoey's emphatic assertions of determination, by 1908 the association had indeed given up on its ambitions to place the statue at the Department of the Treasury. That year, the association worked with the General Herkimer chapter of the Daughters of the American Revolution to erect the statue of Spinner in Herkimer County, New York, the place of his birth.[10] In June 1909, the bronze statue of the former treasurer was finally unveiled to the public, hundreds of miles and hundreds of thousands of pairs of eyes away from where the association had intended it reside. The pedestal bears

Spinner's words: "The fact that I was instrumental in introducing women to employment in the offices of the Government gives me more real satisfaction than all the other deeds of my life."[11]

The saga of the Spinner statue is, in some ways, reminiscent of women's entrance into the federal workforce. Despite women's proven abilities and many contributions, the government failed to adequately acknowledge, recognize, or reward their service. The failure to have the statue of Spinner erected at the Treasury Department was a truly sad and galling defeat for the association, but perhaps ultimately appropriate. Although Spinner was credited with bringing women into the government service, he was also instrumental in creating and maintaining the infrastructure that paid them less for performing the same work and limited their advancement, based on his preconceived and prejudicial notions of what women were and were not capable of doing. He was, after all, the man who had told a Washington, D.C., newspaper that "a Woman Can't Reason a [damn] bit."[12]

A far more fitting testament to the importance of Spinner's opening of the federal civil service to women was women's consistent demonstration of proficiency and competency in full view of the nation. Whether they were aware of it or not, these labor feminists were doing important work by serving as visible and constant reminders to politicians and the entire country that women were valuable workers, who were capable of intellectually challenging labor. In setting this example, early female federal employees began to dismantle some of the economic and cultural restraints that limited the opportunities of nineteenth-century middle-class white women.

Over the Civil War era, women gained some ground in government employment, incrementally exploiting and expanding new opportunities. In her 1861 letter to Lincoln, New Yorker Sarah A. Robison self-consciously joked that she did "not aspire to a foreign mission" in her request for federal employment.[13] By 1867, Mrs. Francis Lord Bond was applying to the State Department for appointment as British consulate. Her application enjoyed congressional support, and President Johnson instructed his Cabinet to treat her application "in the same manner as those of the males." She did not receive the position in 1867, but kept trying. In 1868, Ohio senator Benjamin Wade and other men sent Johnson a letter, which stated, "Believing as we do, that the time has come when women of capacity and talent may properly represent this Government at foreign courts and in foreign countries, we, the undersigned, most cheerfully solicit for and recommend the appointment of Mrs. Francis Lord Bond to such embassy as may be compatible with the interests and the honor of the country."[14] Jane Wadden Turner became the

Smithsonian Institution librarian in 1868 and held the position until 1887. In her first year as librarian, Joseph Henry, secretary of the Smithsonian, reported to Congress that Turner "vindicates by her accuracy and efficiency the propriety of employing her sex in some of the departments of government."[15]

Chief Justice Salmon Chase's dissenting vote in *Bradwell v. Illinois* (1873) also demonstrates the power of the example set by early female federal employees. Myra Bradwell had studied law under her husband (a lawyer), drafted legislation, and edited the *Chicago Legal News*, a well-respected national law and business publication. Although she passed the Illinois bar exam, the Supreme Court of Illinois denied her admission to the Illinois State Bar because she was a woman. Bradwell challenged the Illinois Supreme Court decision under the privileges and immunities clause of the still fairly recent Fourteenth Amendment. In an 8-to-1 decision, the Supreme Court of the United States denied Bradwell's claim. One concurring opinion proclaimed, "The natural and proper timidity and delicacy which belongs to the female sex evidently unfits it for many of the occupations of civil life." Chief Justice Salmon Chase cast the only dissenting vote. Chase only wrote dissents in what he deemed "*very important* cases," and there is evidence that he had " 'hoped' " to write a dissent in *Bradwell*, but he was grievously ill and would be dead of a stroke less than three weeks after the court issued its opinion. Because he did not write an opinion, we can only speculate as to why he dissented in *Bradwell*, and why he felt so strongly about her case. In his *Louisiana Law Review* article, "*Bradwell v. Illinois*: Chief Justice Chase's Dissent and the 'Sphere of Women's Work,' " author Richard L. Aynes posits that it was, perhaps, Chase's role as "a pioneer in the employment of women in government" that led him to dissent from the majority. Although Chase was not a supporter of female equality in the federal workforce and may have been more influenced by his relationship with his intellectual daughter, the Department of the Treasury under his stewardship was the first to hire women in large numbers, and he had years of experience watching women demonstrating that they were "fit" for "the occupations of civil life."[16]

Motivated by women's proven abilities and the economy of paying women less, private businesses also ramped up their employment of women in the late nineteenth century. Historian Margery W. Davies found that "the employment of women as clerks in the United States Treasury Department during the Civil War established a precedent that may have eased the entrance of women into offices ten and fifteen years later."[17] The number of women working in clerical positions in private businesses increased sharply in the late nineteenth century. Historian Angel Kwolek-Folland calculated that women comprised only 2.5 percent of the clerical labor force in America in 1870, yet by 1900 their numbers had grown to over 30 percent.[18] The government's employment of women during the Civil War era established the precedent of hiring women to do intellectual work, but also set the precedent for paying them less than their male counterparts.

So, was the "experiment" of employing women successful? In a remarkably short time women became not only an accepted, but also a vital component of the federal workforce. Yet women were underpaid, underutilized, and underappreciated. Federal department supervisors and the national press generally stereotyped female federal employees in one of two ways. Supporters of the practice tended to portray female government employees as needy and deserving women who, because of the tragic loss of a male breadwinner, were forced to support themselves. Alternatively, opponents of female federal employment or of the Republicans, who were in power, branded female federal employees as prostitutes. This need to categorize female federal employees as either Civil War widows or dangerous prostitutes was an effort to fit women's employment into existing theories of gender. Such labels marginalized and maligned the women who sought government jobs for personal and financial fulfillment and limited the opportunities and remuneration of all female federal employees. The manner in which the government employed women reinforced on a national stage the notion that a woman's gender mattered more than her abilities, intelligence, and skills, which confined all but the most resourceful and ambitious women to low-paying positions with little room for advancement.

Women were not passive players in the evolution of their subordinate position in the federal civil service. Men created and controlled the manner in which they would allow women to be employed. Those who aggressively pursued federal employment outside the narrative supervisors favored, including Clara Scott, Sophia B. Gay, and Mary Walker, failed. Thus, many female federal employees learned to present themselves as helpless and needy, and to use their interpersonal skills to keep themselves in the good graces of male supervisors to obtain and retain coveted jobs. These practices served to reify the government's practice of treating women as lesser employees and gave a degree of credence to the stereotypes that female federal employees were either war widows or whores. Some women did resist this construct, including those advocating for equal pay and advancements, and worked to create cracks in the edifice of their subordination. However, as women lacked the power and tools to mount a true fight against the discrimination and were dissuaded from collective action, cracks and incremental advances were all they could achieve.

The "grand experiment" was flawed from the outset. It purported to ascertain whether women could be successful federal civil service employees. What it actually tested was whether men could find a way to incorporate middle-class white women into the federal civil service in a way that allowed them to remain ladies, not become workers. Overall, the key achievement of female federal employees in the Civil War era was, as Frances Hoey phrased it in relation to the Spinner statue, not giving up despite repeated failures, opposition, and unfairness.

Notes

Abbreviations Used in Notes

NA-USH	National Archives, Records of the U.S. House of Representatives
NA-USS	National Archives, Records of the U.S. Senate
NA-Tr	National Archives, Records of the U.S. Treasury Department
NA-WD	National Archives, Records of the U.S. War Department
ALP	Abraham Lincoln Papers, Library of Congress
Federal Register	U.S. Department of State, *Register of All Officers and Agents, Civil, Military, and Naval, in the Service of the United States*

Introduction

1. There were exceptions. During the antebellum period, women worked at the Government Hospital for the Insane, the Government Printing Office, and the Patent Office. These exceptions are discussed in the chapters that follow. Women were also sometimes employed as postmasters across the United States and as contract laborers in other cities, but as this book is focused on women's federal employment in Washington, D.C., such female federal employees are not discussed here.

2. The *Register of All Officers and Agents, Civil, Military, and Naval, in the Service of the United States* will be referred to herein as the "*Federal Register.*" It was published every other year on odd years. Note that this publication has been found to underreport employees of both sexes, but as it is a consistent measure of federal employment over the time period covered in this book, it is referred to as a gauge. For the underreporting issue, see Aron, "'To Barter Their Souls for Gold,'" 835. Most notably for present purposes, the publication does not include statistics on the men and women employed in the Government Printing Office or most of the men and women employed in the Treasury Department's Bureau of Engraving and Printing.

3. Swisshelm, *Letters to Country Girls*, 78.

4. U.S. GPO, *Keeping America Informed*, 13; Annual Report of Superintendent of Public Printing, 1862. (Note that 44.56 percent of the names listed in this report are female, but it appears some are duplicated. One-third is a conservative estimate.)

5. The term "feminism" came into use in America in the 1910s. Cott, *The Grounding of Modern Feminism*, 3.

6. DuBois, *Woman Suffrage & Women's Rights*.

7. Cobble, Gordon, and Henry, *Feminism Unfinished*, xi.

8. Cobble, *The Other Women's Movement*, 3, 7–8.

9. Thank you to Cindy Aron for helping me pull out and better articulate my ideas about female federal employees and the women's movement.

10. "[Women Workers]," *St. Cloud Democrat*, Dec. 21, 1865. Newspapers also characterized female federal employment during the 1860s as an "experiment." See "Female Clerks," *Daily State Gazette*, Nov. 11, 1865, 2; "Foreign News!," *Pacific Commercial Advertiser*, Jan. 20, 1866, 3; "The Departments," *Daily Morning Chronicle*, Dec. 13, 1866, 1; "The Removal of Female Clerks from the Departments at Washington," *Evening Bulletin*, Dec. 19, 1866; "The Department Bagnios at Washington," *Salt Lake Daily Telegraph*, Feb. 6, 1867, 4; "Hon. Thomas A. Jenckes's Bill: Women in the Civil Service," *The Revolution*, June 18, 1868, 378; "Women as Government Clerks," *New York Times*, Feb. 18, 1869, 2.

11. Giesberg, *Civil War Sisterhood*; Attie, *Patriotic Toil*; Ginzberg, *Women and the Work of Benevolence*.

12. Faulkner, *Women's Radical Reconstruction*, 5.

13. Schultz, *Women at the Front*; Schultz, "Race, Gender, and Bureaucracy."

14. Giesberg, "From Harvest Field to Battlefield"; Osterud, "Rural Women during the Civil War"; Aley and Anderson, eds., *Union Heartland*.

15. Varon, *Southern Lady, Yankee Spy*; Blanton, *They Fought Like Demons*; Leonard, *All the Daring of a Solider*; Elizabeth D. Leonard, Introduction to Edmonds, *Memoirs of a Soldier*.

16. Dudden, *Fighting Chance*; Faulkner, *Women's Radical Reconstruction*; Zaeske, *Signatures of Citizenship*; Sizer, *The Political Work of Northern Women Writers*; Venet, *Neither Ballots nor Bullets*; DuBois, *Feminism and Suffrage*; Flexner, *Century of Struggle*; Whites, *Gender Matters*.

17. Gustafson, *Women and the Republican Party*; Edwards, *Angels in the Machinery*.

18. Giesberg, *Army At Home*; Silber, *Daughters of the Union*; Giesberg, "'Noble Union Girls'"; Wilson, *The Business of the Civil War*.

19. Giesberg, *Civil War Sisterhood*, 6.

20. Silber, *Daughters of the Union*, 283.

21. Aron, *Ladies and Gentlemen*; Aron, "Their Souls for Gold"; Claussen, "Gendered Merit"; Baker, "Entry of Women into Federal Job World"; U.S. Civil Service Commission, *Women in the Federal Service*.

22. The date range of 1859 through 1871 was chosen for two reasons. First, since the *Federal Register* was published only every other year, starting in 1859 and ending in 1871 allows the entire 1860s to be captured. Second, Congress began to revise the civil service system in 1871, which changed the dynamic of women's employment. For more on early civil service reform efforts, see Van Riper, *History of the United States Civil Service*.

23. I have created files for 192 women who applied for jobs with the federal government between 1859 and 1871 but did not receive them, and files for 3,146 women who did at some point in the time period under examination work for the federal government.

24. For example, I searched for every female name located in the *Federal Register* or in application materials. I also browsed the 1870 U.S. Census searching for women employed by the federal government. I located 662 female federal employees in the 1870 census. I also reviewed the employee files of 273 women in the War and Treasury Departments. I did not contain these biographical files to only female federal employees

or applicants and assembled files on over 5,300 men and women who were in Washington, D.C., during the Civil War era.

25. The *Evening Star*, the *Daily Morning Chronicle*, and the *Daily National Intelligencer* were Republican newspapers. The *Daily Constitutional Union* was a Democratic newspaper. One historian of Washington described the *Daily National Intelligencer* as a "lofty, conservative and, in the old-fashioned sense, Southern [newspaper, which] seldom condescended to local items"; the Washington *Evening Star* as "a saltier sheet altogether [with] the largest circulation of any local newspaper in the District [and which] strongly supported the administration"; the *Daily Morning Chronicle* as an important "first-class Washington . . . newspaper," which in a bawdy house trial "refused to pander to 'morbid and impure readers' for the sake of gaining circulation"; and the *Daily Constitutional Union*, as "antagonistic to Lincoln." Leech, *Reveille in Washington*, 92, 200, 332, 491. See also Whyte, "Divided Loyalties." A fifth Washington, D.C., newspaper used in this dissertation, the *Critic-Record*, started publication in August 1868.

26. Diary of Julia A. Wilbur, May 17, 1870—May 2, 1871; July 10, 1870.

27. *Cong. Globe*, 41st Cong., 2nd Sess. 1412–1417; 1415 (Feb. 1870).

Chapter One

1. Sarah A. Robison to Abraham Lincoln, Feb. 25, 1861, ALP, accessed Oct. 22, 2010.

2. Lydia Sayer Hasbrouck to Abraham Lincoln, Mar. 8, 1861, ALP, accessed Oct. 22, 2010. Hasbrouck did not obtain a job with the federal government but did continue to push for women's rights and dress reform. See "City Intelligence," *Daily Morning Chronicle*, Apr. 27, 1869, 4; "City Intelligence," *Daily Morning Chronicle*, Apr. 28, 1869, 4; "City Intelligence," *Daily Morning Chronicle*, Apr. 30, 1869, 4.

3. Elsie Marsteller to Abraham Lincoln, Mar. 19, 1861, ALP, accessed Oct. 22, 2010.

4. Rockman, *Scraping By*, 101.

5. Saint, "Women in the Public Service," 14.

6. Baker, "Entry of Women," 83, 86–87.

7. Ames, *Ten Years*, 371.

8. U.S. Senate, *Report of the Secretary of the Senate*, 38, 59, 80, 83, 85, 87. The Treasury Department also employed "laborers" Mrs. Hamlin, Mrs. Collins, and Miss Hynes, and paid Polly Hawkins for washing towels and Sarah Duvall for making them. Treasury Department, *Letter from the Secretary of the Treasury* (1862), 6, 32–34.

9. Prandoni, "St. Elizabeths Hospital," 5–6. See also U.S. Congress, *Management of the Government Hospital for the Insane* (1876), 409–10; Millikan, "Wards of the Nation," 29–32.

10. When soldiers began to be treated for physical injuries at the Government Hospital for the Insane during the war, they began calling the institution "St. Elizabeths" since they did not want to write home from "The Government Hospital for the Insane." "St Elizabeths" was the colonial name of the parcel of land on which the hospital stood. McMillen, "Institutional Memory," https://www.archives.gov/publications/prologue/2010/summer/institutional.html.

11. Department of the Interior, *Annual Report of Board of Visitors of Government Hospital for Insane* (1865), 828–29. Women at other mental health institutions frequently sent him unsolicited applications for employment. See Records of the Superintendent [of the Government Hospital for the Insane], 1855–1967.

12. Women had been in the printing industry prior to the establishment of the Government Printing Office. One historian estimates that in 1850, 1,400 women comprised 16 percent of the total workforce in the newspaper industry. DuBois, *Feminism and Suffrage*, 129; Baker, *Technology and Women's Work*, 37–49.

13. GPO, *Annual Report of Superintendent of Public Printing* (1860), 15; GPO, *Keeping America Informed*, 7–8.

14. Ibid., 20, 22–23, 32.

15. In addition to the women described above, A. M. Richardson worked in the General Land Office "in clerical duties" prior to September 1861. Her former supervisor from that office wrote her a letter of recommendation to the Treasury Department when she had been let go from the Land Office for lack of work. File of A. M. Richardson, "Application and Recommendations," Box 487 (Ric), NA-Tr. Newspaper articles also make mention of individual women clerking under previous administrations. See "The Female Clerks," *Evening Star*, Oct. 14, 1870, 1 (Mrs. Ridgate working in the Treasury under Buchanan); "Romantic Histories," *Lowell Daily Citizen and News*, Mar. 22, 1870, 2 (a widow working for the federal government during the Pierce administration).

16. Lomax, *Leaves from an Old Washington Diary*, 18, 25, 27, 38, 40, 41. See also Benjamin, *Washington during Wartime*, 204.

17. Sellers, "Commissioner Charles Mason and Clara Barton," 809.

18. Ibid., 811, 813; Baker, "Entry of Women," 83; Oates, *A Woman of Valor*, 11. See also Bacon-Foster, "Clara Barton: Humanitarian," 283. But see Civil Service Commission, *Women*, 5 (noting that while Barton claimed to be the first woman to obtain a clerkship on par with men, "no record has been preserved of such an appointment. . . . The only remaining evidence of Clara Barton's employment possessed by the Department of the Interior consists of vouchers for payments to 'Miss. C. H. Barton' for copying services during 1855–1857 and 1860–1865").

19. On August 3, 1855, acting commissioner of the Patent Office Samuel T. Shugert sent the secretary a note that read, in part: "Sir: I have communicated to the Ladies employed in the patent office that they must vacate their room within the present month." Sellers, "Commissioner Mason," 815–17.

20. Ibid., 817–18.

21. Ibid., 819–20.

22. Employee files for certain women cite previous work for the Patent Office during the 1860s. This was most likely work that was done at their homes and sent to and from the Patent Office via messenger. "Letter from Washington," *Sun*, May 13, 1869, 4. ("The Patent Office, although employing females as copyists and other clerical duties, has never had them regularly assigned to rooms in the Department building, but their work has been done at home.")

23. *Federal Register*, 1863. Women were listed as working at the Government Hospital for the Insane (37 women), and the Treasury (137 women), Post Office (16 women), and War Departments (30 women).

24. Civil Service Commission, *Women*, 3–4. See also Oates, *Woman of Valor*, 11; Aron, *Ladies and Gentlemen*, 73; "From Washington," *Public Ledger*, Sept. 18, 1861, 2 ("The demand for Treasury notes is so great that additional clerks, including some ladies, have been employed to cut and fill them up"); *Registers and Lists of Treasury Employees Register of Female Clerks, 1861–1868*, vol. 3, NA-Tr (noting Emma G. Manning was hired in October 1861).

25. Martin, *Behind the Scenes*, 465; Ames, *Ten Years*, 372. Salmon Chase, secretary of the Treasury in 1861, also described women's entrance into the federal workforce as through the backdoor. S. P. Chase to Augustus French Boyle, Dec. 11, 1872, in Niven, *The Salmon P. Chase Papers*, 363–64.

26. "General Spinner and the Women Clerks," *Women's Journal*, Jan. 10, 1891, 16–17.

27. Ibid.; Ames, *Ten Years*, 372; Deutrich, "Propriety and Pay," 68, citing *Washington Post*, July 24, 1886.

28. Gallman, *The North Fights the Civil War*, 106; Abbott, *Political Terrain*, 93; Davies, *Woman's Place is at the Typewriter*, 51. See also Stanton, *History of Woman Suffrage*, 808.

29. For example, see *Report of the Secretary of the Treasury . . . 1862*, 129–30.

30. There are conflicting stories as to who was the "Eve" of women's work in the Treasury Department. An early newspaper retrospective on female employment in the Treasury gives the honor to Mrs. Fanny Steele, sister-in-law of then assistant secretary of the Treasury George Harrington. The local newspaper claimed that Steele joined the Treasury on July 1, 1861, at $50 per month. The article also claims that Steele worked in the Treasury Secretary's office until 1869. "The Female Clerks," *Evening Star*, Oct. 14, 1870, 1. Local newspaper articles from 1863 announced that Steele was appointed to the Post Office in November. "A Lady Clerk," *Daily Morning Chronicle*, Nov. 28, 1863, 3; "Washington," *Sun*, Nov. 28, 1863, 4. Since the 1870 *Evening Star* article is the only source I have found citing Steele as the inaugural female employee in the Treasury Department in 1861, I have chosen to privilege the more widely circulated Douglass story.

31. "General Spinner," *Women's Journal*, 16–17. This article states that women entered in early spring, 1862, but evidence cited herein indicates that women were employed in the summer and early fall of 1861. See "From Washington," *Public Ledger*, Sept. 18, 1861, 2; "Women in the U.S. Treasury," *Wheeling Sunday Register*, Sept. 3, 1893, 11; "Washington Gossip," *Idaho Falls Times*, May 7, 1896, 3; "Women in Business," *Fortune* 12 (July 1935): 50–57, 90–96, 53.

32. The role Spinner played in employing women was one he was immensely proud of. In 1891, he told a reporter: "I am conscious that I have done some good in the world, and that I have not lived entirely in vain; but the fact that I first introduced women clerks into a department of the National Government at Washington is the one act of my life with which I am entirely satisfied, and in which I feel an honest pride." "General Spinner," *Women's Journal*, 16–17.

33. U.S. Congress, *Loyalty of Clerks*, 8. See also "Late Local News [Second Edition]," *Evening Star*, Nov. 10, 1862, 2 (referencing over three hundred women employed in Arsenal). For more on women working in arsenals in and outside Washington, D.C., see, for example, Giesberg, *Army at Home*; Wilson, *Business of the Civil War*.

34. "Romantic Histories," *Lowell Daily Citizen and News*, Mar. 22, 1870, 2.

35. For sailors and soldiers not needing postage on their mail, see, for example, Act of January 21, 1862, ch. 9, 12 *Stat.* 332 (An Act in Relation to the Letters of Sailors and Marines in the Service of the United States).

36. "Washington City Post Office," *Daily Morning Chronicle*, May 18, 1863, 3 (reporting that for the quarter ending March 31, *"one million sixty-four thousand four hundred and thirty-six"* (emphasis in original) "free" letters and packages were received at the Washington Post Office). See also "Unprecedented Mail Reception," *Daily Morning Chronicle*, July 15, 1864, 2.

37. Act of January 21, 1862, ch. 8, 12 *Stat.* 332 (An Act to Promote the Efficiency of the Dead Letter Office). See also *Congressional Globe*, 37th Cong., 2nd Sess. (1862), 435 (act approved and signed by the president); U.S. Post Office Department, *Annual Report of Postmaster General, 1862*, 136.

38. "Our Washington Letter," *Philadelphia Inquirer*, Feb. 5, 1862, 2. See also "From Washington," *Public Ledger*, Feb. 5, 1862.

39. Civil Service Commission, *Women*, 6. See also "A Lady Clerk," *Daily Morning Chronicle*, Nov. 28, 1863, 3; "[Female Clerk]," *Sun*, Nov. 28, 1863, 4.

40. "Local News," *Evening Star*, Nov. 25, 1862, 4.

41. "Late Local News [Second Edition]," *Evening Star*, Dec. 12, 1862, 2. Meigs did not receive formal approval from Congress for the expansion of his workforce or the employment of women until February 1863. "Late Local News [Second Edition]," *Evening Star*, Feb. 5, 1863, 2. See also "Local Items," *Daily National Intelligencer*, Jan. 1, 1863, 3.

42. *Federal Register*, 1863. In 1863, 137 of the 993 total employees in the Treasury Department at Washington listed in the *Federal Register* were women. The *Federal Register* did not include the men and women in the Treasury Department's Bureau of Printing and Engraving and in calculating the 14 percent figure I did not account for the men employed by the Treasury Department but working outside of the city of Washington.

43. An Act to Supply Deficiencies in the Appropriations for Service of Fiscal Year ending June 30, 1864. See also Silber, *Daughters of the Union*, 78. But see Civil Service Commission, *Women*, 4 ("The first law Congress enacted to attempt to provide a uniform pay scale for Federal clerks set up a separate class for women, who were to be employed in subordinate clerical work or 'temporarily' in the duties of a clerkship."). For more on women's salaries, see chapter 7.

44. Silber, *Daughters of the Union*, 79; S. P. Chase to Augustus French Boyle, Dec. 11, 1872, in Niven, *Chase Papers*, 363–64; Martin, *Behind the Scenes*, 465–66; "The Investigation into the Treasury Department at Washington—The Female Clerk System," *The Daily Age*, May 21, 1864, 1; "The Female Clerks," *Evening Star*, Oct. 14, 1870, 1.

45. But see letter from Chase to reporter that concludes, "It is true, however, that I have always favored the enlargement of the sphere of woman's work and the payment

of just compensation for it," although he instructed the reporter that his letter was intended for private use only. S. P. Chase to Augustus French Boyle, Dec. 11, 1872, in Niven, *Chase Papers*, 363–64.

46. None of the departments placed want ads or announcements with the exception of the Government Hospital for the Insane, which did occasionally run help wanted ads in local papers. See "[Want ad]," *Daily National Intelligencer*, Oct. 1, 1862, 3. Although it appears that no newspaper ran any story announcing the government's employment of women, several newspapers did begin to mention specific women's employment in short articles. See "From Washington," *Public Ledger*, Feb. 5, 1862; "Our Washington Letter," *Philadelphia Inquirer*, Feb. 5, 1862, 2; "Late Local News [Second Edition]," *Evening Star*, Dec. 12, 1862, 2; "Local News," *Evening Star*, Feb. 16, 1863, 3.

47. Ames, *Ten Years*, 372–73. Local residents set up several societies and organizations to help women in need including the Home for Friendless Women and a society to help indigent but "worthy" women. "Some Account of the Home for Friendless Women," *Daily National Intelligencer*, Sept. 19, 1864; "Local News," *Evening Star*, Jan. 17, 1870, 4.

48. Calculated from the *Federal Register*, 1863.

49. File of Rosa Perry, "Application and Recommendations," Box 455 (Per–to Pet), NA-Tr. Their request was granted. Rosa, or Rose, was listed on the *Federal Register* in the Treasury in 1863 and 1865. U.S. Census Office, *Eighth Census of the United States* (1860), Washington, D.C.; *Federal Register*, 1865, 1867.

50. File of Annie Adams, "Application and Recommendations," Box 2 (Acc–Ada), NA-Tr. Jane Reynolds, another female Patent Office employee, who was let go when the "kind of work on which she was engaged was discontinued," similarly applied to the Treasury Department when it began hiring women. Reynolds was also unsuccessful. See File of Jane Reynolds, "Application and Recommendations," Box 495 (Rey–Rhy), NA-Tr.

51. Letter from Letitia Arnold to S. P. Chase, Feb. 17, 1862, File of Letitia Arnold, "Application and Recommendations," Box 13 (Arm–Arr), NA-Tr; Letter from [illeg.— Thos M. Edmunds?] to W. Harrington, Feb. 27, 1862, File of Jarvis Adams, "Application and Recommendations," Box 2 (Acc–Ada), NA-Tr; Letter from Adelaide D. Adams to Secretary of the Treasury, July 21, 1862, File of Adelaide Adams, "Application and Recommendations," Box 2 (Acc–Ada), NA-Tr.

52. For example, see letter from M. A. Locke to J. F. Callen, Dec. 16, 1861, File of M. A. Locke, "Application and Recommendations," Box 352 (Loc–Log), NA-Tr.

53. Letter from Julia Richards to A. Lincoln, Apr. 17, 1862, File of Julia Richards, "Application and Recommendations," Box 487 (Ric), NA-Tr.

54. Martin, *Behind the Scenes*, 466.

55. "From Washington," *Public Ledger*, Nov. 16, 1865, 1.

56. "Washington Items," *Troy Weekly Times*, Dec. 15, 1866, 3. Washington's *Evening Star* also described the Treasury as "besieged" in 1868. "Washington News and Gossip," *Evening Star*, Feb. 15, 1868, 1.

57. "The Removal of Female Clerks from the Departments at Washington." *Evening Bulletin*, Dec. 19, 1866.

58. "Clerkships in Washington," *Sun*, Aug. 27, 1867, 1.

59. Ames, *Ten Years*, 372–73.

60. Penny, *The Employments of Women*, vii.

61. Gallman, *Defining Duty*, 128.

62. C. Montgomery to War Department, Mar. 29, 1865, File of C. Montgomery, "Correspondence Relating to the Hiring of Clerks," Box 4, NA-WD.

63. Penny, *The Employments of Women*, 10–11, 16.

64. Kessler-Harris, *Women Have Always Worked*, 63–63; Montgomery, *Beyond Equality*, 34; Aron, "Their Souls for Gold," 847; Silber, *Daughters of the Union*, 79. The government remained one of the highest paying employers of women through the nineteenth century. Srole, *Transcribing Class*, 168.

65. "Experiences of a Bureau Officer," *Cincinnati Daily Gazette*, May 17, 1871, 4.

66. The remaining 6 percent worked in a variety of jobs including printing, medicine, and clerical work. DuBois, *Feminism and Suffrage*, 128 (citing Montgomery, *Beyond Equality*).

67. Yoe didn't find employment in the Departments. File of Rachel M. Yoe, "Correspondence Relating to the Hiring of Clerks," Box 4, NA-WD.

68. Wilson, *Business of the Civil War*, 226.

69. Though the pay did give one woman pause. In 1864, Mary E. Reynolds wrote to her recommender for a job in Washington and said that her father's health was failing and she needed to obtain work, "and although I feel that I will not be able to *save* much money at a salary of $600 a year I cannot help thinking that it will be better than doing nothing." File of Mary E. Reynolds, "Application and Recommendations," Box 495 (Rey–Rhy), NA-Tr.

70. That is, if they were paid at all. In November 1867, for example, Washington, D.C., public school teachers had not been paid since June because of a dispute in the City Council over the appropriation for schools for African Americans. "Washington News and Gossip," *Evening Star*, Nov. 1, 1867, 2.

71. "From Washington," *Public Ledger*, Nov. 16, 1865, 1.

72. Jane Perry had "earned her living by the needle for years" before applying to the Treasury Department in 1865. File of Jane Perry, "Application and Recommendations," Box 455 (Per–Pet), NA-Tr. Her application was unsuccessful.

73. File of Mary A. Locke, "Application and Recommendations," Box 352 (Loc–Log), NA-Tr.

74. File of Mary F. Shockley, "Application and Recommendations," Box 526 (Shi–Sho), NA-Tr.

75. File of Annie M. Peters, "Application and Recommendations," Box 455 (Per–Pet), NA-Tr.

76. "Letter from Washington City," *Galveston Tri-Weekly News* (Texas), June 21, 1869, 3. The article claims that Postmaster Cresswell, a man "not possessed with an overabundance of the milk of human kindness," did not give the woman a job, and "the poor woman went straight away and drowned herself in the canal."

77. Teaching was a popular employment of literate women in the mid to late nineteenth century. See e.g. Davies, *Woman's Place*, 71. Many female federal employees had been teachers.

78. File of Emily W. Abbott, "Application and Recommendations," Box 1 (Aa–Ab), NA-Tr.

79. File of Annie M. T. Adams, "Application and Recommendations," Box 2 (Acc–Ada), NA-Tr.

80. File of Mary F. Shockley, "Application and Recommendations," Box 526 (Shi–Sho), NA-Tr. See also File of P. Anna Taft, "Application and Recommendations," Box 506 (Syp–Tal), NA-Tr.

81. Margaret A. Shermer ran a boardinghouse in 1863 and was an employee in the "Seed Rooms, Museum, and Laboratory" of the Agriculture Department in 1867. *Hutchinson's*, 182; *Federal Register*, 1867. Alexina Getty also ran a boardinghouse before clerking in the Treasury. File of Alexina Getty, "Application and Recommendations," NA-Tr. See also "Romantic Histories," *Lowell Daily Citizen and News*, Mar. 22, 1870, 2. In 1868, Spinner provided examples of former occupations of his clerks, male and female. Although he did not specify which sex held which positions, included in his list were a washerwoman and a housekeeper. U.S. Congress, Joint Select Committee on Retrenchment, *Civil Service of the United States*, 40.

82. Larsen, *Crusader and Feminist*, 27–28. Swisshelm was a correspondent for the Minnesota newspaper during the war years.

83. *St. Cloud Democrat*, July 23, 1863, in Larsen, *Crusader and Feminist*, 237–42. See also *St. Cloud Democrat*, Aug. 6, 1863, in ibid., 242–47.

84. There was certainly a need for such positions. See "City Intelligence," *Daily Morning Chronicle*, Aug. 6, 1868, 1 (reporting that a typographical error changed a want ad for a private clerical position from "Wanted–'An intelligent boy, sixteen or seventeen years of age, who can read and write'" to "Wanted—An intelligent girl" and the businessman "was astonished to have call upon him yesterday, in the space of a few hours, some thirty young and blooming females, all desiring situation.")

85. Faulkner, *Women's Radical Reconstruction*, 31; Harrison, "Welfare and Employment Policies of the Freedmen's Bureau," 89.

86. "Editress in the City," *Daily Morning Chronicle*, Feb. 7, 1863, 3; Larsen, *Crusader and Feminist*.

87. Leasher, *Letter from Washington*; Leasher, "Lois Bryan Adams," *Federal Register*, 1867; 1869.

88. Faulkner, *Women's Radical Reconstruction*, 15–26.

89. Historian David Montgomery estimated that at the end of the 1860s, hundreds of thousands of women had to support themselves because of a gender imbalance in the population. Montgomery, *Beyond Equality*, 33.

90. File of S. Bridges, "Application and Recommendations," Box 59 (Bre–Bri), NA-Tr. There is no evidence she received the job.

91. Maria E. Baker, "Correspondence Relating to the Hiring of Clerks," Box 4, NA-WD.

92. Neither Bridges nor Baker appear to have received a job with the government.

93. Lydia Sayer Hasbrouck to Abraham Lincoln, Mar. 8, 1861, ALP, accessed Oct. 22, 2010.

94. Ames, *Ten Years*, 357. For more on Ames, see Billings, "Early Women Journalists of Washington," 95–96; Beasley, "Mary Clemmer Ames"; Fleischner, *Mrs. Lincoln and Mrs. Keckley*, 236. In her meticulous work, *Ladies and Gentlemen of the Civil Service*, Cindy Sondik Aron describes "'typical' nineteenth-century female federal clerk[s]" as coming "from respectable middle-class families that had fallen into some kind of financial trouble." Aron also found that the typical female clerk was young and relatively well educated. Aron's research is exhaustive and her findings are undoubtedly true when one generalizes and typifies all female federal clerks over the period examined in her book, 1860 to 1900. Because of availability, however, Aron's data is largely from the later part of the period she examines: 1880 and 1890. For example, only 8.6 percent of the sample Aron uses to calculate the women's class is from the period 1860 to 1870. Only 1.9 percent of the women analyzed for educational backgrounds were from that time period. Aron, *Ladies and Gentlemen*, 40, 43, 45.

95. For an examination of the difficulties of using the concept of "middle class" as a tool to examine clerical workers in the late nineteenth century, see Kwolek-Folland, *Engendering Business*, 13. Ultimately Kwolek-Folland chooses to "emphasize that a shared ethos marked the middle-class experience—a set of values that elevated female domesticity and male breadwinning, the nuclear family, respectability, education, and clean or physically undemanding work." See also Srole, *Transcribing Class*, 4.

96. "Letter from Washington," *Daily Ohio Statesman*, Oct. 26, 1865.

97. The Census Commission tried to ascertain the occupations of Washington's citizens, but because of vague answers—especially with regard to government service—the Commission found the returns to be frustratingly unusable. It did calculate, however, the following numbers: "Public officers, clerks, and in other literary or scientific employments: 3,762. In civil employment, not otherwise described, 1,155 whites and 242 colored." Commissioner of Education, *Special Report of the Commissioner of Education*, 39–40. In addition to the women described, African American women also worked for government hospitals as cooks, laundresses, and nurses. Forbes, *African American Women during the Civil War*, 51, 61.

98. Masur, "Patronage and Protest." For African Americans' experience in the civil service in the early twentieth century, see Yellin, *Racism in the Nation's Service*.

99. Whether or not to make such an indication appears to have been at the discretion of the supervisors of the offices and bureaus. Supervisors often noted the race of African American men, but not always. For example, in 1863, three watchmen in the War Department's Provost Marshal General's Bureau are noted as "colored," but the census for 1870 reveals several male African American messengers in the Treasury Department whose race was not noted in the *Federal Register* for that Department. *Federal Register*, 1863, 146.

100. 1870 Census, Washington, D.C.

101. *Federal Register*, 1863, 1865, 1867; 1860 and 1870 Censuses, Washington, D.C.

102. *Federal Register*, 1863, 1865, 1867; 1860 Census, Washington, D.C.

103. *Federal Register*, 1867; 1870 Census, Washington, D.C.

104. *Federal Register*, 1865, 1867; 1870 Census, Washington, D.C.

105. *Federal Register*, 1865, 48. The women listed as Messengers, including Nancy White and Clara Washington, are not noted as "colored" in 1867. *Federal Register*, 1867, 52.

106. The federal government acknowledged its African American employees as a group in 1869, for example, when it allowed "Colored Employees in the several Executive Departments" to be absent from work on November 4 so that they could attend Baltimore's emancipation celebration. "Washington News and Gossip," *Evening Star*, Nov. 3, 1869, 1.

107. For example, Solomon Johnson, Abraham Lincoln's barber had been a messenger in the Treasury Department and befriended Salmon Chase who promoted him to a first-class clerkship in 1867. "Local News," *Evening Star* [Second Edition], Feb. 14, 1867, 2. In 1870 Isaac Myers, "a well-known colored man," was appointed to the Post Office at $1,200 per year. "Washington News and Gossip," *Evening Star*, Mar. 8, 1870, 1. Later that year, William A. Freeman, an African American messenger in the Third Auditor's office, received a promotion to a clerkship. "Washington News and Gossip," *Evening Star*, July 20, 1870, 1. Within a month, Freeman was promoted from a second to a third class clerkship. "Washington News and Gossip," *Evening Star*, Aug. 3, 1870, 1.

108. "Local News," *Evening Star*, Feb. 12, 1870, 4.

109. "Colored Female Clerks," *Sun*, Mar 29, 1869, 4. Slade was daughter of former White House steward H. M. Slade. Emma V. Brown had been a schoolteacher to African American children in the district. She had attended Oberlin College. Masur, *An Example for All the Land*, 41, 82; Faulkner, *Women's Radical Reconstruction*, 141–147.

110. "Letter from Washington," *Sun*, May 23, 1870, 4.

111. Ibid.; "The City," *The Critic*, May 24, 1870, 3. Ketchum was likely one of the first African American females appointed to a clerkship in the Treasury Department, but her name may have been "Agnes," not Eleanor. In 1869, the Colored National Labor Convention recognized Agnes, whose mother was a black Bermudian woman and whose uncle was a prominent white attorney and abolitionist, as an important woman, a leader who "illustrate[s] an aptitude and ability among colored women" that must be "recognized and encouraged by colored men." Masur, *Example for All the Land*, 160. See also *New York World*, May 22, 1869; and *Philadelphia Enquirer*, July 7, 1869, quoted in *Weekly Georgia Telegraph*, July 16, 1869.

112. "Letter from Washington," *Sun*, May 23, 1870, 4.

113. "Washington News & Gossip," *Evening Star*, Jan. 13, 1867, 1.

114. Commissioner of Education, *Special Report of the Commissioner of Education*, 272–74; Forbes, *African American Women*, 140.

115. 1870 Census, Washington, D.C., 2WD.

116. Aron also found that female federal clerks' definition of "need" varied widely, from educating relatives to acquiring food and shelter. Aron, "Their Souls for Gold," 839.

117. 1860 and 1870 Censuses, Washington, D.C., *Federal Register*, 1865, 1867. See also Jenny Stevens in 1870 Census, Washington, D.C. (listed as Treasury Department employee).

118. "Letter from Washington City," *Galveston Tri-Weekly News,* June 21, 1869, 3.

119. For example, Ellen Gary was a cook and a waitress at the Government Hospital for the Insane in 1867, 1869, and 1870. *Federal Register,* 1867, 1869; 1870 Census, Washington, D.C., Washington PO. Gary's father was an illiterate Irish day laborer; her Irish-born mother was also illiterate. In 1860, twelve-year-old Ellen lived in Vermont with her parents and five brothers and sisters in the same house as a teamster and his wife and children. 1860 Census, Vermont, Burlington. See also "The Explosion Yesterday at the Arsenal; Further Details and Particulars—The Coroner's Inquest," *Evening Star,* June 18, 1864, 1 (describing female arsenal employee as "a poor girl").

120. *Federal Register,* 1865, 1867, 1869, and 1871. 1870 Census, Washington, D.C., Washington PO.

121. Davis: *Federal Register,* 1865, 1867, 1869, 1871; 1870 Census, Washington, D.C., 1WD; Hull: *Federal Register,* 1869, 1871; 1870 Census, Washington, D.C., Washington PO.

122. "Petition of Employees in the Government Printing Office Praying for an Increase in Compensation," NA-USS; 1870 Census, Washington, D.C., 6WD.

123. Only 20.1 percent of African Americans were literate in 1870. See Snyder, *120 Years of American Education: A Statistical Portrait.*

124. See File of Jennie S. Abbott, "Application and Recommendations," Box 1 (Aa–Ab), NA-Tr; File of E. L. Cady, "Application and Recommendations," Box 81 (Byr–Cal), NA-Tr; File of Jane James, "Application and Recommendations," NA-Tr; File of Kate Cain, "Application and Recommendations," Box 81 (Byr–Cal), NA-Tr. Aron found that the female Treasury Department clerks "received uncommonly long educations" but she only had information on 19 women from 1870 (none from 1862/63). The rest of the women she examined were from 1880 and 1890. Her total sample size was 953, thus only 1.9 percent of the women she examined were from the time period under examination here. Aron, *Ladies and Gentlemen,* 43, FN 8. The lower numbers from this time could reflect either that the women seeking positions were not as well educated as the women seeking positions in the 1880s and 1890s, or that listing educational achievements was not yet a general practice for female applicants. The latter may have been because, as we will see in the following chapter, emphasizing one's intellect over one's need was not a successful strategy for obtaining a government position.

125. 1870 Census, Washington, D.C.. Annie McWilliams also worked in the Treasury Department in 1865 and 1867. *Federal Register,* 1865, 1867. But see McWilliams's signature on 1866 petition for increased pay at "Petition of Female Treasury Clerks for Increased Pay," NA-USH.

126. "Letters from Washington," *Sun,* June 22, 1869, 4.

127. Ames, *Ten Years,* 356.

128. "Some Treasury Girls," *New-York Evangelist,* Aug. 7, 1873, 7.

129. Ames, *Ten Years,* 358; Baker, "Entry of Women," 87; Martin, *Behind the Scenes,* 469.

130. 1860 Census, Washington, D.C., no TWP listed.

131. "Inauguration of the College for The Deaf and Dumb," *Daily Morning Chronicle,* June 29, 1864, 2.

132. 1867 *Federal Register,* 21. Ann also worked for the Treasury Department in 1869.

133. 1869 *Federal Register*, 25. Szymanoskie married William Smithson sometime before her death on November 9, 1871. "Died," *The Critic*, Nov. 10, 1871, 2. Szymanoskie was not the only hearing-impaired female clerk in the 1860s. Laura C. Redden described herself in an 1863 letter of application to the Commissioner of the Interior as "a semi-mute," but assured him that she had "yet to find that this fact interferes with the transaction of any ordinary business." File of Laura C. Redden, "Application and Recommendations," Box 479 (Rea–Red), NA-Tr. She did receive the job sometime in the 1860s. Redden, whose married name was Searing, became an authoress of some note during the Civil War under the penname "Howard Glyndon."

134. In addition to the three examples provided herein, Esther E. Spanier was forced to find a way to care for her two small children after her husband abandoned them. District Courts of the U.S., *Equity Case Files 1863–1938*, Box 125, File 2147. Esther supported herself and children by obtaining a job with the government before John had abandoned them. She appears in the 1867 and 1869 *Federal Registers* in the Treasury Department earning $900 per year. Rose A. Pierce worked in the Treasury Department under Spinner from 1863 until at least 1871. *Federal Register*, 1863 to 1871 and 1870 D.C. Censuses, Washington, D.C., 2WD. Rose married John A. Pierce in New York on December 23, 1861. The couple did not live together for long. Rose's 1869 petition for divorce includes allegations of John's infidelity in the Sandwich Islands, California, and New York. By the time she filed for divorce, John was living with another woman in New York "in open and notorious adultery." She asked the court for $40 per month in alimony ($480 per year). The court awarded her $200 per year, which is likely why Pierce kept her job in the Treasury Department. District Courts of the U.S., *Equity Case Files 1863–1938*, Box 96, File 1657. Catherine Dodson, born Catherine Brown, worked in the Treasury Department in 1864. In 1867, she divorced her husband, a flagrant adulterer who worked at the Capitol. In 1868 she worked in the Ladies Retiring Room of the U.S. Senate; "Local News," *Evening Star*, Oct. 7, 1867, 3; Committee on the District of Columbia. *Report* (1868), 12; Masur, *Example for All the Land*, 87, 97; Masur, "Patronage and Protest."

135. "Local News," *Evening Star*, Nov. 4, 1867, 3.

136. "Local News," *Evening Star*, Jan. 9, 1867, 3.

137. *Federal Register*, 1869, 1871; 1870 Census, Washington, D.C., 7WD.

138. Information provided by Lisa Tuttle, descendent of Margaret Ash from District Courts of the U.S., *Equity Case Files 1863–1938*, Box 270, file 4206; "They Have Served Uncle Sam Half A Century," *Miami Herald Record*, Jan. 17, 1917, 10; File of Margaret Ash, "Application and Recommendations," Box 14 (Arr–Ash), NA-Tr.

139. File of Alexina Getty, "Application and Recommendations," NA-Tr.

140. Ibid.

141. "Love and Crime," *New York Herald*, Aug. 14, 1865, 1. The article suppressed the names of the parties involved, "at the earnest request of an injured wife," but a clipping from a related article in Getty's file confirms that that "injured wife" was Alexina Getty.

142. "Love and Crime," *New York Herald*, Aug. 14, 1865, 1.

143. "Love and Crime," *New York Herald*, Aug. 14, 1865, 1.

144. File of Alexina Getty, "Application and Recommendations," NA-Tr.

145. "Love and Crime," *New York Herald*, Aug. 14, 1865, 1.

146. File of Alexina Getty, "Application and Recommendations," NA-Tr.

147. Ibid., *Federal Register*, 1867.

148. Of the 662 women identified in the 1870 census as working for the federal government in Washington, D.C., 126 women were born in Washington, 80 were born in New York, 74 were born in Maryland, 60 were born in Virginia, and 61 were born in Pennsylvania.

149. "Experiences of a Bureau Officer," *Cincinnati Daily Gazette*, May 17, 1871, 4. ("A lady resident in Washington could always commend more congressional friends than one from a distance. The poor soldier's widow or daughter in the country had but her one representative. The young miss of the capital brought in her train a couple of senators, four or five members of the lower house, a general or two, and perhaps a gruff admiral or commodore.")

150. In 1863, 67 out of 137 female employees in the Treasury Department were from or had been appointed in Washington, D.C. (49 percent). In 1865, that percentage dropped to 32.5 percent (145 of 441 female employees). *Federal Register*, 1863, 1865.

151. I have found 76 female federal employees from southern states out of the 662 I have examined in the 1870 census. The overwhelming majority of these women came from Virginia (60). The remainder came from Alabama (2), Georgia (5), Louisiana (2), Mississippi (1), North Carolina (3), South Carolina (1), and Tennessee (2).

152. Letitia G. Plunkett who worked under Spinner in 1865 and 1867 was born in Africa (country unspecified). *Federal Register*, 1865, 1867. Miss C. Albrecht, an 1863 Treasury Department employee, was from Switzerland. *Federal Register*, 1863. Postal Employee Magdalena Wetzel was also from Switzerland. *Federal Register*, 1865, 1867, 1869, 1871; 1870 Census, Washington, D.C., 5WD. In 1870, of the 662 female federal employees examined, 61 were from Ireland, 15 from England, 5 from Germany, 2 each from France and Scotland, and 1 each from Prussia, Canada, Saxony, and Switzerland. Places of birth also included Spain (M. G. Meade, Pension Office: *Federal Register*, 1871), Germany (Augusta Cook, Treasury Department employee: *Federal Register*, 1865, 1867; and Ernestine Becker, Treasury Department employee in 1865 and 1867, and in 1870: *Federal Register*; 1870 Census, Washington, D.C.), Prussia (Willa Leonard, Treasury Department: *Federal Register*, 1865, 1867; note the *Register* states she was from Germany; 1870 Census, Washington, D.C., states that she was from Prussia), and the Danish West Indies (M. F. Foster: *Federal Register*, 1867, 1869, 1871).

153. Sprigg would have been approximately 68 years old in 1867. 1870 Census, Washington, D.C.; *Federal Register* 1867. Sprigg also worked in the Treasury Department in 1865.

154. 1870 Census, Washington, D.C.

155. Columbia N. Payne worked in the Patent Office as early as 1869 and worked there until at least 1871. 1870 Census, Washington, D.C., 1WD; *Federal Register*, 1869, 1871. Sarah's last name appears to be Teulon in the Census but it is difficult to read. 1870 Census, Washington, D.C., 4WD. Joanna Looney worked as a "table girl" or "table

maid" in the Government Hospital for the Insane in 1865 and 1867. *Federal Register*, 1865, 1867. The 1870 Census shows then fifteen-year-old Joanna living with her parents and sister. She was then working as a seamstress. 1870 Census, Washington, D.C., Washington PO. A newspaper article from 1917 claims Emma Brown, who joined the Treasury Department in 1865 at age eleven, was "the youngest person who has been in Government employed for half a century." "They Have Served Uncle Sam Half a Century," *Miami Herald Record*, Jan. 17, 1917, 10.

156. The average age of the female federal employees identified in the 1870 federal census was 29.963 years.

157. Aron, *Ladies and Gentlemen*, 44.

158. 1870 Federal Census

159. Aron, *Ladies and Gentlemen*, 50–51.

160. Commissioner of Education, *Special Report of the Commissioner of Education*.

Chapter Two

1. For example, in March 1864, Sloan received a letter of appreciation from the surgeon at the Pest House near Providence Louisiana, for her donation of underclothing. The letter stated: "When . . . I took charge of this institution, not one of the unfortunates had yet had a change of underclothing since coming in; and in some cases their coarse woolen Army shirts were literally festering in their putrid flesh. So long unused to cool, soft, cotton undergarments they seem to look upon such luxuries as a kind of fabulous thing; or, like maternal caresses, as a matter of long-ago, that is to come back no more forever. I cannot find language to convey to you the knowledge of how deeply grateful the poor soldier-boys were upon the receipt of your donation." File of Mary Sloan, "Application and Recommendations," Box 531 (Sla–Slo), NA-Tr.

2. Ibid.

3. Ibid.

4. Ibid.

5. Of the 273 files that were reviewed, only 35 percent of the women who were successful in obtaining jobs in the department to which they initially applied referenced the military service of male relatives in their applications (16 of 45 successful applications).

6. "Clerkships in Washington," *Sun*, Aug. 27, 1867, 1. See also "Local News," *Evening Star*, Aug. 24, 1867, 3 (citing the *Providence Journal*).

7. The files of the Treasury Department are the most comprehensive employee files available for women in this time period. They are located in the National Archives at College Park, Maryland. They are arranged alphabetically by the surname of the applicant or employee and span from approximately 1830 to 1910. "Application and Recommendations," NA-Tr. The War Department files are less organized. They can be found at the National Archives in Washington, D.C. "Correspondence Relating to the Hiring of Clerks," NA-WD. The files not containing application materials for new appointments contained materials including, but not limited to, requests to be retained

or rehired, resignation letters, and oaths of office. Some files do not contain application material because the woman requested that her letters of recommendation be returned to her, either because she did not receive the job sought or was let go from the civil service. For instance, an 1880 letter in Clara G. Scott's file indicates that she sent or caused to be sent to the Treasury Department at least eighteen letters—two in 1864, two in 1866, three in 1867, one in 1868, nine in 1869, and one in 1870, all of which were returned to her and are no longer in the file. File of Clara Scott, "Application and Recommendations," Box 515 (She–Sco), NA-Tr. It appears that by 1877 it was forbidden to return letters of recommendation or application materials to the employee if their appointment was based on those materials. See file of Kate Cain, "Application and Recommendations," Box 81 (Byr–Cal), NA-Tr.

8. An additional nineteen women eventually did obtain jobs with the federal government, although in departments other than that to which they had originally applied. Note that these figures may be inflated. Presumably because appointments in the 1860s were less formalized than they would become in later years, most women—even those who did work for the government—may not have left behind files in the Treasury or War Departments.

9. Jenckes, *Speech of Hon. Thomas A. Jenckes*; Aron, *Ladies and Gentlemen*, 97–106; "Shameful Disclosures," *The Revolution*, Apr. 1, 1869, 203.

10. "[Women Workers]," *St. Cloud Democrat*, Dec. 21, 1865, in Larsen, *Crusader and Feminist*, 307–13.

11. For example, see "Washington Letter," *The Revolution*, May 21, 1868, 309–10.

12. File of Mary Sloan, "Application and Recommendations," Box 531 (Sla–Slo), NA-Tr.

13. File of Priscilla H. Braislin, "Correspondence Relating to the Hiring of Clerks," Box 4, NA-WD; File of Hettie Jacobs, "Application and Recommendations," NA-Tr; Maria Baker, "Correspondence Relating to the Hiring of Clerks," Box 4, NA-WD. See also letter from File of Julia Richards, "Application and Recommendations," Box 487 (Ric), NA-Tr (did not receive a job); File of Elizabeth Silver, "Application and Recommendations," Box 531 (Slo–Slo), NA-Tr (did not receive a job); Jennie Gaughran to Abraham Lincoln, July 14, 1864, ALP, accessed Oct. 22, 2010; Aron, *Ladies and Gentlemen*, 100–101.

14. Lincoln, *Collected Works of Abraham Lincoln*, 8:126 (the ladies have not been identified). See also Burlingame, *Lincoln Observed*, 85.

15. File of N. J. Brent, "Application and Recommendations," Box 59 (Bre–Bri), NA-Tr (undated, but based on other documents in the file, the letter was likely from 1866). Brent did receive a position sometime in 1867, but she also had acquired a recommendation from Senator James Nye of Nevada.

16. File of Laura M. Hoffman, "Application and Recommendations," NA-Tr (does not appear to have obtained job); File of Alexina Getty, "Application and Recommendations," NA-Tr (eventually obtained job with a significant amount of support from influential recommenders). In what appears to have been a similar type of recycling, Bell Lyon's application to the Confederate government appears in the U.S. Treasury

Department records. File of Bell Lyon, "Application and Recommendations," Box 360 (Lyo–Mac), NA-Tr (does not appear to have obtained job).

17. Epstein, *The Lincolns: Portrait of a Marriage*, 381. For a woman seeking influence of another woman, see also File of Sarah Cahill, "Application and Recommendations," Box 81 (Byr–Cal), NA-Tr.

18. *St. Cloud Democrat*, Aug. 13, 1863, in Larsen, *Crusader and Feminist*, 247–53. Swisshelm also raised the issue of applicants seeking her assistance in a June 1863 letter to the *New York Tribune*: "I get so many letters from women who want me to get them positions as clerks and nurses . . . I cannot answer them, and have no power to serve them." "The Sick and Wounded Soldiers," *New York Tribune*, June 19, 1863, 2.

19. These letters did not earn Sprigg the job. Lincoln's second request in 1864 did succeed, however. Ann G. Sprigg appears on the *Federal Register* in the Treasury in 1865, 1867, and 1869. Abraham Lincoln and Mary Todd Lincoln to Caleb B. Smith, May 31, 1861, ALP, accessed Oct. 22, 2010; Letter from A. Lincoln to W. P. Fessenden, July 21, 1864, Lincoln, *Collected Works of Abraham Lincoln*, vol. 7; *Federal Register*, 1865, 1867, 1869. See also Aron, *Ladies and Gentlemen*, 98.

20. "Application and Recommendations," Box 479 (Rea–Red), NA-Tr (letter of recommendation dated Aug. 22, 1868; did not receive a job).

21. Dodson obtained a divorce in 1867 on the grounds of adultery and regained her maiden name. "Local News," *Evening Star*, Oct. 7, 1867, 3.

22. She also claimed to have had "letters from other Senators and citizens elsewhere." U.S., Congress, *Certain Charges against the Treasury Department*, 220. For more on Kate Brown/Dodson, see Masur, "Patronage and Protest."

23. File of Margaret Lockwood, "Application and Recommendations," Box 352 (Loc–Log), NA-Tr.

24. File of Ada Rennedy, "Application and Recommendations," Box 476 (Ran–Rat), NA-Tr (did not receive the job).

25. File of Mary E. Bennett, "Application and Recommendations," Box 38 (Ben–Ben), NA-Tr. (did not receive a job). Her sister Margaret did obtain a job, apparently on a different recommendation from Wilkinson. This letter stated: "She is 22—well-educated—the daughter of a college classmate whom I tenderly loved—of the best stock on both sides. Do give her employment and oblige." File of Margaret Bennett, "Application and Recommendations," Box 38 (Ben–Ben), NA-Tr. Margaret appears in the *Federal Register* in the Treasury Department in 1865 and 1867.

26. File of Sallie M. Madden, "Application and Recommendations," Box 362 (Mac–Maf), NA-Tr (Madden was a ward of Margaret Meade). See also File of Eliza McCully, "Application and Recommendations," Box 382 (McC–McD), NA-Tr (asked for a recommendation from Sherman to the Agriculture Department); File of Mary Gibbin, "Application and Recommendations," NA-Tr; File of Kate Cahill, "Application and Recommendations," Box 81 (Byr–Cal), NA-Tr.

27. "Lists of Employees," Records of the GPO.

28. "Washington," *New York Herald*, Mar. 28, 1869, 9.

29. As the pressure of female applicants intensified, even Ulysses S. Grant felt that his influence might not be enough to secure a woman a position. In an 1868 letter to his father, Grant wrote: "I spoke to Sec McCulloch about giving Mrs. Porter a clerkship in the Treasury and he promised me he would do it, but has not yet. Now I fancy I would not have much influence and if I had would be very careful about using it." Simon (ed.), *The Papers of Ulysses S. Grant*, 18:143–44.

30. Berebitsky, *Sex and the Office*, 31.

31. Ames, *Ten Years*, 374.

32. Martin, *Behind the Scenes*, 470; Ames, *Ten Years*, 374. This distress narrative became the "standard format" for female stenographer applications later in the century as well. Srole, *Transcribing Class*, 143.

33. Aron, *Ladies and Gentlemen*, 102–3. For examples of women needing to support themselves, see File of Mrs. St. Abbe, "Application and Recommendations," Box 1 (Aa–Ab), NA-Tr; File of Jennie S. Abbott, "Application and Recommendations," Box 1 (Aa–Ab), NA-Tr; File of Rebecca J. Abbott, "Application and Recommendations," Box 1 (Aa–Ab), NA-Tr; File of Elizabeth and Columbia Adams, "Application and Recommendations," Box 2 (Acc–Ada), NA-Tr; File of Annie Gibb, "Application and Recommendations," NA-Tr; File of Kate Cahill, "Application and Recommendations," Box 81 (Byr–Cal), NA-Tr.

34. Of the 45 applicants who obtained positions in the departments to which they applied, 31 made it clear they needed to support themselves and 22 made it clear they needed to support others. For female applicants supporting children, see File of Julia Holmes Abbot, "Application and Recommendations," Box 1 (Aa–Ab), NA-Tr; File of Sarah Cahill, "Application and Recommendations," Box 81 (Byr–Cal), NA-Tr; File of Alexina Getty, "Application and Recommendations," NA-Tr; File of Lillie Madison, "Application and Recommendations," Box 362 (Mac–Maf), NA-Tr; File of Hester A. Peters, "Application and Recommendations," Box 455 (Per–Pet), NA-Tr; File of Mrs. Scott, "Application and Recommendations," Box 515 (She–Sco), NA-Tr; File of Theodosia Talcott, "Application and Recommendations," Box 506 (Syp–Tal), NA-Tr. For women supporting parents, see File of Adelaide D. Adams, "Application and Recommendations," Box 2 (Acc–Ada), NA-Tr; File of Elizabeth Arnold, "Application and Recommendations," Box 13 (Arm–Arr), NA-Tr; File of Ann Byus, "Application and Recommendations," Box 81 (Byr–Cal), NA-Tr; File of Rosa Perry, "Application and Recommendations," Box 455 (Per–Pet), NA-Tr; File of Hettie Jacobs, "Application and Recommendations," NA-Tr; File of Sallie Abrams, "Application and Recommendations," Box 1 (Aa–Ab), NA-Tr; File of Helen Ivey, "Application and Recommendations," NA-Tr; File of Malonia Aburn, "Application and Recommendations," Box 1 (Aa–Ab), NA-Tr. For women supporting siblings, see File of Malonia Aburn, "Application and Recommendations," Box 1 (Aa–Ab), NA-Tr.

35. File of E. Scott ("destitute poverty"), "Application and Recommendations," Box 515 (She–Sco), NA-Tr; File of Mary Rhyon ("very poor"), "Application and Recommendations," Box 495 (Rey–Rhy), NA-Tr; File of F. M. Krebs (job would relieve her from "impending suffering and privation"), "Correspondence Relating to the Hiring of

Clerks," Box 4, NA-WD; File of R. P. Reynolds ("indigent"), "Application and Recommendations," Box 495 (Rey–Rhy), NA-Tr; File of Elizabeth Arnold (in "extreme need"), "Application and Recommendations," Box 13 (Arm–Arr), NA-Tr; File of S. Peters ("poverty"), "Application and Recommendations," Box 455 (Per–Pet), NA-Tr; File of Maggie Jackson ("needy"), "Application and Recommendations," NA-Tr; File of Annie M. Peters ("in need"), "Application and Recommendations," Box 455 (Per–Pet), NA-Tr; File of M. Peters ("want stares us and our children in the face"), "Application and Recommendations," Box 455 (Per–Pet), NA-Tr; File of T. Talcott (widow with five children under the age of eight "without a dollar for their support" and "oppressed with poverty"), "Application and Recommendations," Box 506 (Syp–Tal), NA-Tr.

36. Schultz, *Women at the Front*, 42–44, 47. See also Leonard, *Yankee Women*, 3–4, 27.

37. Attie, *Patriotic Toil*, 31, 83.

38. See Srole, *Transcribing Class*, 44.

39. For example, see File of Maggie Jackson, "Application and Recommendations," NA-Tr.

40. File of Addie Getty, "Application and Recommendations," NA-Tr.

41. Occasionally, the lost male breadwinner had been a federal employee, and giving his female relation, most typically his daughter, a job in that man's office served as an acknowledgment of the male employee's faithful service and posthumously allowed that man to provide for his family. Elizabeth Ryan, for example, received a clerkship in the Post Office after her father died at his desk in the Sixth Auditor's Office. "Letter from Washington," *Sun*, Nov. 22, 1871, 4. (Ryan's father "had been for more than a quarter of a century a prominent clerk in that office." Elizabeth Ryan's appointment was "the first female appointment ever made in the Sixth Auditor's office.") See also File of Rosa Perry, "Application and Recommendations," Box 455 (Per–Pet), NA-Tr (Treasury clerks recommending daughter of deceased coworker).

42. Townsend, *Washington, Outside and Inside*, 698.

43. File of Margaret C. Peters, "Application and Recommendations," Box 455 (Per–Pet), NA-Tr. There is no evidence that either woman obtained a position.

44. File of Anna Howard, "Correspondence Relating to the Hiring of Clerks," Box 4, NA-WD. See also File of S. T. M. Babb, "Correspondence Relating to the Hiring of Clerks," Box 4, NA-WD (did not receive a job); File of Maude Reddick "Application and Recommendations," Box 479 (Rec–Red), NA-Tr (had job in the Treasury by 1865).

45. File of Sarah Peters, "Application and Recommendations," Box 455 (Per–Pet), NA-Tr.

46. File of Hannah Slater, "Application and Recommendations," Box 531 (Sla–Slo), NA-Tr; File of Mary Wanton, "Correspondence Relating to the Hiring of Clerks," Box 4, NA-WD; File of Lucy O. Marsh, "Correspondence Relating to the Hiring of Clerks," Box 4, NA-WD; McPherson, *Battle Cry of Freedom*; U.S. Treasury Department, "Registers and Lists of Treasury Employees Register of Female Clerks, 1861–1868," vol. 3; File of Mary Gibbin, "Application and Recommendations," NA-Tr. See also File of Adelaide D.

Adams, "Application and Recommendations," Box 2 (Acc–Ada), NA-Tr; File of E. A. Jacobs, "Application and Recommendations," NA-Tr; File of Jennie Tall, "Application and Recommendations," Box 506 (Syp–Tal), NA-Tr.

47. For example, see File of Phoebe Anna Taft, "Application and Recommendations," Box 506 (Syp–Tal), NA-Tr; File of Anna Carpenter, "Application and Recommendations," Box 87 (Car—Car), NA-Tr; File of K. Cahill, "Correspondence Relating to the Hiring of Clerks," Box 4, NA-WD.

48. File of M. E. Lloyd, "Application and Recommendations," Box 351 (Lit–Loc), NA-Tr.

49. File of Jennie Gaylord, "Application and Recommendations," Box 216 (Gas–Gar), NA-Tr. Gaylord's husband had died in a battle in Georgia. She did not receive a job.

50. For the *Chenango* explosion, see "Local Intelligence: The Chenango Disaster," *New York Times*, Apr. 21, 1864; "Chenano on the Seas, Part II: The First USS Chenango," *Evening Sun*, May 26, 2010.

51. File of Sarah Cahill, "Application and Recommendations," Box 81 (Byr–Cal), NA-Tr.

52. Andrew Johnson did issue a circular to the department heads in April 1866 directing them to preference former soldiers in hiring and promotion decisions, but it did not direct officials to fire women to make room for such men. "Official," *Daily Constitutional Union*, Apr. 9, 1866, 1.

53. "Further from the North," *Daily Picayune*, Aug. 31, 1865, 2.

54. Mackall had not made it clear in her application whether she could make such a claim. Letter from Meigs to Mackall, July 9, 1868, U.S. War Department, "Letters Sent by the Office of the QMG," M745, Roll #58, vol. 100, 35. See also Meigs to Mrs. Anastasia Kearney, Nov. 25, 1866, ibid., Roll #55, vol. 94, 299.

55. "Employment of Female Clerks," *Daily Morning Chronicle*, Dec. 19, 1866, 1. See also *Journal of the House*, 1866–1867, Dec. 18, 1866, 96.

56. Of the 45 successful applications for employment, 29 did not claim the military service of male relatives (64.4 percent).

57. See "Washington," *Daily Age*, May 29, 1866, 1; "The Treasury Scandal," *Weekly Dakotian*, July 30, 1864, 1; "The Women Clerks at Washington," *Springfield Weekly Republican*, Apr. 17, 1869, 2; "Discharges from the Departments," *Daily Morning Chronicle*, Aug. 11, 1868, 2; "Washington," *The Daily Age*, May 29, 1866, 1. For congressional examples, see, for example, statement of Mr. Farnsworth, Mr. Negley, and Mr. Kelly, *Congressional Globe*, 41st Cong., 2nd sess. 1412–17, 1414–16 (Feb. 18, 1870).

58. Skocpol, *Protecting Soldiers and Mothers*, 83.

59. Even though women were disenfranchised, they could still be negatively affected by the political winds. See File of M. Reddick, "Application and Recommendations," Box 479 (Rec–Red), NA-Tr. See also chapter 7.

60. File of Sallie Bridges, "Application and Recommendations," Box 59 (Bre–Bri), NA-Tr. Bridges does not appear to have been successful. See also File of Mary F. Bennett, "Application and Recommendations," Box 38 (Ben–Ben), NA-Tr. Bennett

received a job in 1864. See also File of Emily C. Brent, "Application and Recommendations," Box 59 (Bre–Bri), NA-Tr; File of Annie E. Byus, "Application and Recommendations," Box 81 (Byr–Cal), NA-Tr; File of Fannie Lockwood, "Application and Recommendations," Box 352 (Loc–Log), NA-Tr; File of Rebecca Lyon, "Application and Recommendations," NA-Tr; File of Mary Locke, "Application and Recommendations," Box 352 (Loc–Log), NA-Tr; File of Laura E. Bend, "Application and Recommendations," Box 37 (Bem–Ben), NA-Tr; File of Emily C. Benedict, "Application and Recommendations," Box 37 (Bem–Ben), NA-Tr; File of Sophia B. Gay, "Application and Recommendations," Box 216 (Gas–Gaz), NA-Tr; File of Hattie Reynolds, "Application and Recommendations," Box 495 (Rey–Rhy), NA-Tr; File of Caroline L. Holmes, "Application and Recommendations," Box 276 (Hol–Hol), NA-Tr; File of Emma C. McDevitt, "Application and Recommendations," Box 382 (McC–McD), NA-Tr.

61. See File of Miss Sallie Abrams, "Application and Recommendations," Box 1 (Aa–Ab), NA-Tr.

62. File of Ada B. Bridges, "Application and Recommendations," Box 59 (Bre–Bri), NA-Tr.

63. See File of Lettia Arnold, "Application and Recommendations," Box 13 (Arm–Arr), NA-Tr; File of Lucy M. Baily, "Correspondence Relating to the Hiring of Clerks," Box 4, NA-WD; File of E. B. Ranney, "Application and Recommendations," Box 476 (Ran–Rat), NA-Tr; File of Caroline Ramsey, "Application and Recommendations," Box 475 (Ram–Ram), NA-Tr; File of Fannie Lockwood, "Application and Recommendations," Box 352 (Loc–Log), NA-Tr; File of Catherine Lloyd, "Application and Recommendations," Box 351 (Lit–Loc), NA-Tr; File of T. Talcott, "Application and Recommendations," Box 506 (Syp–Tal), NA-Tr; File of Sophia Gay, "Application and Recommendations," Box 216 (Gas–Gaz), NA-Tr; File of Annie Young, "Application and Recommendations," Box 645 (Yir–You), NA-Tr.

64. File of Margaret C. Atkinson, "Application and Recommendations," Box 15 (Ash–Aug), NA-Tr.

65. Leasher, "Adams and the Household Department," 117. The representative was also the Chairman of the Committee on Agriculture of the House of Representatives.

66. Leasher, *Letter from Washington*.

67. A woman's qualifications did become increasingly important as the decade progressed, alongside a general civil service reform that began in the late 1860s. The Patent Office, for example, began to administer competitive examinations for positions. "Washington," *The Leavenworth Bulletin*, July 2, 1869, 1.

68. Millikan, "Wards of the Nation," 65.

69. U.S. Congress, *Management of the Government Hospital for the Insane* (1876), 78–79, 188.

70. See, for example, File of Emily W. Abbott, "Application and Recommendations," Box 1 (Aa–Ab), NA-Tr; File of Mrs. E. A. Jacobs, "Application and Recommendations," NA-Tr; File of Jane F. James, "Application and Recommendations," NA-Tr; File of Lucy M. Bailey, "Correspondence Relating to the Hiring of Clerks," Box 4, NA-WD; File of Hattie A. Cromwell, "Correspondence Relating to the Hiring of Clerks," Box 4,

NA-WD; File of Caroline L. Holmes, "Application and Recommendations," Box 276 (Hol–Hol), NA-Tr; File of Annie Haliday, "Correspondence Relating to the Hiring of Clerks," Box 4, NA-WD; File of Lillie Madison "Application and Recommendations," Box 362 (Mac–Maf), NA-Tr; File of Louisa C. Holman, "Application and Recommendations," Box 276, (Hol–Hol), NA-Tr.

71. See File of Adelaide D. Adams, "Application and Recommendations," Box 2 (Acc–Ada), NA-Tr; File of Jennie S. Abbott, "Application and Recommendations," Box 1 (Aa–Ab), NA-Tr; File of Rebecca J. Abbott, "Application and Recommendations," Box 1 (Aa–Ab), NA-Tr; File of Annie Young, "Application and Recommendations," Box 645 (Yir–You), NA-Tr; File of Eve Benton, "Application and Recommendations," Box 38 (Ben–Ben), NA-Tr; File of Annie Young, "Application and Recommendations," Box 645 (Yir–You), NA-Tr; File of Sarah B. Berry, "Application and Recommendations," Box 39 (Ben–Ben), NA-Tr; File of Margaret C. Atkinson, "Application and Recommendations," Box 15 (Ash–Aug), NA-Tr; File of Sophia Gay, "Application and Recommendations," Box 216 (Gas–Gaz), NA-Tr; File of Kate Littig, "Application and Recommendations," Box 350 (Lin–Lit), NA-Tr.

72. As is discussed in chapter 3, many women didn't know what they were applying to do, and so struggled with what skills they should tout. N. J. Brent, for example, wrote: "Vouching my eligibility to office, I doubt not but this would depend wholly upon the nature of the duties to be performed. In the matter of penmanship, I have but little to say in my favor—this letter, in all respects, being equal to my average ability in this special art. But, in the event of my application meeting with favor, I am lead to believe that there are other, and less important departments of labor within the gift of the Secretary which might be filled with advantage to myself, and entire satisfaction to my employers" (she did earn a job). N. J. Brent, "Application and Recommendations," Box 59 (Bre–Bri), NA-Tr.

73. She did not receive a job. File of Helen Ivey, "Application and Recommendations," NA-Tr.

74. File of Laura Redden, "Application and Recommendations," Box 479 (Rea–Red), NA-Tr. Redden did receive a job. She had four letters of recommendation, including one from an Ohio Congressman and had lost two brothers in war.

75. She did not receive a job. File of Jane F. James, "Application and Recommendations," NA-Tr.

76. Although this recommender, the mother of a girl who was a student at the school at which Isams taught, wrote two letters on Isams's behalf, she did not receive a job. File of Isams, "Correspondence Relating to the Hiring of Clerks," Box 4, NA-WD. The file is marked "not a war claim," and the Quartermaster's Office hired only women who had lost male support in the war.

77. Although women were not allowed to be soldiers, Deanne Blanton and Lauren M. Cook uncovered 250 women soldiers in the Union and Confederate Armies and believe that there were many more. Blanton and Cook, *They Fought Like Demons*.

78. File of Jane F. Adams, "Application and Recommendations," Box 2 (Acc–Ada), NA-Tr. She did not receive a job. See also File of Miss E. M. Zook, "Correspondence Relating to the Hiring of Clerks," Box 4, NA-WD; File of Judith Plummer, "Correspondence Relating to the Hiring of Clerks," Box 4, NA-WD; File of Ada B. Bridges, "Application and Recommendations," Box 59 (Bre–Bri), NA-Tr; File of Ann Byus, "Application and Recommendations," Box 81 (Byr–Cal), NA-Tr; File of Hester A. Peters, "Application and Recommendations," Box 455 (Per–Pet), NA-Tr; File of E. Jane Gay, "Correspondence Relating to the Hiring of Clerks," Box 4, NA-WD; Serene Littiger, "Application and Recommendations," Box 350 (Lin–Lit), NA-Tr.

79. File of Jane F. James, "Application and Recommendations," NA-Tr.

80. File of S. L. Atkinson, "Application and Recommendations," Box 15 (Ash–Aug), NA-Tr. Atkinson did receive a job, though she also had male relatives in war.

81. "The Women Clerks at Washington," *Springfield Weekly Republican*, Apr. 17, 1869, 2. This may have been Miss Susan Wright, who worked in the Treasury Department in 1863 and 1865. *Federal Register*, 1863, 1865.

82. This was echoed in another of Gay's letters. File of Sophia B. Gay, "Application and Recommendations," Box 216 (Gas–Gaz), NA-Tr.

83. Other female applicants expressed similar sentiments. See File of Mary F. Shockley, "Application and Recommendations," Box 526 (Shi–Sho), NA-Tr.

84. File of Sophia B. Gay, "Application and Recommendations," Box 216 (Gas–Gaz), NA-Tr.

85. Masur, *Example for All the Land*, 180. Mocking of Walker was not a new practice for the press. See "Miss Mary Walker," *Macon Daily Telegraph*, Feb. 24, 1866, 6; "Items," *Boston Daily Journal*, June 11, 1866, 2. Walker was also involved in the Universal Franchise Association, which earlier that year was advocating for the vote for African Americans and women. See "City Intelligence," *Daily Morning Chronicle*, Jan. 30, 1869, 4; "City Intelligence," *Daily Morning Chronicle*, Feb. 12, 1869, 4. Walker was also involved in dress reform. See "City Intelligence," *Daily Morning Chronicle*, Apr. 30, 1869, 4. For more on Walker, see Leonard, *Yankee Women*, ch. 3; Clinton and Silber, *Battle Scars*, in "Mary Walker, Mary Surratt, and Some thoughts on Gender in the Civil War," ed. Elizabeth D. Leonard, ch. 6; Furgurson, *Freedom Rising*, 238–39.

86. Articles on Walker's 1869 attempt to obtain government employment include: "Letter from Washington," *Sun*, May 11, 1869, 4; "Washington," *Sun*, May 12, 1869; "Our Folks and Other Folks," *Leavenworth Evening Bulletin*, May 19, 1869, 2; "City Intelligence," *Daily Morning Chronicle*, May 21, 1869, 4; "Washington," *New York Herald*, May 21, 1869, 10; "City Intelligence," *Daily Morning Chronicle*, May 22, 1869, 4; "By Telegraph from Washington," *Boston Daily Journal*, May 25, 1869, 4; "Freezing Out a Candidate," *Daily Evening Bulletin*, June 4, 1869, 2; "Mary Walker," *Flake's Bulletin*, June 5, 1869, 6; "Mrs. Dr. Mary Walker," *Cincinnati Commercial Tribune*, June 7, 1869, 4; "Letter from Washington City," *Galveston Tri-Weekly News*, June 21, 1869, 3; "Letter from Washington City," *Galveston Tri-Weekly News*, June 23, 1869, 2; "The Departments," *Daily Morning Chronicle*, July 2, 1869, 4; "The City," *The Critic*, July 14, 1869, 2; "[Dr. Maj.

Mary Walker, Washington]," *Daily State Gazette*, July 23, 1869, 2; "Personal," *Hartford Daily Courant*, July 27, 1869, 2.

87. "Letter from Washington," *Sun*, May 11, 1869, 4; "Mary Walker," *Flake's Bulletin*, June 5, 1869, 6.

88. "Our Folks and Other Folks," *Leavenworth Evening Bulletin*, May 19, 1869, 2.

89. "Washington," *Sun*, May 12, 1869.

90. "By Telegraph from Washington," *Boston Daily Journal*, May 25, 1869, 4.

91. "Washington," *New York Herald*, May 21, 1869, 10.

92. "City Intelligence," *Daily Morning Chronicle*, Mar. 23, 1868, 4.

93. His main argument against applying to clerical jobs, however, does not apply to women. The author stresses the folly of young men quitting good jobs to come to Washington, D.C. Women typically did not have access to the "situations from which they can obtain a fair salary," which the article's author insists men keep in lieu of attempting government employment.

94. Women were aware of the competition they faced. See File of Annie M. T. Adams, "Application and Recommendations," Box 2 (Acc–Ada), NA-Tr; File of E. L. Cady, "Application and Recommendations," Box 81 (Byr–Cal), NA-Tr.

95. "City Intelligence," *Daily Morning Chronicle*, Mar. 23, 1868, 4.

96. "The Female Clerks," *Evening Star*, Oct. 14, 1870, 1. See also "City Intelligence," *Daily Morning Chronicle*, Feb. 17, 1868, 4; "Washington News and Gossip," *Evening Star*, Feb. 15, 1868, 1; "By Telegraph from Washington," *Boston Daily Journal*, Mar. 10, 1869, 4; "Washington Items," *Troy Weekly Times*, Dec. 15, 1866, 3.

97. "Local News," *Evening Star*, Nov. 16, 1867, 3. The article continued that the man made the girl his mistress in Georgetown, but then tired of her. When he abandoned her, she became a prostitute. Another young man tried to help her, but she did not accept his assistance until, on her deathbed, she gave him the address of her father so he could collect her body.

98. Although the story is likely exaggerated, it is not entirely implausible. At least one man was arrested for "blackmailing young ladies, carrying on a so-called 'big game' in attempting to procure situations for females." See "City Intelligence," *Daily Morning Chronicle*, Dec. 6, 1869, 4; "City Intelligence," *Daily Morning Chronicle*, Dec. 7, 1869, 4.

99. File of N. J. Brent, "Application and Recommendations," Box 59 (Bre–Bri), NA-Tr. She did receive the job.

100. File of B. W. Quince, "Application and Recommendations," Box 473 (Que–Rad), NA-Tr. Quince did get a job.

101. "City Intelligence," *Daily Morning Chronicle*, Aug. 12, 1867, 1.

102. Of the 64 successful applications, it took 11 women over 2 years, 9 women 1–2 years, 5 women 6 months–1 year, 3 women 4–6 months, 8 women 1–3 months, and 10 women less than 1 month. The time from application to appointment for 18 women could not be determined.

103. I have identified over thirty women who applied to multiple departments.

104. Gay began to apply to the War Department in July 1863. File of E. Jane Gay, "Correspondence Relating to the Hiring of Clerks," Box 4, NA-WD. Gay applied to the

Patent and Pension Offices in 1865. Graf, *The Papers of Andrew Johnson*, vol. 7: 1864–1865, 546 (letter from C. M. Melville to Andrew Johnson soliciting his assistance for Gay's applications). Gay finally appeared on the federal payroll in the 1869 *Federal Register* in the Post Office Department. *Federal Register*, 1869; 1871; 1870 Census, Washington, D.C., 4WD (showing Gay working in Post Office).

105. File of Mary E. Stabler, "Correspondence Relating to the Hiring of Clerks," Box 4, NA-WD.

106. File of M. K. Guthrie, "Correspondence Relating to the Hiring of Clerks," Box 4, NA-WD. Guthrie obtained a job in the War Department that year.

107. File of Fannie E. Gause, "Application and Recommendations," Box 216 (Gas–Gar), NA-Tr.

108. File of Mary Shockley, "Application and Recommendations," Box 526 (Shi–Sho), NA-Tr.

109. *Federal Register*, 1869. File of Mary F. Shockley, "Application and Recommendations," Box 526 (Shi–Sho), NA-Tr.

110. Secretary of the Treasury Hugh McCulloch was not appreciative of current employees—male or female—telling applicants about possible openings. "The Departments," *Daily Morning Chronicle*, Feb. 13, 1867, 1.

111. Women also used the news of other women being hired as encouragement. See File of J. Gaylord, "Application and Recommendations," Box 216 (Gas–Gar), NA-Tr.

112. File of Laura C. Redden, "Application and Recommendations," Box 479 (Rea–Red), NA-Tr.

113. File of Maria E. Baker, "Correspondence Relating to the Hiring of Clerks," Box 4, NA-WD; File of Mary F. Poor, "Correspondence Relating to the Hiring of Clerks," Box 4, NA-WD (she did not receive a job).

114. File of M. Ream, "Application and Recommendations," Box 479 (Rea–Red), NA-Tr.

115. File of Mary Sloan, "Application and Recommendations," Box 531 (Sla–Slo), NA-Tr.

116. File of Tenie Sloan, "Application and Recommendations," Box 531 (Slo–Slo), NA-Tr. Sloan did receive a job by March 1869.

117. Eleanor J. Ketchum to Benjamin Butler, March 16, 1869 from Box 48 of the Benjamin Butler Papers; Masur, "Patronage and Protest," 1056; Masur, *Example for All the Land*, 158–59.

118. "The City," *The Critic*, May 24, 1870, 3

119. "Washington News and Gossip," *Evening Star*, Mar. 27, 1868, 1.

120. Ibid., Mar. 28, 1868, 1.

121. "Washington," *The Farmers' Cabinet*, May 18, 1871, 2; see also "Washington Pressure for Positions in the Departments," *Cincinnati Commercial*, May 3, 1871, 1; "Washington News," *Jamestown Journal*, May 12, 1871, 1; "Washington Reported," *Pittsfield Sun*, May 11, 1871, 3; "Notes," *Albany Evening Journal*, May 5, 1871, 2. Several of the papers stressed that the women applying had strong recommendations from respectable men in high positions.

122. She did not receive a job. File of D. Daily, "Correspondence Relating to the Hiring of Clerks," Box 4, NA-WD; File of Mary Locke, "Application and Recommendations," Box 352 (Loc–Log), NA-Tr (did not receive a job); File of Annie Gaston, "Application and Recommendations," Box 216 (Gas–Gaz), NA-Tr (did not receive job); File K. Cahill, "Application and Recommendations," Box 81 (Byr–Cal), NA-Tr (obtained a job in the Treasury). See also File of Margaret Ackerman, "Application and Recommendations," Box 2 (Acc–Ada), NA-Tr.

123. Faulkner, *Women's Radical Reconstruction*, 15–16, 85, 96.

124. Diary of Julia A. Wilbur, Sept. 6, 1868–Mar. 27, 1869.

125. Ibid.; March 12, 1869.

126. Ibid.; March 23, 29, 1869.

127. Diary of Julia A. Wilbur, Mar. 30, 1869–May 14, 1870; Apr. 7, 8, 9, 12, 19, 20, 1869.

128. Julia A. Wilbur, Diary of Julia A. Wilbur, Mar. 30, 1869–May 14, 1870; Apr. 22, 26, 1869.

129. Diary of Julia A. Wilbur, Mar. 30, 1869–May 14, 1870; Apr. 27–30, 1869.

130. Ibid., May 1, 1869.

131. Ibid., May 10, 12, 13, 1869.

132. Ibid., May 14, 1869.

133. Ibid., May 17, 1869.

134. Ibid., July 1–2, 1869; 1869; *Federal Register*, 1871.

135. "Experiences of a Bureau Officer," *Cincinnati Daily Gazette*, May 17, 1871, 4.

136. Ibid.

137. Martin, *Behind the Scenes*, 468–69. A subsequent Department of Agriculture secretary felt the same way. In December 1897, Secretary of Agriculture Wilson stated, "Finding places for deserving women on the request of Senators who righteously plead their cause is the greatest difficulty I meet with." Baker, "Women in the U.S. Department of Agriculture," 190. One newspaper had little sympathy for the supervisors or understanding of the situations faced by the applicants: "These gentlemen should remember that it is their predestined fate to be bored by place-hunters, and to our notion it is much less annoying to be bothered by a pretty, blooming woman, than by a great rough, ugly bearded man." "Guillotoning [*sic*] the Ladies," *Flake's Bulletin*, Apr. 7, 1869, 4.

138. "Women's Work in the Departments," *Daily Morning Chronicle*, Aug. 17, 1865, 2.

Chapter Three

1. "Late Local News [Second Edition]," *Evening Star*, Dec. 12, 1862, 2.

2. File of S. F. Wainwright, "Correspondence Relating to the Hiring of Clerks," Box 4, NA-WD.

3. Ibid.

4. 1870 Census, Washington, D.C., 1 WD. In 1870, her children were Richard (age twenty), Dallis (age seventeen), and Virginia (age fourteen). Wainwright would have been approximately thirty-nine years old in 1864.

5. *Federal Register* 1863; "List of Clerks, Messengers, and Laborers Employed in the Office of the QMG," NA-WD; Martin, *Behind the Scenes*, 469–70.

6. File of S. F. Wainwright, "Correspondence Relating to the Hiring of Clerks," Box 4, NA-WD.

7. Ibid.

8. Wainwright first appears in the *Federal Register* in 1863 at a salary of $600. She appears under "Ladies Employed in the Quartermaster General's Office." In the 1865, 1867, 1869, and 1871 *Federal Registers*, she is listed with men under "Clerks."

9. See, for example, U.S. Department of the Interior, *Annual Report of Secretary of Interior, 1869*, 24; U.S. Congress, Joint Select Committee on Retrenchment. *Civil Service of the United States*; Jenckes, *Speech of Hon. Thomas A. Jenckes*; Van Riper, *History of the United States Civil Service*, 65–68.

10. Cobble, *The Other Women's Movement*, 3, 7–8.

11. "The Departments," *Daily Morning Chronicle*, Nov. 30, 1869, 1.

12. For an examination of these issues in a later period in private industry, see, for example, Tentler, *Wage-Earning Women*, ch. 2; Kwolek-Folland, *Engendering Business*, ch. 4; Cobble, *The Other Women's Movement*.

13. File of Julia Richards, "Application and Recommendations," Box 487 (Ric), NA-Tr. Of the 273 women whose files I examined, over fifty files contained a statement to the effect that the applicant sought a "woman's" job. In her study of women workers at a radio-manufacturing plant in Philadelphia in the early 1900s, Patricia Cooper also found women placing importance on the idea that they were doing "women's" jobs. See Baron, *Work Engendered*, ch. 13, in "The Faces of Gender: Sex Segregation and Work Relations at Philco, 1928–1938," ed. Patricia Cooper.

14. File of Julia Richards, "Application and Recommendations," Box 487 (Ric), NA-Tr. See also File of Rachel M. Yoe, "Correspondence Relating to the Hiring of Clerks," Box 4, NA-WD; File of Sarah Cahill, "Application and Recommendations," Box 81 (Byr–Cal), NA-Tr; File of Carrie Montgomery, "Correspondence Relating to the Hiring of Clerks," Box 4, NA-WD; File of M. A. Locke, "Application and Recommendations," Box 352 (Loc–Log), NA-Tr.

15. See File of Mrs. Holmes, "Application and Recommendations," Box 276 (Hol–Hol), NA-Tr; File of M. K. Guthrie, "Correspondence Relating to the Hiring of Clerks," Box 4, NA-WD; File of Louisa C. Holman, "Application and Recommendations," Box 276 (Hol–Hol), NA-Tr; File of Ellen M. Rhodes, "Application and Recommendations," Box 495 (Rey–Rhy), NA-Tr; File of Lillie Madison, "Application and Recommendations," Box 362 (Mac–Maf), NA-Tr; File of Anna Rhodes, "Application and Recommendations," Box 495 (Rey–Rhy), NA-Tr; File of J. Sleigh, "Application and Recommendations," Box 531 (Slo–Slo), NA-Tr.

16. See File of Laura C. Redden, "Application and Recommendations," Box 479 (Rea–Red), NA-Tr; File of Mary F. Poor, "Correspondence Relating to the Hiring of Clerks," Box 4, NA-WD; File of Mary Ream, "Application and Recommendations," Box 479 (Rea–Red), NA-Tr; File of Emma Ashdowns, "Application and

Recommendations," Box 15 (Ash–Aug), NA-Tr; File of E. L. Cady, "Application and Recommendations," Box 81 (Byr–Cal), NA-Tr.

17. For the importance of class to female workforce applicants, see, for example, Aron, *Ladies and Gentlemen*, 9, 56–57; Srole, *Transcribing Class*, 44.

18. See File of Emeline M. Richardson, "Application and Recommendations," Box 487 (Ric), NA-Tr; File of Mary E. Bennett, "Application and Recommendations," Box 38 (Ben–Ben), NA-Tr; File of E. S. Hassler, "Correspondence Relating to the Hiring of Clerks," Box 4, NA-WD; File of Maggie Bremmer, "Application and Recommendations," Box 58 (Bra–Bre), NA-Tr; File of Caroline Roderique, "Correspondence Relating to the Hiring of Clerks," Box 4, NA-WD; File of Mary F. Holman, "Application and Recommendations," Box 276 (Hol–Hol), NA-Tr; File of Maggie Jackson, "Application and Recommendations," NA-Tr; File of Lucy O. Marsh, "Correspondence Relating to the Hiring of Clerks," Box 4, NA-WD; File of M. M. Lockwood, "Application and Recommendations," Box 352 (Loc–Log), NA-Tr; File of Anna Benson, "Application and Recommendations," Box 38 (Ben–Ben), NA-Tr; File of Emma W. Abbott, "Application and Recommendations," Box 1 (Aa–Ab), NA-Tr; File of Sallie Bridges, "Application and Recommendations," Box 59 (Bre–Bri), NA-Tr; File of Caroline Ramsey, "Application and Recommendations," Box 475 (Ram–Ram), NA-Tr.

19. This fictional divide between male and female labor was neither new nor confined to Washington, D.C., and government work. See, for example, Stansell, *City of Women*, 132.

20. "Our Washington Letter: the Storehouse of the Agricultural Department," *Detroit Advertiser and Tribune*, Feb. 1, 1864, 1 (in Leasher, *Letter from Washington*, 59–62); "Deferred Local Articles," *Evening Star*, Nov. 11, 1862, 4. At the end of the 1860s, the Department of Agriculture started employing men instead of women to do this job, and the practice was mocked because sewing seed bags was seen as not being "masculine." "Women Clerks in the Executive Departments at Washington," *The Revolution*, Apr. 16, 1868, 230–31. See also U.S. Department of Agriculture, *Annual Report of Commissioner of Agriculture, 1867*, 17.

21. Ames, *Ten Years*, 317–18.

22. Rockman, *Scraping By*, 102.

23. "The Departments," *Daily Constitutional Union*, Sept. 29, 1869, 1; Ames, *Ten Years*, 527–29. The GPO was not alone in employing women in the printing industry. Stansell, *City of Women*, 142.

24. "I did not inform her that she looked as if she soon would be," Ames remarked to her readers. Ames, *Ten Years*, 528.

25. Aron, *Ladies and Gentlemen*, 86–91 (arguing that since different supervisors adopted different protocol for the use of machines in their bureaus and divisions, mechanization did not lead to feminization (or vice versa) in federal office work in the nineteenth century).

26. Ames, *Ten Years*, 319–20.

27. "Sketches in Washington: The Government Printing Office," *Detroit Advertiser and Tribune*, Feb. 22, 1864, 4 (in Leasher, *Letter from Washington*, 80–82); "City Intelligence," *Daily Morning Chronicle*, Nov. 14, 1865, 4.

28. Townsend, *Washington, Outside and Inside,* 249.

29. Prandoni, "St Elizabeths," 5; U.S. Congress, House of Representatives. *The Management of the Government Hospital for the Insane,* 3 (testimony of Theodore F. Wilson who was an attendant in 1864, and complained, "There was a great deal of work which I had never been used to, such as scrubbing"). Regarding pay, in 1871, for example, female attendants earned between $8 and $12 per month while men earned $13 to $20 per month.

30. Aron, *Ladies and Gentlemen,* 71.

31. In 1867, 514 women worked for the Treasury Department as follows: Ladies, 133; Copyists, 87; Copyists/Counters, 136; Clerks, 13; Female Clerks, 126; Messengers, 9; Laborers, 9, Superintendent, 1 (she was the superintendent of the recording division and earned as much as the women she supervised).

32. "The Government and Wages of Women," *Cincinnati Commercial Tribune,* June 16, 1870, 4.

33. *Congressional Globe,* 40th Cong., 3rd sess. 1773–1780 (March 2, 1869).

34. See "The Departments," *Daily Morning Chronicle,* Nov. 12, 1869, 2; "The Departments," *Daily Morning Chronicle,* Nov. 30, 1869, 1.

35. For example, see File of M. A. Stetson, "Correspondence Relating to the Hiring of Clerks," Box 4, NA-WD.

36. Aron, *Ladies and Gentlemen,* 67.

37. "The Female Clerks," *Evening Star,* Oct. 14, 1870, 1.

38. "Consolidated Report of the Time and Conduct of the Copyists," Box 2, NA-WD, Dec. 1866.

39. Ames, *Ten Years,* 358 (describes women in the War Department as "copying, recording, and registering letters of the department"). Women appear as "copyists" in the *Federal Register* in the named departments.

40. Diary of Julia A. Wilbur, Mar. 30, 1869–May 14, 1870; Jan. 3, 5, 6, 7; July 2, 19, 20, 22; Aug. 9; Sept. 20, 30; Oct. 1, 4, 14; Dec. 14, 1870.

41. Diary of Julia A. Wilbur, May 5, 1871–Apr. 21, 1872; Oct. 9; Dec. 14, 1871.

42. Diary of Julia A. Wilbur, Mar. 30, 1869–May 14, 1870; Jan. 8; Feb. 1, 1870.

43. Ames, *Ten Years,* 327.

44. "The Currency," *New York Tribune,* Sept. 4, 1867, 2 (emphasis in original).

45. Ames, *Ten Years,* 322–23.

46. "The Currency," *New York Tribune,* Sept. 4, 1867, 2. Ames informed her readers that every legal note that the U.S. had issued from the beginning of the war until the time of her writing had passed through the hands of these women, and calculated that as of July 1872, that amounted to "about two thousand and twenty-three million dollars." Ames, *Ten Years,* 328.

47. "The Women Clerks at Washington," *Evening Bulletin,* Apr. 17, 1867, 5; "The Women Clerks at Washington," *Springfield Weekly Republican,* Apr. 17, 1869, 2.

48. U.S. Department of the Treasury, *Report of the Secretary of the Treasury . . . 1868,* 253.

49. *Congressional Globe,* 40th Cong., 3rd sess. 1773–1780, 1777 (Mar. 2, 1869).

50. *Congressional Globe*, 41st Cong. 2nd sess., pt. 4, 3449–52 (May 13, 1870). (Senate discussion on H.R. no. 974.)

51. "The Departments," *Daily Morning Chronicle*, Nov. 11, 1869, 1; "Telegraph News from Washington," *The Sun*, Nov. 10, 1869, 1. See also "By Telegraph, from Washington," *Boston Daily Journal*, Nov. 10, 1869, 4; "Washington," *Cincinnati Commercial*, Nov. 10, 1869, 1; Ames, *Ten Years*, 327.

52. "The Departments," *Daily Morning Chronicle*, Nov. 12, 1869, 2.

53. Ibid., Nov. 23, 1869, 1.

54. Ames, *Ten Years*, 351.

55. "Washington," *New York Daily Tribune*, Oct. 26, 1869, 1; Ames, *Ten Years*, 354.

56. Ames, *Ten Years*, 352.

57. "Department News," *Daily Morning Chronicle*, July 21, 1869, 1.

58. Diary of Julia A. Wilbur, Sept. 6, 1868–Mar. 27, 1869; Jan. 22, 1869.

59. "Departmental," *Daily Morning Chronicle*, Mar. 31, 1870, 1.

60. "Women in the U. S. Treasury," *Wheeling Sunday Register*, Sept. 3, 1893, 11.

61. Ames, *Ten Years*, 352–54; "Washington," *New York Daily Tribune*, Oct. 26, 1869, 1.

62. *Congressional Globe*, 40th Cong., 3rd sess. 1773–1780, 1775 (Mar. 2, 1869).

63. Aron, *Ladies and Gentlemen*, 92.

64. "City Intelligence," *Daily Morning Chronicle*, May 22, 1867, 4; "Miscellany. Down among the Dead Letters," *Jamestown Journal*, Jan. 21, 1870, 2.

65. "The Dead Letter Office," *Daily Morning Chronicle*, July 21, 1869, 4; U.S. Post Office Department, *Annual Report of Postmaster General, 1868*.

66. That year the office was comprised of eight women and twenty-five men, all earning $1,000 per year. *Federal Register*, 1871.

67. Ames, *Ten Years*, 366.

68. Ibid., 360–61.

69. *Bohn's Hand-Book of Washington, D.C.*, 89.

70. Ames, *Ten Years*, 327.

71. Leasher, *Letter from Washington*, 18. Note, however, that she is not listed in the *Federal Register* until 1867.

72. Martin, *Behind the Scenes*; Ames, *Ten Years*, 367.

73. Ames, *Ten Years*, 367. T. Drexler is listed in the 1869 and 1871 *Federal Register* for the Agriculture Department under "Copyists and Attendants in Museum." In the 1870 Census, she lists her profession as "taxidermist." 1870 Census, Washington, D.C., 7 WD; "Local News," *Evening Star*, Jan. 9, 1867, 3.

74. "About Women," *The Revolution*, Aug. 18, 1870, 10. See also *Congressional Globe*, 41st Cong., 2nd sess., 1412–17, 1416 (Feb. 18, 1870); *Federal Register*, 1871.

75. Martin, *Behind the Scenes*, 472; "Women as Government Clerks," *New York Times*, Feb. 18, 1869, 2; "Personal," *Cincinnati Commercial Tribune*, Feb. 22, 1869, 1.

76. "Women as Government Clerks," *New York Times*, Feb. 18, 1869, 2; "Women Clerks in the Executive Departments at Washington," *The Revolution*, Apr. 16, 1868, 230–31. This "merely mechanical" work also gave men the opportunity to steal. In 1867, police arrested Asa D. Wood, a first-class clerk in the Dead Letter office, "on

the charge of purloining money from letters." "Local News," *Evening Star*, July 14, 1867, 4.

77. "The Departments," *Daily Morning Chronicle*, May 7, 1870, 1. "From Washington," *The Revolution*, Oct. 27, 1870, 262.

78. Historian Brian P. Luskey has found this to be an old argument. Luskey, *On the Make*, 29 (citing a 1740 article from the *Boston Gazette*).

79. *Congressional Globe*, 41st Cong. 2nd sess., pt. 4, 3449–52 (13 May 1870). (Senate discussion on H.R. no. 974). See also "Local Intelligence," *Daily Constitutional Union* [Second Edition], Feb. 19, 1866, 2; "Washington Letter," *The Revolution*, May 21, 1868, 309–10.

80. U.S. Department of the Treasury, *Report of the Secretary of the Treasury . . . 1865*, 138, 145–46.

81. But see "Washington," *The Revolution*, Apr. 16, 1868, 226 (arguing that men's praise could be patronizing).

82. U.S. Department of the Treasury, *Report of the Secretary of the Treasury . . . 1864*, 109.

83. U.S. Department of the Treasury, *Report of the Secretary of the Treasury . . . 1865*, 145–46.

84. U.S. Department of the Treasury, *Report of the Secretary of the Treasury . . . 1866*, 173. Spinner repeated this assertion in 1868. U.S. Department of the Treasury, *Report of the Secretary of the Treasury . . . 1868*, 253.

85. Treasurer F. E. Spinner, who was incensed at the inadequacy of pay of his male clerks, began to push for the reorganization of his office in 1866. He listed out how many employees he needed, in what positions, and how much they should be paid. Congress did not take Spinner's advice, and he continued to push for the reorganization. In 1866, he requested an overhaul that would provide him with 191 employees—102 women and 89 men (53.4 percent female staff) with women receiving a salary capped at $1,100. U.S. Department of the Treasury, *Report of the Secretary of the Treasury . . . 1866*, 173. In 1868, he asked for 226 employees—119 women and 107 men (52.7 percent female) with women receiving a salary capped at $1,200. U.S. Department of the Treasury, *Report of the Secretary of the Treasury . . . 1868*, 253. In 1869, Spinner recommended that his office be staffed with 238 employees—114 men and 124 women (52.1 percent female), with women having a salary capped at $1,200. U.S. Department of the Treasury, *Report of the Secretary of the Treasury . . . 1869*, 287. In 1870, he recognized Congress's new legislation allowing for women to be appointed to the graded class of clerkships so it is unclear how many total women and men he anticipated. He suggested 180 employees (gender not specified) and 64 specifically female, noting that women would be included in the 180 figure. U.S. Department of the Treasury, *Report of the Secretary of the Treasury . . . 1870*, 238.

86. U.S. Department of the Treasury, *Report of the Secretary of the Treasury . . . 1868*, 404.

87. Ibid., 131.

88. Martin, *Behind the Scenes*, 477. See also "Washington," *New York Daily Tribune*, Oct. 26, 1869, 1; Ames, *Ten Years*, 351, "Women as Government Clerks," *The Revolution*, Jan. 13, 1870, 28.

89. U.S. Department of the Treasury, *Report of the Secretary of the Treasury . . . 1868*, 253.

90. U.S. Department of the Treasury, *Report of the Secretary of the Treasury . . . 1869*, 286.

91. "The Female Clerks," *Evening Star*, Oct. 14, 1870, 1.

92. U.S. Congress, Joint Select Committee on Retrenchment. *Civil Service of the United States*, Appendix C, Reply of N. Sargent (Commissioner of Customs).

93. Ibid., Reply of J. P. Murphy (Assessor 29th District, New York). In an 1891 interview, Treasurer Spinner asserted that women employees had "failings." "She talks too much, often talking without saying anything," he claimed, adding, "Then she has little regard for punctuality. "General Spinner," *Women's Journal*, Jan. 10, 1891, 16–17.

94. U.S. Department of the Treasury, *Report of the Secretary of the Treasury . . . 1865*, 98.

95. U.S. Department of the Treasury, *Report of the Secretary of the Treasury . . . 1866*, 173–74. This was echoed in later reports. See, for example, U.S. Department of the Treasury, *Report of the Secretary of the Treasury . . . 1869*, 286–87.

96. U.S. Department of the Treasury, *Report of the Secretary of the Treasury . . . 1868*, 252.

97. For an examination of repetitive and routine work for women in manufacturing in the early twentieth century, see chapter 2 of Tentler, *Wage-Earning Women* (esp. pages 31–32).

98. "Mr. Jenckes' Speech on the Workforce Bill," *Daily Morning Chronicle*, Feb. 4, 1867, 1.

99. "Washington Letter," *The Revolution*, July 2, 1868, 411. For more on advancement in the workforce see Aron, *Ladies and Gentlemen*, 120–28. Aron's evidence for women's promotions is all dated from the 1870s and later.

100. 1860 Census, Washington, D.C., 2 WD; 1870 Census, Washington, D.C., 2 WD; *Federal Register*, 1863, 1867.

101. "Women in the Treasury Department," *The Woman's Journal*, July 23, 1892.

102. File of R. Biggs, "Application and Recommendations," Box 37 (Bem–Ben); NA-Tr; *Federal Register* 1869; 1870 Census, Washington, D.C., 1 WD. Mary Linden and Margaret James (both white women) were promoted from laborer to messenger sometime between 1867 and 1869. *Federal Register* 1869. Polly Taylor, Ella Sampson, Kate Swann, and Martha Trimble advanced from laborers to messengers under Spinner between 1869 and 1871. *Federal Register*, 1869, 1871. Miss M. C. E. Kearney, Lucy A. Rallo, and Kate M. Wheat advanced from laborer to clerk (Kearney between 1867 and 1869 and Rallo and Wheat between 1869 and 1871). *Federal Register*, 1867, 1869, 1871.

103. *Federal Register*, 1865, 1867, 1869.

104. The female supervisor in the Patent Office in the late 1860s was Mary Capen of Massachusetts. See "Washington," *Philadelphia Inquirer*, June 22, 1869, 1; "Letters from Washington," *Sun*, June 22, 1869. Jane Seavy was the female superintendent in the Post Office in 1865. She earned $860 a year, a good deal more than the other women's wages of $720. See *Federal Register*, 1865. The Government Hospital for the Insane hired a female "Chief Cook" and a female "Chief Laundress" to oversee the other cooks and laundresses. *Federal Register*, 1863, 1865, 1867, 1869, and 1871. In 1870, the secretary of the Treasury appointed "Mrs. Eliza Scidmore to supervise the female employees of the Trea-

sury Department who clean the halls, rooms, &c." "Washington News and Gossip," *Evening Star*, July 21, 1870, 1.

105. The Bureau of Internal Revenue's female supervisor did earn more than the women under her in 1865 ($860 versus $720) but in 1867, all of the women in that bureau earned $900. *Federal Register*, 1865, 1867. Martin, *Behind the Scenes*, 473–74.

106. In August 1866, Wainwright began to make suggestions as to how her employees should be tasked. There is no evidence as to whether this came from her own initiative or whether she was requested to do so. Next to Miss Cowperthwaite's name, she wrote, "Copies miscellaneous letter books, is at date Dec 6, 1862. More ladies could be put on this work" and next to Miss Wilcox's, "copying claim books, is at date May 1, 1864, Vol 12. More ladies could be put on this work if it is thought proper." "Consolidated Report of the Time and Conduct of the Copyists," Box 2, NA-WD, Aug. 1866.

107. File of S. F. Wainwright, "Correspondence Relating to the Hiring of Clerks," Box 4, NA-WD.

108. Miss Gangwere's task was shifted from "incidental" to "book" the following month, but by October was back to "incidental" work. "Consolidated Report of the Time and Conduct of the Copyists," Box 2, NA-WD, Aug.–Oct. 1866. Meigs made no other reassignments in September.

109. *Congressional Globe*, 41st Cong., 2nd sess., pt. 4, 3449–52, 3451 (May 13, 1870). (Senate discussion on H.R. no. 974). See also *Congressional Globe*, 40th Cong., 3rd sess. 1773–1780, 1774 (Mar. 2, 1869). (Allegation that men obtain job and "sublet" it to a woman who does it for a lower salary and the man [who does nothing] pockets balance.)

110. Ames, *Ten Years*, 361; "The Women Clerks in Washington," *The Revolution*, Sept. 22, 1870, 187.

111. File of Helen C. Briggs, "Application and Recommendations," Box 59 (Bre–Bri), NA-Tr. It appears Briggs was transferred. She had a somewhat choppy career in the Treasury Department that seems to have ended in July 1878.

112. "Miscellany. Down among the Dead Letters," *Jamestown Journal*, Jan. 21, 1870, 2.

113. "[Women Workers]," *St. Cloud Democrat*, Dec. 21, 1865 (in Larsen, *Crusader and Feminist*, 307–13).

114. File of Mary A. Brennan, "Application and Recommendations," Box 58 (Bra–Bre), NA-Tr. Three of Brennan's brothers had served in the war. One died, one emigrated to Australia, and the third relied on Brennan's support because he was "suffering from lung disease contracted in the Army."

115. These examples are from women working in the highest paid female positions. Supervisors probably did not accord women working in lower-paying positions at the Government Hospital for the Insane, Government Printing Office, or parts of the Treasury Department the same kind of care and consideration. Male supervisors of female laborers, for example, did not always take their workplace concerns seriously. In 1864, "An Employee" wrote a letter to the *Daily Morning Chronicle* claiming that the floors of the Government Printing Office were collapsing, the machinery "jars and shakes every floor," and the walls "seem very much like puff-paste." The author wrote that employees, half of whom were female, went to work "nervously every morning."

"We desire, having regard for our lives and limbs, a feeling of *certainty* in respect to the safety of the building where we work day and night," asserted the letter writer. The superintendent responded through the newspaper a few days later, dismissing the letter writer's concerns as the hysteria of "a few girls." "The Government Printing Office Building," *Daily Morning Chronicle*, Feb. 5, 1864, 3.

116. "The Departments," *Daily Morning Chronicle*, Feb. 13, 1867; "Washington News & Gossip," *Evening Star*, Nov. 6, 1867, 1; "Washington News and Gossip," *Evening Star*, Nov. 29, 1867, 1.

117. In 1883, Congress standardized the workday (9:00 A.M. to 4:00 P.M., six days a week with a 12 to 12:30 P.M. lunch break) for all federal agencies. Aron, *Ladies and Gentlemen*, 94.

118. "Miscellany. Down among the Dead Letters," *Jamestown Journal*, Jan. 21, 1870, 2.

119. In April 1870, a visitor claimed that women employees "were so wearied by 3 o'clock that the remaining hour was of but little good." "Correspondence Cincinnati Commercial," *Cincinnati Commercial Tribune*, Apr. 18, 1870, 2.

120. Diary of Julia A. Wilbur, Sept. 6, 1868–Mar. 27, 1869, Nov. 15, 1869; "The Departments," *Daily Morning Chronicle*, May 6, 1870, 4.

121. "The Departments," *Daily Morning Chronicle*, May 6, 1870, 4.

122. Ibid., Sept. 9, 1869, 1.

123. "Washington Terrible Indignities offered to Female Clerks," *Leavenworth Bulletin*, Sept. 18, 1869, 1. See also "Washington News & Gossip," *Evening Star*, Sept. 16, 1869, 1.

124. "Our Washington Letter," *The Galveston Tri-Weekly News*, Sept. 24, 1869, 1.

125. "The Departments," *Daily Morning Chronicle*, Sept. 18, 1869, 1.

126. "Washington Fact and Gossip," *Albany Journal*, Oct. 2, 1869, 2.

127. "The Female Clerks," *Evening Star*, Oct. 14, 1870, 1. As women moved into more positions in the workforce, they began to lose some of the privileges accorded to them as women. "Times Are Changed," *Evening Star*, June 11, 1870, 1.

128. Martin, *Behind the Scenes*, 469.

129. "Experiences of a Bureau Officer," *Cincinnati Daily Gazette*, May 17, 1871, 4.

130. "Consolidated Report of the Time and Conduct of the Copyists," Boxes 1 and 2, NA-WD (contains monthly reports for January–June 1865, all of 1866 except February, and all of 1867).

131. There is also a column to note "General Conduct," though Wainwright did not make heavy use of that column.

132. "Consolidated Report of the Time and Conduct of the Copyists," May 1866, NA-WD. The sick child in question was John Brown, presumably Augusta's son. In 1866, he would have been eleven years old. 1870 Census, Washington, D.C., 1 WD. When she applied for the position in the War Department in 1863, Brown had written that she was "entirely dependent on my own exertion to support my invalid mother, and child." File of Augusta Brown, "Correspondence Relating to the Hiring of Clerks," Box 4, NA-WD. In the 1870 Census, Augusta and John, both from New York, were living in a mixed-sex boarding house without Brown's mother and perhaps they had had a similar living situation in 1866, with no one for Augusta to call on to care for him.

133. See chapter 6.

134. Miss Bates, Mrs. Brown, Miss Bull, Miss Cowperthwaite, Miss Hebb, Miss Howard, Miss Hagner, Miss Janney, Miss E. E. Janney, Mrs. Knight, Miss Leach, Mrs. Neale, Mrs. Page, Miss Pillsbury, Miss Richardson, Miss M. Richardson, Miss Swan, Miss Sherman, Miss Sedgwick, and Miss Wilcox appear on all twenty-nine of Wainwright's monthly reports.

135. I did not find any other files containing recommendations for female employees from current employees (aside from those current employees who were resigning and recommending someone to fill their place). File of Margaret D. King, "Correspondence Relating to the Hiring of Clerks," Box 4, NA-WD; File of Mrs. S. T. M. Babb, "Correspondence Relating to the Hiring of Clerks," Box 4, NA-WD; File of E. M. Zook, "Correspondence Relating to the Hiring of Clerks," Box 4, NA-WD. Catherine M. Melville of the War Department also wrote to Andrew Johnson (then Vice President) to try to get a job for her "friend, Miss E. Jane Gay." Graf, *The Papers of Andrew Johnson, 1864–1865*, 7:546.

136. "[Women Workers]," *St. Cloud Democrat*, Dec. 21, 1865 (in Larsen, *Crusader and Feminist*, 307–13).

137. When he failed to repay her, she filed a complaint against him for fraud with Major General D. H. Rucker. The coworker claimed that Baldwin had "promised him money to repair his own house," a contention Baldwin described as "preposterous." Rucker agreed and sided with Baldwin. She thanked him, stating: "I did not wish to injure him, but to have quietly born with such premeditated fraud, would be awarding a premium to dishonesty. File of Jane D. Baldwin, "Correspondence Relating to the Hiring of Clerks," Box 4, NA-WD. Historian Cindy Aron found that there was a culture of lending and borrowing money in the federal departments between coworkers and that women participated—though only as lenders. Aron found evidence of this practice in the 1890s in the Pension Office. Aron, *Ladies and Gentlemen*, 178–80.

138. File of A. G. Emery, "Correspondence Relating to the Hiring of Clerks," Box 4, NA-WD. See chapter 5 for a full discussion of this affair.

139. "Personal," *Cincinnati Commercial Tribune*, Feb. 22, 1869, 1; "Letter from Washington," *Sun*, May 13, 1869, 4.

140. "Washington," *Philadelphia Inquirer*, June 22, 1869, 1; "Letters from Washington," *Sun*, June 22, 1869; "By Telegraph from Washington," *Boston Daily Journal*, June 22, 1869, 4.

141. Martin, *Behind the Scenes*, 270; *Federal Register*, 1869. Capen's name is variously spelled as "Capan," "Capen," and "Capon" in the *Federal Register*, newspapers, and census. As Wilbur knew her personally and spelled her name "Capen" most often, I prefer that spelling.

142. "Correspondence Cincinnati Commercial," *Cincinnati Commercial Tribune*, Apr. 18, 1870, 2.

143. Diary of Julia A. Wilbur, Mar. 30, 1869–May 14, 1870; July 2, 20, 22, 1869.

144. Ibid., July 24, 29; Aug. 10, 1869.

145. Ibid., July 24, 29; Aug. 30, 1869.

146. Ibid., Sept. 3, 7, 1869; May 2, 1870.

147. Women of the Post Office also petitioned their male supervisor to change an aspect of their workspace." "Miscellany. Down among the Dead Letters," *Jamestown Journal*, Jan. 21, 1870, 2.

148. "Experiences of a Bureau Officer," *Cincinnati Daily Gazette*, May 17, 1871, 4.

149. Diary of Julia A. Wilbur, May 17, 1870–May 2, 1871.

150. The women also disliked one part of their workspace because it "had the look of a prison" owing to a "high grate running through it." One day, a group of visitors came through on a tour of the Post Office, and one of the young female employees told them that behind the grate the Postmaster kept silver stolen from a Confederate general. The young woman explained this was "a two-fold revenge . . . it was punishing the visitors for their inquisitiveness, and 'old ____ ' for having the grating put up there." Women later petitioned to have the grating removed, but the correspondent did not know whether or not they had been successful. The women in this office had a "lady superintendent" but also reported directly to a male "Superintendent." "Miscellany. Down among the Dead Letters," *Jamestown Journal*, Jan. 21, 1870, 2.

151. They also claimed, "that sudden death, among their number, has been caused by the air poison that invades this gallery." Ames, *Ten Years*, 398.

152. Martin, *Behind the Scenes*, 471–72. Martin also claimed that a woman had died because of the foul air. I could not find corroboration of this assertion in any of the local newspapers.

153. For descriptions of the operation of the GPO, see "Sketches in Washington: The Government Printing Office," *Detroit Advertiser and Tribune*, Feb. 22, 1864, 4 (in Leasher, *Letter from Washington*, 80–82); "City Intelligence," *Daily Morning Chronicle*, Nov. 14, 1865, 4; "The Largest Printing Office in the World," *Easton Gazette*, Mar. 28, 1868, 1.

154. As shown in chapter 5, this request likely arose from an investigation going on that spring into the operations of Clark's office. Clark drew a distinction between "clerks" and "employees." He had "but one clerk" and he worked in Clark's office "in which two ladies are also employed," but he took the inquiry to cover "to what extent different sexes are employed in the same rooms" so he provided a "tabulated statement of the number of rooms occupied, their use, the number of males & females in each, their pay, and general duties." Most of Clark's employees are not listed in the *Federal Register*. In 1863, the National Currency Bureau employed two women as copyists.

155. Letter from Clark to Harrington, Mar. 7, 1864, "Letters Received Relating to the Bureau of Engraving and Printing," NA-Tr. A later observer described the work in more detail. Women laid a damp sheet of paper in the ink-lined plate, and removed it after her male coworker, operating the press, had made the impression upon it. Ames, *Ten Years*, 318–19.

156. "Washington News & Gossip," *Evening Star*, Sept. 21, 1870, 1.

157. The newspaper reported that: "Some of the girls lost their underskirts and others their what-do-you-call 'ems; but none would consent to confess proprietorship when some of the gentlemen bashfully inquired for the owners." "Terrible Scare and Grand Stampede at the Government Printing Office," *The Constitution*, Jan. 4, 1865, 2;

see also "Terrible Scare and Grand Stampede at the Government Printing Office," *Milwaukee Daily Sentinel*, Jan. 4, 1865, 3.

158. For an example of women bestowing gifts, see "Late Local News [Second Edition]," *Evening Star*, Apr. 7, 1863, 2; "City Intelligence," *Daily Morning Chronicle*, Oct. 3, 1865, 4; "News of the Day," *New York Daily Tribune*, Apr. 24, 1865, 4; "City Intelligence," *Daily Morning Chronicle*, June 3, 1867, 1.

159. Diary of Julia A. Wilbur, May 17, 1870–May 2, 1871; Nov. 10, 1870.

160. "Local News," *Evening Star*, Dec. 27, 1869, 4; "City Intelligence," *Daily Morning Chronicle*, Nov. 6, 1866, 4.

161. "Local News," *Evening Star*, Sept. 17, 1867, 3.

162. U.S. Department of the Treasury, *Report of the Secretary of the Treasury . . . 1866*, 173.

163. U.S. Department of the Treasury, *Report of the Secretary of the Treasury . . . 1868*, 253. In 1866, the women had inadvertently passed $500 in counterfeit currency and they had "yet not been able, on account of their insufficiency of pay, to make restitution." U.S. Department of the Treasury, *Report of the Secretary of the Treasury . . . 1866*, 174.

164. U.S. Department of the Treasury, *Report of the Secretary of the Treasury . . . 1868*, 253. See also, "The Women Clerks at Washington," *Springfield Weekly Republican*, Apr. 17, 1869, 2.

165. Diary of Julia A. Wilbur, May 17, 1870–May 2, 1871; June 16, 1870.

166. "Sketches in Washington: The Government Printing Office," *Detroit Advertiser and Tribune*, Feb. 22, 1864, 4 (in Leasher, *Letter from Washington*, 80–82).

167. "City Intelligence," *Daily Morning Chronicle*, Aug. 28, 1869, 4; "City Intelligence," *Daily Morning Chronicle*, Sept. 10, 1869, 4.

168. This was likely the Pension Office since in 1866 women working for the Patent Office performed work at home and women working for the Government Hospital for the Insane worked on site.

169. "Local Intelligence," *Daily Constitutional Union*, Jan. 12, 1866, 3.

170. For example, Clara Barton, who joined the Patent Office in the mid-1850s, reported being aggressively and viciously harassed by her male colleagues. At the time, Barton was purportedly earning the pay of a second-class clerk and her male coworkers resented her for it, slandering her with remarks about her sexuality. According to Barton's biographer, the men daily "glared and whistled at her and stooped to taunts and catcalls. They also impugned her character, spreading rumors that she was a 'slut' with illegitimate 'negroid' children." Oates, *Woman of Valor*, 11–12, citing Blackwell, "Clara Barton Kept a Secret," *Woman's Journal*, Feb. 24, 1888. Oates writes that Barton's supervisor, Commissioner Mason, "took her side" and "when one malcontent complained to him about Clara's 'moral character' and insisted that she be fired, the commissioner demanded proof by five o'clock that afternoon. 'But understand,' Mason said, 'things will not remain just as they are in this office. If you prove this charge, Miss Barton goes; if you fail to prove it, you go.' When the deadline passed without the proof, the man went. And that put a stop to the harassment of Clara."

171. "Washington News & Gossip," *Evening Star*, Jan. 13, 1867, 1.

172. Ames, *Ten Years*, 371.

173. Luskey, *On the Make*, ch. 3; Srole, *Transcribing Class*, ch. 3.

174. "Almost Serious," *Daily Morning Chronicle*, June 10, 1864, 2.

175. "The Currency," *New York Tribune*, Sept. 4, 1867, 2. Two years later, Mrs. Amelia M. Meacham, who had previously worked at the Government Printing Office, badly jammed two fingers of her right hand in the running gears of a printing press of the Treasury Department. "The Departments," *Daily Morning Chronicle*, Aug. 19, 1869, 1; "Local News," *Evening Star*, Aug. 19, 1869, 4. Meacham was one of the signers of the 1867 petition from women of Government Printing Office for higher pay. "Petition from Women of Government Printing Office for More Money," NA-USH. In the GPO, Kate Webber crushed three of her fingers in a machine. "City Intelligence," *Daily Morning Chronicle*, Apr. 15, 1868, 4.

Chapter Four

1. File of Mary F. Holmes, "Application and Recommendations," Box 276 (Hol–Hol), NA-Tr.

2. For overviews on life in Washington, D.C., during the Civil War era, see, for example, Winkle, *Lincoln's Citadel*; Leech, *Reveille in Washington*; and Furgurson, *Freedom Rising*.

3. The enemy seriously threatened twice during the war, once when General R. E. Lee was in Maryland (1863), and the following year, when Jubal Early attacked Fort Stevens. Whyte, "Divided Loyalties," 120; Winkle, *Citadel*, 392–94.

4. Cooling, "Defending Washington during the Civil War," 326.

5. See, for example, Wood, *The Freedom of the Streets*, 6 (noting: "By the 1870s and 1880s . . . middle-class women began to demand the same freedom of the streets that men took for granted").

6. See, for example, Stansell, *City of Women*; Wood, *The Freedom of the Streets*, 6–7.

7. 1860 Census, Vol. 1, Population, District of Columbia Table 1 (Population by Age and Sex), 586–87; 1860 Census, Vol. 1, Recapitulation of the Tables of Population, Nativity, and Occupation, 592–97; 1870 Census, Volume 1, Table 22—The United States—1870, 606–9.

8. U.S. Department of the Interior, *Report of the Board of Metropolitan Police . . .* 1864, 761. The growth had occurred steadily over the war years. See, for example, U.S. Department of Interior, *Report of the Board of Metropolitan Police . . .* 1862, 649; U.S. Department of the Interior, *Report of the Board of Metropolitan Police . . .* 1863, 720.

9. Winkle, *Lincoln's Citadel*, xiv; Kauffman, *American Brutus*, 3.

10. "City Intelligence," *Daily Morning Chronicle*, Mar. 5, 1867, 4.

11. 1860 Census, Population, District of Columbia Table 1 (Population by Age and Sex), 586–87; 1860 Census, Recapitulation of the Tables of Population, Nativity, and Occupation, 592–97; 1870 Census, Table 22—The United States—1870, 606–9.

12. "Life in Washington: First Impressions, The City, Its Crowds, Living Prices, Changes," *Detroit Advertiser and Tribune*, Oct. 15, 1863, 4 (in Leasher, *Letter from Washington*, 33–35).

13. "Letter from Washington: The Capital as It Is, Fine Arts, Improvements and Evidence of their Prosperity, Visitors and Their Views, Hospital Life, the Armies That Have Gone." *Detroit Advertiser and Tribune*, Aug. 16, 1864, 4 (in Leasher, *Letter from Washington*, 181–83).

14. "Life in Washington: First Impressions, The City, Its Crowds, Living Prices, Changes," *Detroit Advertiser and Tribune*, Oct. 15, 1863, 4 (in Leasher, *Letter from Washington*, 33–35).

15. See, for example, "City Intelligence," *Daily Morning Chronicle*, Aug. 12, 1867, 1.

16. He specifically referenced "Treasury clerks, men and women" as being battered by the wind. "On Being a Washington Clerk," *Evening Bulletin*, Jan. 19, 1867, 3. See also, "Miscellany: On Being a Washington Clerk," *Jamestown Journal*, Jan. 25, 1867.

17. *St. Cloud Democrat*, Aug. 13, 1863 (in Larsen, *Crusader and Feminist*, 247–53). See also "Our City," *Daily Morning Chronicle*, Nov. 18, 1863, 3.

18. *St. Cloud Democrat*, Sept. 24, 1863 (in Larsen, *Crusader and Feminist*, 264–69).

19. "Life in Washington: First Impressions, The City, Its Crowds, Living Prices, Changes," *Detroit Advertiser and Tribune*, Oct. 15, 1863, 4 (in Leasher, *Letter from Washington*, 33–35).

20. Leech, *Reveille*, 337. The Baltimore scheme enjoyed a fairly long run and a significant amount of research and planning went into it, but it does not appear to have ever been implemented. See, for example, "Meeting in Regard to Removing to Baltimore," *Daily Morning Chronicle*, Sept. 12, 1863, 3; "Local News," *Evening Star*, Sept. 12, 1863, 3.

21. Penfield, *A Tale of the Rebellion*, 6. See also Townsend, *Washington, Outside and Inside*, 42–43.

22. "Washington Items," *Daily Constitutional Union*, Aug. 15, 1866, 3; "Letter to Congress from Committee of Clerks of Treasury Employees," NA-USH.

23. The largest general pay disparity in the period under examination was prior to 1865, when women were paid a maximum of $600 per year and fourth-class male clerks earned $1,800 per year. The smallest pay disparity was after July 1866, when female clerks earned $900 per year as compared to first class male clerks' salaries of $1,200 per year.

24. "Life in Washington: First Impressions, The City, Its Crowds, Living Prices, Changes," *Detroit Advertiser and Tribune*, Oct. 15, 1863, 4 (in Leasher, *Letter from Washington*, 33–35).

25. "Female Department Clerks," *Flake's Bulletin*, Aug. 3, 1866; "Women in Washington," *Albany Journal*, July 20, 1866; "Life and Society in Washington," *Semi-Weekly Telegraph*, Sept. 6, 1866, 4; "Life and Society in Washington," *Evening Bulletin*, Aug. 22, 1866, 3. See chapter 7 for more on women's federal salaries.

26. "Women Clerks in the Executive Departments at Washington," *The Revolution*, Apr. 16, 1868, 230–31.

27. *St. Cloud Democrat*, Apr. 9, 1863 (in Larsen, *Crusader and Feminist*, 201).

28. "[Washington]," *Lowell Daily Citizen and News*, Apr. 23, 1870, 2.

29. Townsend, *Washington, Outside and Inside*, 377.

30. Diary of Julia A. Wilbur, May 5, 1871–Apr. 21, 1872; June 1, 2, 3, 4, 9, 22; July 4, 5; Aug. 1, 1871.

31. In the years 1861 to 1869, the *Federal Register* for the hospital lists boarding as part of the employees' compensation.

32. U.S. Congress, House of Representatives, *The Management of the Government Hospital for the Insane*, 177–78 (Testimony of Annie Creighton), 75–76 (Testimony of Charles H. Nichols).

33. Ibid., 168.

34. Women living with male relatives are more difficult to identify in the 1870 census than are single women, however, and thus the data are to some extent skewed to over-represent women living on their own or as heads of households.

35. Margaret Campbell, "Single Women versus Boarding-House Keepers," *The Woman's Journal*, Nov. 26, 1870, 374.

36. Wood, *Freedom of the Streets*, 17.

37. "Late Local News [Second Edition]," *Washington Star*, Sept. 3, 1862, 3. See also "Local News," *Washington Star*, June 26, 1862, 3; Smith, *The Enemy Within*, 103.

38. Smith, *The Enemy Within*, 103.

39. Furgurson, *Freedom Rising*, 207. For more on prostitution in Washington, D.C., during the Civil War, see chapter 6 of Lowry, *The Story the Soldiers Wouldn't Tell*, and Jordan, "The Capital of Crime," 4–9, 44–47.

40. "City Intelligence," *Daily Morning Chronicle*, Aug. 10, 1866, 2.

41. 1870 Census, Washington, D.C., 2 WD.

42. "Female Department Clerks," *Flake's Bulletin*, Aug. 3, 1866; "Women in Washington," *Albany Journal*, July 20, 1866; "Life and Society in Washington," *Semi-Weekly Telegraph*, Sept. 6, 1866, 4; "Life and Society in Washington," *Evening Bulletin*, Aug. 22, 1866, 3.

43. "City Intelligence," *Daily Morning Chronicle*, Oct. 27, 1865, 4.

44. "Boarding," *Daily Morning Chronicle*, Oct. 27, 1865, 3.

45. Ibid., Nov. 20, 1865, 2.

46. "Boarding," *Evening Star*, July 31, 1865, 4; "Boarding," *Evening Star*, Aug. 1, 1865, 4. See also "Boarding," *Daily Morning Chronicle*, Aug. 3, 1865, 2.

47. Groneman and Norton, "*To Toil the Livelong Day*," in "Gender Relations and Working-Class Leisure: New York City, 1880–1920," ed. Kathy Peiss, 103–6; Cross, "'We Think We Are of the Oppressed,'" 25.

48. This figure excludes mothers who lived with adult male relatives and mothers who had at least one adult, employed child (even if they also had unemployed children and children under 18 years old). Of these 98 women, 93 were white, 4 were black, and 1 was listed as "mulatto." Most of these single mothers (71) worked in the Treasury Department, though in what capacity is unknown. The remainder worked in the GPO (15 women); Post Office (5 women); Patent Office (4 women); War Department (2 women); and Pension Office (1 woman). For an examination of working-class employed mothers from 1900 to 1930, see chapter 6 of Tentler, *Wage-Earning Women*.

49. 1870 Census, Washington, D.C., 2 WD. Boston signed a petition for higher pay in 1871. "Petition of Women Employed as Sweepers and Scrubbers," NA-USH.

50. "Men and Women—Work and Wages," *The Revolution*, Mar. 4, 1869, 140.

51. 1870 Census, Washington, D.C., 2 WD; *Federal Register*, 1869.

52. Martin, *Behind the Scenes*, 476.

53. "Men and Women—Work and Wages," *The Revolution*, Mar. 4, 1869, 140.

54. See, for example, "Our City," *Daily Morning Chronicle*, Nov. 18, 1863, 3. There were hundreds of eating establishments in Washington as early as 1863. See, for example, *Hutchinson's* (listing 283 restaurants, 15 with female proprietors, and 43 oyster saloons, 1 with a female proprietor). See also Townsend, *Washington, Outside and Inside*, 176.

55. Freedman, "Women and Restaurants," 2–3, 13. But see "Woman in Congress," *The Revolution*, Mar. 10, 1870, 148–49 (describing women dining in the restaurant at the Supreme Court).

56. See, for example, Freedman, "Women and Restaurants," 10 (noting that establishments catering to working women's lunch needs were not common until the end of the nineteenth century); Kwolek-Folland, *Engendering Business*, 122 (examining the development of corporate lunch rooms as a "response to the fact that in the earlier period, few if any public lunchrooms on the outside were available to women"). For women bringing lunches to work, see, for example, "Miscellany. Down among the Dead Letters," *Jamestown Journal*, Jan. 21, 1870, 2. In 1864, Catherine Dodson kept a "confectionary stand" at the Treasury. U.S. Congress, House of Representatives, *Certain Charges against the Treasury Department*, 154 (Testimony of Beattie Pumphrey).

57. "Correspondence: Our Washington Letter," *Pomeroys Democrat*, Sept. 8, 1869, 3.

58. Townsend, *Washington, Outside and Inside*, 179–80; "Life in Washington: First Impressions, The City, Its Crowds, Living Prices, Changes," *Detroit Advertiser and Tribune*, Oct. 15, 1863, 4 (in Leasher, *Letter from Washington*, 33–35).

59. *St. Cloud Democrat*, Aug. 13, 1863 (in Larsen, *Crusader and Feminist*, 247–53). See also "Life in Washington: First Impressions, The City, Its Crowds, Living Prices, Changes," *Detroit Advertiser and Tribune*, Oct. 15, 1863, 4 (in Leasher, *Letter from Washington*, 33–35).

60. "Letter to Congress from Committee of Clerks of Treasury Employees," NA-USH.

61. Martin, *Behind the Scenes*, 476.

62. "Romantic Histories," *Lowell Daily Citizen and News*, Mar. 22, 1870, 2.

63. District Courts of the U.S., *Equity Case Files 1863–1938*, Box 39, 642–662, File #655, E69.

64. Brewster's appointment was delivered on September 24, 1868, and her file stated that she had a brother-in-law in the secretary's office. File of V. Brewster, "Application and Recommendations," NA-Tr. She appeared in the 1869 *Federal Register* as a "Lady Clerk" in Custom-House Bonds. It was a small department. She was the only female clerk and earned $900 per year. By 1871, Brewster had moved to the Records and Files division and was one of 23 female clerks. *Federal Register* 1871. Her salary remained at $900 per year.

65. 1870 Census, Washington, D.C., 2 WD.

66. Green, *Washington Village and Capital*, 209.

67. Kelly, "Memories of a Lifetime in Washington."

68. After working for the Department of the Interior, Dudley left Washington, D.C., and married Edwin A. Davis. She is referred to by the last name "Dudley" herein. Diary of Annie G. Dudley Davis, Aug. 3, 1861.

69. Mearns, "A View of Washington in 1863," 212; Furgurson, *Freedom Rising*, 241.

70. I identified 414 women working in the Treasury Department in the 1870 Census. The Treasury Department was located between the first ward (where 44 women lived) and the second ward (where 154 women lived). I identified 33 women working in the Post Office Department and 29 in the Patent Office, located in close proximity to the second, third, and fourth wards (where 16 out of 33 female Post Office employees and 14 out of 29 female Patent Office employees lived).

71. 1870 Census, Washington, D.C., Tenally Town PO.

72. "Washington Letter," *The Revolution*, May 21, 1868, 309–10.

73. Perhaps because she enjoyed those she lived with so much, she did not actually make firm plans to move until May 1871. Diary of Julia A. Wilbur, May 17, 1870–May 2, 1871; June 29; July 14; Sept. 23, 24, 28, 1870; Diary of Julia A. Wilbur, May 5, 1871–Apr. 21, 1872; May 26, 1871.

74. U.S. Department of the Interior, *Report of the Board of Metropolitan Police . . .* 1867, 508; U.S. Department of the Interior, *Report of the Board of Metropolitan Police . . .* 1865, 845; U.S. Department of the Interior, *Report of the Board of Metropolitan Police . . .* 1868, 877; U.S. Department of the Interior, *Report of the Board of Metropolitan Police . . .* 1869, 1134.

75. Green, *Washington Village and Capital*, 211.

76. For more on sanitation issues in D.C. during this time period, see Winkle, *Citadel*, 121–124.

77. Kelly, "Memories of a Lifetime in Washington," 123.

78. U.S. Department of the Interior, *Report of the Board of Metropolitan Police . . .* 1868, 873. A year later, he reported further progress on the construction of sewers. U.S. Department of the Interior, *Report of the Board of Metropolitan Police . . .* 1869, 1126.

79. Green, *Washington Village and Capital*, 28, 33, 72.

80. Kelly, "Memories of a Lifetime in Washington," 119. The citizens of Washington, D.C., submitted a petition to the 38th Congress in spring 1864 to address the Washington canal, because it was "detrimental to the health of the city." "Petition of citizens of Washington City, D.C . . . for cleansing and improving the Washington Canal."

81. U.S. Department of the Interior, *Report of the Board of Metropolitan Police . . .* 1869, 1126. The next year, the board wrote: "in view of the alarming spread of cholera . . . which at any moment may be wafted to our own shores, [we] request that the speedy attention of our city authorities be directed toward the removal of [the canal's] foul and festering bed." U.S. Department of the Interior, *Report of the Board of Metropolitan Police . . .* 1870, 934.

82. During the war, smallpox was a significant concern. In 1863, the superintendent reported that it had been rare in the city, but had "increased greatly since the army and its

accompanying attendants and followers have been in this region of the country, and there is now no season when cases of this horrible disorder may not be found in our midst." U.S. Department of the Interior, *Report of the Board of Metropolitan Police . . . 1863*, 726.

83. In 1867, the superintendent of police reported, "By far the greater number of complaints . . . are from a lack of an adequate system of drainage, or more properly . . . from a want of any artificial system of drainage whatever." U.S. Department of the Interior, *Report of the Board of Metropolitan Police . . . 1867*, 507.

84. U.S. Department of the Interior, *Report of the Board of Metropolitan Police . . . 1863*, 727. See also U.S. Department of the Interior, *Report of the Board of Metropolitan Police . . . 1867*, 507.

85. *St. Cloud Democrat*, Sept. 24, 1863 (in Larsen, *Crusader and Feminist*, 264–69).

86. Winkle, *Citadel*, 124; Leech, *Reveille*, 307. See also "Washington Items," *Daily Constitutional Union*, July 28, 1866, 3.

87. Diary of Annie G. Dudley Davis, March 1863.

88. Of course Washington, D.C., was not unique in this regard. Other mid-nineteenth century American cities also had sanitation problems. See, for example, Stansell, *City of Women*, 49.

89. "City Intelligence," *Daily Morning Chronicle*, Dec. 11, 1865, 4. See also *St. Cloud Democrat*, Sept. 24, 1863 (in Larsen, *Crusader and Feminist*, 264–69).

90. "City Intelligence," *Daily Morning Chronicle*, Mar. 13, 1867, 2. See, "Local Intelligence," *Daily Constitutional Union*, Feb. 1, 1865, 2; Briggs, *The Olivia Letters*, 23 (letter dated March 9, 1866); Billings, "Early Women Journalists of Washington," 93.

91. "City Intelligence," *Daily Morning Chronicle*, Mar. 28, 1868, 4.

92. Diary of Julia A. Wilbur, Sept. 6, 1868–Mar. 27, 1869; Mar. 6, 1869; Mar. 30, 1869–May 14, 1870; Apr. 19; Aug. 12; Nov. 7, 1869; Jan. 8; Apr. 15, 16, 28, 1870; May 17, 1870–May 2, 1871; Sept. 20; Oct. 18, 29, 31; Dec. 6, 24, 1870; March 23; April 11, 12, 22; May 1, 1871; May 5, 1871–Apr. 21, 1872; May 26; Aug. 27; Sept. 26, 1871.

93. "Run over by a Hack," *Daily National Intelligencer*, Jan. 28, 1864, 3.

94. U.S. Department of the Interior, *Report of the Board of Metropolitan Police . . .* 1862, 649.

95. U.S. Department of the Interior, *Report of the Board of Metropolitan Police . . .* 1865, 843.

96. Jordan, "The Capital of Crime," 5; U.S. Department of the Interior, *Report of the Board of Metropolitan Police . . . 1861*; Winkle, *Citadel*, 188.

97. U.S. Department of the Interior, *Report of the Board of Metropolitan Police . . .* 1863, 725–26.

98. U.S. Department of the Interior, *Report of the Board of Metropolitan Police . . .* 1865, 843.

99. Nineteenth century concerns about urban crime were not unique to Washington. See, for example, Ryan, *Women in Public*, 68–69.

100. "City Intelligence," *Daily Morning Chronicle*, Oct. 2, 1865, 4.

101. "An Ungallant Thief," *Daily Morning Chronicle*, Apr. 10, 1863, 3. See also "City Intelligence," *Daily Morning Chronicle*, Apr. 15, 1869, 4 (reporting on the arrest of

"Rachel Ann Harris, a colored girl" for "stealing a pocket-book containing $20, and numerous other articles, from Mrs. Adeline Heath and Mrs. Catherine Goldsmith"). Goldsmith had been one of the women working at the Washington Arsenal when it exploded in 1864. She suffered severe burns on her hands, arms, and face, but survived. "Frightful Explosion at the Arsenal," *Washington Star* [Second Edition], June 17, 1864.

102. Diary of Annie G. Dudley Davis, May 21, 1864.

103. "Local Intelligence," *Daily Constitutional Union*, Mar. 28, 1866, 3; File of Mary Gatewood, "Application and Recommendations," Box 216 (Gas–Gaz), NA-Tr; Records of the Government of the District of Columbia, Records of the Metropolitan Police, Detective Office, Daily Record, Box 2—January 11–May 16, 1866.

104. Diary of Julia A. Wilbur, Sept. 6, 1868—Mar. 27, 1869; Dec. 3, 1869.

105. "The Smithsonian Grounds," *Evening Star*, July 31, 1865, 3.

106. "Local Intelligence," *Daily Constitutional Union*, Feb. 1, 1865, 2.

107. "Washington News & Gossip," *Evening Star*, Nov. 6, 1867, 1. On poor street lighting, see also Kelly, "Memories of a Lifetime in Washington," 123.

108. U.S. Congress, House of Representatives, *Certain Charges against the Treasury Department*, 153 (Testimony of Sarah Lulley); 210 (Testimony of Clara Donaldson); 213 (Testimony of James Lamb).

109. "Sketches in Washington: The Government Printing Office," *Detroit Advertiser and Tribune*, Feb. 22, 1864, 4 (in Leasher, *Letter from Washington*, 80–82). Ames reported that a day's work in the GPO was from 8 A.M. to 5 P.M. Ames, *Ten Years*, 529.

110. Masur, *Example for All the Land*, 113–14.

111. Diary of Julia A. Wilbur, May 17, 1870–May 2, 1871; Jan. 26, 1871; May 5, 1871–Apr. 21, 1872; Nov. 17, 1871.

112. For women experiencing the male gaze in other nineteenth century American cities, see, for example, Ryan, *Women in Public*, 69–70.

113. "Local News," *Evening Star*, Nov. 29, 1869, 4.

114. Winkle, *Citadel*, 395–96.

115. See, for example, "Local News," *Evening Star*, Aug. 25, 1870, 4.

116. Diary of Julia A. Wilbur, Mar. 30, 1869–May 14, 1870; Feb. 21; Mar. 12, 1870.

117. African American federal employee Kate Brown reportedly resisted a conductor's instruction to move to a segregated car "because there were some persons there who were disorderly." Committee on the District of Columbia, *Report*, 8. For more on Kate Brown, see Kate Masur, "Patronage and Protest."

118. Such close quarters was perhaps the reason one woman got on the train and paid twice the normal fare (ten cents) and when the conductor tried to give her change to her she replied, " 'Don't give me change, but give me room,' and taking a seat in a corner which happened to be vacant, spread her skirts over the space usually allotted to half a dozen of the masculine species, where she was left undisturbed until the end of her journey." "Local News," *Washington Star*, Oct. 3, 1862, 3.

119. "City Intelligence," *Daily Morning Chronicle*, Oct. 12, 1866, 4.

120. "Local News," *Evening Star*, July 29, 1870, 4.

121. "Washington Items," *Daily Constitutional Union*, July 25, 1866, 4; "Local News," Washington *Evening Star*, Aug. 2, 1862, 3.

122. Diary of Julia A. Wilbur, Sept. 6, 1868–Mar. 27, 1869; Jan. 13, 1869.

123. Leech, *Reveille*, 316–17; Winkle, *Citadel*, 292–93.

124. Cooling, "Defending Washington," 314–37; Winkle, *Citadel*, xii, 163–64, 392–94; Leech, *Reveille*, 417–23.

125. Winkle, *Citadel*, 213–19, 265–75, 410; Briggs, *The Olivia Letters*, 10 (letter dated January 31, 1866); Larsen, *Crusader and Feminist*, 237–42 (*St. Cloud Democrat*, July 23, 1863). The Civil War also changed the composition of patients at the Government Hospital for the Insane; in the first year of the war, 75 percent of new cases came from the military. Millikan, "Wards of the Nation," 77.

126. Winkle, *Citadel*, 368–69.

127. Masur, *Example for All the Land*, 1.

128. For more on working women's changing the spatial character of a city, see, for example, Deutsch, *Women and the City*.

129. "Woman in Congress," *The Revolution*, Mar. 10, 1870, 148–149.

130. "Letter from Washington," *Detroit Advertiser and Tribune*, Aug. 24, 1864, 4.

131. "Life in Washington," *Detroit Advertiser and Tribune*, Oct. 15, 1863, 4 (Leasher, *Letter from Washington*, 33–35).

132. "Woman in Congress," *The Revolution*, Mar. 10, 1870, 148–49.

133. Abbott, *Political Terrain*, 95.

134. "Local News," *Evening Star*, July 3, 1867, 3; "Washington Items," *Daily Constitutional Union*, June 29, 1867, 3.

135. "Washington," *Cincinnati Commercial*, Aug. 17, 1870, 5; "The City," *The Critic*, Aug. 17, 1870, 3; "Personal," *Lowell Daily Citizen and News*, Aug. 22, 1870, 2; "Latest News Items," *Daily Evening Bulletin*, Sept. 2, 1870, 4; "Washington News and Gossip," *Evening Star*, Aug. 16, 1870, 1. When she was hired, Green was not a member of the Printers' Union, which did not admit women. The year prior, the union and the Government Printing Office were at odds over the hiring of an African American man as a compositor. Shortly after Green was hired, the Columbia Typographical Union unanimously admitted her to their ranks. "The City," *The Critic*, Sept. 19, 1870, 3; "Washington News and Gossip," *Evening Star*, Aug. 16, 1870, 1; "Woman's Rights in the District," *Evening Star*, Sept. 19, 1870, 2. The *Cincinnati Commercial* declared: "As negroes are now employed by Mr. Clapp, the beautiful future so long prayed for has come to the Government Printing Office, at least, when no distinction is made on account of race, sex, color or condition." "Washington," *Cincinnati Commercial*, Aug. 17, 1870, 5. Ames reported that Green later went on "to become the editor of a real-estate journal in Indianapolis, Indiana." Ames, *Ten Years*, 526.

136. "The Attractions and Celebrities of Washington City, D.C.," *Cincinnati Commercial*, Sept. 29, 1869, 2.

137. Diary of Julia A. Wilbur, Sept. 6, 1868–Mar. 27, 1869; Jan. 23, 1869; Mar. 30, 1869–May 14, 1870; Apr. 21, 1869; Jan. 1, 1870; May 17, 1870–May 2, 1871; Jan. 1, 1871; May 5, 1871–Apr. 21, 1872; Dec. 11, 1871.

138. Deutsch, *Women and the City*, 91; Stansell, *City of Women*, 85; Tentler, *Wage-Earning Women*, 117 ("Probably a majority of women living without family chose to board in private homes"). Of the 662 women identified in the 1870 Census in Washington, D.C., 42 were under the age of eighteen. Of these 42, 12 lived entirely on their own. According to the 1870 Census in Washington, D.C., 325 women lived without family members. Of these, 131 lived in large boarding houses and 43 lived in "other" situations—mostly at the Government Hospital for the Insane. Only 45 percent lived in smaller boarding homes, defined herein to mean having three or fewer of any one family name.

139. See, for example, Leech, *Reveille*, 11.

140. Stansell, *City of Women*, 84–85.

141. In the mid-1870s, the federal government began to prohibit the employment of more than one family member. Aron, *Ladies and Gentlemen*, 52.

142. McKenna is listed in the Treasurer's Office in the 1865, 1867, and 1869 *Federal Registers*.

143. 1870 Census, Washington, D.C., Georgetown PO. A fourth child, a fourteen-year-old boy, was at home.

144. 1870 Census, Washington, D.C., 5 WD; *Federal Register* 1865, 1867.

145. 1870 Census, Washington, D.C., 1 WD. Becker appears as a Treasury clerk in the 1865, 1867, 1869, and 1871 *Federal Register*. She worked in the Treasurer's Office. Tenner does not appear in the *Federal Register* in the period under examination.

146. For these purposes, I define "large" boarding house as housing four or more persons or families of different last names, excluding domestic servants.

147. 1870 Census, Washington, D.C., 2 WD.

148. Diary of Annie G. Dudley Davis.

149. Stansell, *City of Women*, 85.

150. "The Sick and Wounded Soldiers," *New York Tribune*, June 19, 1863, 2.

151. Historian Elizabeth Clark-Lewis found a similar peer-group interaction in her study of African American women in 1910–1940 Washington, D.C. See Elizabeth Clark-Lewis, "This Work Had an End: African American Domestic Workers in Washington, D.C., 1910–1940," in Groneman and Norton, *"To Toil the Livelong Day,"* 205–6.

152. File of A. G. Emery, "Correspondence Relating to the Hiring of Clerks," Box 4, NA-WD. Female federal clerks' relationships with men are discussed in more detail in chapter 5.

153. Diary of Annie G. Dudley Davis, January 1863.

154. Stansell, *City of Women*, 85.

155. Gemmill, *Notes on Washington*, 88–89.

156. Stansell, *City of Women*, 56.

157. "Letter from Washington," *Detroit Advertiser and Tribune*, Aug. 24, 1864, 4 (in Leasher, *Letter from Washington*, 183–86).

158. Diary of Julia A. Wilbur, Sept. 6, 1868–Mar. 27, 1869; Mar. 2, 1869; Mar. 30, 1869–May 14, 1870; Apr. 6; May 4; Jan. 1, 13; Feb. 22, 24, 1870; May 17, 1870–May 2, 1871; Jan. 10, 20; Feb. 18, 1871. On February 11, 1870, Wilbur attended Speaker James G. Blaine's reception. Diary of Julia A. Wilbur, Mar. 30, 1869–May 14, 1870; Feb. 11, 1870.

159. Diary of Annie G. Dudley Davis, Feb. 1863; Feb. 1864; May 1864; Feb. 1869.

160. Records of the Post Office Department, *Miscellaneous File*, Box 1, Clerks Library Association, Subscription for Purchasing Books for the Post Office Library; "Local News," *Evening Star*, Nov. 20, 1867, 3; Johnston, "The Earliest Free Public Library Movement in Washington, 1849–1874." "Woman in Congress," *The Revolution*, Mar. 10, 1870, 148–49; "Washington Letter: Women as Clerks," *The Revolution*, Apr. 30, 1868, 261–62.

161. "City Intelligence," *Daily Morning Chronicle*, Dec. 13, 1869, 4.

162. Diary of Julia A. Wilbur, Mar. 30, 1869–May 14, 1870; Apr. 1; May 11; Aug. 23, 1869; Jan. 26, 27; Feb. 5, 6, 1870; May 17, 1870–May 2, 1871; May 23; Oct. 11; Nov. 20, 23; Dec. 22, 1870; Feb. 7, 8, 15; March 14, 18; Apr. 27, 30, 1870; May 5, 1871–Apr. 21, 1872; May 17, 18; June 28; Aug. 5, 9, 10, 27, 28; Sept. 18; Oct. 21, 23, 25, 26; Nov. 28; Dec. 18, 1871.

163. "Washington," *The Revolution*, Apr. 16, 1868, 226.

164. Diary of Annie G. Dudley Davis, Dec. 1861; Apr. 1864.

165. Diary of Julia A. Wilbur, Sept. 6, 1868–Mar. 27, 1869; Mar. 16, 23; Mar. 30, 1869–May 14, 1870; Mar. 29; Apr. 7, 8, 22, 23; May 4, 1869; Jan. 11, 14, 17, 21; Feb. 16, 23, 28; Mar. 7, 14, 16, 22; July 4, 1870; May 17, 1870–May 2, 1871; June 24; Dec. 5, 1870; Jan. 9, 25; Feb. 7, 23, 24; Mar. 4, 7, 10, 17, 20, 21, 24, 27; Apr. 7, 19, 1871.

166. Ibid., May 17, 1870–May 2, 1871; Jan. 7; Mar. 13, 15, 28; Apr. 25, 1871.

167. Ibid., Mar. 30, 1869–May 14, 1870; May 15; July 31; Sept. 7, 9; Oct. 2, 9, 27, 1869; May 17, 1870–May 2, 1871; Aug. 6; Oct. 20; Dec. 16, 1870; Jan. 21; Feb. 3; Mar. 1; Apr. 25, 1871; May 5, 1871–Apr. 21, 1872; May 27; Aug. 23; Sept. 22, 1871.

168. Ibid., Mar. 30, 1869–May 14, 1870; Apr. 2, 1870.

169. Ibid., Sept. 6, 1868–Mar. 27, 1869; Mar. 4, 1869; Mar. 30, 1869–May 14, 1870; Apr. 16, 1869; Apr. 2, 1870; May 17, 1870–May 2, 1871; May 30, 31, 1870; Feb. 20; Apr. 17, 1871; May 5, 1871–Apr. 21, 1872; May 30, 31, 1871.

170. Diary of Annie G. Dudley Davis, Apr. 1863; July 1863; Nov. 1863; Jan. 1864.

171. Diary of Julia A. Wilbur, Sept. 6, 1868–Mar. 27, 1869; Mar. 7, 25, 26, 27, 1869; Mar. 30, 1869–May 14, 1870; Apr. 7, 18, 25; May 2; Sept. 12; Oct. 12, 17; Nov. 14, 28; Dec. 5, 1869; Feb. 15, 20; Mar. 6, 1870; May 17, 1870–May 2, 1871; Jan. 1; Feb 18, 19, 26, 1871; May 5, 1871–Apr. 21, 1872; Oct. 29, 1871.

172. Diary of Annie G. Dudley Davis, Apr. 1863; July 1863; Nov. 1863; Jan. 1864. For more on Dickinson, see Gustafson, *Women and the Republican Party*, 24–26.

173. Diary of Julia A. Wilbur, May 17, 1870–May 2, 1871; Sept. 27, 1870.

174. Ibid., Sept. 6, 1868; Mar. 27, 1869; Jan 22, 1869; Mar. 30, 1869–May 14, 1870; Apr. 15; Oct. 11; Nov. 15, 17; Dec. 4, 1869; Jan. 24; Mar. 15, 1870; May 17, 1870–May 2, 1871; July 27; Oct. 24; Nov. 21, 24; Dec. 19, 1870; Jan 16; Feb. 1, 1871; May 5, 1871–Apr. 21, 1872; May 22; Dec. 27, 1871; "Personal," *Cincinnati Daily Gazette*, Dec. 28, 1869, 1.

175. Diary of Julia A. Wilbur, Sept. 6, 1868–Mar. 27, 1869; Mar. 8, 20, 1869; May 17, 1870–May 2, 1871; Nov. 7, 9; Dec. 10, 1870; Feb. 11, 19, 1871.

176. Ibid., Sept. 6, 1868–Mar. 27, 1869; Mar. 19, 1869; Mar. 30, 1869–May 14, 1870; Feb. 21, 1870; May 17, 1870–May 2, 1871; Oct. 17; Dec. 8, 1870; Jan. 5, 1871; May 5, 1871–Apr. 21, 1872; Nov. 3, 1871.

177. Ibid., May 17, 1870–May 2, 1871; Nov. 3, 7, 14, 28; Dec. 17, 1870; May 5, 1871–Apr. 21, 1872; Nov 4, 9, 1871.

178. Ibid., May 17, 1870–May 2, 1871; Oct. 31, 1870.

179. Gemmill, *Notes on Washington*, 10.

180. Smith, "My Recollections of Civil War Days," 36. The Treasury clerk was likely Miss H. A. Sweeney, who worked for the Treasury Department from 1863 to 1865. *Federal Register*, 1863–1865; Record of Clerks in the Office of the Commissioner of Internal Revenue 1862–1869, NA-Tr.

181. Diary of Julia A. Wilbur, May 17, 1870–May 2, 1871; May 5, 1870.

182. Ibid., Mar. 30, 1869–May 14, 1870; Feb. 28; Mar. 7; May 13, 1870; May 17, 1870–May 2, 1871; Oct. 25, 1870; Feb. 18, 1871.

183. Townsend, *Washington, Outside and Inside*, 252.

184. Diary of Julia A. Wilbur, Mar. 30, 1869–May 14, 1870; Feb. 28; May 13, 1870.

185. Ibid., May 5, 1871–Apr. 21, 1872; June 5, 1871.

186. "General Spinner's Camp," *The Revolution*, Sept. 29, 1870, 203; "Letter from Washington," *Sun*, Sept. 10, 1870, 4.

187. "General Spinner's Camp," *The Revolution*, Sept. 29, 1870, 203.

188. "General Spinner," *The Inter Ocean*, Aug. 7, 1875, 5.

189. Diary of Julia A. Wilbur, May 5, 1871–Apr. 21, 1872; Dec. 6, 1871.

190. "Washington Items," *Daily Constitutional Union*, June 28, 1866, 3; "Washington Items," *Daily Constitutional Union*, June 30, 1866, 2.

191. "City Intelligence," *Daily Morning Chronicle*, July 3, 1866, 4.

192. When the rink was open, they would place a "red ball" on the streetcars to inform the public. "City Intelligence," *Daily Morning Chronicle*, Jan. 17, 1867, 4; "City Intelligence," *Daily Morning Chronicle*, Jan. 19, 1867, 4. See also "City Intelligence," *Daily Morning Chronicle*, Jan. 2, 1867, 4. Ice skating was also popular in other cities. See, for example, Ryan, *Women in Public*, 81.

193. "[Advertisement]," *Evening Star*, Apr. 28, 1870, 2. See also, ads in *Evening Star* on Apr. 29, Apr. 30, May 2, May 3, May 4, May 5, and May 6. Wilbur's diary contains multiple entries referencing buying photographs. See, for example, Wilbur, Diary of Julia A. Wilbur, Mar. 30, 1869–May 14, 1870; Apr. 22, 1869.

194. Diary of Julia A. Wilbur, Mar. 30, 1869–May 14, 1870; Sept. 6; Dec. 3, 1869; Apr. 4, 1870; May 17, 1870–May 2, 1871; Oct. 22, 1870. See also Nov. 15, 1871 ("In evening went to hear Vincent Collger[?] but 50 cts. was more than I cd. afford to pay + I came away!").

195. "City Intelligence," *Daily Morning Chronicle*, Dec. 21, 1867, 2; "Local News," *Evening Star*, Dec. 3, 1869, 4.

196. "City Intelligence," *Daily Morning Chronicle*, Jan. 30, 1868, 4. A January 1869 advertisement for the same school also touted the importance of learning usable skills and by doing so, "young people [and] men and women of maturer years" would "Resolve Not To Be Poor." "City Intelligence," *Daily Morning Chronicle*, Jan. 1, 1869, 4. See also, "For Women," *The Critic*, Oct. 3, 1870, 4 (Grace Greenwood endorsing Washington's Business College because women "can not all be supported, depend and cling as we may" and needed to "learn how to take care of ourselves").

197. Such schools had been established by the 1840s and 1850s. Davies, *Woman's Place*, 72. The numbers of commercial bookkeeping schools increased greatly in the 1860s and 1870s, however. Historian Carole Srole found that private commercial schools increased in number from 30 in 1860 to 1,620 in 1880. Srole, *Transcribing Class*, 34.

198. "Local News," *Evening Star*, Dec. 3, 1869, 4.

199. Diary of Julia A. Wilbur, May 5, 1871–Apr. 21, 1872; Oct. 16, 17, 19, 20, 1871.

200. "City Intelligence," *Daily Morning Chronicle*, Dec. 21, 1867, 2; "Washington Business College," *Daily Morning Chronicle*, July 2, 1869, 4. Washington business colleges also served as a center for women's political activity. In 1871, fifty female Washingtonians met at "the Ladies Department of the Business College" after a failed attempt at registering to vote. The women, most of whom had attempted to register at City Hall, used the Business College as a place to regroup and plan "further steps for the enforcement of their rights and the attainment of their ambition." Women's entrance into business and education helped them take further steps into politics. "Woman's Rights," *The Critic*, Apr. 19, 1871, 2.

201. "Law School for Young Ladies," *Daily Morning Chronicle*, Oct. 29, 1869, 4.

202. "Washington Letter," *Cincinnati Commercial Tribune*, Aug. 19, 1871, 2.

203. "Words and Works," *The Revolution*, Dec. 16, 1871, 6.

204. For more on Barton's work, see, for example, Oates, *Woman of Valor*.

205. "The Widow's Mite," *Daily Morning Chronicle*, Dec. 25, 1862, 3.

206. "City Intelligence," *Daily Morning Chronicle*, Dec. 29, 1869, 4; "City Intelligence," *Daily Morning Chronicle*, Dec. 30, 1869, 4; "City Intelligence," *Daily Morning Chronicle*, Jan. 1, 1870, 4.

207. "City Intelligence," *Daily Morning Chronicle*, Oct. 23, 1867, 1.

208. "Visitors to the Poor," *Daily Morning Chronicle*, Jan. 8, 1870, 4; 1870 Census, Washington, D.C., 3 WD. Freeman is listed as a "laborer" in the 1871 *Federal Register*.

209. "A Sewing Circle for the Benefit of Refugee Women and Children," *Daily Morning Chronicle*, Feb. 13, 1865, 2.

210. She also stayed on past her tenure until her successor was appointed. "City Intelligence," *Daily Morning Chronicle*, Dec. 16, 1865, 4. She was still serving as Secretary in April 1865. "Ladies' National Union Relief Association," *Daily Morning Chronicle*, Apr. 27, 1865, 2.

211. "Ladies' National Union Relief Association," *Daily Morning Chronicle*, Apr. 27, 1865, 2.

212. "The Ladies' Union Relief Association," *Daily Morning Chronicle*, Mar. 28, 1865, 2.

213. See e.g. Masur, *Example for All the Land*, 174; Sneider, *Suffragists in an Imperial Age*, 23; "City Intelligence," *Daily Morning Chronicle*, Sept. 13, 1867, 1; "City Intelligence," *Daily Morning Chronicle*, Sept. 21, 1867, 1; "Local News," *Evening Star*, Sept. 21, 1867, 2; "Equal Rights Meeting," *Evening Star*, July 6, 1867, 1; "City Intelligence," *Daily Morning Chronicle*, July 20, 1867, 4; "Local News," *Evening Star*, July 20, 1867, 1; "City Intelligence," *Daily Morning Chronicle*, Dec. 16, 1868, 4; "City Intelligence," *Daily Morning Chronicle*, Jan. 1, 1869, 4; "City Intelligence," *Daily Morning Chronicle*, Jan. 8, 1869, 4; "City Intelligence," *Daily Morning Chronicle*, Jan. 20, 1869, 4; "City Intelligence," *Daily*

Morning Chronicle, Jan. 21, 1869, 4; "City Intelligence," *Daily Morning Chronicle*, Jan. 22, 1869, 4; "City Intelligence," *Daily Morning Chronicle*, Jan. 23, 1869, 4; "City Intelligence," *Daily Morning Chronicle*, Feb. 26, 1869, 4; "City Intelligence," *Daily Morning Chronicle*, Apr. 2, 1869, 4; "City Intelligence," *Daily Morning Chronicle*, April 16, 1869, 4; "City Intelligence," *Daily Morning Chronicle*, Apr. 27, 1869, 4; "City Intelligence," *Daily Morning Chronicle*, May 26, 1869, 4; "City Intelligence," *Daily Morning Chronicle*, May 26, 1869, 4; "City Intelligence," *Daily Morning Chronicle*, Sept. 20, 1869, 4; "City Intelligence," *Daily Morning Chronicle*, Oct. 4, 1869, 1; "City Intelligence," *Daily Morning Chronicle*, Oct. 11, 1869, 1; "City Intelligence," *Daily Morning Chronicle*, Dec. 2, 1869, 4; "City Intelligence," *Daily Morning Chronicle*, Dec. 27, 1869, 4; "Local News," *Evening Star*, Dec. 27, 1869, 4; "Universal Suffrage," *Daily Morning Chronicle*, Jan. 19, 1870, 4; "Universal Suffrage," *Daily Morning Chronicle*, Jan. 20, 1870, 4; "City Intelligence," *Daily Morning Chronicle*, Jan. 24, 1870, 4; "Woman's Suffrage," *Daily Morning Chronicle*, May 12, 1870, 1; "[No Title]," *Evening Star*, May 12, 1870, 1; "Wailing Women: American Amazons in Council and Political Females Let Loose," *New York Herald*, May 12, 1870, 10; "City Intelligence," *Daily Morning Chronicle*, Jan. 6, 1871, 4.

214. For an example of Griffing's work with freedmen, see, for example, "Local Intelligence," *Daily Constitutional Union*, Mar. 15, 1865, 3.

215. Harrison, "Welfare and Employment Policies of the Freedmen's Bureau"; "Local News," *Evening Star*, Mar. 25, 1867, 3.

216. Harrison, "Welfare and Employment Policies of the Freedmen's Bureau," 31–33. See also, "City Intelligence," *Daily Morning Chronicle*, Mar. 27, 1867, 2.

217. "Washington," *New York Herald*, Mar. 12, 1869, 3.

218. *Federal Register*, 1867, 1869.

219. *Federal Register*, 1871. See also 1870 Census, Washington, D.C., 5 WD. A third daughter, Cora, was fourteen years old in 1870.

220. See, for example, Diary of Julia A. Wilbur, Mar. 30, 1869–May 14, 1870; Dec. 31, 1869; Jan. 1; Mar. 5, 1870; May 17, 1870–May 2, 1871; Mar. 14, 1871.

221. Ibid., Sept. 6, 1868–Mar. 27, 1869; Jan. 12, 1869; Mar. 30, 1869–May 14, 1870; Jan. 11, 1870; May 17, 1870–May 2, 1871; Jan. 10, 1871.

222. Ibid., Sept. 6, 1868–Mar. 27, 1869; Dec. 11, 1869; May 17, 1870–May 2, 1871; Feb. 2, 1871.

223. Ibid., May 5, 1871–Apr. 21, 1872; Sept. 8, 9, 10, 12, 16, 22, 30; Oct. 7, 14, 25; Nov. 18, 25; Dec. 16, 26, 30, 1871.

224. Ibid., May 5, 1871–Apr. 21, 1872; Dec. 2, 3, 1871.

225. Stanton, *History of Woman Suffrage*, 808.

226. Masur, *Example for All the Land*, 179.

227. Dudden, *Fighting Chance*.

228. Ibid., 7.

229. "City Intelligence," *Daily Morning Chronicle*, Jan. 20, 1869, 4; "City Intelligence," *Daily Morning Chronicle*, Oct. 4, 1869, 1; "Universal Suffrage," *Daily Morning Chronicle*, Jan. 19, 1870, 4; "Woman's Suffrage," *Daily Morning Chronicle*, May 12, 1870, 1; "City Intelligence," *Daily Morning Chronicle*, Jan. 8, 1869, 4.

230. Larsen, *Crusader and Feminist*.

231. "Department News," *Daily Morning Chronicle*, June 28, 1869, 1; *Federal Register*, 1871.

232. "Universal Suffrage," *Daily Morning Chronicle*, Jan. 19, 1870, 4.

233. Hall appears on the *Federal Register* in 1865, 1867, 1869, and 1871 and is listed as a Treasury Department clerk in the 1870 D.C. Census. 1870 Census, Washington, D.C., 5 WD. "City Intelligence," *Daily Morning Chronicle*, Sept. 13, 1867, 1.

234. Julia Holmes was listed in the *Federal Register* for the Treasury Department in 1863 and 1865. Holmes's husband, James, worked as a clerk in the Interior Department. 1870 Census, Washington, D.C., 5 WD. Elizabeth Cady Stanton and Susan B. Anthony reported that James and Julia Holmes called a meeting at their residence to organize the Universal Franchise Association in 1867. Stanton, *History of Woman Suffrage*, 809.

235. "City Intelligence," *Daily Morning Chronicle*, Dec. 16, 1868, 4; "Equal Rights," *Daily Morning Chronicle*, July 13, 1867, 4; "City Intelligence," *Daily Morning Chronicle*, Sept. 13, 1867, 1; "City Intelligence," *Daily Morning Chronicle*, Jan. 20, 1869, 4; "City Intelligence," *Daily Morning Chronicle*, Feb. 2, 1869, 4.

236. "City Intelligence," *Daily Morning Chronicle*, Sept. 21, 1867, 1; "Local News," *Evening Star*, Sept. 21, 1867, 2.

237. *Federal Register*, 1865, 1867.

238. "Woman's Rights," *Evening Star*, Jan. 22, 1870, 1.

239. "Editorial Correspondence: National Suffrage Convention," *The Revolution*, Jan. 28, 1869, 49–50.

240. Voter names available at "Voter name: April 1871. Washington, DC," The Elizabeth Cady Stanton & Susan B. Anthony Papers Project. I cross-referenced these names with my database of female federal employees. The women came from the War Department, Treasury Department, Government Printing Office, Patent Office, and Freedmen's Bureau. For more on the argument that the Fourteenth Amendment granted women the right to vote, and on this April 1871 attempt, see Sneider, *Suffragists in an Imperial Age*, 30–32, 53.

241. DuBois, *Woman Suffrage & Women's Rights*, 99, chapter 7.

242. Diary of Julia A. Wilbur, Mar. 30, 1869–May 14, 1870; Apr. 22, 26, 1869.

243. Ibid., May 17, 1870–May 2, 1871; Apr. 15, 1871.

244. Ibid., Sept. 6, 1868–Mar. 27, 1869; Jan. 21, 1869.

245. Ibid., May 17, 1870–May 2, 1871; Jan. 11, 12, 1871.

246. Ibid., Sept. 6, 1868–Mar. 27, 1869; Nov. 29, 1869; May 17, 1870–May 2, 1871; May 25, 1870.

247. Ibid., Mar. 30, 1869–May 14, 1870; Jan. 11, 18, 19, 20, 1870; May 17, 1870–May 2, 1871; Dec. 14, 1870; Jan. 11, 12, 25, 26; Feb. 1, 7, 10, 15, 16; Mar. 3, 5, 17, 1871; May 5, 1871–Apr. 21, 1872; Aug 11, 25; October 6; Nov. 17; Dec. 8, 9, 10, 11, 12, 1871; Jan. 10, 12, 1872.

248. Ibid., May 17, 1870–May 2, 1871; Jan. 11, 12, 13, 1871.

249. Stanton, *History of Woman Suffrage, Volume 2*, 485. The following month the women were moved to the Agricultural Committee rooms.

250. DuBois, *Woman Suffrage & Women's Rights*, 101.

251. Diary of Julia A. Wilbur, May 17, 1870–May 2, 1871; Jan 25, 26, 1871.

252. "A Lecture on Constitutional Equality," Library of Congress.

253. Diary of Julia A. Wilbur, May 17, 1870–May 2, 1871; Feb. 15, 16, 17, 1871.

254. Ibid., May 5, 1871–Apr. 21, 1872; Dec. 10, 1871; see also Jan. 12, 1872.

255. Ibid., Jan 10, 1872.

256. "Washington," *The Revolution*, Apr. 16, 1868, 226.

257. "Men and Women—Work and Wages," *The Revolution*, Mar. 4, 1869, 140.

258. "City Intelligence," *Daily Morning Chronicle*, Jan. 23, 1869, 4; "The Washington Convention," *The Revolution*, Jan. 27, 1869, 52–57 (two out of three sessions during the day).

259. "City Intelligence," *Daily Morning Chronicle*, Nov. 25, 1869, 4.

260. Ibid., Dec. 2, 1869, 4.

261. "All about the Sex," *Daily Evening Bulletin*, Feb. 19, 1870, 6.

262. "City Intelligence," *Daily Morning Chronicle*, Jan. 20, 1869, 4 (Woman's Rights Convention's evening sessions began at 7:00 P.M.).

263. "City Intelligence," *Daily Morning Chronicle*, Jan. 18, 1870, 4; see also "The Washington Convention," *The Revolution*, Jan. 27, 1869, 52–57.

264. "Equal Rights Meeting," *Evening Star*, July 6, 1867, 1 ("a meeting was held last evening").

265. "City Intelligence," *Daily Morning Chronicle*, Apr. 2, 1869, 4. See also "City Intelligence," *Daily Morning Chronicle*, Feb. 26, 1869, 4 (meeting on woman suffrage "did not adjourn until a late hour").

266. "Woman's Rights," *The Critic*, Apr. 19, 1871, 2.

267. "Washington Suffrage Association," *The Revolution*, Dec. 9, 1869, 366; "Washington Correspondence," *The Revolution*, Dec. 2, 1869, 342.

268. "Washington Correspondence," *The Revolution*, Dec. 9, 1869, 359; Masur, *Example for All the Land*, 179.

Chapter Five

1. "Died," *Evening Star*, May 4, 1864, 3.

2. "Startling Developments, Abortion and Death, Terrible Disclosures," *Daily Constitutional Union*, May 5, 1864, 2.

3. "Died," *Evening Star*, May 4, 1864, 3.

4. "The Late Mystery," *Daily Constitutional Union*, May 6, 1864, 3.

5. "A Painful Affair and Singular Developments," *Evening Star*, May 5, 1864, 2; "The Late Mystery," *Daily Constitutional Union*, May 6, 1864, 3; Smith, *The Enemy Within*, 100–101. For the color of Baker's eyes, see Velazquez, *The Woman in Battle*, 396; Baker, *History of the United States Secret Service*, 20; Leech, *Reveille*, 183.

6. "A Painful Affair and Singular Developments," *Evening Star*, May 5, 1864, 2.

7. "Local News—The Death of Maggie Duvall," *Evening Star*, May 6, 1864, 2; "A Painful Affair and Singular Developments," *Evening Star*, May 5, 1864, 2.

8. Prior to her employment in the Treasury Department, Maggie (or Margaret) had been a dressmaker. 1860 Census, Washington, D.C., 3 WD.

9. Smith, *The Enemy Within*, 98.

10. For an overview of the images of female federal Treasury clerks in *Frank Leslie's Illustrated Newspaper, Harper's Weekly, The Days' Doings,* and *Harper's Bazar,* see Green, "Visual Fictions and the U.S. Treasury Courtesans" (arguing that the images "aided in the creation of stereotypes that continued well into the twentieth century, in turn contributing to the devaluation of white-collar women and their work").

11. Smith, *The Enemy Within*, 125.

12. "From Washington," *Public Ledger,* Sept. 18, 1861, 2.

13. See, for example, "From Washington," *Public Ledger,* Feb. 5, 1862; "The Arsenal," *Daily Morning Chronicle,* Dec. 13, 1862, 3; "News from Washington," *The New York Herald,* Feb. 25, 1863, 5; "The Treasury Building—Business of the Department—Printing Treasury Notes," *Sun,* Oct. 30, 1863, 4; "Observance of Thanksgiving Day—Arrival of Surgeons from Richmond—Female Clerk . . ." *Sun,* Nov. 28, 1863, 4; "[No title]," *Daily Evening Bulletin,* June 7, 1862.

14. "Our Omnibus Budget," *Evening Saturday Gazette,* Apr. 11, 1863, 1.

15. "A Lady Clerk," *Daily Morning Chronicle,* Nov. 28, 1863, 3.

16. "All Sorts of Paragraphs," *Portland Daily Advertiser,* June 3, 1863, 2.

17. I have been unable to locate any statements in newspapers prior to the Treasury Department Scandal of 1864 concerning rumors of sexual immorality in the Treasury Department. Detective Lafayette Baker claimed that prior to 1864, "It was more than intimated, by those who ought to have known, that among the hundreds of females employed there, some were not virtuous." Baker, *History of the Secret Service,* 261. Several secondary sources cite the existence of rumors of sexual impropriety in the Treasury Department. Aron, "Their Souls for Gold," 848; Smith, *The Enemy Within,* 99; Mogelever, *Death to Traitors,* 248; U.S. Department of the Treasury, *History of the Bureau of Engraving and Printing,* 16; Leech, *Reveille,* 391.

18. Congress provided for greenbacks in the Legal Tender Act of February 25, 1862. Nussbaum, *A History of the Dollar;* Unger, *The Greenback Era,* 15.

19. Smith, *The Enemy Within,* 106–8. See also Weber, *Copperheads,* 4–6.

20. Gurney and Gurney, *United States Treasury,* 97; U.S. Department of the Treasury, *History of the Bureau of Engraving and Printing,* 2.

21. Gurney and Gurney, *United States Treasury,* 97, 98; U.S. Department of the Treasury, *History of the Bureau of Engraving and Printing,* 2, 6–7. U.S. Congress, House of Representatives, *Certain Charges against the Treasury Department,* 1 (Majority Report); 251 (Appendix C); 2 (Majority Report).

22. U.S. Congress, House of Representatives, *Certain Charges against the Treasury Department,* 112 (Testimony of S. M. Clark).

23. Baker, *History of the Secret Service,* 274. See also U.S. Congress, House of Representatives, *Certain Charges against the Treasury Department,* 1 (Majority Report).

24. See, for example, "A Thousand Dollar Bond Missing," *Daily Constitutional Union,* Dec. 26, 1863, 3; "[ ]aling all Round—The Places of Trust Abound with Thieves," *Daily Constitutional Union,* Dec. 28, 1863, 3; "Foul, Festering Corruption," *Daily Constitutional Union,* Jan. 2, 1864, 1; "Conspiracy to Defraud," *Daily Morning*

Chronicle, Jan. 9, 1864, 3; "Frauds on Government," *Daily Constitutional Union*, Jan. 13, 1864, 1; "Frauds on the Government," *Daily Morning Chronicle*, Jan. 16, 1864, 2; "A Case of Crime in the Treasury Department," *Daily Constitutional Union*, Mar. 14, 1864, 3.

25. U.S. Congress, House of Representatives, *Certain Charges against the Treasury Department*, 13 (Majority Report); Smith, *The Enemy Within*, 104–6. Baker was the head of a semisecret federal police force known as the National Detectives or the Secret Service and well known in Washington for his liquor-spilling, gambler-arresting, brothel-breaking crusade against vice crime. Leech, *Reveille*, 329. He is a self-aggrandizing, highly suspect source.

26. Baker arrested Treasury employee James Cornwall for embezzling over $30,000. U.S. Congress, House of Representatives, *Certain Charges against the Treasury Department*, 20 (Minority Report); 13 (Majority Report).

27. Baker, *History of the Secret Service*, 274, 263; U.S. Congress, House of Representatives, *Certain Charges against the Treasury Department*, 13 (Majority Report).

28. Baker, *History of the Secret Service*, 264, 288.

29. U.S. Congress, House of Representatives, *Certain Charges against the Treasury Department*, 14 (Majority Report); "Dr. Gwynne's [*sic*] Case," *Daily Constitutional Union*, Apr. 21, 1864, 3; "Dr Gwynne's [*sic*] Case," *Daily Morning Chronicle*, Apr. 21, 1864, 2.

30. U.S. Congress, House of Representatives, *Certain Charges against the Treasury Department*, 14 (Majority Report); 48 (Testimony of Jordan).

31. Baker, *History of the Secret Service*, 261.

32. Baker, *History of the Secret Service*, 261, 292 (quoting letter from Baker to Jordan, dated April 13, 1864).

33. Baker, *History of the Secret Service*, 292 (quoting letter from Baker to Jordan, dated April 13, 1864). The first statements were taken April 9, 1864, just eight days after Jordan denied Baker's request for legal protection. Whether or not the women's confessions were true, bought, or coerced is, at present, impossible to determine.

34. U.S. Congress, House of Representatives, *Certain Charges against the Treasury Department*, 14 (Majority Report). Ada Thompson was an interesting character. She claimed to have been "one of the first seven ladies who were sent to [Washington, D.C.] by the Chamber of Commerce in New York to act as nurses in our hospitals." She also claimed that she "had studied two years at the New York Medical College." Thompson was offended when the *Star* incorrectly reported she worked at the Treasury, sending a letter to the editor of the paper, which stated: "I am happy to be able to say that I am not, and never have been employed in the Treasury, and was never inside of the building but once." Further, although she seems very quick to judge the sexual morality of Treasury employees, it appears she and another witness in the case were cohabitating lovers. Thompson never admitted T. C. Spurgeon was her live-in lover, but when asked if it was true, Thompson did not deny it, instead asserting that it had no relevance on the Jackson case. Finally, there is a suggestion in her testimony in the Jackson case that she was one of Baker's detectives. Jackson's attorney asked her if she was, and she replied: "If I am, I'm sharp enough not to answer that question." "A Card from Miss Ada Thompson—She Is Not That Sort of a Woman," *Evening Star*, May 6, 164,

2; "The Alleged Abortion Case," *Evening Star*, May 11, 1864, 3. To read Thompson/Spurgeon's own account of her service as a nurse, see Holland, ed., *Our Army Nurses*, 454–65. I owe thanks to Lisa Tuttle for sharing her research on Thompson and the Treasury Department Scandal with me.

35. U.S. Congress, House of Representatives, *Certain Charges against the Treasury Department*, 14 (Majority Report), 410–12 (Diary of Miss Ella Jackson); "The Late Mystery," *Daily Constitutional Union*, May 6, 1864, 3. Jackson was also an actress. There are two photographs of her at the Library of Congress. In both, she is in white, wearing tights and a shoulder-baring top. Ella Jackson [between 1855 and 1865] (Library of Congress Prints and Photographs Division); Ella Jackson, full-length portrait, standing, with right hand held up to chest, facing left [no date recorded on caption card] (Library of Congress Prints and Photographs Division).

36. Further complicating an already complicated story, there were two Miss Duvalls, who both worked in the Treasury Department and were involved in this scandal. One was Laura Duvall. Her testimony was taken by Baker in April 1864, and is described herein. Another was Maggie Duvall, who was introduced in the beginning of this chapter as having died in May 1864. Maggie and Laura were cousins. "The Alleged Abortion Case," *Evening Star*, May 11, 1864, 3. Even members of the Congressional Committee were confused. One of the members remarked: "Miss Duvall is dead," referring to Laura Duvall who had provided a statement, but the woman who died was Maggie Duvall. U.S. Congress, House of Representatives, *Certain Charges against the Treasury Department*, 71 (Discussion among committee after questioning of Clark).

37. U.S. Congress, House of Representatives, *Certain Charges against the Treasury Department*, 14 (Majority Report). See also Testimonies of Jackson, Duvall, and Thompson, 405–9. It is not clear if it was Duvall or Germon who lived with Jackson. Jackson is silent on the issue, Duvall claims to live with her mother and Germon claims to live with her sister. The remaining testimony and evidence is contradictory. I believe Laura Duvall was Jackson's roommate because Baker allegedly gathered the roommates' testimonies on the same day, and both Jackson's and Duvall's statements are dated April 9, 1864, whereas Germon's statement is dated three days later.

38. Old Capitol was a much-feared prison in Civil War–era Washington, D.C. Leech, *Reveille*, 174–96.

39. U.S. Congress, House of Representatives, *Certain Charges against the Treasury Department*, 14 (Majority Report), 405–9 (testimonies of Jackson, Duvall, and Thompson).

40. Ibid.

41. U.S. Congress, House of Representatives, *Certain Charges against the Treasury Department*, 405–6 (Statement of Miss Ella Jackson), 410–12 (Diary of Miss Ella Jackson).

42. U.S. Congress, House of Representatives, *Certain Charges against the Treasury Department*, 408–9 (Statement of Miss Ada Thompson). Jackson also "frequently" told Thompson "that whenever new girls applied for situations in the Currency Bureau, Clark would come to her and ask her to find out all about them; that she would make the inquiries, and if she (Miss Jackson) reported that she thought they [the girls] could be improperly used by Clark, they were employed."

43. Christine Stansell found this kind of causal prostitution in mid-nineteenth century New York City as well and notes that prostitution was tied to women's low pay. Stansell, *City of Women*, 171–92.

44. U.S. Congress, House of Representatives, *Certain Charges against the Treasury Department*, 406–7 (Statement of Miss Jennie Germon).

45. Anthony Lulley, for example, worked at a soda stand in front of the Treasury Department. Lulley stated that in fall 1863, he and his brother saw Clark and another man meet two women outside No. 276 Pennsylvania Avenue and followed the four to a restaurant. U.S. Congress, House of Representatives, *Certain Charges against the Treasury Department*, 415 (Statement of Anthony Lulley), 414 (Statement of Mano Lulley).

46. U.S. Congress, House of Representatives, *Certain Charges against the Treasury Department*, 416 (Letter from Jordan to Chase dated April 19, 1864).

47. U.S. Congress, House of Representatives, *Certain Charges against the Treasury Department*, 49–50 (Testimony of Edward Jordan).

48. U.S. Congress, House of Representatives, *Certain Charges against the Treasury Department*, 50 (Testimony of Edward Jordan).

49. For more on Brooks's involvement, see Smith, *The Enemy Within*, 114–16.

50. U.S. Congress, House of Representatives, *Certain Charges against the Treasury Department*, 1 (Majority Report).

51. "Startling Developments. Abortion and Death," *Daily Constitutional Union*, May 5, 1864, 2. The paper incorrectly reported that Clark had been arrested "charged with the crime of being an accessory to the act of abortion." Clark had not been arrested. In fact, the man purported to be the father of Duvall's unborn baby was Enoch Lewis, son of Judge Lewis of the Internal Revenue Department (a bureau in the Treasury Department). "A Painful Affair and Singular Developments," *Evening Star*, May 5, 1864, 2.

52. "Local News—The Death of Maggie Duvall," *Evening Star*, May 6, 1864, 2. Simultaneous to that inquest, Ella Jackson was forced to answer charges of "feloniously aiding and abetting . . . in attempting or in procuring an abortion on [Duvall] of which malpractice [Duvall] died." The charges were based on the testimony of Thompson and her live-in lover, who claimed Jackson had been administering abortifactient medicine to Duvall. "Further Developments in the Shocking Case of Miss Margaret Ann Duvall," *Evening Star*, May 5, 1864, 2; "The Alleged Abortion Case," *Evening Star*, May 11, 1864, 3.

53. "Local News—The Death of Maggie Duvall," *Evening Star*, May 6, 1864, 2. Indeed, the case was reported on at least as far away as Chicago. "Death of Margaret Ann Duval, Late Employee in the Treasury Department—The Cause—Arrest of Miss Ella Jackson," *Chicago Tribune*, May 10, 1864, 3.

54. *Evening Star*, May 10, 1864, 2.

55. Weber, *Copperheads*, 139. These losses were incurred at numerous battles, including the battles of the Wilderness (May 5–7, 1864), Spotsylvania (May 8–19, 1864), and Cold Harbor (May 31–June 12, 1864).

56. Weber, *Copperheads*, 135.

57. Ibid., 142 (quoting *Niles Republican*, June 18, 1864).

58. For more on Garfield's involvement, see Smith, *The Enemy Within*, 116–17, 121–25.

59. The majority report was supported by James A. Garfield, James F. Wilson, Thomas A. Jenckes, and Henry Winter Davis. Reuben E. Fenton, representative of New York, wrote a concurrence. Leech, *Reveille*, 391.

60. The minority report was signed by James Brooks, John T. Stuart, W. G. Steele, and John L. Dawson. U.S. Congress, House of Representatives, *Certain Charges against the Treasury Department*, 29 (Minority Report).

61. On the first issue—the printing of national securities—the Democrats' minority report stated that Clark's Bureau of Engraving and Printing was "loose, slovenly, unsatisfactory, and susceptible of a considerable amount of fraud." U.S. Congress, House of Representatives, *Certain Charges against the Treasury Department*, 24, 26 (Minority Report). The Republican majority reached far different conclusions about Clark and the Treasury Department. Their report fully supported Clark.

62. The committee failed to call Germon, Jackson, Duvall, or Thompson to provide testimony at the hearings, "not deeming it just to put the personal and official character of any public officer on trial before such parties." U.S. Congress, House of Representatives, *Certain Charges against the Treasury Department*, 17 (Majority Report).

63. U.S. Congress, House of Representatives, *Certain Charges against the Treasury Department*, 17 (Majority Report).

64. U.S. Congress, House of Representatives, *Certain Charges against the Treasury Department*, 21 (Minority Report). In statements during the investigation, Brooks made it clear that he believed that the majority of women in the Treasury were virtuous. U.S. Congress, House of Representatives, *Certain Charges against the Treasury Department*, 71. (Discussion among committee after questioning of Clark). See also U.S. Congress, House of Representatives, *Certain Charges against the Treasury Department*, 23 (Minority Report).

65. See, for example, Aron, *Ladies and Gentlemen*, 166; Cooney, "The State of the Treasury," 40–43; Leech, *Reveille*, 391. For a balanced, thorough account of the scandal, see Smith, *The Enemy Within*, chapter 4, and Green, "Visual Fictions and the U.S. Treasury Courtesans." Other exceptions include Baker's own account of the events in his book and subsequent biographies of Baker that track his story. Baker, *History of the Secret Service*; Mogelever, *Death to Traitors*; Treasury, *History of the Bureau of Engraving and Printing*, 15–17; Goodwin, *Greenback*, 219. The Goodwin reference includes a balanced account of the scandal, but lacks footnotes and takes some extreme literary licenses ("Pretty Ella [Jackson] stretches and waggles her fingers over her head. She looks at Clark and her eyes go wide. Mr. Clark smiles back").

66. That is not to say that I do not believe there were concerns about sexual immorality. Although I have not yet found contemporary newspaper articles to support the contention, the public was very likely concerned with women entering the workforce. See, for example, Aron, *Ladies and Gentlemen*, 166; Cutter, *Domestic Devils, Battlefield Angels*, 184–85.

67. Scholars of sex scandals have argued that when, as in the Treasury Department Scandal, elements of sex are mixed with fraud, sex usually overshadows fraud in the public mind because it is easier to understand. Many citizens likely found Baker's

concerns with the inefficiency of dry printing less gripping than Jennie Germon's testimony that she and Clark spent the night in his marital bed while his wife was out of town. Sex scandals also require a much lower burden of proof than do scandals focused on finances or fraud. Apostolidis and Williams, *Public Affairs: Politics in the Age of Sex Scandals*, in "Introduction: Sex Scandals and Discourses of Power," ed. Paul Apostolidis and Juliet A. Williams, 4–6.

68. For articles discussing the scandal outside Washington, D.C., see, for example, "The Investigation into the Treasury Department and Washington—the Female Clerk System," *The Daily Age*, May 21, 1864, 1; "The Investigations in the Treasury Department," *The Daily Age*, July 4, 1864, 1; "Mr Lincoln's Officeholders," *The Daily Age*, Oct. 1, 1864, 2; "Letter from New York," *Daily Evening Bulletin*, Aug. 1, 1864, 1; "From Washington," *New York Tribune*, Apr. 28, 1864, 4; "The Treasury on Trial," *Springfield Republican*, May 7, 1864, 2; "From Washington," *Springfield Weekly Republican*, May 7, 1864, 4; "The Treasury Investigation," *Springfield Republican*, July 23, 1864, 5; "Horrible Immorality," *New Hampshire Patriot and Gazette*, May 11, 1864, 2; "Interesting from Washington . . . the Charges against the Treasury Department," *New York Herald*, May 2, 1864; "General News," *New York Herald*, July 1, 1864, 4; "Shocking Developments," *New York Herald*, May 7, 1864, 8; "News Summary," *Troy Weekly Times*, May 14, 1864, 1; "The United States Treasury Scandal," *Times-Picayune*, May 18, 1864, 1; "More of the Treasury Building Scandal—Death of One of the 'Clerks' by Abortion," *Columbian Register*, May 14, 1864, 1; "The Treasury Scandal," *Weekly Dakotian*, July 30, 1864, 1.

69. Ellis, *The Sights and Secrets of the National Capital*, 383.

70. Ibid., 383–86.

71. Ibid., 387. The fear of prostitutes passing as respectable women was one that preoccupied many Americans in the mid-nineteenth century. Cutter, *Domestic Devils*, 48.

72. Townsend, *Washington, Outside and Inside*, 162.

73. Smith, *The Enemy Within*, 126.

74. This reputational harm was especially unfortunate because a close reading of the House Report reveals a level of respect for the female clerks working in the Treasury. During questioning, Clark was asked to name the superintendents of the divisions, and he provided eighteen names—eleven of the superintendents are women. U.S. Congress, House of Representatives, *Certain Charges against the Treasury Department*, 69 (Testimony of S. M. Clark). When the committee questions the women, the questioning is in the same tenor as their questioning of the men—professional and respectful. See, for example, U.S. Congress, House of Representatives, *Certain Charges against the Treasury Department*, 78, 81, 87 (Questioning Mrs. S. R. Wilkins), 85 (Questioning of Miss Ella C. Mitchell), 87 (Questioning of Miss M. C. Douglass), 92 (Questioning of Miss Emma Cooper).

75. Stansell, *City of Women*, 148.

76. Weber, *Copperheads*, 1–2, 135–36.

77. For more on this, see Smith, *The Enemy Within*, chapter 4.

78. J. Henry Mullford to Abraham Lincoln, Wednesday, Apr. 27, 1864, ALP, accessed Oct. 22, 2010.

79. "Behind the Scenes" (1864), Library of Congress, Prints and Photographs Division, Washington, D.C., Call Number: PC/US-1864.A000.

80. "The Treasury Investigation," *Daily Constitutional Union*, July 9, 1864, 1.

81. "The Treasury Investigation," *Daily Constitutional Union*, July 9, 1864, 1. The *Daily Constitutional Union* was so enamored with the story they printed the article again, in its entirety, two days later. "The Treasury Investigation," *Daily Constitutional Union*, July 11, 1864, 2. This restraint may have been due to the local newspaper's knowledge that the women specifically implicated in the scandal—Germon, Jackson, and Duvall—worked in the Treasury's Bureau of Engraving and Printing. The employees in this bureau were considered to be manual laborers, as opposed to clerks.

82. "Horrible Immorality," *New Hampshire Patriot and Gazette*, May 11, 1864, 2; Smith, *The Enemy Within*, 117 (citing *New York World* as quoted in *Pittsburgh Post*, May 5, 1864).

83. Smith, *The Enemy Within*, 119 (citing *Chicago Times* May 11 and May 19, 1864).

84. "The Treasury on Trial," *Springfield Republican*, May 7, 1864, 2.

85. Smith, *The Enemy Within*, 97–98 (citing "[no title]," *Newark* (Ohio) *Advocate*, May 6, 1864).

86. "The United States Treasury Scandal," *Times-Picayune*, May 18, 1864, 1.

87. "Employment of Female Clerks." *Houston Union*, Mar. 15, 1869, 1. For more on the Republican Party's relationship with women during this era, see Gustafson, *Women and the Republican Party*.

88. "[No Title]," *The New Hampshire Patriot*, Dec. 1, 1869, 1.

89. "The Department Women at Washington," *Pomeroy's Democrat*, May 5, 1869, 4.

90. "Various Items," *Lowell Daily Citizen and News*, Oct. 19, 1866, 2.

91. *Pomeroy's Democrat*, May 3, 1871, 1 (emphasis added). A related rumor circulating the streets of Washington, D.C., and the pages of the press was that women employed by the government were low class criminals. "City Intelligence," *Daily Morning Chronicle*, Sept. 3, 1866, 4; "Brief Topics," *Jamestown Journal*, Mar. 18, 1870, 4; "Washington Correspondence," *The Revolution*, Feb. 24, 1870, 119.

92. See Aron, *Ladies and Gentlemen*, 167–69. Aron includes a story of a well-known Washington, D.C., madam testifying before a judge during the Wilson administration in which she stated, "Your Honor, everybody knows I run the second-best house in the city.... The Treasury runs the best." See also Buel, *Mysteries and Miseries*, 192.

93. Smith, *The Enemy Within*, 124.

94. "Letter from Washington," *Daily Ohio Statesman*, Oct. 26, 1865; "Letter from Washington," *Daily Picayune*, Nov. 26, 1865.

95. "Guillotoning [*sic*] the Ladies," *Flake's Bulletin*, Apr. 7, 1869, 4.

96. "The Department Women at Washington," *Pomeroy's Democrat*, May 5, 1869, 4.

97. "Depravity at the Capitol," *Jamestown Journal*, Feb. 11, 1870, 4; "Depravity at the Capitol," *The Revolution*, Feb. 3, 1870, 75.

98. "Women of the Lobby," *Daily Evening Bulletin*, Jan. 15, 1870, 4. See also "The Investigation into the Treasury Department and Washington—The Female Clerk System," *The Daily Age*, May 21, 1864, 1.

99. "The Federal Capital," *The Revolution*, Feb. 5, 1868, 76.

100. "The Department Bagnios at Washington," *Salt Lake Daily Telegraph*, Feb. 6, 1867, 4.

101. Townsend, *Washington, Outside and Inside*, 389.

102. "Life and Society in Washington," *Semi-Weekly Telegraph*, Sept. 6, 1866, 4; "Life and Society in Washington," *Evening Bulletin*, Aug. 22, 1866, 3; "Female Department Clerks," *Flake's Bulletin*, Aug. 3, 1866; "Women in Washington," *Albany Journal*, July 20, 1866.

103. "Washington Correspondence," *Georgia Weekly Telegraph*, Nov. 26, 1869, 1. In 1891, Lewis V. Bogy, a former federal clerk, wrote a novel set in Reconstruction-era Washington, D.C., about a female Treasury Department clerk who was plagued by repeated seduction attempts from male superiors and the immoral influence of female coworkers. She escaped damnation by marrying outside of the Treasury. Bogy, *In Office*. For an analysis of this book, see Srole, *Transcribing Class and Gender*, 54–56.

104. Wood, *Freedom of the Streets*, 16.

105. Srole, *Transcribing Class and Gender*, 53, 67–68.

106. "Treasures of the Treasury," *Pomeroy's Democrat*, Sept. 24, 1871, 2. I could find no further information on the "Jolly Independents" or "Selina Tewksbury."

107. Aron, *Ladies and Gentlemen*, 165.

108. Srole, *Transcribing Class and Gender*, 56. Stansell found a similar discomfort in New York City with "factory girls" in the mid-nineteenth century, and the Jolly Independents also resemble Bowery girls—"members of a high-spirited peer group, reveling in their association with each other." Stansell, *City of Women*, 93, 125.

109. "Foreign News!" *Pacific Commercial Advertiser*, Jan. 20, 1866, 3. The same article appeared in "Female Clerks," *Daily State Gazette*, Nov. 11, 1865, 2. See also "The Lady Clerks in the Departments," *New York Times*, Nov. 10, 1865, 4; "The Female Clerks," *Evening Star*, Oct. 14, 1870, 1.

110. "The Man in the Door Was Secretary George S. Boutwell" (1869), reproduced in "Women in Business," *Fortune* 12 (July 1935): 50–57, 90–96, 56. See also Davies, "Woman's Place," 12 (analyzing the cartoon and ascribing to it a 1875 publication date, citing Bruce Bliven, Jr., *The Wonderful Writing Machine* [New York: Random, 1954], 73).

111. Diary of Julia A. Wilbur, Mar. 30, 1869–May 14, 1870; Jan. 3, 1870; May 2, 1870; Diary of Julia A. Wilbur, May 17, 1870–May 2, 1871; July 16; Sept. 22; Nov. 12, 30; Dec. 1, 1870; Jan. 19, 1871; Diary of Julia A. Wilbur, May 5, 1871—Apr. 21, 1872; Aug. 2, 1871.

112. For more on Swisshelm's prewar civil rights work, see, for example, Isenberg, *Sex and Citizenship*, 48, 119, 250n.142.

113. This was not Swisshelm's first instance of making negative remarks about fellow working-women. In 1868, Julia Archibald chided Swisshelm in the pages of *The Revolution* for her disparaging remarks about sculptor, and former Post Office Department employee, Vinnie Ream. "Washington Letter," *The Revolution*, May 21, 1868, 309–10 ("It would seem that [she] must consider any appreciation which another woman receives as just so much of honor and fame detracted from [herself]. Every demonstra-

tion of genius by a woman should be hailed by her sisters with joy. Women should rejoice at every evidence that the slaveries of fashion and false education have not entirely extinguished in her sex the fire of genius. No true woman will cast the shadow of an obstacle in the way of a toiling sister, and no woman with any degree of self-respect will pander to that vicious appetite for slander, which, like a hideous ulcer, consumes the vitals of society").

114. "[Women Workers]," *St. Cloud Democrat*, Dec. 21, 1865 (in Larsen, *Crusader and Feminist*, 307–13).

115. "A Woman on Women Clerks," *Sun*, Mar. 26, 1869, 2.

116. "Washington Letter," *The Revolution*, May 21, 1868, 309–10.

117. "The Department Women at Washington," *Pomeroy's Democrat*, May 5, 1869, 4. See also "The Women Clerks—A Voice to the Rescue," *Sun*, Apr. 3, 1869, 1 (author might have been Harriet C. Heald, a Treasury Department clerk in 1865, 1867, and 1870. *Federal Register*, 1865, 1867; 1870 Census, Washington, D.C.).

118. This paper also noted that it appeared that there was "no such woman as Hannah Tyler among the clerks" and that the statements made were false.

119. Mrs. H. C. Ingersoll worked in the office of the Comptroller of the Currency in 1866. U.S. Department of the Treasury, *Report of the Secretary of the Treasury . . . 1866*, 76. She was a relatively wealthy woman from New Hampshire who as of 1870 no longer worked in the Treasury Department. Ingersoll's nineteen-year-old daughter, Fanny Ingersoll, was working in the Treasury in 1870. 1870 Census, Washington, D.C., 4 WD.

120. "The Women Clerks at Washington," *Springfield Weekly Republican*, Apr. 17, 1869, 2.

121. Stansell, *City of Women*, 98.

122. "Washington Letter," *The Revolution*, July 2, 1868, 411.

123. Aron, *Ladies and Gentlemen*, 173.

124. "The Laborer and Her Hire," *The Revolution*, June 23, 1870, 396.

125. "Washington Letter," *The Revolution*, July 2, 1868, 411.

126. To some degree validating the criticism of women for their attention to appearance, women did care about the way the appeared in the workplace. In 1867, the *Evening Star* reported on an employee of the Currency Bureau who fainted from a too-tightly laced corset "which has reduced the dimensions of her naturally small waist to the size of an hour glass." The woman was presumably wearing the corset—at work—to make herself appear more attractive to the opposite sex. "Local News," *Evening Star*, July 29, 1867, 3.

127. Billings, "Early Women Journalists of Washington," 93; Leasher, *Letter from Washington*, 24–25.

128. Briggs, *The Olivia Letters*, 95, 182.

129. Ames, *Ten Years*, 308.

130. Gemmill, *Notes on Washington*, 34–35.

131. File of A. G. Emery, "Correspondence Relating to the Hiring of Clerks," Box 4, NA-WD.

132. Ibid.

133. See, for example, "Local News," *Evening Star*, Dec. 17, 1866, 3; "Scandal in Washington: One of the Treasury Female Clerks the Subject," *Albany Journal*, Dec. 28, 1866, 2; "Local News," *Evening Star*, Oct. 19, 1867, 3; "Local News," *Evening Star*, Jan. 10, 1867, 2.

134. The *Evening Star* reported on local matters more so than other local papers so I believe this is why these stories are all from that paper. I did not see these same stories reported on in the other local papers. For more on local newspapers during the Civil War, see Whyte, "Divided Loyalties," 103–22 (noting "The *Star* covered the local scene in greater detail than any other newspaper").

135. Kavender had been employed in the Treasury since at least 1865. The *Federal Register* spells her last name "Cavender." *Federal Register,* 1865, 1867. Based on newspaper articles regarding her daughter Leona's acting career, "Cavender" appears to be the correct spelling. See, for example, "The Diamond Comedienne," *The Critic*, Jan. 24, 1870, 2; "Critic Gossip," *The Critic*, Jan. 25, 1870, 4; "Miss Leona Cavender," *The Critic*, Mar. 16, 1871, 3.

136. "Local News," *Evening Star*, July 29, 1867, 3.

137. Ibid., Nov. 11, 1867, 3. I could not corroborate Harrison's employment.

138. Ibid., Sept. 16, 1869, 4. I could not corroborate Kendrick's employment.

139. As historian Sharon E. Wood has noted, "A woman's reputation was more fragile than a man's, its loss more devastating." Wood, *The Freedom of the Streets*, 7.

140. U.S. Congress, House of Representatives, *Certain Charges against the Treasury Department*, 45 (Testimony of L. C. Baker).

141. U.S. Congress, House of Representatives, *Certain Charges against the Treasury Department*, 17 (Majority Report). The third woman "left of her own accord." Presumably that woman was Jennie Germon, who had married Frank Clover, a captain and a scout under Fremont. U.S. Congress, House of Representatives, *Certain Charges against the Treasury Department*, 151 (Testimony of Anthony Lulley).

142. U.S. Department of the Treasury, *History of the Bureau of Engraving and Printing*, 20. Clark's Printing Division continued to be accused of fraud while it was under his supervision. "The Reported Frauds at the Treasury Department," *New York Times*, Mar. 18, 1867, 1.

143. See, for example, *New York Times*, Mar. 15, 1866, 4; *New York Times*, Mar. 19, 1864, 5; "Local Intelligence," *Daily Constitutional Union*, Mar. 27, 1866, 3. See also Goodwin, *The Almighty Dollar*, 245; U.S. Department of the Treasury, *History of the Bureau of Engraving and Printing*, 12. Spurred by Clark's action, Congress passed a law "forbidding the likeness of anyone living to be used on US currency, stamps, or coins." Goodwin, *The Almighty Dollar*, 245; U.S. Department of the Treasury, *History of the Bureau of Engraving and Printing*, 12.

144. File of A. G. Emery, "Correspondence Relating to the Hiring of Clerks," Box 4, NA-WD. Aron has found that men faced a lower standard of behavior and had more latitude in indiscretions in the federal departments in the period she examined as well. Aron, *Ladies and Gentlemen*, 171.

145. "Local News," *Evening Star*, Sept. 16, 1869, 4.

146. Wood, *The Freedom of the Streets*, 7.

147. Aron, *Ladies and Gentlemen*, 165; Srole, *Transcribing Class and Gender*, 59.

148. "Letters Received by the Secretary of War, Irregular Series, 1861–1866," NA-WD, 607.

149. Ibid.

150. Record of Clerks in the Office of the Commissioner of Internal Revenue 1862–1869, NA-Tr; *Federal Register*, 1863.

151. "Death of Rev. James Cook Richmond," *Salem Register*, July 26, 1866; "The Murder of Rev. James Cook Richmond," *Boston Journal*, July 23, 1866, 2.

152. Letter from Richmond to Bielaski, April 4, 1863, "Letters Received by the Secretary of War, Irregular Series, 1861–1866," NA-WD, 618 (describing the first time he met her "for you came so unlooked for 'In that new ward called K' "). Hertford's report indicated that a Reverend at the Armory Square Hospital was "well acquainted" with Richmond. Ibid., 609–11 (Letter from J. Hertford to J. J. Lewis, May 16, 1863).

153. "Death of Rev. James Cook Richmond," *Salem Register*, July 26, 1866, 2. Richmond was apparently the poet of his Harvard class.

154. Letter from Richmond to Bielaski, April 4, 1863, "Letters Received by the Secretary of War, Irregular Series, 1861–1866," NW-WD, 619.

155. Ibid., Letter from Richmond to Bielaski, April 29, 1863 ("and that my lips will [illeg.] those between thy tapering marble, but warm columns, be allowed to meet your *middle bearded lips*—[for you too, O sweet, *have a beard round the best of your two sets of lips*] in infinite kisses, where the odors are more fragrant & divine than the perfumes of Damascus. I would give more for one smack *there*, or even for one prolonged *smell* of the *odors of Rose*, than I would for all proved and great [illeg.] Atter of Roses") (emphasis in original).

156. Ibid., Letter from Richmond to Bielaski ("I shall poetically fancy that thy two greater mountains in thy rear (not thy twin hillocks with coral-tops in front) of my Rose, all yet *untrodd* by *man*—though I confess it seems very *poetical* to think so, and will *make you laugh* and I really care nothing for the *footsteps that may have gone before*, or even if several men have been on *thy great mountains* of joy, provided always and *strictly & absolutely* that *hereafter*, my [illeg] private property Rose, *no man but me shall touch or ascend them again*") (emphasis in original).

157. Ibid., Letter from Richmond to Bielaski, April 29, 1863. ("So much pleased you in that part of the poem which I read you on the walk, when I told you that in his talk of 'ramrod and bullocks' I really think your shameless beau meant to allude to—and what the men call 'bollocks' i.e. the two balls as the foot of—.")

158. Ibid., 608 (Richmond "was in the habit of visiting the Treasury Department almost daily and writing the letters at one of the tables at which doorkeepers usually sit and requesting one of the messengers to deliver them to the ladies").

159. Ibid., Letter from Richmond to Bielaski, May 1, 1863.

160. Ibid., 620, Letter from Richmond to Bielaski, undated. See also Letter from Richmond to Bielaski dated May 7, 1863, directing her to a secret message in a local newspaper. The message can be found at "To Clara," *Daily National Intelligencer*, May 7, 1863, 1.

161. Letter from Richmond to Bielaski, May 1, 1863, "Letters Received by the Secretary of War, Irregular Series, 1861–1866," NA-WD.

162. Ibid., 609–11, Letter from J. Hertford to J. J. Lewis, May 16, 1863.

163. Ibid. Rose Bielaski's reputation seems to have survived Richmond's advances. She retained her job until January 1864 and I have been unable to locate Bielaski's name or reporting of the events in any newspapers from the 1860s. Bielaski was removed from office for reasons unknown on January 13, 1864. Record of Clerks in the Office of the Commissioner of Internal Revenue 1862–1869, NA-Tr. Richmond was murdered in July 1866 in Poughkeepsie, New York, by Richard Lewis. Richmond had called Lewis's mother and sister "strumpets" and in response, Lewis struck Richmond in the temple, causing his death. "The Murder of Rev. James Cook Richmond," *Boston Journal*, July 23, 1866, 2; "Death of Rev. James Cook Richmond," *Salem Register*, July 26, 1866, 2. For more on the Richmond/Bielaski story, see Jordan, "The Capital of Crime," 44; Lowry, *The Story the Soldiers Wouldn't Tell*, 160–63 (note, however, that Lowry transcriptions of Richmond's letters contain many mistakes, most of them minor).

164. McLean, "Confided to His Care or Protection."

165. Aron, *Ladies and Gentlemen*, 172.

166. Oates, *Woman of Valor*, 11–12 (citing Blackwell, "Clara Barton Kept a Secret," *Woman's Journal*, Feb. 24, 1888, and "A Woman Clerk," *Washington Sunday Chronicle*, Mar. 11, 1883).

167. U.S. Congress, House of Representatives, *Certain Charges against the Treasury Department*, 151–52 (Testimony of Sarah Lulley).

168. Ibid., 148–49 (Testimony of Mano Lulley). Mano tried to speak to Gray personally after the incident, saying, "I should face him as a father and a man, not in the office but out of it" but he did not see Gray.

169. Pumphrey also testified that Clark "said he made a good friend, but a bad enemy." Ibid., 154–55 (Testimony of Beattie Pumphrey).

170. Letter from Chas. Drummer to Secretary of the Treasury Fessenden, November 8, 1864, "Letters Received Relating to the Bureau of Engraving and Printing (1862–1911)," NA-Tr.

171. Aron, *Ladies and Gentlemen*, 170 (citing letter of Addie Tyrrell to Secretary of the Treasury, 7 January 1868).

172. Ibid.

173. "The City," *The Critic*, July 29, 1870, 3.

174. "Post-Mortem Examination," *Daily Constitutional Union*, May 6, 1864, 3; "The Alleged Abortion Case," *Evening Star*, May 11, 1864, 3.

175. "Local News—The Death of Maggie Duvall," *Evening Star*, May 6, 1864, 2.

176. "The Post-Mortem Examination," *Daily Constitutional Union*, May 6, 1864, 3.

177. "Local News—The Death of Maggie Duvall," *Evening Star*, May 6, 1864, 2. See also "The Post-Mortem Examination," *Daily Constitutional Union*, May 6, 1864, 3.

178. "The Post-Mortem Examination," *Daily Constitutional Union*, May 6, 1864, 3. Whyte, "Divided Loyalties," 103–22 (noting that the *Daily Constitutional Union* "appeared in June 1863, as the organ of the Democratic Party").

179. For more on the explosion, see Bergin, *The Washington Arsenal Explosion*.

180. "Friday's Tragedy," *Daily Morning Chronicle*, June 20 1864, 2; "Terrible Calamity: Explosion at the Washington Arsenal," *Daily Morning Chronicle*, June 18, 1864, 2; "Washington Arsenal Calamity: Imposing Funeral Solemnities," *Daily Morning Chronicle*, June 20, 1864, 2.

181. "Local News: The Funeral of the Victims of the Arsenal Explosion," *Evening Star*, Monday, June 20, 1864. At least one newspaper called on the government to stop employing women in such dangerous occupations. "Friday's Tragedy," *Daily Morning Chronicle*, June 20, 1864, 2. In 1865, the citizens of Washington, D.C., erected a monument to the women who were killed in the Congressional Cemetery.

182. "Terrible Explosion at the Washington Arsenal," *Daily Evening Bulletin*, July 13, 1864.

183. "The Explosion Yesterday at the Arsenal; Further Details and Particulars—The Coroner's Inquest," *Evening Star*, Saturday, June 18, 1864, 1; "Terrible Calamity: Explosion at the Washington Arsenal," *Daily Morning Chronicle*, June 18, 1864, 2.

184. "The Explosion Yesterday at the Arsenal; Further Details and Particulars—The Coroner's Inquest," *Evening Star*, June 18, 1864, 1.

185. See, for example, Faust, *This Republic of Suffering*, 123.

186. "The Explosion Yesterday at the Arsenal; Further Details and Particulars—The Coroner's Inquest," *Evening Star*, June 18, 1864, 1; "Further of the Explosion—More of the Bodies Recognized—Preparations for Interment," *Evening Star*, June 18, 1864 (Second Edition, 4 o'clock).

187. The article mentions "persons" working in the room but only describes the searching of the women. In 1864, only women (15) worked in the separating room, so it may have been an exclusively female workspace. See Letter from S. M. Clark to George Harrington, Mar. 7, 1864, "Letters Received Relating to the Bureau of Engraving and Printing (1862–1911)," NA-Tr.

188. The superintendent "compelled" them "to sign a paper agreeing to pay her pro rata of the $750 lost." "The City," *The Critic*, Nov. 30, 1869, 3.

189. "Washington Letter," *The Revolution*, July 2, 1868, 411.

190. Ibid., May 21, 1868, 309–10.

191. File of Sallie Bridges, "Application and Recommendations," Box 59 (Bre–Bri), NA-Tr. There is no evidence that Bridges obtained a job with the government in the 1860s. See also Silber, *Daughters of the Union*, 119.

192. Historian Cindy Aron has found evidence of women losing jobs in later periods due to allegations of immorality. Aron, *Ladies and Gentlemen*, chapter 7.

193. Aron, for example, found that allegations of sexual misconduct in the late 1870s resulted in the discharge of a woman from the Treasury Department, but the Pension Office supervisor treated similar allegations against two of his female clerks in the early 1890s much more leniently. Aron, *Ladies and Gentlemen*, 170.

194. Ibid., 171–72.

195. "The City," *The Critic*, Aug. 21, 1872, 3; "Letter from Washington," *Sun*, Aug. 22, 1872, 4.

196. File of Minnie Brien, "Application and Recommendations," Box 59 (Bre–Bri), NA-Tr.

197. "General Spinner's Camp" *The Revolution*, Sept. 29, 1870, 203; "Washington Gossip," *Daily Picayune*, Sept. 11, 1869, 1; "General Spinner," *Inter Ocean*, Aug. 7, 1875, 5.

198. "Correspondence: Our Washington Letter," *Pomeroy's Democrat*, Sept. 8, 1869, 3.

199. "Washington Gossip," *Daily Picayune*, Sept. 11, 1869, 1.

200. Thorp, *Female Persuasion*, 67.

201. "The Laborer and Her Hire," *The Revolution*, June 23, 1870, 396.

202. Martin, *Behind the Scenes*, 473.

203. U.S. Department of the Treasury, *Report of the Secretary of the Treasury . . . 1862*, 129–30; U.S. Department of the Treasury, *Report of the Secretary of the Trea-sury . . . 1863*, 103–4; U.S. Department of the Treasury, *Report of the Secretary of the Trea-sury . . . 1864*, 72; U.S. Department of the Treasury, *Report of the Secretary of the Treasury . . . 1865*, 41; U.S. Department of the Treasury, *Report of the Secretary of the Treasury . . . 1866*, 172; U.S. Department of the Treasury, *Report of the Secretary of the Treasury . . . 1868*, 73. There were no overtly negative comments about the female employees in any of the Annual Reports of the Secretary of the Treasury to Congress in the 1860s.

204. See "The United States Treasury Scandal," *Times-Picayune*, May 18, 1864, 1; "The Investigation into the Treasury Department and Washington—The Female Clerk System," *Daily Age*, May 21, 1864, 1.

205. Here Hendricks is undoubtedly referring to the 1864 Treasury Department Scandal.

206. *Congressional Globe*, 39th Cong., 2nd sess., 1149–63, 1155 (Feb. 11, 1867).

207. The reasons for the timing of this are unclear. Several newspaper articles discuss how frustrated McCulloch was with number and persistence of female applicants, and his annoyance may have been the cause. McCulloch received a good deal of resistance to the idea and did not fire all of the female employees. In fact, soon after this move-ment began the first of the debates in Congress calling for equal pay for women. See, for example, "The Departments," *Daily Morning Chronicle*, Dec. 13, 1866, 1; "The De-partments," *Daily Morning Chronicle*, Sept. 5, 1866, 1.

208. See, for example, "From Washington," *Pittsfield Sun*, Dec. 20, 1866, 2; "The De-partments," *Daily Morning Chronicle*, Dec. 13, 1866, 1; "Washington Items," *Troy Weekly Times*, Dec. 15, 1866, 3; "The Departments," *Daily Morning Chronicle*, Dec. 15, 1866, 1; "The Removal of Female Clerks from the Departments at Washington," *Evening Bulle-tin*, Dec. 19, 1866.

209. "The Removal of Female Clerks from the Departments at Washington," *Eve-ning Bulletin*, Dec. 19, 1866.

210. Srole, *Transcribing Class and Gender*, 61.

211. U.S. Congress, House of Representatives, *Certain Charges against the Treasury Department*, 17 (Majority Report), 59 (Testimony of Lucius E. Chittenden).

212. "The Treasury Scandal," *The Weekly Dakotian*, July 30, 1864, 1. See also "The Women Clerks at Washington," *Springfield Weekly Republican*, Apr. 17, 1869, 2. See, for example, statements of Mr. Farnsworth, Mr. Negley, and Mr. Kelly, *Congressional Globe*,

41st Cong., 2nd sess., 1412–17, 1414–16 (Feb. 18, 1870). Employee files reveal that some of the female federal employees were related to Union soldiers, and several department heads were vocal in their preference for hiring and retaining soldiers' relatives. "Further from the North," *Daily Picayune*, Aug. 31, 1865, 2; "Washington," *New York Herald*, Nov. 16, 1868, 4; *Daily Morning Chronicle*, Dec. 19, 1866, 1.

213. See chapter 1.

214. "The Female Clerks," *Evening Star*, Oct. 14, 1870, 1.

215. "The City," *The Critic*, July 13, 1871.

Chapter Six

1. "Amusing Dilemma of a Female Clerk," *Sun*, May 3, 1869, 4.

2. Aron, *Ladies and Gentlemen*, 116.

3. File of Letitia Arnold, "Application and Recommendations," Box 13 (Arm–Arr), NA-Tr.

4. "Our Washington Letter," *Galveston Tri-Weekly News*, Sept. 24, 1869, 1.

5. "The Returning Masses," *North American and United States Gazette*, June 19, 1865, 2.

6. See "A Heavy Furlough," *Daily Morning Chronicle*, Sept. 1, 1865, 4; "City Intelligence," *Daily Morning Chronicle*, Oct. 3, 1865, 4; "Correspondence," *The Sun*, Nov. 7, 1865, 4; "Female Clerks," *Daily State Gazette*, Nov. 11, 1865, 2; "Foreign News!," *The Pacific Commercial Advertiser*, Jan. 20, 1866, 3; "From Washington," *Public Ledger*, Nov. 16, 1865, 1; "By Telegraph," *Boston Daily Advertiser*, Dec. 16, 1865, 1; "Correspondence," *Sun*, Dec 29, 1865, 4; "Local Intelligence," *Daily Constitutional Union*, Mar. 3, 1866, 3; "Washington Items," *Daily Constitutional Union*, June 30, 1866, 2; "City Intelligence," *Daily Morning Chronicle*, Oct. 1, 1866, 4; "Correspondence," *Sun*, Nov. 12, 1866, 4; "Local News," *Evening Star*, Dec. 11, 1866, 3; "The Departments," *Daily Morning Chronicle*, December 13, 1866, 1; "Washington Items," *Troy Weekly Times*, Dec. 15, 1866, 3; "The Departments," *Daily Morning Chronicle*, Dec. 15, 1866, 1; "Washington," *New York Daily Tribune*, Dec. 17, 1866, 1; "The Removal of Female Clerks from the Departments at Washington," *Evening Bulletin*, Dec. 19, 1866; "From Washington," *Pittsfield Sun*, Dec. 20, 1866, 2.

7. See "City Intelligence," *Daily Morning Chronicle*, Jan. 1, 1867, 4; "Female Clerks," *Evening Star* [Second Edition], Feb. 7, 1867, 2; "By Telegraph from Washington," *Boston Daily Journal*, Feb. 8, 1867, 4; "Washington," *New York Herald*, June 8, 1867, 5; "Local News," *Evening Star*, June 8, 1867, 3; "City Intelligence," *Daily Morning Chronicle*, June 13, 1867, 1; "Local News," *Evening Star*, July 9, 1867, 3; "Dismissal of Clerks at the Treasury Department," *Evening Star*, Aug. 17, 1867, 2; "From the Daily of August 20," *Weekly Patriot and Union*, Aug. 22, 1867, 5; "Clerkships in Washington," *Sun*, Aug. 27, 1867, 1; "Removals," *Evening Star*, Aug. 31, 1867, 2; "Reduction of the Force at the Treasury," *Evening Star*, Sept. 2, 1867, 2; "Local News," *Evening Star*, Oct. 16, 1867, 3; "The Force of the Quartermaster General's Office," *Evening Star*, Oct. 31, 1867, 2; "Washington News and Gossip," *Evening Star*, Nov. 2, 1867, 2; "Washington News and Gossip," *Evening Star*, Dec. 12, 1867, 1; "Washington New & Gossip," *Evening Star*, Dec. 12, 1867, 1; "Times' Special Dispatches," *New-Orleans Times*, Dec. 13, 1867, 1.

8. See "Washington News & Gossip," *Evening Star*, Jan. 25, 1868, 1; "Washington News & Gossip," *Evening Star*, Jan. 28, 1868, 1; "City Intelligence," *Daily Morning Chronicle*, Jan. 30, 1868, 4; "Local News," *Evening Star*, Feb. 4, 1868, 4; "City Intelligence," *Daily Morning Chronicle*, Feb. 5, 1868, 4; "Washington News and Gossip," *Evening Star*, Feb. 20, 1868, 1; "Washington News and Gossip," *Evening Star*, Mar. 27, 1868, 1; "City Intelligence," *Daily Morning Chronicle*, July 2, 1868, 1; "City Intelligence," *Daily Morning Chronicle*, July 14, 1868, 4; "Washington," *Sun*, July 16, 1868, 2; "By Telegraph from Washington," *Boston Daily Journal*, July 27, 1868, 4; "Discharges from the Departments," *Daily Morning Chronicle*, Aug. 11, 1868, 2; "Telegraph News From Washington," *Sun*, Oct. 5, 1868, 1; "From Washington," *Boston Daily Journal*, Oct. 6, 1868, 2; "Washington," *New York Herald*, Oct. 22, 1868, 7; "Washington News," *Philadelphia Inquirer*, Oct. 22, 1868, 1; "Letter from Washington," *The Sun*, Oct. 24, 1868, 4; "Washington," *New York Herald*, Nov. 8, 1868, 7; "City Intelligence," *Daily Morning Chronicle*, Nov. 14, 1868, 1; "Washington," *New York Herald*, Nov. 16, 1868, 4; "Letter from Washington," *Sun*, Nov. 21, 1868, 4; "City Intelligence," *Daily Morning Chronicle*, Nov. 27, 1868, 4; "Scene at the United States Treasury in Discharging Female Clerks," *Sun*, Dec. 7, 1868, 3; "News of the Day," *Cincinnati Daily Gazette*, Dec. 9, 1868, 2; "Review of the Week," *Springfield Weekly Republican*, Dec. 12, 1868, 1.

9. "Washington," *New York Herald*, Nov. 8, 1868, 7.

10. U.S. Treasury Department, *Reduction of Employees in Treasury Department*, House Ex. Doc. No 49, 40th Cong, 3rd sess. (Jan. 19, 1869); "City Intelligence," *Daily Morning Chronicle*, Feb. 26, 1869, 4; "Washington," *New York Herald*, Mar. 28, 1869, 9; "From Washington," *Hartford Daily Courant*, Apr. 2, 1869, 3; "By Telegraph Washington," *Boston Daily Advertiser*, Apr. 2, 1869, 1; "Correspondence," *The Sun*, Apr. 10, 1869, 4; "By Telegraph, Washington," *Boston Daily Advertiser*, Apr. 12, 1869, 1; "By Telegraph, Washington," *Boston Daily Advertiser*, Apr. 15, 1869, 1; "Washington," *Cincinnati Commercial Tribune*, Apr. 16, 1869, 1; "Latest by Telegraph, Washington," *Cincinnati Daily Gazette*, Apr. 26, 1869, 3; "Washington," *New York Daily Tribune*, Apr. 28, 1869, 1; "This Week's Washington News," *Pomeroy's Democrat*, May 5, 1869, 8; "The Departments," *Daily Morning Chronicle*, May 12, 1869, 1; "The Departments," *Daily Morning Chronicle*, June 1, 1869, 1; "The Departments," *Daily Morning Chronicle*, June 16, 1869, 1; "Washington," *Cincinnati Commercial Tribune*, June 24, 1869, 1; "From Washington," *Hartford Daily Courant*, June 24, 1869, 1; "From Washington," *Daily State Register*, June 24, 1869, 4; "Department News," *Daily Morning Chronicle*, June 28, 1869, 1; "[No title]," *Cincinnati Daily Gazette*, June 28, 1869, 2; "Latest by Telegraph. Washington," *Cincinnati Daily Gazette*, June 28, 1869, 3; "Washington," *Cincinnati Commercial Tribune*, June 30, 1869, 1; "The Departments," *Daily Morning Chronicle*, July 2, 1869, 4; "[No title]," *Public Ledger*, Nov. 3, 1869, 2.

11. "[No title]," *Public Ledger*, Nov. 3, 1869, 2.

12. Every above named office increased in size between 1859 and 1871, as follows: the Patent Office grew from 87 employees in 1859 to 349 in 1871; the Post Office grew from 101 employees in 1859 to 337 in 1871; the Pension Office grew from 77 employees in 1859 to 323 in 1871; the Treasury Department grew from 439 employees in 1859 to 2,496 in

1871; the War Department grew from 93 employees in 1859 to 453 in 1871; the Agricultural Office grew from 5 employees in 1859 to the Agricultural Department of 84 employees in 1871; and the Government Hospital for the Insane grew from 48 employees in 1859 to 139 in 1871. Numbers from the *Federal Register*, 1859 and 1871. Treasury Department figures exclude the Coast Survey from the *Federal Register*.

13. "Local News," *Evening Star*, Apr. 25, 1867, 3. Numbers from the *Federal Register*, 1859 and 1871. Treasury Department figures exclude the Coast Survey from the *Federal Register*.

14. "City Intelligence," *Daily Morning Chronicle*, July 23, 1868, 1.

15. "Latest by Telegraph, Washington," *Cincinnati Daily Gazette*, Apr. 26, 1869, 3.

16. I analyzed the 2,936 women I found who worked for the federal government between 1859 and 1871. In my analysis, I both overestimated and likely underrepresented the time a woman worked for the government. For example, if I had evidence that a woman worked for the government in 1863 and 1865, I assumed that she worked there for at least three years and had no break in her employment. My data likely in some ways underrepresents the facts, however. For example, I have very limited data on women who worked for the Government Printing Office, so I may have only captured one year of a woman's long career at the GPO and if a woman worked during an even-numbered year (outside of the *Federal Register*) and I did not find evidence of her work elsewhere, I may have underestimated the length of her tenure in the federal government.

17. See "Departmental," *Daily Morning Chronicle*, Nov. 23, 1869, 1; "Washington News & Gossip," *Evening Star*, Nov. 29, 1869, 1; "Departmental," *Daily Morning Chronicle*, Nov. 30, 1869, 1; "The Departments," *Daily Morning Chronicle*, Dec. 3, 1869, 1; "Letter from Washington," *Sun*, Sept. 8, 1870, 4.

18. See File of Elizabeth Arnold, "Application and Recommendations," Box 13 (Arm–Arr), NA-Tr; File of Maria Linton, "Application and Recommendations," Box 350 (Lin–Lit), NA-Tr. When Emma C. Duncanson resigned from the War Department in the fall of 1866, Quartermaster General Meigs informed the secretary of war that he had a memorandum instructing him to appoint Annie Donaldson to the first vacancy, but that Meigs did not have Donaldson's address. He recommended that if Donaldson could not be found, they appoint one of the other women whose applications were on file. Demonstrating the pressure for jobs, Meigs also added the application of another woman, Mary K. Smith, "widow of Lieut. Col. E. Kirby Smith, killed in the command of his regiment which he was leading to the assault of Molino del Rey during the Mexican war, and mother of Col. J. E. K. Smith, of the 43d Ohio Volunteers, who was killed at the head of his regiment in [Corinth, Mississippi]." Meigs also included in his letter to the secretary of war "the applications of Mrs. Annie Dixon, Mrs. T. Youngs, and Mrs. Judith Plummer, for employment as copyists." "Correspondence Relating to the Hiring of Clerks," Box 4, NA-WD.

19. "City Intelligence," *Daily Morning Chronicle*, Mar. 28, 1868, 4.

20. Letter from U. S. Grant to Hugh McCulloch, July 25, 1866, Simon, *The Papers of Ulysses S. Grant*, 18:260. Curtis may also have been physically impaired, leaving her

with limited work options. In 1862, a local paper reported that her dress had accidentally caught fire, "and she was badly burned before the flames could be extinguished." "Local News," Washington *Evening Star*, Mar. 1, 1862, 3.

21. Letter from William E. Chandler, July 28, 1866. Simon, *The Papers of Ulysses S. Grant*, 16:260.

22. "[Correspondence of the Baltimore Sun]," *Sun*, May 28, 1863, 4; "The Great Christmas Dinner," *Daily Morning Chronicle*, Dec. 19, 1862, 3. Middleton either never lost her job or got it back. She was listed as a copyist in the Fourth Auditor's Office (Treasury Dept.) in 1867. *Federal Register*, 1867.

23. Diary of Julia A. Wilbur, May 17, 1870–May 2, 1871; Apr. 3, 1871.

24. File of Elizabeth J. Scott, "Application and Recommendations," Box 515 (She–Sco), NA-Tr.

25. In 1861, for instance, one of the earliest female employees of the Agricultural Bureau, Mrs. S. Crooks, was the only female name on the list of employees reported to the secretary of the interior by the Committee of Investigation, and she presumably lost her job. U.S. Congress, House of Representatives, *Loyalty of Clerks and Other Persons Employed by Government*, 35.

26. "Congress Matters," *Sun*, Feb. 28, 1866, 4; Larsen, *Crusader and Feminist*, 28.

27. "The Reconstructionist," *The Reconstructionist*, Feb. 10, 1866, 4. For a negative review of the paper, see "Local Intelligence," *Daily Constitutional Union*, Mar. 28, 1866, 3.

28. "Local Intelligence," *Daily Constitutional Union*, Mar. 1, 1866, 3; "Local Intelligence," *Daily Constitutional Union*, Feb. 28, 1866, 3; Larsen, *Crusader and Feminist*, 28. Removal letter from Meigs can be found in "Letters Sent by the Office of the QMG," M745, Roll #53, vol. 90, 130.

29. "Departmental," *Daily Morning Chronicle*, Apr. 8, 1870, 1. Maggie worked in the Government Printing Office and her sister Johanna worked in the Treasury. Their father, Michal Fenton, was a forty-five-year-old stonemason from Ireland. 1870 Census, Washington, D.C., 7 WD. Maggie was appointed in November 1869. Government Printing Office, "Lists of Employees and Their Employment Status, compiled 1870?–1907, documenting the period ca. 1858–1907."

30. Aron, *Ladies and Gentlemen*, 118.

31. Diary of Julia A. Wilbur, May 17, 1870–May 2, 1871; Nov. 9, 10, 1870; Feb. 6, 1871.

32. File of Sallie M. Madden, "Application and Recommendations," Box 362 (Mac–Maf), NA-Tr.

33. Testimony of Harriet J. Bennett, *Management of the Government Hospital for the Insane*, (1876), 6.

34. File of Ella Ladde, "Application and Recommendations," Box 352 (Loc–Log), NA-Tr.

35. "Correspondence Relating to the Hiring of Clerks," Box 4, NA-WD.

36. "Consolidated Report of the Time and Conduct of the Copyists," Boxes 2–3, NA-WD, Mar. 1866, Dec. 1867.

37. "Correspondence Relating to the Hiring of Clerks," Box 4, NA-WD; see also "Letters Sent by the Office of the QMG," NA-WD, M745, Roll #59, 103:223.

38. For women being replaced by men after World War II, see, for example, Milkman, *Gender at Work*. Between 1865 and 1867, the percentage of females employed in the Treasury Department dipped slightly, the only time it did so in the period under examination. In 1865, the Treasury Department was 21.45 percent female, but in 1867 it was 20.36 percent female (439 females out of 2,047 employees in 1865 and 514 females out of 2,525 employees in 1867). Although this dip may be explained by women leaving jobs because male relatives had returned from the war and could now provide for them, it may also have reflected women losing jobs to men. See "The Departments," *Daily Morning Chronicle*, Oct. 21, 1865, 1; but see File of Emeric Szabad, "Application and Recommendations," Box 506 (Syp–Tal), NA-Tr (letter in file suggesting that not enough room was made for returning soldiers).

39. See "Discharges from the Departments," *Daily Morning Chronicle*, Aug. 11, 1868, 2.

40. "Washington," *New York Herald*, Nov. 16, 1868, 4; "Scene at the United States Treasury in Discharging Female Clerks," *Sun*, Dec. 7, 1868, 3.

41. See *Lowell Daily Citizen and News*, July 12, 1864, col, E; "Washington," *New York Daily Tribune*, Dec. 17, 1866, 1; "From Washington," *Public Ledger*, Nov. 16, 1865, 1; "Washington," *New York Herald*, Mar. 28, 1869, 9; "Correspondence," *Sun*, Apr. 10, 1869, 4.

42. "Female Department Clerks," *Flake's Bulletin*, Aug. 3, 1866.

43. "A Hard Case," *Daily Star Gazette*, Apr. 23, 1869, 2.

44. "Telegraph News from Washington," *Sun*, Oct. 5, 1868, 1; see also "From Washington," *Boston Daily Journal*, Oct. 6, 1868, 2.

45. There is only brief mention of both of these attempts in the newspapers. "City Intelligence," *Daily Morning Chronicle*, Dec. 6, 1869, 4; "City Intelligence," *Daily Morning Chronicle*, Dec. 7, 1869, 4 (John Seitz Jr. was reported to have carried on a "so-called 'big game' in blackmailing and attempting to procure situations for females"); "Jottings About Town," *Critic-Record*, Nov. 16, 1871, 5 ("The trial of T. Z. Hoover, the ex-Postmaster, for blackmailing female Treasury employés, is postponed until Friday next").

46. "Discharges from the Departments," *Daily Morning Chronicle*, Aug. 11, 1868, 2.

47. Anthony represented Arnold's home state of Rhode Island in the Senate. She had begun as a copyist but had been promoted to a clerkship. File of Mary Arnold, "Application and Recommendations," Box 13 (Arm–Arr), NA-Tr. See also File of Alexina Getty, "Application and Recommendations," NA-Tr. Perhaps because of women like Anthony were let go from government work with limited options, men of standing in Washington agreed to serve as references for an association formed in 1868 "for the purpose of furnishing employment to ladies who are dependent upon their own exertions for a livelihood." "City Intelligence," *Daily Morning Chronicle*, Oct. 16, 1868, 1.

48. Scott, C. (file of), NA-USH.

49. File of Clara G. Scott, "Application and Recommendations," Box 515 (She–Sco), NA-Tr. Her file in the Treasury Department records is slim because she recalled her letters in 1880. See also "Correspondence Relating to the Hiring of Clerks," Box 4, NA-WD.

50. Scott, C. (file of), NA-USH; File of Clara G. Scott, "Application and Recommendations," Box 515 (She–Sco), NA-Tr.

298 Notes to Chapter Six

51. Ibid. Scott sent at least three letters to the Committee between October 1866 and December 1867. File of Clara G. Scott, "Application and Recommendations," Box 515 (She–Sco), NA-Tr.

52. Of the forty-three women reapplying, twenty-five were successful (with two finding jobs in other departments, however) and eighteen failed.

53. Tall also appears in the *Federal Register* for the years 1867, 1869.

54. File of Jennie Tall, "Application and Recommendations," Box 506 (Syp–Tal), NA-Tr.

55. File of Alexina Getty, "Application and Recommendations," NA-Tr.

56. "Scene at the United States Treasury in Discharging Female Clerks," *The Sun*, Dec. 7, 1868, 3.

57. File of Hester A. Peters, "Application and Recommendations," Box 455 (Per–Pet), NA-Tr. See also File of Mollie Lloyd, "Application and Recommendations," Box 351 (Lit–Loc), NA-Tr; File of Maria Linton, "Application and Recommendations," Box 350 (Lin–Lit), NA-Tr; File of Jane W. Little, "Application and Recommendations," Box 350 (Lin–Lit), NA-Tr.

58. File of Jennie Tall, "Application and Recommendations," Box 506 (Syp–Tal), NA-Tr.

59. File of Maude A. Reddick, "Application and Recommendations," Box 479 (Rec–Red), NA-Tr.

60. "Experiences of a Bureau Officer," *Cincinnati Daily Gazette*, May 17, 1871, 4.

61. "Local News," *Evening Star*, Dec. 11, 1866, 3.

62. "Washington," *New York Daily Tribune*, Apr. 28, 1869, 1; "Washington," *New York Herald*, Nov. 16, 1868, 4; "Washington," *New York Herald*, Nov. 8, 1868, 7; "From Washington," *The Pittsfield Sun*, Dec. 20, 1866, 2; "Reduction of the Force at the Treasury," *Evening Star*, Sept. 2, 1867, 2.

63. File of Alexina Getty, "Application and Recommendations," NA-Tr.

64. Aron, *Ladies and Gentlemen*, 96.

65. File of Sallie Bridges, "Application and Recommendations," Box 59 (Bre–Bri), NA-Tr (letter from Sallie Bridges to "My Dear Colonel" stating in part: "As you have several times offered me your friendly services in my endeavors to render myself independent, and as I have perfect confidence in your kindly disposition towards me, I venture once more to intrude upon your memory and notice, with a request for your influential assistance in my pursuit of this object"); "By Telegraph from Washington," *Boston Daily Journal*, Mar. 10, 1869, 4 ("there are hundreds of women here begging offices for themselves and for their friends or relatives, and besieging Congressmen at their lodgings, in the streets and at the Capitol").

66. File of M. Aubrey, "Application and Recommendations," Box 15 (Ash–Aug), NA-Tr. See also file of Laura Hanger, "Correspondence Relating to the Hiring of Clerks," Box 4, NA-WD.

67. *Federal Register*, 1871; "General Spinner," *Inter Ocean*, Aug. 7, 1875, 5.

68. "Washington News & Gossip," *Evening Star*, Dec. 14, 1867, 1.

69. Despite her hard work, it does not appear that Linton was successful in regaining her job in 1875. File of Maria Linton, "Application and Recommendations," Box 350 (Lin–Lit), NA-Tr. See also File of Sylvia Bemis, "Application and Recommendations," Box 37 (Bem–Ben), NA-Tr; File of Kate Cain, "Application and Recommendations," Box 81 (Byr–Cal), NA-Tr; File of A. M. Richardson, "Application and Recommendations," Box 487 (Ric), NA-Tr; File of Mary Shockley, "Application and Recommendations," Box 526 (Shi–Sho), NA-Tr.

70. File of Jennie Tall, "Application and Recommendations," Box 506 (Syp–Tal), NA-Tr; File of Maria Linton, "Application and Recommendations," Box 350 (Lin–Lit), NA-Tr.

71. Diary of Julia A. Wilbur, May 17, 1870–May 2, 1871; May 23, 1870; June 30; July 1, 1871; 1870 Census Georgetown, File of T. Talcott, "Application and Recommendations," Box 506 (Syp–Tal), NA-Tr.

72. Diary of Julia A. Wilbur, May 17, 1870–May 2, 1871; Oct. 7, 1870.

73. File of Mary Arnold, "Application and Recommendations," Box 13 (Arm–Arr), NA-Tr; File of Hester A. Peters, "Application and Recommendations," Box 455 (Per–Pet), NA-Tr.

74. File of Hester A. Peters, "Application and Recommendations," Box 455 (Per–Pet), NA-Tr; File of Maria Linton, "Application and Recommendations," Box 350 (Lin–Lit), NA-Tr; File of Jane Little, "Application and Recommendations," Box 350 (Lin–Lit), NA-Tr; File of Alexina Getty, "Application and Recommendations," NA-Tr. See also File of Maude Reddick, "Application and Recommendations," Box 479 (Rec–Red), NA-Tr; File of Jennie Tall, "Application and Recommendations," Box 506 (Syp–Tal), NA-Tr.

75. Bemis appears on the *Federal Register* in 1869.

76. File of Sylvia Bemis, "Application and Recommendations," Box 37 (Bem–Ben), NA-Tr.

77. The letter stated that the men had "been informed that the clerical force in your department is likely to be reduced, respectfully request that Mrs. Jane W. Little be retained in her position when such change occurs." File of Jane Little, "Application and Recommendations," Box 350 (Lin–Lit), NA-Tr.

78. "Correspondence Relating to the Hiring of Clerks," Box 4, NA-WD. See also File of Mary Gatewood, "Application and Recommendations," Box 216 (Gas–Gaz), NA-Tr.

79. Diary of Julia A. Wilbur, May 5, 1871–Apr. 21, 1872; June 14, 1871.

80. File of Eliza McCully, "Application and Recommendations," Box 382 (McC–McD), NA-Tr.

81. This geographic quota survived the restructuring of the civil service under the Pendleton Act. Aron, *Ladies and Gentlemen*, 108. I have found evidence of at least ninety-nine women shifting the state from which they were appointed in the *Federal Register*.

82. File of A. Byus, "Application and Recommendations," Box 81 (Byr–Cal), NA-Tr.

83. File of Helen Briggs, "Application and Recommendations," Box 59 (Bre–Bri), NA-Tr.

84. I have found evidence of at least ninety-one women changing jobs within a department.

85. *Federal Register,* 1863, 1865, 1867, 1869; Government Printing Office, "Lists of Employees and Their Employment Status, compiled 1870?–1907, documenting the period ca. 1858–1907"; Records of the Superintendent [of the Government Hospital for the Insane], Box 2, 272.

86. I have found evidence of at least fifty-nine women changing departments.

87. For example, Emma Rawlings, Clementina Downs, and Mattie Pendergast all worked in the GPO in 1864 and in the Treasury Department in 1870. Government Printing Office, *Annual Report of Superintendent of Public Printing 1865*; 1870 Census, Washington, D.C. M. Falconer was transferred from the GPO to the Treasury in 1871. Government Printing Office, "Lists of Employees and Their Employment Status, compiled 1870?–1907, documenting the period ca. 1858–1907."

88. *Federal Register,* 1867, 1869; Government Printing Office, "Lists of Employees and Their Employment Status, compiled 1870?–1907, documenting the period ca. 1858–1907."

89. For Frances Richardson, see *Federal Register,* 1865, 1867 (Treasury Department), *Federal Register,* 1871 (Pension Office). For H. M. Barnard, see *Federal Register,* 1867, 1869 (Treasury Department), 1871 (Pension Office). For Frances Plummer, see *Federal Register,* 1865, 1867, 1869 (Treasury Department), 1871 (Pension Office).

90. *Federal Register,* 1867 (Treasury Department); "Letter from Washington," *Sun,* Sept. 8, 1870, 4.

91. For S. P. King, see Record of Clerks in the Office of the Commissioner of Internal Revenue 1862–1869; *Federal Register,* 1867, 1869 (Post Office). For Alice Martin, see *Federal Register,* 1867 (Treasury Department), 1870 Census, Washington, D.C. (Post Office). For Alice White, see *Federal Register,* 1863, 1865, 1867 (Treasury Department), 1870 Census D.C. (Post Office).

92. *Federal Register,* 1863 (Post Office); *Federal Register,* 1867 (Treasury Department).

93. *Federal Register,* 1867, 1871; "Department News," *Daily Morning Chronicle,* June 28, 1869, 1.

94. Other women also sought jobs in multiple departments. When Hester Peters encountered difficulty in getting her job at the Treasury Department back, she tried applying to the Post Office Department, but was unsuccessful. The secretary of the navy wrote a letter to Quartermaster General Meigs on behalf of Mrs. Rudd, explaining that she was the widow of a Navy Officer and that she had, "lost her position in the Treasury Department under the recent curtailment of the force in that Department." The secretary asked the quartermaster general to use his "influence to obtain her a position in your Department," but his attempt was unsuccessful. Three days later another man tried to get Rudd a job in the Pension Office. This too was unsuccessful. Two weeks later, Rudd asked that all of her papers be returned to her. File of Hester A. Peters, "Application and Recommendations," Box 455 (Per–Pet), NA-Tr; File of E. A. Rudd, "Correspondence Relating to the Hiring of Clerks," Box 4, NA-WD. Mrs. Jane Reynolds was one of the earliest female employees in the Patent Office, but the type of work she performed "was discontinued." Reynolds caused to be sent four letters of

recommendation, including two from commissioner of patents David Holloway and one from the Mayor's Office, to the Department of the Treasury. The letters explained that Reynolds was "very anxious to procure employment" clipping Treasury notes so that she could support her sick sister and children, but Reynolds appears to have been unsuccessful in making the lateral move. "Application and Recommendations," Box 495 (Rey–Rhy), NA-Tr.

95. It took Breedin two years to get the job she sought in the Treasury Department. File of Fannie Kemp Breedin, "Application and Recommendations," Box 58 (Bra–Bre), NA-Tr.

96. Nancy D. Bishop was appointed to the Treasury Department on March 1, 1869. She appears in the 1869 *Federal Register* and the 1871 *Federal Register*, but listed no occupation in the 1870 census. Department of the Treasury, "Registers and Lists of Treasury Employees Register of Female Clerks, 1861–1868," vol. 3.

97. File of Jennie Tall, "Application and Recommendations," Box 506 (Syp–Tal), NA-Tr. In another letter, Tall complained that Bishop was making more than Tall had made, though Tall had performed additional duties. Young was from Nova Scotia and was a contract assistant surgeon during the war. Bishop was also from Nova Scotia. See also File of Mary A. Lyons, "Application and Recommendations," Box 360 (Lyo–Mac), NA-Tr.

98. Oates, *Woman of Valor*, 19.

99. Ibid., 65. Upperman's motivations are unclear. Perhaps he was trying to gain favor through indirectly assisting with soldier relief. Upperman had been accused of disloyalty in 1862 and temporarily lost his job. U.S. Congress, House of Representatives, *Loyalty of Clerks and Other Persons Employed by Government*, 34, 44.

100. Oates, *Woman of Valor*, 200–201.

101. Letter from Clara Barton to Holloway, December 11, 1863, as copied in diary. *Clara Barton Papers*, Diaries and Journals, 1849–1911, Box 1, Reel 1. Barton was reinstated. Oates, *Woman of Valor*, 203.

102. See File of Elizabeth Arnold, "Application and Recommendations," Box 13 (Arm–Arr), NA-Tr; File of Annie Carpenter, "Application and Recommendations," Box 87 (Car–Car), NA-Tr; File of Mrs. M. R. Gibbs, "Application and Recommendations," NA-Tr; U.S. Congress, House of Representatives, *The Management of the Government Hospital for the Insane* (Testimony of Jane Beatty); U.S. War Department, "List of Clerks, Messengers, and Laborers Employed in the Office of the QMG, 1861–1864"; Government Printing Office, "Lists of Employees and Their Employment Status, compiled 1870?–1907, documenting the period ca. 1858–1907"; File of Mary B. Ratcliffe, "Application and Recommendations," Box 476 (Ran–Rat), NA-Tr; File of Margaret C. Atkinson, "Application and Recommendations," Box 15 (Ash–Aug), NA-Tr; File of Marion T. Litchfield, "Application and Recommendations," Box 350 (Lin–Lit), NA-Tr; War Department, "Letters Sent by the Office of the QMG," M745, Roll #59, 102:310.

103. *Federal Register*, 1863, 1865; 1870 Census, Washington, D.C., Georgetown PO. See also Louisa Burgdorf (*Federal Register*, 1863, 1865; 1870 Census, Washington, D.C., Georgetown PO); Ellen Webster (*Federal Register*, 1863, 1865; 1870 Census, Washington,

D.C., Georgetown PO); S. E. Thomason (*Federal Register*, 1865, 1867; "Petition of Female Treasury Clerks for Increased Pay," NA-USH; 1870 Census, Washington, D.C., Georgetown PO).

104. *Federal Register*, 1865, 1867, 1870; Census, Washington, D.C., 2 WD.

105. File of Mary Ream, "Application and Recommendations," Box 479 (Rea–Red), NA-Tr.

106. "City Intelligence," *Daily Morning Chronicle*, Jan. 14, 1867, 4.

107. She appeared happy in her work, and it was a shock to her friends when Kinney killed herself by taking laudanum and chloroform, allegedly because of an unplanned and out-of-wedlock pregnancy. "Suicide in Alleghany," *New York Herald*, Oct. 14, 1870, 8.

108. *Federal Register*, 1869; 1870 Census, Washington, D.C.

109. *Federal Register*, 1865, 1867, 1869; 1870 Census, Washington, D.C., 5 WD.

110. *Federal Register*, 1865, 1867; 1870 Census, Washington, D.C.

111. "Two Women Washington Correspondents," *San Francisco Bulletin*, Feb. 22, 1871, 1; Richardson, "Recollections of a Washington Newspaper Correspondent," 36.

112. "Departmental," *Daily Morning Chronicle*, Sept. 1, 1869, 1.

113. File of Kate Cain, "Application and Recommendations," Box 81 (Byr–Cal), NA-Tr.

114. *Federal Register*, 1867, 1869; 1870 Census, Washington, D.C.

115. *Federal Register*, 1865, 1867, 1869; 1870 Census, Washington, D.C., 2WD.

116. "General Spinner," *Women's Journal*, 16–17; *Federal Register* 1863, 1865, 1867, 1869; 1870 Census, Washington, D.C.; 1880 Census, Washington, D.C.

117. *Federal Register*, 1865, 1867, 1870 Census, Washington, D.C.

118. Government Printing Office, *Annual Report of Superintendent of Public Printing 1865*; 1870 Census, Washington, D.C.

119. File of Mary Lyons, "Application and Recommendations," Box 360 (Lyo–Mac), NA-Tr.

120. Aron, "Their Souls for Gold," 851–52.

121. File of Jane Little, "Application and Recommendations," Box 350 (Lin–Lit), NA-Tr; 1870 Census, Washington, D.C., 4 WD.

122. Quote from email to author from Lisa Tuttle, one of Ash's descendants.

123. File of Fannie Kemp Breedin, "Application and Recommendations," Box 58 (Bra–Bre), NA-Tr.

124. Although President Grant attempted to institute civil service reform in the early 1870s, real reform did not come until the Pendleton Civil Service Act in 1883. Aron, *Ladies and Gentlemen*, 107.

Chapter Seven

1. "Memorial to Congress of the Clerks and Other Civil Employees" NA-USH; "Changes in the Clerical Force of the Attorney General's Office," *Evening Star* [Second Edition], Nov. 14, 1866, 2.

2. U.S. Department of the Treasury, *Report of the Secretary of the Treasury . . . 1868*, 73. Male federal clerks were divided into four classes and each of the classes had an as-

signed salary: first class received $1,200 a year, second class received $1,400 a year, third class received $1,600 a year, and fourth class received $1,800 a year. Penfield, *A Tale of the Rebellion.*

3. Women employed by the government working outside Washington, D.C., also petitioned for higher pay during the Civil War era. See, for example, Giesberg, *Army at Home*, 119–23.

4. File of A. Benedict, "Application and Recommendations," Box 37 (Bem–Ben), NA-Tr; *Federal Register*, 1869; *Federal Register*, 1871; "Petition of Female Employees in the Treasury Department Praying an Increase of Salary," NA-USS; 1870 Census, Washington, D.C., 2 WD.

5. "Petition from Officers and Employees of the Department of Interior for More Pay," NA-USH (6 female signatures among male signatures); "Petition of Female Employees in the Treasury Department Praying an Increase of Salary," NA-USS (42 women signing); "Petition of Citizens of Massachusetts, Clerks in the War Department, Praying an Increase in Salary," NA-USS (3 female signatures among male signatures); "Petition of Female Treasury Clerks for Increased Pay," NA-USH (59 women signing); "Petition of Female Postal Workers for Increased Compensation," NA-USH (27 women signing); "Petition of Employees in the Government Printing Office Praying for an Increase in Compensation," NA-USS (co-ed petition, 139 women signing); "Petition of Females Employed as Folders in the Post Office Department Praying for an Increase of Compensation," NA-USS (3 women signing as a committee); "Petition of Female Employees in the Folding Room of the Government Printing Office, Praying for an Increase of Compensation," NA-USS (104 women signing); "Petition from Women of Government Printing Office for More Money," NA-USH (285 women signing); "Petition of Kate Fannie Keene to Honorable Members of the Fortieth Congress," NA-USH (1 woman signing); "Petition of Women Employed as Sweepers and Scrubbers in the Treasury Department praying for an increase of Compensation," NA-USS (71 women signing; 48 signing own name, 23 "x-ing" next to name). Note that there were likely additional petitions from women than the ones above cited. For example in 1866 a local newspaper referenced female petitioners from the Government Printing Office, but I was unable to find a petition from the women of the GPO dated around the time of the article. "Local Intelligence," *Daily Constitutional Union*, Mar. 23 1866, 3; "[Correspondence]," *Sun*, Mar. 24, 1866, 4.

6. Kessler-Harris, *Out to Work*; Kessler-Harris, *A Woman's Wage*; Stansell, *City of Women*, 130–31.

7. Kessler-Harris, *Out to Work*, 68–69, 128.

8. Kessler-Harris, *A Woman's Wage*, 83. Kessler-Harris finds that the slogan "equal pay for equal work" became "popular in the United States at the end of the nineteenth century," but that it did not "seem to carry very much emotional resonance" until the United States entered World War I. There is also evidence of women working in white-collar jobs in Pennsylvania in the late 1890s who expressed their desire for equal pay. See also Cross, "'We Think We Are of the Oppressed'," 45–49; Cobble, *The Other Women's Movement*, 94–115.

9. Aron, *Ladies and Gentlemen*, 82–86.

10. Stansell, *City of Women*, 131; Masur, *Example for All the Land*, 3.

11. Reis, *African Americans and the Civil War*, 12, 86–87.

12. Edwards, *Angels in the Machinery*, 5–6, 29. See also Gustafson, *Women and the Republican Party*.

13. Women in nonclerical positions were also underpaid. Female laborers and messengers in the executive departments earned less than their male counterparts, as did female positions in the Government Hospital for the Insane. Millikan, "Wards of the Nation," 64–66; Townsend, *Washington, Outside and Inside*, 377.

14. "An Act to Supply Deficiencies in the Appropriations for Service of Fiscal Year ending June 30, 1864, and for Other Purposes."

15. Aron, *Ladies and Gentlemen*, 58, 209n61; Aron, "Their Souls for Gold," 847; Massey, *Bonnet Brigades*, 132; Kessler-Harris, *Out to Work*, 148; Wilson, *Business of the Civil War*, 226.

16. Massey, *Bonnet Brigades*, 132; Letter from Reynolds to Spalding, January 13, 1864, "Application and Recommendations," Box 495 (Rey–Rhy), NA-Tr.

17. Montgomery, *Beyond Equality*, 96.

18. In addition to the annual reports, see, for example, "Local Items," *Daily National Intelligencer*, Nov. 23, 1864, 3; "The Departments," *Daily Morning Chronicle*, Aug. 15, 1866, 1; "Washington Items," *Daily Constitutional Union*, Aug. 15, 1866, 3; "Starvation Pay," *Evening Star*, Nov. 30, 1866, 2.

19. Penfield, *A Tale of the Rebellion*. See, for example, "Committee on Ways and Means, Increase of Government Salaries," NA-USH; "Petition from Officers and Employees of the Department of Interior For More Pay," NA-USH (the petition was undated but the 38th Congress met from March 4, 1863, to March 4, 1865). Men also formed groups to consider ideas such as moving their families to Baltimore (where the cost of living was reportedly lower) and commuting to Washington, D.C. See, for example, "Local News," *Evening Star*, Sept. 12, 1863, 3.

20. "Sketches in Washington: The Government Printing Office," *Detroit Advertiser and Tribune*, Feb. 22, 1864, 4 (in Leasher, *Letter from Washington*, 80–82). For more on women in the bookbinding trade in the nineteenth century, see Kessler-Harris, *Out to Work*, 48.

21. "Strike of the Female Press Feeders at the Government Printing Office," *Daily Morning Chronicle*, Feb. 19, 1863, 3.

22. "A Gentleman Presented with a Petticoat," *Daily Morning Chronicle*, Feb. 21, 1863, 3. In December the women struck again for higher wages but this second strike failed. "At Work Again," *Daily Morning Chronicle*, Dec. 11, 1863, 2; "News Items," *Albany Journal*, Dec. 12, 1863, 2.

23. "Petition from Officers and Employees of the Department of Interior For More Pay," NA-USH; "Petition of Citizens of Massachusetts, Clerks in the War Department, Praying an Increase in Salary," NA-USS. For women arguing for higher pay based on cost of living increases, see, for example, *Congressional Globe*, 39th Cong., 2nd sess. 1149–1163, 1154 (Feb. 11, 1867).

24. The petitioners cited boarding expenses of $360 to $480 per year "independent of fuel, washing, and other incidental expenses." "Petition of Female Employees in the Treasury Department Praying an Increase of Salary," NA-USS.

25. See, for example, "A Bill to Provide for the Temporary Increase of the Compensation of Certain Clerks and Employees in the Civil Service of the Government" (setting pay for female clerks at $800 per year); U.S. Congress, *Journal of the House of Representatives*, 62 (Mar. 2, 1865), 391 (Congress voted down a bill to increase female salaries to $800 per year).

26. "[Treasury Department, Washington]," *Flake's Bulletin*, Apr. 4, 1866, 4.

27. "Petition of Female Treasury Clerks for Increased Pay," NA-USH. The petition was accompanied by a reserved cover letter from Hugh McCulloch, secretary of the Treasury. Although he had endorsed the men's petitions for higher wages in December 1865 as "absolutely necessary" and "justly due from the Government," he did not "think it would be advisable for Congress to increase the pay of female Clerks in the Treasury Department indiscriminately." He did believe, however, that "there are many ladies employed in the Department who are earning much more money then they receive." He hoped that "Congress would authorize a classification of these Clerks with proper provisions for the payment of their services according to their merit." "Letter to Congress from Committee of Clerks of Treasury Employees," NA-USH.

28. "Petition of Female Treasury Clerks for Increased Pay," NA-USH.

29. Ibid.

30. The first signer was Miss H. H. Webber. Webber joined the Post Office in 1865 and was also listed as an employee of the Post Office in 1867, 1869, and 1871. *Federal Register*, 1865, 1867, 1869, 1871.

31. "Petition of Female Postal Workers for Increased Compensation," NA-USH (emphasis in original).

32. "An Act making Appropriations for the Legislative, Executive, and Judicial Expense of the Government." See also U.S. Congress, *Journal of the House of Representatives*, 58 (July 17, 1866), 663–64.

33. *Federal Register*, 1865, 1867; "Petition of Kate Fannie Keene to Honorable Members of the Fortieth Congress," NA-USH (emphasis in original).

34. "Petition of Women Employed as Sweepers and Scrubbers in the Treasury Department praying for an increase of Compensation," NA-USS.

35. "Extra Compensation," *Evening Star*, Feb. 12, 1867, 2.

36. "Women as Government Clerks," *New York Times*, Feb. 18, 1869, 2.

37. "Petition of Females Employed as Folders in the Post Office Department Praying for an Increase of Compensation," NA-USS. Corbin began work at the Post Office in 1866 and appears in the *Federal Register* in the Post Office in 1867 and 1869. The 1870 Census shows her "at home." She signed two petitions. Ann Carver began work at the Post Office in 1867. She appears on the *Federal Register* in the Post Office in 1867, 1869, and 1871. The 1870 Census shows her "at home." Martha Collier began work at the Post Office in 1865. She appears on the *Federal Register* in the Post Office in 1865, 1867, 1869, and 1871. She signed two petitions.

38. "Petition from Women of Government Printing Office for More Money," NA-USH.

39. The women in the Post Office, for instance, requested that they be included in the distribution of "the two hundred and forty thousand ($240,000) appropriated to clerks receiving small salaries." "Petition of Female Postal Workers for Increased Compensation," NA-USH.

40. Wives of male clerks also wrote to newspapers to argue for increases to their husbands' salaries. See, for example, "Local News," *Evening Star*, Apr. 18, 1868, 4; "The Twenty Per Cent.," *Daily Morning Chronicle*, June 1, 1868, 1.

41. "Twenty Per Cent.," *Evening Star*, Dec. 14, 1867, 1.

42. "A Woman's Plea," *Daily Morning Chronicle*, Mar. 18, 1867, 2 (emphasis in original). See also, "[No title]," *Daily Morning Chronicle*, Mar. 18, 1867, 2.

43. The *Daily Morning Chronicle* letter to the editor is dated March 5 but was not published until April 1. "The Pay of Female Clerks," *Daily Morning Chronicle*, Apr. 1, 1868, 4.

44. "Washington News and Gossip," *Evening Star*, Feb. 8, 1867, 1 (emphasis in original); "The Pay of Female Clerks," *Daily Morning Chronicle*, Apr. 1, 1868, 4.

45. "Women in Government Departments," *The Revolution*, Dec. 16, 1869, 370–71 (emphasis in original).

46. "Clerical Compensation," *Evening Star*, Jan. 30, 1868, 1. See also "Clerical Compensation," *Evening Star*, Feb. 1, 1868, 2.

47. "Clerical Compensation," *Evening Star*, Jan. 30, 1868, 1. See also letter from "Truth," who argued that messengers and women should receive the pay increase (even though women had "received a permanent increase of pay within the year past"), "Washington News & Gossip," *Evening Star*, Feb. 1, 1868, 1; Letter from "Justice," arguing that men and women in the federal departments should receive the 20 percent increase, "The Twenty Per Cent.," *Daily Morning Chronicle*, June 15, 1868, 1. For a rebuttal to the J. H. R. letter, see "Washington News & Gossip," *Evening Star*, Feb. 1, 1868, 1, in which "*Justitia fiat*" claimed that women had already received a raise and did not need another.

48. "Women as Government Clerks," *New York Times*, Feb. 18, 1869, 2. See also "Employment of Female Clerks." *Houston Union*, Mar. 15, 1869, 1.

49. "Correspondence Cincinnati Commercial," *Cincinnati Commercial Tribune*, Apr. 18, 1870, 2. See also "Some Treasury Girls," *New-York Evangelist*, Aug. 7, 1873, 7.

50. "A Good Word for the Female Clerks," *Evening Star*, Nov. 11, 1869, 2.

51. But see "Washington Letter: Women as Clerks," *The Revolution*, Apr. 30, 1868, 261–62 (describing suffragists who were in Washington, D.C., to make it a "special point" to survey senators and congressmen on the issue of equal pay).

52. "A Woman's Work and Wages," *The Revolution*, Apr. 22, 1869, 249–50; DuBois, *Feminism and Suffrage*, 162.

53. "The Revolution," *The Revolution*, Jan. 8, 1868, 1. See also Montgomery, *Beyond Equality*, 396.

54. "Local News," *Evening Star*, July 20, 1867, 1; "City Intelligence," *Daily Morning Chronicle*, Jan. 21, 1869, 4; "City Intelligence," *Daily Morning Chronicle*, Jan. 23, 1869, 4;

"Woman Suffrage," *Evening Star*, Jan. 19, 1870, 4; "Universal Suffrage," *Daily Morning Chronicle*, Jan. 19, 1870, 4; "City Intelligence," *Daily Morning Chronicle*, Jan. 21, 1869, 4; "Local News," *Evening Star*, Dec. 20, 1869, 4; "Woman Suffrage," *Evening Star*, Jan. 19, 1870, 4; "Universal Suffrage," *Daily Morning Chronicle*, Jan. 19, 1870, 4; Briggs, *Olivia Letters*, 150; "Wailing Women: American Amazons in Council and Political Females Let Loose," *New York Herald*, May 12, 1870.

55. "The Washington Convention," *The Revolution*, Jan. 27, 1869, 52–57. The woman inquiring may have been Leonora Edson, who worked at the Treasury Department in 1863. *Federal Register*, 1863.

56. For a detailed examination of this issue, see chapters 4 and 5 of DuBois, *Feminism and Suffrage*. See also Kessler-Harris, *Out to Work*, 95–97; Montgomery, *Beyond Equality*, 395–400; and Stansell, *City of Women*, 153, 220.

57. For more on the women's suffrage movement in the Civil War era, see generally Dudden, *Fighting Chance*; Sneider, *Suffragists in an Imperial Age*; Gustafson, *Women and the Republican Party*; Edwards, *Angels in the Machinery*; DuBois, *Feminism and Suffrage*; Flexner, *Century of Struggle*; chapter 5 of DuBois, *Woman Suffrage & Women's Rights*; and "From Seneca Falls to Suffrage? Reimagining a 'Master' Narrative in U.S. Women's History," in Hewitt, *No Permanent Waves*, ed. Nancy A. Hewitt.

58. Gustafson, *Women and the Republican Party*, 26–27, 34.

59. See, for example, Edwards, *Angels in the Machinery*, 51.

60. DuBois, *Feminism and Suffrage*, 126.

61. Ibid., 133.

62. Ibid., 134–35. For another example of feminists clashing with working women over strategy, see "Work and Wages," *The Revolution*, June 9, 1870, 362.

63. DuBois, *Feminism and Suffrage*, 153, 160.

64. Ibid., 162.

65. Sneider, *Suffragists in an Imperial Age*, 20–23.

66. "Votes and Wages," *The Woman's Journal*, Feb. 26, 1870, 61.

67. "[No title]," *The Revolution*, Apr. 22, 1869, 251. For more on the split between the African American rights movement and women's rights movement at this time, see Dudden, *Fighting Chance*.

68. "Something Better Than the Ballot for Women," *The Revolution*, Oct. 14, 1869, 226.

69. "Civil Service Reform," *The Revolution*, Dec. 2, 1869, 345; "Women as Government Clerks," *The Revolution*, Mar. 10, 1870, 153.

70. "Work and Wages," *The Revolution*, June 9, 1870, 362.

71. The 20 percent pay increase was a major issue in the mid- to late 1860s, especially between 1866 and 1868. Local newspapers ran dozens of articles on the subject and groups of clerks (apparently all men) came together to fight for the increase. Congress would vote for the 20 percent increase, but as written, it expired in one year and so the cycle would start anew.

72. Historian Rachel A. Shelden makes a compelling argument that historians should read and interpret congressional speechmaking critically because much of it was political theater, meant to garner support from voters back in their districts. Of

course, during these debates, women could not vote. Politicians could be considering women's brothers, fathers, sons, and husbands when making their remarks. Shelden, *Washington Brotherhood*.

73. *Congressional Globe*, 40th Cong., 3d sess. 117–18 (Dec. 16, 1868); "Women as Government Clerks," *New York Times*, Feb 18, 1869, 2.

74. "Correspondence," *Sun*, Feb. 16, 1869, 4.

75. *Congressional Globe*, 40th Cong., 3rd sess. 1773–80, 1774 (Mar. 2, 1869).

76. For the atmosphere of equality in Washington, D.C., in the late 1860s, see Masur, *Example for All the Land*.

77. Yates was an advocate of female suffrage. See, for example, Yates and Pickering, *Richard Yates, Civil War Governor*.

78. Illinois Senator Lyman Trumbull was coauthor of the Thirteenth Amendment, author of the Civil Rights Act of 1866, and a man who would become one of the champions for women in Congress. See, for example, Roske, *His Own Counsel*; Krug, *Lyman Trumbull*; and White, *The Life of Lyman Trumbull*.

79. Pomeroy was a strong supporter of women's rights. He was the president of an equal rights group that met in the district in 1867. "Equal Rights," *Daily Morning Chronicle*, July 13, 1867, 4. He was also reported as being the lone senator at the National Woman Suffrage Convention in Washington in January 1870. Briggs, *The Olivia Letters* (Jan. 18, 1870), 143; (Jan. 20, 1870), 238; (Jan. 12, 1871), 252–53. See also "The Washington Convention," *The Revolution*, Jan. 27, 1869, 52–57.

80. This idea of "simple justice" was a large part of the 1948 hearings on equal pay for women as well. Historian Kessler-Harris's description of those hearings could have been written about the debates of the late 1860s: "the notion of simple justice was echoed so frequently as to appear self-evident and need no defense." The mid- to late twentieth-century debates on equal pay, however, were full of multilayered rhetoric that had been developing over time. The 1860s debates on equal pay, by contrast, were less nuanced. Kessler-Harris, *A Woman's Wage*, 105.

81. *Congressional Globe*, 41st Cong., 2nd sess. 3449–52 (May 13, 1870).

82. *Congressional Globe*, 40th Cong., 3rd sess. 1773–80, 1774 (Mar. 2, 1869).

83. *Congressional Globe*, 41st Cong., 2nd sess. 3451 (May 13, 1870). Trumbull expressed this sentiment frequently—"it does seem to me so just that these persons should be put upon the same footing in regard to pay that I cannot see how we should refuse it."

84. The fact that these equal pay measures passed (though they died in committee) is further evidence that the equal pay movement had supporters.

85. Ibid., 3450. For more on Stewart, see Drabelle, "The Tarnished Silver Senator."

86. *Congressional Globe*, 41st Cong., 2nd sess. 3452 (May 13, 1870).

87. *Congressional Globe*, 39th Cong., 2nd sess. 1149–63, 1155 (Feb. 11, 1867). Conness was staunchly antislavery, supported radical Reconstruction, and broke ways with many of his California constituents in his advocating of Chinese civil rights. Denning, "A Fragile Machine." He was an early supporter of the eight-hour movement as well. Montgomery, *Beyond Equality*, 240–41.

88. *Congressional Globe*, 40th Cong., 3rd sess. 1773–80, 1775 (Mar. 2, 1869).

89. "Congressional News," *Daily Morning Chronicle*, Mar. 22, 1870, 4. See also "By Telegraph. Washington," *Boston Daily Advertiser*, June 11, 1870, 1; "Latest by Telegraph," *Cincinnati Daily Gazette*, June 13, 1870, 3.

90. Whether these men were genuine in their sentiments is unknown. Their remarks could have been motivated by the same idea which caused some Democrats to support woman's suffrage in these years: a desire to embarrass Radical Republicans supporting male African Americans' right to vote. DuBois, *Feminism and Suffrage*, 76.

91. *Congressional Globe*, 41st Cong., 2nd sess. 1412–17, 1416 (Feb. 18, 1870). This "plain, honest proposition" apparently had not held true for Voorhees with respect to African Americans. In a speech Voorhees gave in 1860 at the University of Virginia and entitled "The American Citizen," he stated, "I hold nothing in common with that false and pernicious system of political ethics which proclaims as its favorite dogma the unqualified equality of the whole human family." Jordan, "Daniel Wolsey Voorhees," 534.

92. Foner, *The Fiery Trial*, 174; *Congressional Globe*, 39th Cong., 2nd sess. 1149–63, 1155 (Feb. 11, 1867).

93. *Congressional Globe*, 40th Cong., 3rd sess. 1773–80, 1774 (Mar. 2, 1869).

94. *Congressional Globe*, 41st Cong., 2nd sess. 3450 (May 13, 1870).

95. Ibid., 3451.

96. *Congressional Globe*, 41st Cong., 2nd sess. 1414 (Feb. 18, 1870). Representative William S. Holman of Indiana would have gone even further, and argued that "it would be but in conformity with the spirit of the age for the Government, if it employs females, to give them even a better rate of compensation than is given to men for like services. But I only desire by this amendment to put them upon exactly the same footing." Ibid.

97. Edwards, *Angels in the Machinery*, 39.

98. *Congressional Globe*, 39th Cong., 2nd sess. 1149–63, 1154 (Feb. 11, 1867).

99. *Congressional Globe*, 40th Cong., 3rd sess. 1773–80, 1774 (Mar. 2, 1869).

100. *Congressional Globe*, 41st Cong., 2nd sess. 3450 (May 13, 1870).

101. *Congressional Globe*, 41st Cong., 2nd sess. 1412 (Feb. 18, 1870). Opponents of equal pay argued that its supporters were basing their opinion on sentimentalism and feelings that had no place in Congress. *Congressional Globe*, 40th Cong., 3rd sess. 1777, 1779 (Mar. 2, 1869); *Congressional Globe*, 41st Cong., 2nd sess. 3449–52, 3452 (May 13, 1870).

102. *Congressional Globe*, 40th Cong., 3rd sess. 1776 (Mar. 2, 1869). For more on Howe, who was a supporter of Radical Reconstruction, see Russell, "Timothy O. Howe, Stalwart Republican."

103. S. L. Burlingame, "The Making of a Spoilsman" (for Conkling's financial policies, see iii, 194, 230).

104. The argument of a surplus of female labor reducing female wages was also made in the private sector at this time. Kessler-Harris, *Out to Work*, 99–100.

105. *Congressional Globe*, 40th Cong., 3rd sess. 1779 (Mar. 2, 1869).

106. Ibid., 1779.

107. *Congressional Globe*, 41st Cong., 2nd sess. 3450 (May 13, 1870). For more on Sawyer, see Harvard University, *The Class of 1844*, 194–203.

108. It was, however, convincing to suffragists, who believed this was precisely why women needed to obtain the vote. "Women as Government Clerks," *The Revolution*, Mar. 10, 1870, 153.

109. *Congressional Globe*, 41st Cong., 2nd sess. 1412 (Feb. 18, 1870). Arnell was the Representative who introduced a bill (H. R. No. 1143) "to do justice to the female employés of the Government." *Congressional Globe*, 41st Cong., 2d sess. 1087 (Feb. 7, 1870). In fact, there were men in Washington, D.C., who were desperate for laborer jobs around the time of the equal pay debates. In January 1868, for example, General George D. Ramsay of the Washington Arsenal wrote to the *Evening Star* to ask them to publicize that they were not hiring. Statements in papers to the contrary had "brought to us *hundreds* of the needy and unemployed, only to be disappointed." "Washington News & Gossip," *Evening Star*, Jan. 25, 1868, 1 (emphasis in original).

110. *Congressional Globe*, 40th Cong., 3rd sess. 1775 (Mar. 2, 1869).

111. Ibid., 1779.

112. *Congressional Globe*, 41st Cong., 2nd sess. 3452 (May 13, 1870).

113. Stansell also found this brand of paternalism at play in New York City, in working women's agitation for better pay and conditions. Stansell, *City of Women*, 218–19.

114. *Congressional Globe*, 40th Cong., 3rd sess. 1774 (Mar. 2, 1869). Historian Brian Luskey notes that arguments such as this "parallel the arguments made by free labor proponents who counseled freedpeople to sign contracts with white planters in an arrangement that resembled slavery. Under these terms, economic opportunity could only be enjoyed at the behest of white men with land or capital, and the fault for lost opportunities would be workers', not the economic system's." Luskey, *On the Make*, 233.

115. There were also arguments made that women did not actually perform the same work, but these were quickly refuted. Moreover, opponents of equal pay often conceded that women did perform the same work as men. For example, Senator Sawyer, who was against equalizing female pay with male pay, stated, "I know there are ladies there who are worth to the Government six times as much as some single clerks who received $1,200." *Congressional Globe*, 41st Cong., 2nd sess. 3452 (May 13, 1870).

116. *Congressional Globe*, 40th Cong., 3rd sess. 1774 (Mar. 2, 1869). Harlan was likely generalizing based on his own personal opinions—when he became secretary of the interior in 1865, he dismissed most of the female clerks in that Department. Massey, *Bonnet Brigades*, 133; "Correspondence," *Sun*, Nov. 7, 1865, 4.

117. *Congressional Globe*, 41st Cong., 2nd sess. 3450 (May 13, 1870).

118. Ibid.

119. Ibid., 3452.

120. Ibid., 3451.

121. Stansell, *City of Women*, 111.

122. "Letter from A. E. Fithian Regarding Pay of Women, May 26, 1870," US-USH.

123. *Congressional Globe*, 41st Cong., 2nd sess. 3450 (May 13, 1870).

124. U.S. Department of the Treasury, *Report of the Secretary of the Treasury . . . 1863*, 85.

125. Question 36 asked how many women the officer employed, how much they were paid, how they compared to men "for diligence, attention and efficiency," and

whether they thought women should be appointed "for competency alone," and promoted based on seniority and merit. U.S. Congress, Joint Select Committee on Retrenchment, *Civil Service of the United States*, Appendix B, 18. The major concerns addressed in the report were hiring and promotion practices. Congressman Thomas A. Jenckes, Republican of Rhode Island, submitted the report on behalf of the Joint Select Committee on Retrenchment. Sixteen men provided substantive answers to Question 36. See also Van Riper, *History of the United States Civil Service*, 64–65.

126. In addition to the annual reports, newspapers cited supervisors' praise of female clerks. See, for example, "Women as Government Clerks," *New York Times*, Feb. 18, 1869, 2.

127. See, for example, U.S. Department of the Treasury, *Report of the Secretary of the Treasury* . . . 1864, 109, 118; U.S. Department of the Treasury, *Report of the Secretary of the Treasury* . . . 1865, 145–46.

128. U.S. Department of the Treasury, *Report of the Secretary of the Treasury* . . . 1865, 92.

129. U.S. Department of the Treasury, *Report of the Secretary of the Treasury* . . . 1868, 404.

130. U.S. Department of the Treasury, *Report of the Secretary of the Treasury* . . . 1865, 102.

131. U.S. Department of the Treasury, *Report of the Secretary of the Treasury* . . . 1864, 76.

132. U.S. Department of the Treasury, *Report of the Secretary of the Treasury* . . . 1865, 98.

133. If women miscounted or passed counterfeit bills, they could be liable for the money (see chapter 3). For details on Spinner's proposed reorganization, see U.S. Department of the Treasury, *Report of the Secretary of the Treasury* . . . 1866, 172–74; U.S. Department of the Treasury, *Report of the Secretary of the Treasury* . . . 1868, 251–55; U.S. Department of the Treasury, *Report of the Secretary of the Treasury* . . . 1869, 283–87. Spinner's reorganization proposals changed slightly over time.

134. "Letter from Washington," *Sun*, Dec. 3, 1868, 4; "Female Clerks," *Daily Morning Chronicle*, Dec. 3, 1868, 2; "Washington," *New York Daily Tribune*, Oct. 26, 1869, 1; "Letters from Washington," *Sun*, Oct. 27, 1869, 4; "General Spinner," *Women's Journal*, Jan. 10, 1891, 16–17.

135. U.S. Department of the Treasury, *Report of the Secretary of the Treasury* . . . 1869, 283–87.

136. Female government work also entered the suffrage debates. In 1867, for example, Julia Holmes argued at a meeting of the Universal Franchise Association that, "evidence of [women's] equality with men was the manner in which they had filled Government clerkships. They had given eminent satisfaction." "Local News," *Evening Star*, Sept. 21, 1867, 2.

137. *Congressional Globe*, 41st Cong., 2nd sess. 3449, 3452 (May 13, 1870).

138. Ibid., 3450.

139. *Congressional Globe*, 41st Cong., 2nd sess. 3452 (May 13, 1870).

140. *Congressional Globe*, 41st Cong., 2nd sess. 1415, 1416 (Feb. 18, 1870).

141. Ibid.

142. "Women as Government Clerks," *The Revolution*, Mar. 10, 1870, 153.

143. "The Laborer and Her Hire," *The Revolution*, June 23, 1870, 396 (emphasis in original).

144. "Equal Wages for Equal Work," *Evening Star*, June 13, 1870, 2.

145. *Congressional Globe*, 41st Cong., 2nd sess. 3452 (May 13, 1870).

146. *Congressional Globe*, 40th Cong., 3rd sess. 1779 (Mar. 2, 1869).

147. Ibid., 1776.

148. Ibid., 1774.

149. *Congressional Globe*, 41st Cong., 2nd sess. 1417 (Feb. 18, 1870).

150. Kessler-Harris, *Out to Work*, 59.

151. *Congressional Globe*, 40th Cong., 3rd sess. 1778 (Mar. 2, 1869). Senator Sherman, brother of General William Tecumseh Sherman, characterized women's initial $600 per year salary as one upon which "they were able to maintain their families in comfort and independence." *Congressional Globe*, 39th Cong., 2nd sess. 1149–63, 1154 (Feb. 11, 1867).

152. *Congressional Globe*, 41st Cong., 2nd sess. 3451 (May 13, 1870).

153. *Congressional Globe*, 40th Cong., 3rd sess. 1779 (Mar. 2, 1869).

154. *Congressional Globe*, 41st Cong., 2nd sess. 3451 (May 13, 1870); *Congressional Globe*, 40th Cong., 3rd sess. 1779 (Mar. 2, 1869).

155. *Congressional Globe*, 40th Cong., 3rd sess. 1774 (Mar. 2, 1869). See also *Congressional Globe*, 41st Cong., 2nd sess. 3449 (May 13, 1870).

156. *Congressional Globe*, 40th Cong., 3rd sess. 1779 (Mar. 2, 1869). This basic argument was echoed eighty years later in Congressional hearings on equal pay. Kessler-Harris, *A Woman's Wage*, 106.

157. *Congressional Globe*, 40th Cong., 3rd sess. 1779 (Mar. 2, 1869).

158. *Congressional Globe*, 41st Cong., 2nd sess. 3449 (May 13, 1870).

159. *Congressional Globe*, 39th Cong., 2nd sess. 1155 (Feb. 11, 1867).

160. *Congressional Globe*, 41st Cong., 2nd sess. 1412 (Feb. 18, 1870). Newspaper correspondent Emily Edson Briggs described Rogers as "the man who wanted all the women of the Treasury blown out exactly as the flame of a lamp." Briggs, *Olivia Letters*, 272 (Mar. 7, 1871).

161. *Congressional Globe*, 41st Cong., 2nd sess. 1412 (Feb. 18, 1870).

162. Ibid.

163. Ibid., 1417.

164. Ibid., 1415.

165. Ibid., 1417

166. Kelle was a supporter of Radical Reconstruction and African American civil rights. (His daughter, Florence, was a social welfare crusader in the Progressive Era.) He was also an early endorser of female suffrage. Brown, "William D. Kelley and Radical Reconstruction."

167. *Congressional Globe*, 41st Cong., 2nd sess. 1416 (Feb. 18, 1870).

168. *Congressional Globe*, 41st Cong., 2nd sess. 1931 (Mar. 14, 1870); "City Intelligence," *Daily Morning Chronicle*, Mar. 15, 1870, 4.

169. "Brief Topics," *Jamestown Journal*, Mar. 18, 1870, 4; Kacrick, *Informal English*, 122; Dickson, *War Slang*, 204; Green, *Cassell's Dictionary of Slang*, 868.

170. For examples of women bestowing gifts upon supervisors, see, for example, "City Intelligence," *Daily Morning Chronicle*, Oct. 3, 1865, 4; U.S. Congress, House of Representatives, *Certain Charges against the Treasury Department*, 147–48.

171. Briggs, *Olivia Letters*, 249 (Jan. 14, 1871).

172. "Woman's Pay for Labor," *Daily Morning Chronicle*, Dec. 19, 1868, 4.

173. "Employment of Female Clerks," *Houston Union*, Mar. 15, 1869, 1. The paper praised the Republican Party and rejoiced "to know that a large majority of the educated females of the United States are thorough Republicans."

174. "Women's Work and Wages," *The Revolution*, June 2, 1870, 341–42.

175. "About Women," *The Revolution*, Aug. 18, 1870, 103; "The Women Clerks in Washington," *The Revolution*, Sept. 22, 1870, 187.

176. *Congressional Globe*, 40th Cong., 3rd sess. 117–18 (Dec. 16, 1868); "Woman's Pay for Labor," *Daily Morning Chronicle*, Dec. 19, 1868, 4; "Women as Government Clerks," *New York Times*, Feb. 18, 1869, 2.

177. *Congressional Globe*, 41st Cong., 2nd sess. 1414 (Feb. 18, 1870).

178. *Congressional Globe*, 41st Cong., 2nd sess. 3451 (May 13, 1870).

179. Ibid., 3452.

180. Unfortunately, committee records explaining this failure have not yet been located, and may no longer exist.

181. "Department News," *Daily Morning Chronicle*, June 19, 1869, 1.

182. Letter from R. H. Tayler, First Comptroller of the Treasury to Hon. Wm. A. Richardson, Assistant Secretary of the Treasury, June 24, 1869, Records of the Post Office Department, *Miscellaneous File*, Entry 213, RG 28, Box 1, National Archives, Washington, D.C. See also "Washington," *New York Daily Tribune*, June 19, 1869, 5; "General Press Dispatches," *New York Daily Tribune*, June 29, 1869, 5; "Department News," *Daily Morning Chronicle*, June 29, 1869, 1.

183. *Congressional Globe*, 41st Cong., 2nd sess. 3449, 3451 (May 13, 1870).

184. "Latest by Telegraph," *Cincinnati Daily Gazette*, June 13, 1870, 3.

185. This is questionable, as department heads were given limits on the numbers of clerks they could employ of each class—first through fourth—and female clerks. Men that had promoted women, like the secretary of war's promotion of Wainwright, for example, did so surreptitiously, inserting promoted female women into the list of male clerks with only their first initials (see chapter 7).

186. *Congressional Globe*, 41st Cong., 2nd sess. 3451 (May 13, 1870).

187. Meigs to Emma P. Sedgwick, Nov. 7, 1871, "Letters and Endorsements sent to Officers, Agents, and Employees Relating to Personnel 1871–1883," NA-WD.

188. Ibid.

189. See, for example, "Washington News and Gossip," *Evening Star*, July 21, 1870, 1; Washington, D.C., *Daily Evening Bulletin*, June 15, 1871, 2. According to an analysis of the *Federal Register*, eighteen women were promoted to first-class clerkships and four women were promoted to second-class clerkships: H. C. Keller and Belle Tracy (promoted to $1,200 clerk in Treasurer's Office); Juliette Shearer (promoted to $1,200 clerk in Secretary of the Treasury's Office); Jane M. Seavey, May R. Raymond, Mary Van

Vranken, H. B. Upson, and Jane W. Little (promoted to $1,200 clerks in Internal Revenue Bureau); Hannah M. C. Hanscom, Mattie J. Saulsbury, and Fannie M. Gilbert (promoted to $1,200 clerks in Currency Division); Jane E. Jennings and Helen Godwin (promoted to $1,200 clerk in Fifth Auditor's Office); Fannie E. Wadleigh (promoted to $1,200 clerk in Supervising Architect's Office); Nancy Bishop and M. A. Spencer (promoted to $1,200 clerks in Treasury's Bureau of Statistics); Annie E. Fithian (promoted to $1,200 clerk in Treasury); Kate S. Olds (promoted to $1,200 clerk in Second Comptroller's Office); Abby A. Baker (promoted to $1,400 clerk in the Records and Files Division); F. R. Sprague (promoted to $1,400 clerk in Office of the Comptroller of the Currency); M. M. Watson and Lydia E. Rosenberg (promoted to $1,400 clerk in Treasurer's Office).

190. *Congressional Globe*, 40th Cong., 3rd sess. 1775 (Mar. 2, 1869); Aron, *Ladies and Gentlemen*, 84, Table 4.2.

191. Aron, *Ladies and Gentlemen*, 84, Table 4.2.

192. Kessler-Harris, *Out to Work*, 290.

193. Aron, *Ladies and Gentlemen*, 84

194. Kessler-Harris, *A Woman's Wage*, 88.

195. Ames, *Ten Years*, 379.

196. Martin, *Behind the Scenes*, 473–74.

197. See, for example, Tentler, *Wage-Earning Women*.

198. Aron, *Ladies and Gentlemen*, 6.

199. "Women's Work and Wages," *The Revolution*, June 2, 1870, 341–42.

Epilogue

1. For newspapers reporting on the statue, see "A Friend to Women," *Carroll Herald*, Mar. 11, 1896, 2; "The Statue without A Site," *Pittsburgh Post-Gazette*, Sept. 13, 1908; "[Congressional Matters]," *Age Herald*, Feb. 13, 1900, 7; "Women Strive to Honor Memory of Him Who Fought for Their Cause," *Philadelphia Inquirer*, Sept. 1, 1901, 3; "Was a Hero at Washington," *Macon Telegraph*, Aug. 9, 1903, 5; "[No title]," *Springfield Republican*, June 17, 1908, 8; "Bits of Information," *Evening Telegram*, Sept. 24, 1908, 10; "Unveil Statue of General Spinner," *Fort Worth Star-Telegram*, June 28, 1909, 9; "Women Do Honor to General F. Spinner," *Evening Telegram*, June 28, 1909, 6; "Monument to Gen. Spinner," *Dallas Morning News*, June 29, 1909, 7; "Note and Comment," *Springfield Republican*, July 1, 1909, 8; "Washington Gossip," *Idaho Falls Times*, May 7, 1896, 3. See also U.S. Congress, *Statue of Francis E. Spinner*.

2. For Stoner's start date, see Aron, "Their Souls for Gold," 851–52. For Hoey's start date, see "Registers and Lists of Treasury Employees Register of Female Clerks, 1861–1868," vol. 3, NA-Tr. For Devendorf's start date, see *Federal Register*, 1865. See also "The Vocations of Women," *Dallas Morning News*, Nov. 26, 1893, 5. Stoner continued to work in the Treasury Department until at least 1894 and as president of the association until at least 1896. "Washington Gossip," *Idaho Falls Times*, May 7, 1896, 3.

3. "Women Strive to Honor Memory of Him Who Fought for Their Cause," *Philadelphia Inquirer*, Sept. 1, 1901, 3; "Washington Gossip," *Idaho Falls Times*, May 7, 1896, 3 ("The expense of the monument to Spinner has been borne entirely by women. . . . It will not cost the government a penny, for the funds have all been raised by individual subscriptions, most of them from ladies.") The cost of the statue was reported to be as high as $25,000. "Unveil Statue of General Spinner," *Fort Worth Star-Telegram*, June 28, 1909, 9.

4. "A Friend to Women," *Carroll Herald*, Mar. 11, 1896, 2; U.S. Congress, House of Representatives, *Statue of Francis E. Spinner*.

5. "Women Strive to Honor Memory of Him Who Fought for Their Cause," *Philadelphia Inquirer*, Sept. 1, 1901, 3.

6. Based on their ages in the 1870 Census for Washington, D.C., in 1896, Stoner was sixty-eight, Devendorf was sixty-six, and Hoey was fifty-six. U.S. Congress, House of Representatives, *Statue of Francis E. Spinner*.

7. "Women Strive to Honor Memory of Him Who Fought for Their Cause," *Philadelphia Inquirer*, Sept. 1, 1901, 3; "Was a Hero at Washington," *Macon Telegraph*, Aug. 9, 1903, 5.

8. "A Friend to Women," *Carroll Herald*, Mar. 11, 1896, 2. See also "The Statue without a Site," *Pittsburgh Post-Gazette*, Sept. 13, 1908.

9. "[No title]," *Springfield Republican*, June 17, 1908, 8.

10. "Bits of Information," *Evening Telegram*, Sept. 24, 1908, 10.

11. "Unveil Statue of General Spinner," *Fort Worth Star-Telegram*, June 28, 1909, 9.

12. "The Female Clerks," *Evening Star*, Oct. 14, 1870, 1.

13. Sarah A. Robison to Abraham Lincoln, Feb. 25, 1861, ALP, accessed Oct. 22, 2010.

14. "City Intelligence," *Daily Morning Chronicle*, Mar. 8, 1867, 2; "Washington News & Gossip," *Evening Star*, Mar. 21, 1868, 1.

15. *Annual Report of the Board of Regents of the Smithsonian Institution*, 44.

16. Aynes, "*Bradwell v. Illinois*," 525–29, 537. See also Hyman, *The Reconstruction Justice of Salmon P. Chase* (though note I could not find confirmation of some of Aynes's claims about Chase's thoughts on female employment).

17. Davies, *Woman's Place*, 58; Davies, "Woman's Place," 7; "Women in Business," *Fortune* 12 (July 1935): 50–57, 90–96.

18. Kwolek-Folland, *Engendering Business*, 4; Srole, *Transcribing Class*; Luskey, *On the Make*; Kwolek-Folland, *Incorporating Women*; Tentler, *Wage-Earning Women*.

Bibliography

Archives

Haverford College, PA
    Haverford College Quaker and Special Collections
        Julia Wilbur Papers, 1843–1908, Manuscript Collection 1158 https://tripod
            .brynmawr.edu/find/Record/.b2159351
            Diary of Julia A. Wilbur, Sept. 6, 1868–Mar. 27, 1869.
            Diary of Julia A. Wilbur, Mar. 30, 1869–May 14, 1870.
            Diary of Julia A. Wilbur, May 17, 1870–May 2, 1871.
            Diary of Julia A. Wilbur, May 5, 1871–Apr. 21, 1872.
Huntington Library, San Marino, CA
    Diary of Annie G. Dudley Davis, Jan. 1, 1861–Mar. 24, 1868, mssHM 58019
Library of Congress, Washington, DC
    Manuscript Division
        Benjamin F. Butler Papers, 1778–1929
        Clara Barton Papers
        Abraham Lincoln Papers, American Memory Project, American Memory
            Project, 2000–2002, http://memory.loc.gov/ammem/alhtml/alhome
            .html
    Rare Book and Special Collections Division
        "A Lecture on Constitutional Equality, delivered at Lincoln Hall, Washington,
            D.C., Thursday, February 16, 1871, by Victoria C. Woodhull," New York:
            Journeymen Printers' Cooperative Association, 1871, National American
            Woman Suffrage Association Collection.
Rutgers, the State University of New Jersey
    The Elizabeth Cady Stanton & Susan B. Anthony Papers Project, available at
        http://ecssba.rutgers.edu/resources/votenames.html, last accessed July 7,
        2014.

Published Government Documents

"Act of January 21, 1862." (An Act to Promote the Efficiency of the Dead Letter
    Office), ch. 8, 12 *Stat.* 332.
"Act of January 21, 1862." (An Act in Relation to the Letters of Sailors and Marines in
    the Service of the United States), ch. 9, 12 *Stat.* 332.
"An Act Making Appropriations for the Legislative, Executive, and Judicial Expense of
    the Government for the Year ending the thirtieth of June, Eighteen Hundred and

Sixty Seven, and for other Purposes," July 23, 1866, 39th Cong., 1st sess., ch. 202, 208.

"An Act to Supply Deficiencies in the Appropriations for Service of Fiscal Year ending June 30, 1864, and for other Purposes," March 14, 1864, 38th Cong., ch. 30, 13 *Stat.* 22.

"A Bill to Provide for the Temporary Increase of the Compensation of Certain Clerks and Employees in the Civil Service of the Government," January 25, 1865, 38th Cong., 2nd sess., H.R. 701.

Committee on the District of Columbia, *Report*, 40th Cong., 2nd sess., S. Rept. Com. 131, 1868.

Jenckes, Thomas A. *Speech of Hon. Thomas A. Jenckes of Rhode Island, on the Bill to Regulate the Civil Service of the United States and Promote the Efficiency Thereof. Delivered to the House of Rep, May 14, 1868*. Washington, DC: F&J Rives & Geo. A. Bailey, 1868.

"Petition of Citizens of Washington City, DC, Praying an Appropriation for Cleansing and Improving the Washington Canal," 1177 S.misdoc.84, March 24, 1864.

U.S. Census Office. *Eighth Census of the United States* (1860).

U.S. Census Office. *Ninth Census of the United States* (1870).

U.S. Civil Service Commission. *Women in the Federal Service*. Washington, DC: GPO, 1938.

U.S. Commissioner of Education. *Special Report of the Commissioner of Education, House of Representatives on the Condition and Improvement of Public Schools in the District of Columbia* (submitted to Senate June 1868, and to the House with additions June 13, 1870), 41st Cong., 2nd sess., Ex. Doc. No. 315. Washington, DC: GPO, 1871.

U.S. Congress. *Congressional Globe.* 1861–1871.

U.S. Congress. *Journal of the House of Representatives of the United States.*

U.S. Congress, House of Representatives. *Annual Report of the Board of Regents of the Smithsonian Institution, 1868.* 40th Cong., 3d sess., 1869.

U.S. Congress, House of Representatives. *Loyalty of Clerks and Other Persons Employed by Government,* 37th Cong., 2d sess., H. Report No. 16, 1862.

U.S. Congress, House of Representatives. *The Management of the Government Hospital for the Insane,* 44th Cong., 1st sess., H. Report No. 793, 1876.

U.S. Congress, House of Representatives. *Report of the Select Committee . . . To Investigate Certain Charges against the Treasury Department,* 38th Cong., 1st sess., H. Rept. no. 140, 1864.

U.S. Congress, House of Representatives. *Statue of Francis E. Spinner,* 54th Cong., 3459 H. Report No. 577, March 2, 1896.

U.S. Congress. Joint Select Committee on Retrenchment. *Civil Service of the United States,* H. Report No. 47, 40th Cong., 2d sess., 1868.

U.S. Department of Agriculture. *Annual Report of Commissioner of Agriculture, 1867,* 1347 H.exdoc.344, November 25, 1867.

U.S. Department of the Interior. *Annual Report of Board of Visitors of Government Hospital for Insane.* H.exdoc.1/12, 39th Cong., Serial 1248, October 1, 1865.

———. *Annual Report of Secretary of Interior, 1869,* 1414 H.exdoc. 1/8, November 15, 1869.

———. *Report of the Metropolitan Board of Police.* 1117 S.exdoc.1/11, 1861.

———. *Report of the Board of Metropolitan Police.* 1157 H.exdoc.1/12, 1862.

———. *Report of the Board of Metropolitan Police.* 1182 H.exdoc.1/14, 1863.

———. *Report of the Board of Metropolitan Police.* 1220 H.exdoc.1/15, 1864.

———. *Report of the Board of Metropolitan Police.* 1248 H.exdoc.1/14, 1865.

———. *Report of the Board of Metropolitan Police.* 1326 H.exdoc.1/11. 1867.

———. *Report of the Board of Metropolitan Police.* 1366 H.exdoc.1/10, 1868.

———. *Report of the Board of Metropolitan Police.* 1414 H.exdoc.1/14, 1869.

———. *Report of the Board of Metropolitan Police.* 1449 H.exdoc.1/17, 1870.

U.S. Department of State. *Register of All Officers and Agents, Civil, Military, and Naval, in the Service of the United States.* Washington, DC: GPO, odd years from 1859 to 1871.

U.S. Department of the Treasury. *History of the Bureau of Engraving and Printing.* 2nd ed. New York: Sanford J. Durst, 1978.

———. *Letter from the Secretary of the Treasury,* 37th Congress, 3rd sess., Ex. Doc. No 12, 1862.

———. *Reduction of Employes in Treasury Department,* House Ex. Doc. No 49, 40th Cong., 3rd sess., Jan. 19, 1869.

———. *Report of the Secretary of the Treasury, on the State of the Finances, for the Year Ending June 30, 1862.* 1149 S.exdoc.1, 1862.

———. *Report of the Secretary of the Treasury, on the State of the Finances, for the Year ending June 30, 1863.* 1186 H.exdoc.3, 1863.

———. *Report of the Secretary of the Treasury on the State of the Finances For the Year 1864.* 1222 H.exdoc.3, 1864.

———. *Report of the Secretary of the Treasury on the State of the Finances For the Year 1865.* 1254 H.exdoc.3, 1865.

———. *Report of the Secretary of the Treasury on the State of the Finances for the Year 1866.* 1287 H.exdoc.4, 1866.

———. *Report of the Secretary of the Treasury on the State of the Finances for the Year 1868.* 1370 H.exdoc.2, 1868.

———. *Report of the Secretary of the Treasury on the State of the Finances For the Year 1869.* 1415 H.exdoc.2, 1869.

———. *Report of the Secretary of the Treasury on the State of the Finances for the Year 1870.* 1451 H.exdoc.2, 1870.

U.S. Government Printing Office (GPO). *Annual Report of Superintendent of Public Printing 1860.* 1103 H.misdoc 11, January 9, 1861.

———. *Annual Report of Superintendent of Public Printing, 1862.* 1171 H.misdoc 6, December 22, 1862.

———. *Annual Report of Superintendent of Public Printing 1865*. 1255 H.Execdoc 23, January 16, 1866.

———. *Keeping America Informed: The U.S. Government Printing Office: 150 Years of Service to the Nation*. Washington, DC: GPO, 2011.

U.S. Post Office Department. *Annual Report of Postmaster General, 1862*, 1159 H. exdoc.1/16, Dec. 1, 1862.

———. *Annual Report of Postmaster General, 1868*, 1369 H.exdoc.1/17, Dec. 3, 1868.

U.S. Senate. *Report of the Secretary of the Senate*. 37th Cong., 2nd sess., Mis. Doc. No. 66, 1862.

Unpublished Government Documents

U.S. GOVERNMENT HOSPITAL FOR THE INSANE

"Letters Sent, 'Executive Series' 1957–1906," Records of the Superintendent [of the Government Hospital for the Insane], 1855–1967. December 21, 1857–February 22, 1864, Entry 9, RG 418. National Archives, Washington, DC.

U.S. GOVERNMENT PRINTING OFFICE

"Lists of Employees and Their Employment Status, compiled 1870?–1907, documenting the period ca. 1858–1907," Records of the Government Printing Office. Entry P40, RG 149, National Archives, Washington, DC.

U.S. HOUSE OF REPRESENTATIVES

"Committee on Ways and Means, Increase of Government Salaries," Records of the United States House of Representatives, Box HR38A-G24.6-24.9. Folder HR 38A-G24.8, RG 233, National Archives, Washington, DC.

"Letter from A. E. Fithian Regarding Pay of Women, May 26, 1870," Records of the United States House of Representatives, Box HR41A-F2.24. Folder 41A. F2.24, Comm. on App. Treasury Department, RG 233, National Archives, Washington, DC.

"Letter to Congress from Committee of Clerks of Treasury Employees," Records of the United States House of Representatives, December, 1864, Box HR 38A-E22.16, Folder HR 38A-E22.16, 38th Congress, Committee on Ways and Means Personnel Affairs, RG 233, National Archives, Washington, DC.

"Memorial to Congress of the Clerks and Other Civil Employees in the Executive Departments at Washington To Revive and Continue the Act of 18th February, 1867 Giving Twenty Per Cent. Additional Compensation," Records of the U.S. House of Representatives, HR 40A, F2.10-HR40A, F 2.11, RG 233, National Archives, Washington, DC.

"Petition from Officers and Employees of the Department of Interior for More Pay," Records of the United States House of Representatives, Box HR 38A-G24.6-24.9; Folder HR 38A, G24.8, RG 233, National Archives, Washington, DC.

"Petition from Women of Government Printing Office for More Money," Records of the United States House of Representatives, December 19, 1867, Box HR 40A-H1.1-H1.2, Folder Committee on Appropriations, 40A-H1.1, RG 233, National Archives in Washington, DC.

"Petition of Female Postal Workers for Increased Compensation," Records of the United States House of Representatives, May 11, 1866, HR39A-H19.5 Committee on Post Office & Post Records, RG 233, National Archives, Washington, DC.

"Petition of Female Treasury Clerks for Increased Pay," Committee on Ways and Means, Records of the United States House of Representatives, April 12, 1866, HR39A-H25.10, RG 233, National Archives, Washington, DC.

"Petition of Kate Fannie Keene to Honorable Members of the Fortieth Congress," Records of the U.S. House of Representatives, July 23, 1868, Box 40A-H1.1-H1.2. Folder 40A H1.1 Committee on Appropriations, RG 233, National Archives, Washington, DC.

Scott, C. (file of), Records of the United States House of Representatives, Box 40A-F27.0-F27.10, Folder—Committee on Ways and Means, 40th Congress, HR40A-F27.9, Government Personnel, RG 233, National Archives, Washington, DC.

U.S. SENATE

"Petition of Citizens of Massachusetts, Clerks in the War Department, Praying an Increase in Salary," Records of the U.S. Senate, January 27, 1865, 38th Congress, 2nd Session, Box No. 81, Folder 38A.H5, RG 46, National Archives, Washington, DC.

"Petition of Employees in the Government Printing Office Praying for an Increase in Compensation," Records of the U.S. Senate, January 16, 1867, 39th Congress, SEN 39A to H5.2, Committee on Finance, Box No 36, Folder January 16, 1867–January 18, 1867, RG 46, National Archives, Washington, DC.

"Petition of Female Employees in the Folding Room of the Government Printing Office, Praying an Increase of Compensation," Records of the U.S. Senate, January 14, 1867, 39th Congress, SEN 39A H5-H5.2, Box No. 36, Folder SEN 39A-H5.1, Jan. 29, 1866–Jan. 15, 1867, RG 46, National Archives, Washington, DC.

"Petition of Female Employees in the Treasury Department Praying an Increase of Salary," Records of the U.S. Senate, January 30, 1865, 38th Congress, 2nd Session, Box No. 81, Folder SEN 38H5—January 27–Feb. 3 1865, RG 46, National Archives, Washington, DC.

"Petition of Females Employed as Folders in the Post Office Department Praying for an Increase of Compensation," Records of the U.S. Senate, January 16, 1867, 39th Congress, Sen 39A H5.-H5.2 Box No. 36, Folder Sen 39A-H5.1, January 16, 1867–January 18, 1867, Committee on Finance, RG 46, National Archives, Washington, DC.

"Petition of Women Employed as Sweepers and Scrubbers in the Treasury Department Praying for an Increase of Compensation," Records of the U.S. Senate,

May 10, 1870, Sen 41A-H71-H7.1, Committee on Finance, Various Subjects, Box #75, Folder March 21, 1870–January 17, 1871, RG 46, National Archives, Washington, DC.

U.S. TREASURY DEPARTMENT

"Applications and Recommendations for Positions in the Washington, DC," Offices of the Treasury Department, 1830–1910. General Records, Records of the Division of Appointments, Entry 210, RG 56, National Archives, College Park, MD.

"Letters Received Relating to the Bureau of Engraving and Printing (1862–1911)." Entry 165, RG 56, National Archives, College Park, MD.

Record of Clerks in the Office of the Commissioner of Internal Revenue 1862–1869, Records of the Internal Revenue Service, Entry 64, RG 58, National Archives, College Park, MD.

"Registers and Lists of Treasury Employees Register of Female Clerks, 1861–1868," Records of the Division of Appointments, RG 56, National Archives, College Park, MD.

U.S. WAR DEPARTMENT

"Consolidated Report of the Time and Conduct of the Copyists employed in the QMG Office Under the Supervision of S. F. Wainwright," Records of the Office of the Quartermaster General, Entry 1160, RG 92, National Archives, Washington, DC.

"Correspondence Relating to the Hiring of Clerks and Messengers 1863–1872," Records of the Office of the Quartermaster General, Entry 1156, RG 92, National Archives, Washington, DC.

"Letters and Endorsements Sent to Officers, Agents, and Employees Relating to Personnel 1871–1883." Records of the Office of the Quartermaster General, Entry 1100, RG 92, National Archives, Washington, DC.

"Letters Received by the Secretary of War, Irregular Series, 1861–1866." July 1861–December 1865, Letters S151-T90, Microfilm, National Archives, Washington, DC.

"Letters Sent by the Office of the QMG." Main Series, 1818–1870. Microfilm, RG 92, National Archives, Washington, DC.

"List of Clerks, Messengers, and Laborers Employed in the Office of the QMG, 1861–1864." Records of the Office of the Quartermaster General, Entry 1161-1162, RG 92, National Archives, Washington, DC.

MISCELLANEOUS

Records of the District Courts of the U.S., *Equity Case Files 1863–1938*, RG 21, National Archives, Washington, DC.

Records of the Government of the District of Columbia, *Records of the Metropolitan Police, Detective Office, Daily Record, Box 2—January 11–May 16, 1866*, Entry 126, RG 351, National Archives, Washington, DC.

Records of the Post Office Department, *Miscellaneous File*, Entry 213, RG 28, National Archives, Washington, DC.

Newspapers and Periodicals

Age Herald (Birmingham, AL)
Albany Journal
Boston Daily Advertiser
Boston Daily Journal
Carroll Herald (Carroll, IA)
Cincinnati Commercial
Cincinnati Daily Gazette
Columbian Register (New Haven, CT)
Constitution (Middletown, CT)
Daily Age (Philadelphia, PA)
Daily Constitutional Union
   (Washington, DC)
Daily Critic (Washington, DC)
Daily Morning Chronicle (Washington,
   DC)
Daily National Intelligencer
   (Washington, DC)
Daily Ohio Statesman (Columbus, OH)
Daily Picayune (New Orleans, LA)
Daily State Gazette (Trenton, NJ)
Daily State Register (Des Moines, IA)
Dallas Morning News
Detroit Advertiser and Tribune
Easton Gazette (Easton, MD)
Evening Bulletin (San Francisco, CA)
Evening Saturday Gazette (Boston, MA)
Evening Star (Washington, DC)
Farmers' Cabinet (Amherst, NH)
Flake's Bulletin (Galveston, TX)
Fort Worth Star-Telegram (Fort
   Worth, TX)
Galveston Tri-Weekly News
   (Galveston, TX)
Hartford Daily Courant (Hartford, CT)
Houston Union
Idaho Falls Times (Idaho Falls, ID)
Inter Ocean (Chicago, IL)
Jamestown Journal (Jamestown, NY)
Leavenworth Bulletin (Leavenworth,
   KS)
Lowell Daily Citizen and News
   (Lowell, MA)

Macon Daily Telegraph (Macon,
   GA)
Miami Herald Record (Miami, FL)
Milwaukee Daily Sentinel (Milwaukee,
   WI)
New Hampshire Patriot and Gazette
   (Concord, NH)
New-Orleans Times
New-York Evangelist
New York Herald
New York Times
New York Tribune
*North American and United States
   Gazette* (Philadelphia, PA)
Pacific Commercial Advertiser
   (Honolulu, HI)
Philadelphia Inquirer
Pittsburgh Post-Gazette
Pittsfield Sun (Pittsfield, MA)
Pomeroy's Democrat (Chicago, IL)
Portland Daily Advertiser (Portland,
   ME)
Public Ledger (Philadelphia, PA)
The Reconstructionist (Washington, DC)
Revolution (New York, NY)
Salt Lake Daily Telegraph
Semi-Weekly Telegraph (Salt Lake
   City, UT)
Springfield Weekly Republican
   (Springfield, MA)
St. Cloud Democrat (St. Cloud, MN)
Sun (Baltimore, MD)
Times-Picayune (New Orleans, LA)
Troy Weekly Times (Troy, NY)
Washington Post (Washington, DC)
Weekly Dakotian (Yankton, SD)
Weekly Patriot and Union (Harrisburg,
   PA)
Wheeling Sunday Register (Wheeling,
   WV)
Woman's Journal (Boston, MA, and
   Chicago, IL)

Primary Sources

Ames, Mary Clemmer. *Ten Years in Washington: Life and Scenes in the National Capital, as a Woman Sees Them.* Hartford, CT: A. D. Worthington, 1873. Page references are to the 1880 edition, which includes additional illustrations.

Baker, General L. C. *History of the United States Secret Service.* Philadelphia, PA: L. C. Baker, 1867.

Benjamin, Marcus, ed. *Washington during Wartime: A Series of Papers Showing the Military, Political, and Social Phases during 1861 to 1865.* Washington City: Official Souvenir of the Thirty-Sixth Annual Encampment of the Grand Army of the Republic, 1902.

Bogy, Lewis Vital. *In Office: A Story of Washington Life and Society.* Chicago, IL: F. J. Schulte, 1891.

Bohn's Hand-Book of Washington. Washington, DC: Casimir Bohn, 1860.

Briggs, Emily Edson. *The Olivia Letters; Being Some History of Washington City for Forty Years as Told By the Letters of a Newspaper Correspondent.* New York: Neale Publishing, 1906.

Buel, J. W. *Mysteries and Miseries: America's Great Cities.* St. Louis, MO: Historical Publishing, 1883.

Edmonds, Sarah Emma. *Memoirs of a Soldier, Nurse and Spy: A Woman's Adventures in the Union Army.* DeKalb, IL: Northern Illinois University Press, 1999.

Ellis, John. *The Sights and Secrets of the National Capital.* New York: United States Publishing Company, 1869.

Gemmill, Jane W. *Notes on Washington or Six Years at the National Capital.* Philadelphia, PA: E. Claxton, 1884.

Green, Constance McLaughlin. *Washington Village and Capital, 1800–1878.* Princeton, NJ: Princeton University Press, 1962.

Harvard University. *The Class of 1844, Harvard College, Fifty Years' After Graduation.* Cambridge, MA: J. Wilson and Son, 1896.

Holland, Mary A. Gardner, ed. *Our Army Nurses: Interesting Sketches, Addresses, and Photographs.* Boston, MA: B. Wilkins, 1895.

Hutchinson's Washington and Georgetown Directory. Washington, DC: Hutchinson & Brother, 1863.

Kelly, Joseph T. "Memories of a Lifetime in Washington." *Records of the Columbia Historical Society*, 31–32 (1930): 117–49.

Lincoln, Abraham. *Collected Works of Abraham Lincoln.* Edited by Roy P. Basler. Ann Arbor, MI: University of Michigan Digital Library Production Services 2001. http://quod.lib.umich.edu/l/lincoln/ (last accessed 8/15/2012).

Martin, Edward Winslow. *Behind the Scenes in Washington.* New York: Continental Publishing, 1873.

Penfield, Alanson *A Tale of the Rebellion. Facts and Figures from the Standpoint of a Departmental Clerk. Proposition for the Government to Solve the Problem of Diminishing the High Prices of House Rent in Washington.* 2nd ed. Washington, DC: Intelligencer Printing House, 1867.

Penny, Virginia. *The Employments of Women: A Cyclopedia of Women's Work*. Boston, MA: Walker, Wise, 1863.

Smith, Mrs. Lathrop E. "My Recollections of Civil War Days." *The Wisconsin Magazine of History* 2, no. 1 (Sept. 1918): 26–39.

Stanton, Elizabeth Cady, Susan B. Anthony, and Matilda Joslyn Gage, *History of Woman Suffrage, Volume 3*. Rochester, NY: Charles Mann, 1887.

Swisshelm, Jane. *Letters to Country Girls*. New York: John C. Riker, 1853.

Townsend, George Alfred. *Washington, Outside and Inside: A Picture and a Narrative of the Origin, Growth, Excellencies, Abuses, Beauties, and Personages of our Governing City*. Hartford, CT: James Betts, 1873.

Velazquez, Loreta Janeta. *The Woman in Battle: A Narrative of the Exploits, Adventures, and Travels of Madame Loreta Janeta Velazquez, Otherwise Known as Lieut. Harry T. Buford, Confederate States Army*. Hartford, CT: T. Belknap, 1876.

Secondary Sources

Abbott, Carl. *Political Terrain: Washington, D.C., from Tidewater Town to Global Metropolis*. Chapel Hill: University of North Carolina Press, 1999.

Aley, Ginette, and J. L. Anderson, eds. *Union Heartland: The Midwestern Home Front during the Civil War*. Carbondale: Southern Illinois University Press, 2013.

Apostolidis, Paul, and Juliet A. Williams, eds. *Public Affairs: Politics in the Age of Sex Scandals*. Durham, NC: Duke University Press, 2004.

Aron, Cindy S. " 'To Barter Their Souls for Gold': Female Clerks in Federal Government Offices, 1862–1890." *Journal of American History* 67, no. 4 (March 1981): 835–53.

———. *Ladies and Gentlemen of the Civil Service: Middle Class Workers in Victorian America*. New York: Oxford University Press, 1987.

Attie, Jeanie. *Patriotic Toil: Northern Women and the American Civil War*. Ithaca, NY: Cornell University Press, 1998.

Aynes, Richard L. "*Bradwell v. Illinois*: Chief Justice Chase's Dissent and the 'Sphere of Women's Work.' " *Louisiana Law Review* 59 (Winter 1999): 521–41.

Bacon-Foster, Corra. "Clara Barton: Humanitarian." *Records of the Columbia Historical Society* 21 (1918): 278–356.

Baker, Elizabeth. *Technology and Women's Work*. New York: Columbia University Press, 1964.

Baker, Gladys L. "Women in the U.S. Department of Agriculture." *Agricultural History* 50, no. 1 (Jan. 1976): 190–201.

Baker, Ross K. "Entry of Women into Federal Job World—At a Price." *Smithsonian* 8, no. 4 (July 1977): 82–91.

Baron, Ava, ed. *Work Engendered: Toward a New History of American Labor*. New York: Cornell University Press, 1991.

———. *Work Engendered*. In "The Faces of Gender: Sex Segregation and Work Relations at Philco, 1928–1938," edited by Patricia Cooper.

Beasley, Maurine Hoffman. "Mary Clemmer Ames: A Victorian Woman Journalist." *Hayes Historical Journal* 2 (1978): 57–63.

Berebitsky, Julie. *Sex and the Office: A History of Gender, Power, and Desire.* New Haven, CT: Yale University Press, 2012.

Bergin, Brian. *The Washington Arsenal Explosion: Civil War Disaster in the Capital.* Edited by Erin Bergin Voorheis. Charleston, SC: History Press, 2012.

Billings, Elden E. "Social and Economic Conditions Washington during the Civil War." *Records of the Columbia Historical Society* 63–65 (1963–1965): 191–209.

———. "Early Women Journalists of Washington." *Records of the Columbia Historical Society* 66–68 (1966–1968): 84–97.

Blanton, DeAnne, and Lauren M. Cook. *They Fought Like Demons: Women Soldiers in the Civil War.* New York: Vintage Books, 2002.

Brown, Ira V. "William D. Kelley and Radical Reconstruction." *Pennsylvania Magazine of History and Biography* 85, no. 3 (Jul. 1961): 316–29.

Burlingame, Michael, ed. *Lincoln Observed: Civil War Dispatches of Noah Brooks.* Baltimore, MD: Johns Hopkins University Press, 1998.

Burlingame, S. L. "The Making of a Spoilsman: The Life and Career of Roscoe Conkling from 1829 to 1873." Ph.D. diss., Johns Hopkins University, 1974.

Claussen, Cathryn L. "Gendered Merit: Women and the Merit Concept in Federal Employment, 1864–1944." *The American Journal of Legal History* 40, no. 3 (July 1996): 229–52.

Clinton, Catherine, and Christine Lunardini. *The Columbia Guide to American Women in the Nineteenth Century.* New York: Columbia University Press, 2000.

Clinton, Catherine, and Nina Silber, eds. *Divided Houses: Gender and the Civil War.* New York: Oxford University Press, 1992.

———. *Battle Scars: Gender and Sexuality in the American Civil War.* Oxford, NY: Oxford University Press, 2006.

Cobble, Dorothy Sue. *The Other Women's Movement: Workplace Justice and Social Rights in Modern America.* Princeton, NJ: Princeton University Press, 2004.

Cobble, Dorothy Sue, Linda Gordon, and Astrid Henry. *Feminism Unfinished: A Short, Surprising History of American Women's Movements.* New York: Liveright Publishing, 2014.

Cooling, Benjamin Franklin. "Defending Washington during the Civil War." *Records of the Columbia Historical Society* 71–72 (1971–1972): 314–37.

Cooney, Charles F. "The State of the Treasury—1864: Nothing More . . . Than a Whorehouse." *Civil War Times Illustrated* 2, no. 8 (December 1982): 40–43.

Cott, Nancy F. *The Grounding of Modern Feminism.* New Haven, CT: Yale University Press, 1987.

Cross, Coy F. *Justin Smith Morrill Father of the Land-Grant Colleges.* East Lansing, MI: Michigan State University Press, 1999.

Cross, Gary and Peter Shergold. "'We Think We Are of the Oppressed': Gender, White Collar Work, and Grievances of Late Nineteenth-Century Women." *Labor History* 28, no. 1 (1987): 23–53.

Cutter, Barbara. *Domestic Devils, Battlefield Angels: The Radicalism of American Womanhood, 1830-1865.* DeKalb, IL: Northern Illinois University Press, 2003.

Davies, Margery. "Woman's Place is at the Typewriter: The Feminization of the Clerical Labor Force." *Radical America* 8, no. 4 (July–August 1974): 1–28.

———. *Woman's Place Is at the Typewriter: Office Work and Office Workers, 1870–1930.* Philadelphia: Temple University Press, 1982.

Denning, R. "A Fragile Machine: California Senator John Conness." *California History* 85, no. 4 (October 2008): 26–49.

Deutrich, Bernice M. "Propriety and Pay." *Prologue* 3, no. 2 (Fall 1971): 67–72.

Deutsch, Sarah. *Women and the City: Gender, Space, and Power in Boston, 1870–1940.* New York: Oxford University Press, 2000.

Dickson, Paul. *War Slang: Fighting Words and Phrases of Americans from the Civil War to the Gulf War.* New York: Pocket Books, 1994.

Drabelle, D. "The Tarnished Silver Senator." *American History* 41, no. 5 (December 2006): 52–59.

DuBois, Ellen Carol. *Feminism and Suffrage: The Emergence of An Independent Women's Movement in America, 1848–1869.* New York: Cornell University Press, 1978.

———. *Woman Suffrage & Women's Rights.* New York: New York University Press, 1998.

Dudden, Faye E. *Fighting Chance: The Struggle over Woman Suffrage and Black Suffrage in Reconstruction America.* New York: Oxford University Press, 2011.

Edwards, Rebecca. *Angels in the Machinery: Gender in American Party Politics from the Civil War to the Progressive Era.* New York: Oxford University Press, 1997.

Epstein, Daniel Mark. *The Lincolns: Portrait of a Marriage.* New York: Ballantine Books, 2008.

Faulkner, Carol. *Women's Radical Reconstruction: The Freedmen's Aid Movement.* Philadelphia, PA: University of Pennsylvania Press, 2004.

Faust, Drew Gilpin. *Mothers of Invention: Women of the Slaveholding South in the Civil War.* Chapel Hill, NC: University of North Carolina Press, 1996.

———. *This Republic of Suffering: Death and the American Civil War.* New York: Alfred A. Knopf, 2008.

Fleischner, Jennifer. *Mrs. Lincoln and Mrs. Keckley.* New York: Broadway Books, 2003.

Flexner, Eleanor. *Century of Struggle: The Woman's Rights Movement in the United States.* Cambridge, MA: The Belknap Press of Harvard University, 1959.

Foner, Eric. *The Fiery Trial: Abraham Lincoln and American Slavery.* New York: W. W. Norton, 2010.

Forbes, Ella. *African American Women during the Civil War.* New York: Garland Publishing, 1998.

Freedman, Paul H. "Women and Restaurants in the Nineteenth-Century United States." *Journal of Social History* 48, no. 1 (Fall 2014): 1–19.

Furgurson, Ernest B. *Freedom Rising: Washington in the Civil War.* New York: Vintage Books, 2004.

Gallman, J. Matthew. *The North Fights the Civil War: The Home Front*. Chicago: Ivan R. Dee, 1994.

———. *Defining Duty in the Civil War: Personal Choice, Popular Culture, and the Union Home Front*. Chapel Hill, NC: University of North Carolina Press, 2015.

Giesberg, Judith. *Civil War Sisterhood: The U.S. Sanitary Commission and Women's Politics in Transition*. Boston, MA: Northeastern University Press, 2000.

———. "From Harvest Field to Battlefield: Rural Pennsylvania Women and the U.S. Civil War." *Pennsylvania History* 72, no. 2 (April 2005): 159–91.

———. *Army At Home: Women and the Civil War on the Northern Home Front*. Chapel Hill, NC: University of North Carolina Press, 2009.

———. " 'Noble Union Girls.' " *Civil War Times* 49, no. 3 (June 2010): 58–64.

Ginzberg, Lori. *Women and the Work of Benevolence: Morality, Politics, and Class in Nineteenth-Century United States*. New Haven, CT: Yale University Press, 1990.

Goodwin, Jason. *Greenback: The Almighty Dollar and the Invention of America*. London: Penguin Group, 2003.

Graf, Leroy P., ed. *The Papers of Andrew Johnson: 1864–1865*. Vol. 7. Knoxville, TN: University of Tennessee Press, 1986.

Green, Jonathon. *Cassell's Dictionary of Slang*. London: Weidenfeld & Nicolson, 2005.

Green, Midori V. "Visual Fictions and the U.S. Treasury Courtesans: Images of 19th-Century Female Clerks in the Illustrated Press." *Belphégor* [En ligne] 13, no. 1 (2015). https://belphegor.revues.org/593 (last accessed Feb. 14, 2017).

Gurney, Gene, and Clare Gurney. *The United States Treasury, A Pictorial History*. New York: Crown Publishers, 1978.

Gustafson, Melanie Susan. *Women and the Republican Party, 1854–1924*. Chicago: University of Illinois Press, 2001.

Harrison, Robert. "Welfare and Employment Policies of the Freedmen's Bureau in the District of Columbia." *Journal of Southern History* 72 (February 2006): 75–110.

Hewitt, Nancy A., ed. *No Permanent Waves: Recasting Histories of U.S. Feminism*. Rutgers, NJ: Rutgers University Press, 2010.

Hyman, Harold M. *The Reconstruction Justice of Salmon P. Chase:* In Re Turner & Texas v. White. Lawrence: University Press of Kansas, 1997.

Isenberg, Nancy. *Sex and Citizenship in Antebellum America*. Chapel Hill: University of North Carolina Press, 1998.

Johnston, W. Dawson. "The Earliest Free Public Library Movement in Washington, 1849–1874." *Records of the Columbia Historical Society* 9 (1906): 1–13.

Jordan, Henry D. "Daniel Wolsey Voorhees." *The Mississippi Valley Historical Review* 6, no. 4 (March 1920): 532–55.

Jordan, Philip D. "The Capital of Crime." *Civil War Times Illustrated* 13, no. 10 (1975): 4–9, 44–47.

Kacrick, Jeffrey. *Informal English: Puncture Ladies, Egg Harbors, Mississippi Marbles, and Other Curious Words and Phrases of North America*. New York: Touchstone, 2005.

Kauffman, Michael W. *American Brutus: John Wilkes Booth and the Lincoln Conspiracies*. New York: Random House, 2004.

Kessler-Harris, Alice. *Women Have Always Worked: A Historical Overview*. New York: McGraw-Hill Book Company, 1981.

———. *Out to Work: A History of Wage-Earning Women in the United States*. Oxford: Oxford University Press 1982.

———. *A Woman's Wage: Historical Meanings & Social Consequences*. Lexington: University Press of Kentucky, 1990.

Krug, Mark M. *Lyman Trumbull: Conservative Radical*. New York: A. S. Barnes, 1965.

Kwolek-Folland, Angel. *Engendering Business: Men and Women in the Corporate Office, 1870–1930*. Baltimore, MD: Johns Hopkins University Press, 1994.

———. *Incorporating Women: A History of Women & Business in the United States*. New York: Palgrave, 1998.

Larsen, Arthur J., ed. *Crusader and Feminist: Letters of Jane Grey Swisshelm, 1858–1865*. Westport, CT: Hyperion Press, 1976.

Leasher, Evelyn. "Lois Bryan Adams and the Household Department of the 'Michigan Farmer.'" *Michigan Historical Review* 21, no. 1 (Spring 1995): 100–119.

Leasher, Evelyn, ed. *Letter from Washington: 1863–1865*. Detroit, MI: Wayne State University Press, 1999.

Leech, Margaret. *Reveille in Washington: 1860–1865*. New York: Time Incorporated, 1941.

Leonard, Elizabeth D. *Yankee Women: Gender Battles in the Civil War*. New York: W. W. Norton, 1994.

———. *All the Daring of a Solider: Women of the Civil War Armies*. New York: W. W. Norton, 1999.

Lomax, Elizabeth Lindsay. *Leaves from an Old Washington Diary: 1854–1863*. Edited by Lindsay Lomax Wood. New York: Books, Inc., distributed by E. P. Dutton, 1943.

Lowry, Thomas P. *The Story the Soldiers Wouldn't Tell: Sex in the Civil War*. Mechanicsburg, PA: Stackpole Books, 1994.

Luskey, Brian P. *On the Make: Clerks and the Quest for Capital in Nineteenth-Century America*. New York: New York University Press, 2010.

Massey, Mary Elizabeth. *Bonnet Brigades*. New York: Alfred A. Knopf, 1966.

Masur, Kate. *An Example for All the Land: Emancipation and the Struggle over Equality in Washington, D.C.* Chapel Hill: University of North Carolina Press, 2010.

———. "Patronage and Protest in Kate Brown's Washington." *The Journal of American History* 99, no. 4 (March 2013): 1047–71.

McLean, Sara. "Confided to His Care or Protection: The Late Nineteenth-Century Crime of Workplace Sexual Harassment." *Columbia Journal of Gender and the Law* 9 (Oct. 1999): 47–88.

McMillen Frances M., and James S. Kane. "Institutional Memory: The Records of St. Elizabeths Hospital at the National Archives," *Prologue Magazine* 43, no. 2 (Summer 2010). https://www.archives.gov/publications/prologue/2010/summer/institutional.html (accessed Jan. 30, 2017).

McPherson, James M. *Battle Cry of Freedom: The Civil War Era*. New York: Ballantine Books, 1988.

Mearns, David C. "A View of Washington in 1863." *Records of the Columbia Historical Society* 63–65 (1963–1965): 210–20.

Milkman, Ruth. *Gender at Work: The Dynamics of Job Segregation by Sex during World War II*. Chicago: University of Illinois Press, 1987.

Millikan, Frank Rives. "Wards of the Nation: The Making of St. Elizabeths Hospital, 1852–1920." Ph.D. diss., George Washington University, 1990.

Mogelever, Jacob. *Death to Traitors: The Story of General Lafayette C. Baker, Lincoln's Forgotten Secret Service Chief*. New York: Doubleday, 1960.

Montgomery, David. *Beyond Equality: Labor and the Radical Republicans, 1862–1872* (Illini Books Edition). Chicago: University of Illinois Press, 1981.

Niven, John, ed. *The Salmon P. Chase Papers: Correspondence, 1865–1872*. Vol. 5. Ohio: Kent State University Press, 1998.

Nussbaum, Arthur. *A History of the Dollar*. New York: Columbia University Press, 1957.

Oates, Stephen B. *A Woman of Valor: Clara Barton and the Civil War*. New York: First Free Press, 1995.

Osterud, Nancy Grey, "Rural Women during the Civil War: New York's Nanticoke Valley, 1861–1865." *New York History* 7, no. 4 (October 1990): 357–85.

Peiss, Kathy. "Gender Relations and Working-Class Leisure: New York City, 1880–1920." In *To Toil the Livelong Day: America's Women at Work, 1780–1980*, edited by Carol Groneman and Mary Beth Norton, 103–6. New York: Cornell University Press, 1987.

Peiss, Kathy, and Christina Simmons, eds. *Passion and Power: Sexuality in History*. Philadelphia, PA: Temple University Press, 1989.

Prandoni, Jogues R., and Suryabala Kanhouwa. "St. Elizabeths Hospital: Photos from 150 Years of Public Service." *Washington History* 17, no. 1 (Fall–Winter 2005): 4–25.

Reis, Ronald A. *African Americans and the Civil War*. New York, Infobase Publishing, 2009.

Richardson, Francis A. "Recollections of a Washington Newspaper Correspondent." *Records of the Columbia Historical Society* 6 (1903): 24–42.

Rockman, Seth. *Scraping By: Wage Labor, Slavery, and Survival in Early Baltimore*. Baltimore, MD: Johns Hopkins University Press, 2009.

Roske, Ralph J. *His Own Counsel: The Life and Times of Lyman Trumbull*. Reno: University of Nevada Press, 1979.

Russell, William H. "Timothy O. Howe, Stalwart Republican." *The Wisconsin Magazine of History* 35, no. 2 (Winter 1951): 90–99.

Ryan, Mary. *Women in Public: Between Banners and Ballots, 1825–1800*. Baltimore, MD: Johns Hopkins University Press, 1990.

Saint, Avice Marion. "Women in the Public Service." *Public Personnel Studies* 9 (January–February 1931): 14–19.

Schultz, Jane E. "Race, Gender, and Bureaucracy: Civil War Army Nurses and the Pension Bureau." *Journal of Women's History* 6, no. 2 (Summer 1994): 45–69.

———. *Women at the Front: Hospital Workers in Civil War America*. Chapel Hill: University of North Carolina Press, 2004.

Sellers, Leila. "Commissioner Charles Mason and Clara Barton." *Journal of the Patent Office Society* 22, no. 11 (November 1940): 803–27.

Shelden, Rachel A. *Washington Brotherhood: Politics, Social Life, and the Coming of the Civil War.* Chapel Hill: University of North Carolina Press, 2013.

Silber, Nina. *Daughters of the Union: Northern Women Fight the Civil War.* Cambridge, MA: Harvard University Press, 2005.

Simon, John Y., ed. *The Papers of Ulysses S. Grant.* Carbondale: Southern Illinois University Press, 1967.

Sizer, Lyde Cullen. *The Political Work of Northern Women Writers and the Civil War, 1850–1872.* Chapel Hill: University of North Carolina Press, 2000.

Skocpol, Theda. *Protecting Soldiers and Mothers: The Political Origins of Social Policy in the United States.* Cambridge, MA: Belknap Press of Harvard University Press, 1992.

Skowronek, Stephen. *Building a New American State: The Expansion of National Administrative Capacities, 1877–1920.* Cambridge, MA: Cambridge University Press, 1982.

Smith, Michael Thomas. *The Enemy Within: Fears of Corruption in the Civil War North.* Charlottesville: University of Virginia Press, 2011.

Sneider, Allison L. *Suffragists in an Imperial Age: U.S. Expansion and the Woman Question, 1870–1929.* New York: Oxford University Press, 2008.

Snyder, Tom, ed. *120 Years of American Education: A Statistical Portrait* (National Center for Education Statistics, 1993). http://nces.ed.gov/naal/lit_history.asp (last accessed August 15, 2012).

Srole, Carole. *Transcribing Class and Gender: Masculinity and Femininity in Nineteenth-Century Courts and Offices.* Ann Arbor: University of Michigan Press, 2010.

Stansell, Christine. *City of Women: Sex and Class in New York, 1789–1860.* Chicago: University of Illinois Press, 1982.

Tentler, Leslie Woodcock. *Wage-Earning Women: Industrial Work and Family Life in the United States, 1900–1930.* New York: Oxford University Press, 1979.

Thorp, Margaret Farrand. *Female Persuasion: Six Strong-Minded Women.* New Haven, CT: Yale University Press, 1949.

Unger, Irwin. *The Greenback Era: A Social and Political History of American Finance 1865–1879.* Princeton, NJ: Princeton University Press, 1968.

Van Riper, Paul P. *History of the United States Civil Service.* Evanston, IL: Row, Peterson and Company, 1958.

Varon, Elizabeth R. *Southern Lady, Yankee Spy: The True Story of Elizabeth Van Lew, A Union Agent in the Heart of the Confederacy.* New York: Oxford University Press, 2003.

Venet, Wendy Hamand. *Neither Ballots nor Bullets: Women Abolitionists and the Civil War.* Charlottesville: University Press of Virginia, 1991.

Weber, Jennifer L. *Copperheads: The Rise and Fall of Lincoln's Opponents in the North.* New York: Oxford University Press, 2006.

White, Horace. *The Life of Lyman Trumbull*. New York: Houghton Mifflin, 1913.

Whites, LeeAnn. *Gender Matters: Civil War, Reconstruction, and the Making of the New South*. New York: Palgrave, MacMillan, 2005.

Whyte, James H. "Divided Loyalties in Washington during the Civil War." *Records of the Columbia Historical Society* 60–62 (1960–1962): 103–22.

Wilson, Mark R. *The Business of the Civil War: Military Mobilization and the State, 1861–1865*. Baltimore, MD: Johns Hopkins University Press, 2006.

Winkle, Kenneth J. *Lincoln's Citadel: The Civil War in Washington, DC*. New York: W. W. Norton, 2013.

"Women in Business." *Fortune* 12 (July 1935): 50–57, 90–96.

Wood, Sharon E. *The Freedom of The Streets: Work, Citizenship, and Sexuality in a Gilded Age City*. Chapel Hill: University of North Carolina Press, 2005.

Yates, Richard, and Catherine Yates Pickering. *Richard Yates, Civil War Governor*. Edited by John H. Krenkel. Danville, IL: Interstate Printers & Publishers, 1966.

Yellin, Eric. *Racism in the Nation's Service: Government Workers and the Color Line in Woodrow Wilson's America*. Chapel Hill: University of North Carolina Press, 2013.

Zaeske, Susan. *Signatures of Citizenship: Petitioning, Antislavery & Women's Political Identity*. Chapel Hill: University of North Carolina Press, 2003.

Index